FAMILY, KIN AND COMMUNITY

A Contemporary Reader

Bernard P. Wong

San Francisco State University

KENDALL/HUNT PUBLISHING COMPANY
4050 Westmark Drive   Dubuque, Iowa 52004

Cover images © 2001 PhotoDisc, Inc.

❧ Contents

Part Three Alternative Lifestyles and New Kinship Patterns   217

Preface

Kinship studies have always played a pivotal role in Anthropology. In fact, it is one of the earliest fields that anthropologists, for a number of historical and even accidental reasons, have immersed themselves in. Consequently, many important anthropological theories recognized today were generated from seminal studies in kinship. Anthropology is a discipline considered to be a relative late-comer to the field of social sciences. The early anthropologists such as Franz Boas, Bronislaw Malinowski and Alfred Kroeber, were giants, whose life-long work were responsible for the construction and acceptance of Anthropology as a recognized academic field in itself. Going to exotic locales to study societies untouched by political scientists, sociologists or economists, these early pioneers opened up virgin territory by examining societies that emphasized kinship as important to social structure.

In the late 19th to early 20th century, many of the tribal societies in Africa, Oceania and Asia became the focus of intensive anthropological investigation by Western scholars. Tribal groups such as the Trobriand Islanders or the Innuit (Eskimo), heretofore-unknown societies, gained worldwide attention due to anthropological findings, one which paid particular attention to kinship organizations in such Third World locales.

Over the years, theories in kinship have evolved as the discipline itself matured and changed. One of the earliest approaches to the study of kinship is the social evolutionary approach which attempted to explain the complexity of cultures in terms of evolutionary stages. Other approaches engendered by different scholars have since arisen, reflecting their current intellectual climate in accordance with the development of new anthropological theories. Developments in theory include genealogical, psychological, functional, structural-functional and the terminological approaches.

During the period of the 1950s to 1970s, kinship theory again moved forward in new directions, with such concepts as componential analysis, alliance theory and sociobiology. In the 1970s to 1990s, once again reflecting major social changes, the teaching of kinship came to include considerations of gender, decision-making and fictive kinship networks.

Despite such a diverse background, all those who toil in the field of kinship studies face a lack of relevant material that can be used in the classroom. I have taught kinship classes for many years now, yet, increasingly, I find it more and more difficult to get relevant reading material for my students. Meanwhile, interest in the study of kinship is rising in the general public, due to its unique applicability in many fields besides anthropology. Currently, there is no book or reader on the market that can meet this demand. Thus, in the past few years, I have had to resort to making my own ad-hoc reader for my classes at San Francisco State University. Still, I found it unsatisfactory because much of the existing literature is outdated and not reflective of current anthropological theory or even social reality.

In the past few years, anthropology has become increasingly interested in how people initiate social actions. Newer theories such as practice theory, actor-oriented approach, activity- or agency-centered analysis are now more useful in understanding human society and human action. Similarly, in anthropological approaches to kinship, we have now moved away from structural analysis towards agency. However, there is no existing text or reader that can be used to illustrate the creation and use of kinship in the ever-changing contemporary social life.

This shortage of relevant reading material is further aggravated by the increased interest in this subject. In teaching kinship, I have been able to use standard kinship books on concepts, methods and theories. There are a number of texts that are useful for inculcating the basic anthropological concepts and theories on kinship. However, when it comes to relevant reading materials, I have to resort to my own compilation. Thus, the present collection represents a concerted effort in bridging the gap in this field. All the papers in this collection deal with contemporary societies and issues, such as continuity and change in kinship, the role of kinship in the formation of self, the new reproductive technologies and their implications for kinship, globalization and family life. These are issues, which the student not only can easily relate to, but also certainly must deal with in their own lives as we enter the 21st century.

In the teaching of kinship, I also found that much attention has been paid to the study of structure, functions and types of kinship systems. However, not enough attention has been paid to the use of kinship in decision-making activities, for the formation of community, social and economic activities. How kinship is used in contemporary societies is another focus of the present collection of readings.

The third goal of this work is to look at the generation of new kinship patterns in contemporary life. This includes friendship and quasi-kinship networks. Contemporary kinship studies have branched out from the study of traditional kinship systems to the study of social networks. Thus, this reader is divided into three parts: Part One deals with continuity and change in kinship systems; Part Two concentrates on the use of kinship in contemporary life; Part Three discusses new kinship patterns and the development of new kinship behavior resulting from interaction between people and changing cultures.

In general, the readings attempt to be both contemporary and relevant. Many of the articles demonstrate how kinship is not just an institution, but a network that plays an important role in our contemporary societies. Many of the articles are tried and true. They are articles received most favorably by my students—the reason for their inclusion here. Other articles in this volume are original papers written by authors who are specialists in their respective fields. All deal with the topic of kinship. Geographically, the book covers a large territory, from Britain to the United States, from China to India. Some of the articles were written with data from Africa and Hawaii. The book has specific articles dealing with the kinship systems and their use by ethnic groups in the U.S. such as the Norwegian Americans, the Asian Americans, the Mexican Americans, the Anglo-Americans and the Afro-Americans. Of the sixteen chapters, eleven have been previously published; five were written specifically for this compilation, and I am pleased to include them.

The ultimate decision for inclusion or exclusion has been guided by, first of all, the interests of students, then relevance, and unavoidably, production and economic factors.

I am grateful to all the authors who contributed original articles for this volume, and to Ms. Lynn Murata Tsang, who did all the copy editing for this work.

Bernard P. Wong, Ph.D. Anthropology
San Francisco State University
Department of Anthropology

Part One

Continuity and Change in Kinship

Introduction

Part One contains readings dealing with continuity and changes in kinship systems in a number of societies. Many anthropologists believe that kinship systems are relatively stable over time. They argue that kinship systems are the backbones of societies, greatly influencing other institutions within a society. An example of this type of thought is found in the work of Francis L.K. Hsu, "The Effect of Dominant Kinship Relations on Kin and Non-Kin behavior: A Hypothesis." In his work, Hsu demonstrated that there are certain relatively permanent kinship configurations that do not easily change. These kinship configurations, which Hsu calls "dominant dyads," tend to transcend the limitation of time. The patterns of dominant dyads can influence other aspects of culture, such as religion, politics and interpersonal social relations. After criticizing the traditional approaches, such as functionalism, structural-functionalism and the terminological approach, Hsu advanced his own "dominant dyad" hypothesis. Hsu argued that the dyadic relations within the family are important keys to culture.

However, some anthropologists believe that kinship patterns are not as immutable. William Jankoviak intimated that changes in kinship do occur in Chinese society. Jankoviak argues that, while certain kinship behaviors continue, change does occur in China as a result of urbanization and political change. Likewise, Lynn Murata examines the continuity and changes in kinship systems for Japanese-Americans in Hawaii. Murata shows how a strong *Nikkeijin* (Japanese-American) community has been built on traditional kinship systems, while gradually changing over many generations due to influences from American culture.

Drawing from fieldwork done in the United States, Carol Stack, Linda Burton and Susan Keefe argue for a similar development in American society, i.e., that certain kinship patterns persist but with modifications. Despite opinions to the contrary, these authors show that kinship is alive and well in urban societies. David Schneider demonstrates that kinship patterns certainly do exist among Anglo-Americans. Kinship patterns are the artifacts of culture.

Dianne Hoffman explores the cultural meanings and value of "self"—a new emphasis in post-modern American anthropology—within the context of the American family. Hoffman compares American child-rearing practices with that of Japan, as reflective of each culture's attitudes towards self and family.

All the readings in this section underscore a common theme: that there are definite kinship patterns in different cultures, and it is possible for anthropologists to discover these patterns of kinship. Some of the authors emphasize the continuity of kinship patterns, while others, their mutability. However, the intimate relationship between kinship and culture is clear among all the authors. Kinship can influence culture. Likewise, culture change can also lead to changes in kinship structure. The authors in this section have, in one way or another, dealt with methodological issues. Francis Hsu's dominant dyad analysis and the life course approach of Carol Stack and Linda Burton provide clear illustrations in the study of kinship. Hoffman focuses on the relationship between psychology and culture, between parent and child, as found in self and society.

Within the context of the reading materials, students can be encouraged to relate their own kinship systems to their particular ethnic cultures. In this age of increased awareness of self-identity and ethnicity, particularly, students from non-Western cultural or ethnic backgrounds will be stimulated to dig into their own personal backgrounds for deeper understanding of kinship systems. Asian systems, long ignored, are now approachable as immediate and meaningful databases. Thus, Japanese-Americans, Korean-American, or even Norwegian-Americans and others from diverse backgrounds can delve into their own kinship systems with enthusiasm.

Instructors will be able to use these readings to stimulate meaningful discussions on kinship in urban societies. Are kinship patterns predictors of social behavior? Do kinship systems die or fall away in industrial societies? What is the relationship between culture and kinship? Or does a relationship even exist? How much influence does a parent have on a child's sense of self? Is "self" really an independent factor, as Americans believe, or is it deeply rooted in accepted cultural norms? Such questions beg to be discussed and answered. Students will also be able to test out some of the kinship methodologies suggested by the authors in this section.

CHAPTER 1

The Effect of Dominant Kinship Relationships on Kin and Non-Kin Behavior: A Hypothesis

Francis L.K. Hsu

The concept of kinship extension was first explained by Radcliffe-Brown. He observed "the tendency" among the Bantu tribes and Nama Hottentots of South Africa to develop patterns for the mother's brother and the father's sister by regarding the former as somewhat of a male mother and the latter to some extent a female father (Radcliffe-Brown 1924 and reprinted 1952:19). He concludes as follows: "In primitive society there is a strongly marked tendency to merge the individual in the group to which he or she belongs. The result of this in relation to kinship is a tendency to extend to all members of a group a certain type of behaviour which has its origin in a relationship to one particular member of the group" (1952:25).

Radcliffe-Brown's use of the term primitive is unnecessary. The kind of behavior he spoke of cannot scientifically be used to separate mankind into "primitive" and "civilized." In fact the very dichotomy of "primitive" versus civilized is to be questioned (Hsu 1964) However the idea of extension of patterns of behavior characteristic of one kinship relationship to that of another has been the basis of much valuable field research. Thus Fred Eggan, among others, has shown that the Hopi not only class mother's mother's mother and the mother's brothers as "siblings" but also extend "the sibling relationship to all the members of one's clan and phratry who are of roughly the same age or generation and also to the children of all men of the father's clan and phratry, including the clans and phratries of the ceremonial and doctor fathers regardless of age" (Eggan 1950:43–44).

However, all of these works, including those aided by precise models such as those of Lévi-Strauss (1949) and White (1963) deal merely with the modification of one kind of kinship relationship by another, the degree to which kinship categories are applied to non-kins, or the bearing of these phenomena on kinship or kinship-connected behavior such as avoidance of intimacy but particularly mate selection. Where the question of relationship between what goes on in the kinship sphere and what goes on outside it is concerned, two approaches have been apparent. The first is the personality-and-culture one, which attempts to relate certain child rearing practices which are little or unrelated to forms of kinship (such as swaddling, permissiveness, sibling rivalry, length of breast-feeding, alleged or real sudden changes in parental attitude when the child reaches a certain age, etc.) to the personality of the individual or culture of the society. The other is that of students of social structure which either ignores the question or tries to explain social development without reference to kinship at all (Lévi-Strauss 1953:534–35 and Hsu 1959:792–93).

Our present hypothesis is designed to do a number of things. First, we hope to go beyond Radcliffe-Brown and others by showing that not only the influences of one kinship relationship upon another is a general phenomenon, but that these influences can originate from one relationship and extend to all other relationships so as to shape the entire kinship system. Second, when these influences exert themselves thusly, the effector relationships do not simply change into secondary versions of the affector relationship, as Radcliffe-Brown and others have observed so far, and the kinship systems in question make no assumptions of such formal changes either. Instead, what occurs much more generally is that the qualities and patterns of interaction in the effector relationships have assumed characteristics similar to those of the affector relationship so that, e.g., the husband-wife relationship or father-son relationship *as husband-wife or father-son relationships* in one kinship system appears drastically different from that in another. Third, we hope to show that the same influence becomes visible in the qualities and patterns of behavior among those other members of the same society who are not related through kinship, acting in non-kinship roles. In other words, we hope firmly to link interaction patterns in a kinship system with the characteristic modes of behavior in the wider society of which that kinship system forms a part. In doing so we hope to convince, on the one hand, many students of psychological anthropology that it is the broader aspects of interpersonal interaction patterns in the nuclear family and not merely certain limited child rearing practices which are crucial to human development and, on the other, many students of social structure that they have unnecessarily restricted the scientific fruitfulness of their efforts by ignoring psychological anthropology. Last, in order to carry out these tasks we have to scrutinize kinship relationships in terms of their attributes, for it is then that we can not only trace their influences where human beings are structurally linked through terminological or other kinship-connected categories but also identify their ramifications outside the kinship organization, far beyond their boundaries throughout the society.

Dominant Relationships and Dominant Attributes

Before going into the hypothesis it is first necessary to define four basic terms: Relationship and Attribute, and Dominant Relationship and Dominant Attribute.

I first dealt with the importance of distinguishing between the structure and content of social organization in a paper entitled "Structure, Function, Content and Process" (1959:790–805).[1] In the present exercise we must distinguish between relationship and attributes, and see structure as consisting of a combination of relationships and content, a combination of attributes. A relationship is the minimum unit into which two or more individuals are or may be linked. In the nuclear family eight such relationships are basic. These are: father-son, mother-son, father-daughter, mother-daughter, husband-wife, brother-brother, sister-sister, and brother-sister. Attribute refers to the logical or typical mode of behavior and attitude intrinsic to each relationship. The words logical, typical, and intrinsic are crucial to this definition. By them we mean that the attributes of each relationship are what David Schneider describes as "constants" (Schneider 1961:5) because they are universally the potential and inherent properties of that relationship.

The easiest example for aid in understanding this is perhaps that of the employer-employee relationship. The intrinsic attributes of this relationship are, for example, functional considerations, calculated obligations and rewards, and specific delineations in duration. A man enters into such a relationship generally because he has work he wants done or he desires wages or their equivalent. Furthermore, the length of time during which the relationship lasts is likely to be understood or made specific in advance. The details vary from society to society but these intrinsic attributes can be found wherever an employer-employee relationship is said to exist. On the other hand, these attributes intrinsic to the employer-employee relationship do not obtain in the case of a romantic relationship. The intrinsic attributes of each relationship are the basic ingredients and determinants of the interactional patterns between parties to that relationship.

No nuclear family would seem to give equal prominence to all its eight basic relationships. What actually occurs is that in each type of nuclear family one (or more) of the latter takes precedence over the others. When a relationship is thus elevated above others it tends to modify, magnify, reduce, or even eliminate other relationships in the kinship group. Such a relationship is designated in our hypothesis as the *dominant relationship* while others in the system are *non-dominant relationships*. For example, if the father-son relationship in the nuclear family is the dominant one, it will increase the social importance of the father-son relationship at the expense of other relationships such as husband-wife so that the father and mother will have more to say about their son's future wife than the son himself. In such an eventuality the kinship group or kinship team as defined by Naroll (1956:696 and 698) tends to extend itself far beyond the nuclear family of parents and unmarried children because of its inclusion of a variety of other consanguineal relatives and their wives and children. Conversely, if the husband-wife relationship is dominant, it will alter the parent-child relationship into a temporary arrangement to be replaced or discarded when the child grows into adulthood. In such a case the kinship group tends to correspond to the nuclear family at all times because of the exclusion of all consanguineal relatives as soon as they are married.

The intrinsic attributes of the dominant relationships are designated in our hypothesis as the *dominant attributes* while those of the non-dominant relationships in the system are designated *non-dominant attributes*.[2] In each form of nuclear family the dominant attributes will so influence the non-dominant attributes that the latter tend to converge in the direction of the dominant attributes.

The dominant attributes prevail over and give shape to all the non-dominant attributes. The sum of all the attributes converging toward the dominant attributes in the kinship system is designated its content, just as the sum of all the relationships under the influence of one or more dominating relationships is its structure.

The interrelationship may be roughly represented in the following diagram:

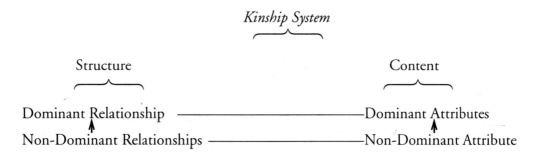

The Hypothesis

Having defined the terms we are then ready to tackle the hypothesis which, in skeletal form, is as follows: *the dominant attributes of the dominant relationship in a given kinship system tend to determine the attitudes and action patterns which the individual in such a system develops towards other relationships in this system as well as towards his relationships outside of the system.*

We shall explicate this hypothesis in three parts: first, an examination of four basic kinship relationships and their attributes; second, the effect of dominant relationships on other kinship relationships in the same kinship system; third, the effect of dominant relationships on non-kin relationships.

Six points should be made clear at the outset. First, the different relationships overlap to a certain extent in their attributes. For example, discontinuity is common to husband-wife, mother-son, and brother-brother relationships. It is the particular combination of attributes, not single attributes, which differentiates one relationship from another. Second, the differences between attributes are rarely if ever absolute, but as a rule used in a comparative sense. Continuity versus discontinuity, or inclusiveness versus exclusiveness are illustrative of this view. In the geometric sense of a line being a set of points, continuity is made up of a set of discontinuities. Third, when an attribute is listed for relationship A but not for relationship B it does not mean that it is entirely absent in the latter. Thus the attribute authority is not entirely absent in the mother-son relationship, but this attribute tends to be so overshadowed by one or more others, or embraced by them, that it is not independently significant. Fourth, some attributes, such as authority and sexuality, are opposed to each other, while others, such as authority and dependence, are intimately related to each other. Fifth, the list of attributes given for each relationship is not exhaustive. Further analysis may yield new ones. Lastly, in this and later analyses the reader should bear in mind the contribution of Parsons in his essay on "Family Structure and Socialization of the Child" (1955a:35–131). Some of our attributes are similar but not identical with some aspects of Parsons' "role structure" of the nuclear family and their differentiations. These will be pointed out as we progress. More pronounced differences between our analysis and Parsons' will occur in later sections of this paper.

Four Relationships and Their Attributes

Relationship	Attributes	Definition of Attributes
Husband-Wife	1. Discontinuity	The condition of not being, or the attitude of desiring not to be, in a sequence or connected with others.
	2. Exclusiveness	The act of keeping others out or unwillingness to share with them.
	3. Sexuality	Preoccupation with sex.
	4. Volition	The condition of being able to follow own inclinations, or of desiring to do so.
Father-Son	1. Continuity	The condition of being, or the attitude of desiring to be, in an unbroken sequence, or connected with others.
	2. Inclusiveness	The act of incorporating or the attitude of wishing to be incorporated.
	3. Authority	Personal power that commands and enforces obedience, or the condition of being under such power.
	4. Asexuality	The condition of having no connection with sex.
Mother-Son	1. Discontinuity	(Already defined above)
	2. Inclusiveness	(Already defined above)
	3. Dependence	The condition of being or the attitude of wishing to be reliant upon others.
	4. Diffuseness	The tendency to spread out in all directions.
	5. Libidinality	Diffused or potential sexuality.
Brother-Brother	1. Discontinuity	(Already defined above)
	2. Inclusiveness	(Already defined above)
	3. Equality	The condition of being or the attitude of wishing to be of the same rank and importance as others.
	4. Rivalry	The act of striving, or the attitude of wishing to strive, for equality with or excellence over others.

Let us examine the links between these relationships and their attributes. The attributes of the husband-wife relationship are discontinuity,[3] exclusiveness, and sexuality. It is discontinuous because, and here I must ask leave for elaboration of the obvious, every husband is never a wife and every wife is never a husband. Every husband-wife relationship is a unit by itself, independent of all other relationships. There is no structural necessity for any husband-wife relationship, as such, to be related to other husband-wife relationships. It is exclusive because, while marriage in every society is a public affair, every husband and wife must universally carry out by themselves alone some activities which are crucial to the conjugal relationship. This remains true regardless of the form of marriage. It is a well known fact that in most of the polygynous societies of Africa each wife in the polygynous situation has her own hut where live her own children and where her husband visits her. It is also well known that the wife in the few known polyandrous societies receives her husbands separately and each of the several husbands usually establishes some kind of individualized ritual relationship with a particular child.

Among these exclusive activities, sexuality occupies an obvious, central place, which is the third attribute of the husband-wife relationship. The connection between sexuality and husband-wife relationship needs no elaboration. Of all the eight basic relationships the husband-wife relationship is the only one in which sexuality is universally an implicit and explicit constant.

The attribute of volition is commensurate with both exclusiveness and sexuality. Of all the eight basic relationships in the nuclear family, that of husband-wife relationship alone is one which, by virtue of sexuality, involves a kind of need for individual willingness unknown or not required in the others. Even in societies where caste or other customary rules exclude individual choice, individual preferences enter into the making, continuation and termination of the relationship. Sometimes the volition may be exercised by parents, or family heads and not the man and woman entering or forming the relationship. But that is a kind of freedom of choice nevertheless which is not naturally true in the other basic relationships in the nuclear family. Furthermore for the male at least there is universally more room for personal manoeuvre no matter what the kinship system he lives in.

The basic attributes of the father-son relationship are continuity, inclusiveness, and authority. It is continuous because every father is a son and every son, in the normal course of events, is a father. Therefore every father-son relationship is but a link in an everlasting chain of father-son relationships. It is inclusive because while every son has only one father, every father actually or potentially has many sons. Therefore the relationship between the father and the son is inherently tolerant rather than intolerant toward sharing with others. The attribute of authority comes from the fact that every father is many years older than his son and is inherently in a position of power over the younger man.

A closer examination will reveal that the several attributes intrinsic to each of the two relationships are mutually commensurate with each other. Take the attributes of the father-son relationship first.

Continuity means relatively lengthy existence of that relationship in time. With normal birth and marriage more lengthy existence in time means greater chances of involvement of others who were not previously in the picture. Thus two bachelors may develop a friendship. If the friendship lasts more than a few years there are chances of each of them being married to a woman. If their friendship had ended before they were married, there would have been no question of inclusion in their friendship of the two women who came later. But if they continue their friendship after marriage, it is reasonable to expect that the new wives will be involved in the relationship. If their friendship continues still further, there is the likelihood of their having children who are also likely to be involved in some way in the friendship of the two older men.

However, the widening of the circle of involvement as this friendship continues is not restricted to birth and marriage. One member of the friendship team may move away, due to business or other reasons, to another locality where he will meet new people and make new friends. If he discontinues his friendship with his older friend, then indeed his circle of friendship need not be more inclusive than before. But if he wants to continue the older friendship, then it becomes obvious that the circle is inevitably enlarged. Thus we may generate the following subsidiary hypothesis: the more continuous a relationship, and the longer it lasts, the more inclusive it will become of other individuals who were not previously in that relationship.

Authority can be exercised generally in one of three ways. First by brutal power on the part of the superior over the subordinates. Second through what Max Weber would designate as charisma or what is popularly known in the United States as sex appeal of the superior. Third by conviction on the part of the subordinates of the superior's right, duty, or privilege to exercise authority just as it is their right, duty, or privilege to obey it. It is obvious that the first two ways of exercising authority are likely to be less permanent than the third. In the first, resentment is likely to occur among those who are subject to the authority so that they may revolt or attempt to get out from under the authority at the first opportunity. In the second way, authority is likely to be disrupted as soon as there is a reduction of charisma on the part of the superior or of his sex appeal through old age or loss of capacity in some manner. At any rate, death is likely to end his position of authority once and for all In the third way, since the subordinates are taught to respect the superior's role of authority, revolts are much less likely.

The lines separating these three ways of authority are relative, but the third way is more likely to characterize authority in the father-son relationship especially since the attribute of continuity enables the sons to cooperate, because they themselves expect to exercise it in the same way when it is their turn to do so. In this situation the idea of authority permeates the relationship and is not tied to the accident of the brutal power or the special qualities of a single person. Under such circumstances authority does not disappear with the death of the person in authority; it tends to continue after his death in the form of the cult of the dead (in the kinship sphere) or worship of the past or tradition (in the society generally). Furthermore, on the basis of what we said before of the relationship between continuity and inclusiveness, we can say that the more continuous the worship of the ancestry of a kinship group or tradition of a society, the more inclusive that authority is likely to apply to wider circles of human beings.

In the same light we may see the attributes of the husband-wife relationship. Discontinuity is more commensurate with exclusiveness and inclusiveness. Going back to the same friendship example discussed before, it is obvious that the shorter the duration of friendship, the less the chances of involvement in friendship with others who are not originally part of that friendship.

Sexuality and exclusiveness are necessary for each other because no matter how widely distributed the sex appeal of a single individual, the core of sexuality, that is the sexual act, is universally carried out between two individuals. There are many forms of self-eroticism such as masturbation which can be restricted to one individual alone, and there are other forms of sexual practices which can involve more than two individuals, but there is no question that the sexual act between one man and one woman is the universal norm.

Sexuality as a physiological phenomenon necessarily waxes and wanes even during that period of the individual's life when the sex drive is strong. Then as the individual grows older the sexual drive diminishes and recedes. There are known differences between the male and the female in this regard and there are also known individual differences. But there is no question that sexuality recedes and then disappears as age advances. Furthermore, death concludes it. Unlike authority, which can be exercised many centuries after a man's death, sexuality cannot be exercised in absentia. Consequently sexuality in contrast to authority is much more commensurate with discontinuity than with continuity.

Turning now to the mother-son relationship we find five differentiable attributes: discontinuity, inclusiveness, dependence, diffuseness, and libidinality. In common with the husband-wife relationship it is discontinuous because no mother is a son and no son is ever a mother. But the next two attributes are more particularly its own. These are dependence and diffuseness, built on two closely related facts. First, since the mother comes into the new born child's life at the earliest possible moment, she caters to its wants at a time when it is at its most ineffectual. For the infant, the mother is the principal agent for all satisfaction. She is his answer-all. Second, the mother's relationship with her infant involves more interaction of an unstructured nature than that of the father's since, as some psychoanalysts would put it, the "mother normally achieves identification with her infant through libidinally charged processes which permit her to become a child with her child again The identification with the baby permits her to enjoy her "regression and to repeat and satisfy her own receptive, dependent needs" (Alexander 1952:104 and 106).[4]

Therefore, though dependence is not entirely absent in some of the other kinship relationships, it is the outstanding ingredient in the mother-son relationship (as it is also naturally in the mother-daughter relationship). Dependence obviously enters into the father-son relationship. But there it is greatly modified by the fact of growth. Intensive interaction between a father and his son usually occurs some months or years after the son's birth when the latter is less ineffectual and helpless than when he first began life with his mother. In Parsons' terms (1955a:47–55) the father-son relationship is one step farther in the process of role differentiation from that of mother-son. This means not only far less dependence, but that dependence when it occurs has changed its nature from one due to sheer inability to comprehend or perform any task to one in which the need is for guidance, channelling, wisdom of experience, or punishment. In Parsons' terms these are characteristic of "instrumentality" rather than "expressiveness" (1955a:45).

In the mother-son situation dependence is found in its pristine state but in the father-son situation dependence is only an element of what can better be described as authority (Parsons' "power"). The attribute authority includes a degree of dependence but it is much higher on "instrumentality" and on "power." Conversely though "power" and some "instrumentality" are not totally absent in the mother-child relationship, these (especially "instrumentality") tend to be overshadowed by other more characteristic attributes. This enables us to understand why diffuseness is an attribute of the mother-son relationship but not of others. Diffuseness is related to lack of differentiation and therefore of specialization. Of the eight basic relationships in the nuclear family, those of mother-son and mother-daughter are the least structured and differentiated in role because the younger member of the dyad is, to begin with, so completely helpless and dependent.

The last attribute, namely libidinality, associated with the mother-son relationship is present whenever the partners of the relationship are not of the same sex. But this attribute is likely to be stronger in the case of mother-son relationship than that of father-daughter or brother-sister because of greater physical intimacy at a time when the son is least differentiated with reference to his place in the social system. In general our libidinality is related to what Parsons designates as "expressiveness" insofar as the latter contains a sexual component, but his concept would seem to embrace our attributes dependence (partially) and diffuseness (entirely).

However, although we derive the term libidinality from the Freudian term libido, it is not identical with the latter in significance. Freudian libido is conceived as the raw material of a sexual nature which is the fountainhead of all psychic energy and which, through socializing mechanisms such as repression or sublimation, becomes greatly modified, warped, diverted, or its sexuality driven from consciousness. It is strictly a matter of personality dynamics. Libidinality in our sense may undergo repression or sublimation in the individual but it is primarily characteristic of general patterns of interpersonal interaction in a society so that it expresses itself throughout the culture in diverse ways in its native state without significant modification or at least with the sexual component still visible.

On the other hand, the attribute libidinality is very different from that of sexuality which is exclusive to the husband-wife relationship. Sexuality involves a specific and recognized urge and motive with relatively clearly defined objects for its satisfaction, while libidinality is more nebulous, undifferentiated, but usually without clearly defined objects for its satisfaction as sexuality. The attraction between two lovers is characterized by sexuality but that between certain types of entertainers and their public, between the temple lingam (male phallic representation) and their worshippers, and even between certain pieces of art and their viewers, contains libidinality in our sense.

The brother-brother relationship is discontinuous because solidarity among brothers marks each generation out from the last and the next. Each set of brothers has no structural connection with the brothers of the generation above or the brothers of the generation below. The brother-brother relationship is inclusive for the same reason that father-son and mother-son relationships are inclusive, for there are likely to be more than two brothers. Brother-brother relationship is not a dyad intolerant of the inclusion of other parties.

Two attributes, equality and rivalry, are peculiar to the brother-brother relationship. Of all the relationships in the nuclear family, brothers are more likely to be equal age-wise and occupy more nearly equivalent positions in the social system than others. Husbands and wives may be more similar in age to each other than some brothers but they seem to be universally complementary in function and differentiated in work. A greater degree of general equality tends to obtain between brothers than between all other related persons in the nuclear family. With greater equality comes greater chances of rivalry. Competition can occur in any situation wherever there are individuals who think they ought to at least be as well situated as others. But it is between equals, within a structural arrangement where they are more equal among themselves than between themselves and others in that configuration, that competition becomes most intense.

The link between equality and rivalry in the brother-brother relationship would seem to suggest that all the attributes intrinsic to this relationship are mutually compatible with each other. This is not the case. While the attributes of father-son relationship are mutually supportive of each other and those of the husband-wife relationship are also mutually supportive of each other, the attributes of mother-son relationship and again those of brother-brother are not always harmonious. In the mother-son relationship dependence is commensurate with diffuseness and libidinality, but it is not always supportive of inclusiveness because the dependent may be so jealous of the person on whom he depends as to be intolerant of other parties. This incompatibility may be moderated by the fact that, since it is usually the depended upon and not the dependent who provides the initiative, the dependent is necessarily tied down in his decisions by the preferences of the depended upon and therefore cannot exclude with as much ease as an independent. But dependence is highly incommensurate with discontinuity because by all psychological evidence, one who is dependent will normally seek the continuation of the relationship in time rather than its breakage. The problems of weaning and of first separation from parents are but two of the most common illustrations of this fact. Finally, discontinuity is also incommensurate with inclusiveness because the two undercut each other. Viewing all five attributes of the mother-son relationship as a whole, we find discontinuity alone to be specially discordant, which must create serious problems for the predominantly dependent.

In the case of brother-brother relationship, the attribute of equality reinforces inclusiveness. It is under such ideals as "all men are brothers" or "all men are created equal" that universalistic religions or political philosophies are usually based. Similarly the attribute of rivalry reinforces discontinuity. The essence of rivalry expresses itself in the effort to excel over others or even the desire to annihilate the others. Therefore it is separatist in consequence no matter what rationalization is used to soft pedal it. One of the most universal signs of status or achievement is separation from the others. Yet these very links between discontinuity and rivalry on the one hand and inclusiveness and equality on the other pit these two sets of attributes against each other. For the former is centrifugal while the latter is centripetal. Not only is discontinuity incompatible with inclusiveness, but rivalry and equality are usually at odds with each other, for, as we noted before, rivalry heightens itself with greater equality.

The Effect of Dominant Kinship Relationships on Other Kinship Relationships

Our next order of business is to examine the way in which the dominant relationships in a kinship system affect other relationships in that system. Since it is impossible in a single paper to analyse the complicated possible effects of each dominant relationship on all the other relationships in a system, we shall illustrate our points by confining ourselves to the effects of the dominant relationship on primarily one non-dominant relationship in each instance. We shall begin with a system where the father-son relationship is the dominant one. Previously we noted in passing that in such an eventuality the parents will have more to say about their son's future wife than the son himself. In the light of the respective sets of attributes intrinsic to the father-son and husband-wife relationships, this means that the attribute of exclusiveness intrinsic to the husband-wife relationship is greatly modified in favor of the attribute of inclusiveness characteristic of that of father-son. Hence married partners in this system seem aloof to each other, for they often place their duties and obligations towards parents before those towards each other. Custom will strongly disapprove of any sign of public intimacy between spouses. Instead it enjoins them to exhibit ardent signs of devotion to their (especially his) elders. In case of a quarrel between the wife and the mother-in-law, the husband must take the side of the latter against the former, especially in public. Polygyny with the ostensible aim of begetting male heirs to continue the father-son line is a structural necessity.

Yet in spite of all this the marital bond in a father-son dominated system tends to endure. Divorce is possible but rare. The attribute of continuity and the attribute of authority militate against the dissolution of the marital bond. Continuity means that all bonds including the marital bond are likely to last once they are formed. Authority, with all that it implies toward the past and the superiors, means that the pleasures or displeasures of the married partners are less important considerations for staying together than those of their elders or of the kinship group as a whole according to tradition.

This form of kinship is likely to be associated with a strong cult of ancestors[5] and a maximum tendency for the development of the clan.

Where the husband-wife relationship is dominant we should expect the father-son relationship to be temporary. In all likelihood that relationship tends to end or nearly so upon marriage of the younger man, after which the father will no longer have strong authority over him. The cohesion between a husband and wife takes precedence over all other relationships and mate selection is at least theoretically entirely in the hands of the prospective spouses. Not only will the father or mother have no right to initiate divorce for his daughter or son, but any over-intimacy between a son and his parents against the objections of his wife is likely to lead to serious marital disharmony. In such a situation monogamy is the only form of marriage possible to satisfy the exclusiveness of the husband-wife relationship. Discontinuity makes for lack of respect for old age, tradition, and the past in general. Therefore there will be sharp gulfs between the generations and no true ancestor cult of any kind.

The attributes of sexuality and exclusiveness make public exhibition of marital intimacy (by such things as terms of endearment and kissing) easy and almost imperative, for in the ardency of their exclusive feelings for each other, they need to pay no attention to the rest of the world. In spite of all this, the marital bond is brittle. Divorce is likely to be far more common than in a father-son dominated system. The attribute of discontinuity and the attribute of sexuality are both conducive to this. Discontinuity means that all relationships including the marital one are not really forever since there is little concern for the past. Sexuality adds to this impermanency since its emphasis means that marriage is likely to be precarious, as sexuality waxes and wanes during any period of time and throughout life. Therefore, while in the father-son dominated system the marital bond is not endangered by long periods of separation, in the husband-wife dominated system even separation of a moderate duration creates great marital hazards.

But a dominant husband-wife relationship has other effects on the father-son relationship than making it temporary. The father-son relationship in a husband-wife dominated system is likely to be imbued with sexuality and exclusiveness. Parents insist on exclusive control of their children, are likely to be extraordinarily sensitive about their rights over them, and resent all advice from grandparents and other relatives (the inclusiveness intrinsic to parent-child relationships is lost). Furthermore there is even likely to be competition between the parents for the affection of the youngsters. Add to this the attribute of sexuality and we have then a most fertile soil for the Oedipus Complex. Since the resolution of the Oedipus Complex involves such mechanisms as repression or sublimation, I submit that it is not at all fantastic to suggest that modern day emphasis on sex education on the part of parents is a devious expression of the repressed or sublimated sexuality rooted in a husband-wife dominated kinship system. By contrast, sex as a subject cannot even be touched upon casually between parents and children in a father-son dominated kinship system.

In a mother-son dominated kinship system the father-son relationship tends to exhibit discontinuity rather than continuity. For one thing the father-son tie is not eternal so that the cult of ancestors, even if it exists, tends to be minimal (according to our scale, see Chapter 15). Authority of the father will be greatly reduced so that the father is less a strong guiding, channelling, and punishing figure than a nourishing, supportive, and succoring one. Furthermore, the father image is blurred so that there tends to be the need for the son to seek other "father" figures, not to replace the real father but to assure himself of adequate sources of nourishment, support, and succor. In fact, the line of distinction between the father figure and the mother figure is often unclear.

The attribute of inclusiveness of the mother-son dominated system, like that of the father-son dominated system, is not incommensurate with polygyny, for the marital bond needs not be exclusive. But lacking the attribute continuity, the custom is not primarily for the purpose of maintenance of the patrilineal line as it would be in the father-son dominated system. Rather it seems to be strongly related to the attribute of libidinality or diffused sexuality, and therefore the mother-son dominated system is likely to be associated with more than just polygyny. If the attributes of exclusiveness and sexuality are commensurate with monogamy, and those of inclusiveness and continuity are in line with polygyny, then those of inclusiveness and libidinality or diffused sexuality favor plurality of spouses in general, including polygyny and polyandry, as well as other practices such as cicisbeism defined by Prince Peter as "an arrangement between the sexes, wherein one or more of the male partners is not related to the woman in marriage" (Prince Peter 1963:22), or conjoint-marriage in which polygyny is combined with polyandry, enabling several males (often related) to be married to several females, or a passing connection between one woman and more than one man for several reasons, including insemination of the childless female by a male other than her husband with the latter's consent.

In a brother-brother dominated society there will be strong tensions between fathers and sons. Rivalry among brothers will spill over to the father-son relationship and the attribute of equality will seriously affect the authority of the old over the young. In fact, these attributes are conducive to sexual competition between fathers and sons. At any rate, the possibility of such emulation is real enough to produce many forms of hostility such as suspicion or witchcraft accusations against each other. Therefore the cult of ancestors is likely to be either non-existent or minimal, and even when some form of ancestor cult may be said to exist, the central effort will be directed toward preventing the spirits of the departed from punishing or performing wrathful acts rather than showing concern for the ancestor's comfort and respect.

In the husband-wife relationship calculatedness tends to rise above everything else. Rivalry and equality reduce the need for protection of one sex by the other. In fact they tend to make the "weaker" versus "stronger" sexes dichotomy superfluous. The complementary element between the sexes is so greatly diminished that the question of devotion, fidelity, and sentiments between married partners are unimportant or subordinated to considerations such as calculated advantages and disadvantages. Their relationship may be marked by a contest of power, economic or otherwise, rather than a depth of intimacy. Polygyny, instead of being rationalized in terms of the need for continuing the family line, as in the father-son dominated systems, is practiced primarily as the man's sign of status or wealth. On the female side a sort of polyandry is practiced, not necessarily fraternal from the point of view of economy among the males, but primarily as the woman's symbol of ability and affluence. This is the only kind of kinship system in which exists the condition for true male concubinage. One feels almost compelled to term it female polygyny (as distinguished from the usual polyandry). In addition, premarital and extra-marital relations are likely to be common in theory and practice. The custom of surrogate fathers whereby a childless woman is inseminated by her husband's brother or someone else is not likely to be rare. For sex is apt to be used as a means for conquest or for other gains rather than as an expression of emotional or moral or social commitment. The marital bond tends to be weak. We can expect divorce to be common especially where it is not mitigated by plurality of spouses or lovers in one form or another.

In an earlier paragraph we noted the observation of Radcliffe-Brown (1952:19) that among the Bantu tribes and Nama Hottentots of South Africa the mother's brother is a male mother of a sort and the father's sister is somewhat of a female father. In the light of the effects of the dominant relationship in each system on some other relationships in that system, we may say with a good deal of justification that husbands in a father-son dominated society are younger fathers, mothers in a husband-wife dominant society tend to be older wives, fathers in a mother-son dominated society tend to be male mothers, while wives in brother-brother dominated societies are to some extent female brothers. However, such observations tend to miss the point and obscure the truly significant effects of each dominant relationship on non-dominant relationships. The fact is *not* that the husband-wife relationship under the dominance of the father-son relationship is changed, in terms of that kinship system, or in the minds of the individuals concerned, into a father-son relationship. What occurs is that *the intrinsic attributes of the husband-wife relationship are so influenced by the intrinsic attributes of the father-son relationship that the characteristic qualities and modes of interaction of the husband-wife relationship in that system, as husband-wife relationship, are very different from those in other systems where the father-son relationship is not dominant.* Furthermore, if our hypothesis is correct, the characteristic qualities and modes of interaction of the husband-wife relationship (or any other basic relationship) in any kinship system become predictable once its dominant relationship is known. Conversely, knowing something of the characteristic qualities and modes of interaction of the husband-wife relationship (or any other basic relationship) in any kinship system will guide us to its dominant relationship (or relationships).[6]

Similarly, for those in husband-wife dominated systems, the male in the father-son dominated society would seem to suffer from lack of ambition; for those in the father-son dominated society, the male and female in the husband-wife dominated system would seem to be oversexed; for those in both of these systems, the male in the mother-son dominated society would seem to be unsure of his sex identity; while for those in all three systems, the male and female in the brother-brother dominated society would seem to be too callous or calculating with reference to the matter of sexual attachments and too lacking in concern for fidelity. Sex seems to be a commodity to be satisfied or conquered through almost commercialized means. But these "problems" from the point of view of outsiders reared in kinship systems with other dominant relationships may be no problem at all in the minds of those persons who exhibit the characteristic behavior in question.[7] Until we appreciate the role of dominant kinship relationship of each system in shaping the other relationships in that system, our understanding of human behavior will hardly be cross-cultural.

The Effect of Dominant Kinship Relationships on Non-Kin Behavior

Had space permitted we would have considered the equally telling effect of each of the dominant relationships on other relationships; however, we must proceed to the next task. In considering the effect of dominant kinship relationships on non-kin behavior we will once more confine ourselves to a limited exercise. We shall only comment upon one cluster of facts: the problem of authority.

Reviewing the four kinds of kinship systems dealt with above, we should expect authority to be less problematic in societies with father-son and mother-son dominated kinship systems than those with husband-wife and brother-brother dominated kinship systems. Authority is a major attribute of the father-son relationship. Nurtured in this attribute, both the father and the son are attuned to its necessity. The superior does not have to disguise his power because he knows this is his due, and the subordinate has no need to disguise his obeisance since it is not necessary to be ashamed of it. Authority and compliance to authority are therefore carried out openly and elaborately with no qualms on either side. Difficulties may arise if the superior becomes too oppressive, but the salvation of the oppressed lies in finding individual relief from it, not in challenging the entire social structure in which such oppression occurs. The individual reared in the father-son dominated system will have no resentment against benevolent authority; in fact, he will love it.

In a mother-son dominated kinship system, authority is a major component of dependence; therefore, its exercise and compliance to it are also undisguised. However, while in the father-son dominated system the child is already conditioned to achieve a good deal of autonomy so that he can proceed independently once the specifications are given, the child in the mother-son dominated kinship system tends to retain more of his undifferentiated outlook and therefore needs continuous guidance, supervision, and restraint in order to conduct himself within the specifications desired by the authority. In a mother-son dominated society authority must be much more elaborately implemented with heavy reliance upon minute negative barriers to make this type possible at all. There will be challenges to authority, but the challenges will be ineffective and have little real impact on the society and culture. The central problem for the leader is not merely to urge his followers to action, but to get them to sustain their efforts toward specific, positive goals without being sidetracked by diverse or unrelated issues.

It is in societies with husband-wife and brother-brother dominated kinship systems that the problem of authority is most acute. In neither system is authority a dominant attribute, or a major element of a dominant attribute. The individual who is a product of such a system tends to resent authority or regard it as an obstacle to be overcome by all means. The difference between these two types of societies in this regard is, however, considerable. In the husband-wife dominated system the complementary nature of sex, pregnancy, and the care of the young provides the basis for two related developments. On the one hand there exists a certain amount of inevitable authority of the male over the female which came from man's primitive past and which, as far as we can see, may last indefinitely into the future. This is a kind of authority to which the female has to submit by voluntary cooperation for her own satisfaction. On the other hand, there is the idea of protection of the weak and the helpless which is at the root of chivalry or noblesse oblige. Therefore the authority can be exercised and maintained, in spite of the waxing and waning of its basis, as long as there exists functional inter-dependence between superiors or leaders and subordinates or followers. However, in exercising and maintaining their authority, the superiors or leaders must disguise their position by minimizing external signs of authority in their interaction with their subordinates or followers, buttressing their own decisions with public opinion, or resorting to other devices which tend to make them appear to be at most authority-transmitters but not authority-originators. Since chivalry is so obviously linked with women and children, adult males welcome the status of being protectors of the weak but resent that of being protected.

In the brother-brother dominated society authority is not an element of any of the attributes. It is true that the older brother can physically coerce his younger brothers but there is no need on the part of the latter which must be satisfied through some inevitable cooperation with the authority-attempting older brother. Consequently the exercise and maintenance of authority is inclined to be brutal (for there is no idea of chivalry to encourage saving or protecting the weak) and easily subject to rebellion and opposition (for the desire for power is widespread). The divisive tendency is extremely apparent. Superiors or leaders will be constantly in fear of harm from their followers and subordinates by assassination or, more diffusedly, by witchcraft. The problem of succession will be most difficult to solve in these societies, for rival claims are not silenced except by force. Yet, in contrast to husband-wife dominated societies, superiors or leaders in such societies do not have to disguise their power to originate decision since being dependent or under protection is a matter of expediency rather than of admission of basic weaknesses as in the other system.

Our analyses of authority in the four systems enable us to question the cross-cultural validity of certain sociological findings concerning the incompatibility of "task" and "emotional" functions A number of sociologists have dealt with this problem (Marcus 1960; Kahn and Katz 1960; and Blau and Scott 1962). Bales has presented evidence from small group experiments to support the position that differentiation between task (our attribute, authority) and emotional functions of group gives stability. Taking five-men groups, Bales gives subjects problem solving tasks requiring cooperation. The researchers, behind a one-way mirror, observed and recorded interaction. (See Bales 1950 for methodology). Some of the findings are as follows: (1) the task leader (best idea and guidance man) was most disliked by other members whereas the emotional leader was most liked; (2) the emotional leader was least likely to be a task leader; and (3) through a series of problem solving sessions, the emotional leader was less likely to be chosen as task leader (over time). In contrast, the task leader was less likely to be chosen as emotional leader through successive trials (Bales 1953:111–161). Our analyses above give us reason to suspect that these findings are probably characteristic of the husband-wife dominated society where authority is resented and where the attribute of exclusiveness makes it additionally necessary to have sharp differentiation and separation of roles as well as everything else, but will not hold true for the father-son, mother-son, and even brother-brother dominated societies. In father-son and mother-son dominated societies submission to and dependence upon authority are not resented and therefore present no conflict with affective relationships between the superior and the subordinate. Furthermore, in both of these and in brother-brother dominated societies the attribute of inclusiveness will make separation of roles far less mandatory.

Our hypothesis on the effect of dominant kinship relationships on non-kin behavior can equally well be applied to illuminate other clusters of facts, from the nature of friendship, sexuality and associations, to forms of economy and patterns of social development, but these exercises can only be attempted in later publications.[8]

The Question of Personality Dynamics

To the extent that our hypothesis is built on the basic premise that early experiences of the individual, especially those associated with members of his nuclear family, are extremely important in shaping the way he relates to the wider world, it is Freudian in orientation. There is no doubt, from what we now know about the dynamics of individual personality, that every person as he goes through life resorts to past experiences to deal with present and future problems which confront him. Since the nuclear family in which he grows up provides him with the structure and content for social action to begin with, the experiences in his early years cannot but serve as the basis for action in the wider human arena.

But here our hypothesis and Freudian psychology part. Freudian psychology puts overwhelming emphasis on the parent-child triad; our hypothesis stresses the fact that, depending upon the social system, the relationship of central importance may be one other than that triad. Furthermore, the dominant relationship in the nuclear family, whether it be that of father-son or brother-brother, may seriously alter the very nature of that triad, as our analyses show, so that no universal Oedipal situation such as Freud and his followers conceived can be assumed. Exclusiveness and sexuality are indispensable attributes inducing the Oedipal problem, this combination is characteristic only of the husband-wife relationship The father-son and the brother-brother relationships have neither attribute, while the mother-son relationship has diffused sexuality but not exclusiveness. In the brother-brother dominated system with its frequent and obvious rivalry between father and son even over sex, there will be many sentiments and expressions which, to observers familiar with the Freudian theory and reared in a husband-wife dominated society, easily suggest the Oedipal situation. According to our hypothesis, on the other hand, there is a distinct possibility that the latter type of observation will, on closer inspection, prove to be wide of the mark. For sexual rivalry between fathers and sons in a brother-brother dominated society is likely to occur when the sons are already adults; it is not likely to be resolved in the Freudian fashion if resolved at all; and it is merely one of many forms of rivalry in a social system where rivalry is a dominant attribute.

There are other differences between our hypothesis and the Freudian position. These particularly bear on the manner in which the individuals in different social systems tend to make use of their early experiences. In the husband-wife dominated society the individual makes use of them by their rejection, suppression, or repression because the dictates of his kinship system encourage him to depart from his parents as quickly as possible and to reject their authority as he grows up. When he chooses a wife because he needs his succoring mother, or cannot tolerate his boss because the latter reminds him of his authoritarian father, he is indeed being affected by his early experiences. But the operation of these early experiences, whether he wants to go back to them or get away from them, is likely to be denied because they are resented or unconscious.

In the father-son dominated society the individual makes use of early experiences by their deliberate maintenance, application, or extension, because the dictates of his kinship system encourage him to remember and cultivate his roots—his parents and his forebears. When he enters into ritual brotherhood with his business partners, or addresses his teachers as fathers, he is also affected by his early experiences. But the operation of these early experiences is likely to be spoken of openly because they are desired and conscious.

In yet another aspect, our hypothesis is different from both the relatively orthodox and certain revised Freudian positions. The relatively orthodox Freudians focus their attention on the influences which come to the individual by way of the erogenic zones. Others primarily deal with developmental problems connected with dependence and aggression (Whiting and Child 1953: Chapter 4; Erikson 1950: Chapters I and II; and Whiting et al. 1958). Our hypothesis, though it is not unconcerned with sexuality, dependence, and aggression, addresses itself far less to individual personality dynamics or its genesis than to that intricate but broad area of social and cultural life where different individuals meet and interact, the patterns of that interaction, which can be scrutinized independently of the actors involved, at least in analytic terms (Chapple and Arensberg 1940: 24–25), and the genesis of those patterns. To do so is not to deny the existence of unconscious motives on the part of the individual in any system.

Finally the reader who has come this far probably realizes that our hypothesis is also very different from that of Parsons (1955a & b). Our hypothesis and that of Parsons begin with the universal elements of the nuclear family. We have seen how some of our attributes and Parsons' differentiated roles are identical or related to each other. But our hypothesis becomes very dissimilar to that of Parsons when we go beyond the universal elements of the nuclear family and see the circumstances under which the same universal elements can help to give rise to different intra-kinship and extra-kinship patterns of interaction. For example, Parsons observes that although power (our attribute, authority) is a basic element in both father-son and mother-son relationships, a "critical change" in the evolution of the personality organization of the child occurs later when "the instrumental-expressive distinction comes to be differentiated out from the power axis" (1955b:135). Our hypothesis leads us to suspect that the extent of the differentiation of parental roles may vary greatly from one kinship system to another depending upon its dominant relationship and attributes. In a father-son dominated society the power or authority role of the father is likely to be greatly accentuated at all stages of personality development. His authority role is accentuated not merely because he wishes to exercise power but also because his sons tend voluntarily to concede it to him. Furthermore, while, according to Parsons, the mother's role is "disassociated" at the stage of "second fission" from power or authority (Parsons 1955b:135), our hypothesis suggests that the mother's role in a father-son dominated society is not likely to be easily separated from the power or authority element. In fact, as she grows older she is ingested with more power or authority rather than less. Consequently the kind of binary differentiation that Parsons discusses as occurring between the roles of the father and of the mother, respectively, into "instrumental" and "expressive" varieties tends neither to be so clear nor so final. In such a society both the father and the mother tend to lean toward "instrumentality" rather than "expressiveness." Following the same line of reasoning our hypothesis will lead us to believe that in a mother-son dominated society where dependence and libidinality (rather than authority as such) are dominant attributes, both the father and the mother tend to lean toward "expressiveness" rather than "instrumentality," while in the brother-brother dominated society both parents tend to be less "instrumental" and "expressive" than in either the father-son or the mother-son dominated societies, because of the greater impact of the sibling relationship. Parsons' analysis fits well with a husband-wife dominated society where, according to our hypothesis, differentiation of parental roles tends to be most pronounced.

The Role of Factors Other Than Kinship

This hypothesis does not attempt to deal with the roles of geography (e.g., isolation or topography), diffusion through historical contact, size of population, political or military conquest, human or natural catastrophe, or hereditary endowment in human affairs. It aims at probing primarily the role of human beings in shaping each other, and within that scope kinship occupies a uniquely central place.

Our hypothesis does not, of course, say that, e.g., any form of marriage or sexual connection will *definitely* occur under the dominance of a certain kinship relationship. What it does say is that certain dominant relationships are compatible with certain forms of marriage or sexual practices, and that, if such a form of marriage or sexual practice is already in existence in a given geographical region for any reason whatever, it has a better chance of continuation with one dominant relationship rather than another.

Antecedental Evidence for the Hypothesis

The bulk of the data in support of this hypothesis from the qualitative point of view is to be found in *Clan, Caste and Club* (a comparative study of Chinese, Hindu, and American ways of life [Hsu 1963]. In this work my main effort was directed toward the relationship between the forces in the kinship organization and the development of what I term "secondary groupings" in the larger society outside of the kinship organization. The present hypothesis identifies the principal of these forces in the kinship organization as dominant relationships and dominant attributes. This hypothesis leads us to expect that these forces affect the behavior patterns within and without the kinship organization, in diverse ways including the development of secondary groupings. The American, Chinese, and Hindu kinship systems fit the picture well if we assume the first to be dominated by the husband-wife relationship, the second by father-son relationship, and the third by mother-son relationship.

Some antecedental evidence on our postulation for the brother-brother relationship is to be found in the African portion of "Kinship and Ways of Life: an Exploration" (Hsu 1961b:400–56). It is also to be found in a very interesting article by Melville and Frances Herskovits entitled "Sibling Rivalry, the Oedipus Complex and Myth" (1959:1–15). If we assume many African societies of the patrilocal type to be dominated by brother-brother relationship we shall find many central features of African life understandable.

In addition, unexpected support for our hypothesis on the mother-son dominated society is found in a recent book by Prince Peter of Greece and Denmark titled *A Study of Polyandry* (1963). It will be recalled that, according to our hypothesis, the mother-son dominated kinship system structurally favors plurality of spouses in different combinations in contrast to the father-son dominated kinship system which structurally favors polygyny, and the husband-wife dominated kinship system which structurally favors monogamy. Our hypothesis also leads us to believe that the brother-brother dominated kinship system tends to be similar in this regard to the mother-son dominated kinship system except to a lesser extent.

According to Prince Peter's survey of a total of 18 societies practicing true polyandry, 11 are to be found in India or nearby such as among the Kandyans of Ceylon and the Tibetans, while three are found in Africa. Of a total of 27 societies practicing some form of cicisbeism,[9] 15 are found in India or nearby, while five are found in Africa. Of a total of four societies where the rule is passing connection between one woman and more than one man, three are found in or near India. Of a total of four societies practicing a combination of polyandry and polygyny, three are found in or near India (Prince Peter 1963:506–11).

Prince Peter's survey does not, obviously, cover the Eskimo and the Chukchee custom of wife-lending as a matter of hospitality. But his figures are highly suggestive for one portion of our hypothesis. The hypothesis in part and as a whole, needs rigorous testing not only by intense field and library analysis but also by cross-cultural statistical research.

Notes

1. A revised and augmented view of the same subject was given in "Kinship and Ways of Life" (Hsu 1961b) and in *Clan, Caste and Club* (Hsu 1963).

2. Among physical scientists the term "property" is generally used in place of our term "attribute." In the original article I used the term "recessive" to designate the non-dominant dyads and attributes.

3. The term discontinuity used in this paper is not identical with the term discontinuity which Parsons regards as one of the basic discoveries of Freud in analyzing the socialization process (Parsons 1955a:40). As our analysis will show, our term discontinuity refers not to an absolute break in the child's socialization process but to a quality of interpersonal relationships in comparative terms throughout life. This relationship is either very long and measured by decades and therefore more continuous, or very short and measured by a few months or a few years and therefore more discontinuous. However, sharp breaks in the socialization process are probably more likely to occur in a social system where discontinuity is one of its dominant attributes than in other systems where it is not.

4. In this presentation we will resort to some specific psychoanalytic observations on parent-child relationships but we do not follow any particular psychoanalytic theory of personality development.

5. Some sort of cult of ancestors is to be found in different parts of the world. So far, the term "ancestral cult" or "ancestor worship" has been applied in anthropological literature to such facts without precision. A research project at Northwestern University attempts to examine the existing ethnographic literature bearing on the subject with greater precision (See Chapter 15).

6. In my earlier publication distinguishing kinship content from kinship structure (Hsu 1959), I accepted the fact, based on Murdock (1949:226–228), that the Eskimos and the Yankees of New England have a similar kinship structure. What I tried to demonstrate in that article was that the contents of their two kinship systems made their behavior patterns so different. In view of our present analysis, it should become obvious that the Eskimos and the New England Yankees do not even share a common kinship structure. In fact the Eskimo pattern of kinship does not belong to any of the four forms analyzed in this paper. Whether the concepts of dominant kinship relationships and attributes defined here or some other factors must be resorted to in order to explain Eskimo behavior is a problem to be tackled by future intensive field research.

7. According to Whiting: "In societies with maximum conflict in sex identity, e.g., where a boy initially sleeps exclusively with his mother and where the domestic unit is patrilocal and hence controlled by men, there will be initiation rites at puberty which function to resolve this conflict in identity" (Burton and Whiting 1961:90. See also Whiting et al. 1958). The situation of Hindu India fits this picture of maximum conflict, but as far as can be ascertained, no initiation rites exist other than the donning of the sacred thread at puberty or before. The initiation rites in Whiting's studies predominantly comprise hazing, genital mutilation, seclusion from women and tests of endurance. There is nothing like them connected with puberty in Hindu India. The sacred thread rite has no trace of overt sex symbolism and is primarily restricted to Brahmins and only occasionally extended to lower castes such as the Pancha Brahma of Shamirpet, Hyderabad, Kayastha of Bengal, or (in modified form) the Lingayat of Deccan, for caste raising purposes. Yet projective materials indicate that Hindu males would seem to have uncertainty of sex identity. Presuming Whiting's hypothesis to be correct, our inference is that this seeming uncertainty is more of a problem to the outside observer

than to the Hindu. The fact that a majority of Hindu males undergo no initiation rite, and that those who do regard it primarily as a matter of caste status, is an important evidence in support of our inference. Whiting's hypothesis on initiation rites has recently been challenged by Yehudi Cohen (1964), whose grounds for the challenge do not, however, eliminate the possibility that initiation rites may be at least partially related to the problem of sex identity in many societies. On the other hand, the Hindu rite connected with the donning of the sacred thread obviously is consonant with Cohen's idea of the need for the society to manipulate "the child in relation to the boundaries of his nuclear family and kin group in order to implant a social emotional identity and values consonant with the culture's articulating principles." In the Hindu case the boundary is that of caste instead of kin group and the principle is hierarchy as explained in our hypothesis.

8. For some of these covariations see Hsu 1961 but especially 1963, and Chapter 15.
9. "So-called boarders in the U.S.A." (quoted by Linton) is listed as one case in Prince Peter's compilation of cicisbeism. This case is dropped from our count.

References Cited

Alexander, Franz. 1952. Development of the fundamental concepts of psychoanalysis. *Dynamic psychiatry*, edited by Franz Alexander and Helen Ross. Chicago, University of Chicago Press.

Bales, Robert F. 1950. *Interaction Process Analysis, A Method for the Study of Small Groups*. Cambridge, Mass., Addison-Wesley press.

———. 1953. The equilibrium problem in small groups *In* Talcott Parsons, Robert F. Bales, and E.A. Shils, *Working Papers*. Glencoe, Free Press.

Blau, P.M. and W.R. Scott. 1962. *Formal Organizations*. San Francisco, Chandler.

Burton, Roger C. and John W.M. Whiting. 1961. The absent father and cross-sex identity. *Merrill-Palmer Quarterly of Behavior and Development*.

Chapple, E.D. and C.M. Arensberg. 1940. *Measuring Human Relations: An Introduction to the Study Of the Interaction of Individuals*. Genetic Psychology Monograph 22:3–147.

Cohen, Yehudi. 1964. The establishment of identity in a social nexus: the special case of initiation ceremonies and their relation to value and legal systems. *American Anthropologist* 66:529–552.

Eggan, Fred. 1950. *Social Organization of the Western Pueblos*. Chicago, University of Chicago Press.

Erikson, E.H. 1950. *Childhood and Society*. New York, Norton.

Herskovits, Melville and Frances. 1959. Sibling rivalry, the Oedipus complex and myth. *Journal of American Folklore* 72:1–15.

Hsu, Francis L. K. 1959. Structure, function, content and process. *American Anthropologist* 61: 790-805.

———. 1961. Kinship and ways of life: an exploration. In Francis L. K. Hsu (editor), *Psychological Anthropology: Approaches to Culture and Personality*. Homewood, Illinois, Dorsey Press.

———. 1963. *Clan, Caste and Club*. Princeton, N.J., Van Nostrand Co.

———. 1964. Rethinking the concept "Primitive." *Current Anthropology*, June 1964.

Kahn, R.L. and D. Katz. 1960. Leadership practices in relation to productivity and morale. In D. Cartwright and A. Zander (editors), *Group Dynamics*. Evanston, Illinois, Row Peterson.

Lévi-Strauss, C. 1949. *Les Structures Elementaires de la Parenté*. Paris, Presses Universitaires de France.

———. 1953. Social structure. *Anthropology Today*, A. L. Kroeber (editor). Chicago, University of Chicago Press.

Marcus, P. M. 1960. Expressive and instrumental groups: toward a theory of group structure. *American Journal of Sociology* LXVI:54–59.

Murdock, G. P. 1949. *Social Structure*. New York, Macmillan Company.

Naroll, Raoul. 1956. Social development index. *American Anthropologist* 58:687-715.

Parsons, Talcott. 1955a. Family structure and the socialization of the child. In Talcott Parsons and Robert F. Bales (editors), *Family, Socialization, and Interaction process*. Glencoe, Ill., Free Press.

———. 1955b. The organization of personality as a system of action. In Talcott Parsons and Robert F. Bales (editors), *Family, Socialization, and Interaction Process*. Glencoe, Ill., Free Press.

Peter, Prince. 1963. *A Study of Polyandry*. The Hague, Mouton and Co.

Radcliffe-Brown, A.R. 1924. The mother's brother in south Africa. *South African Journal of Science* XXI:542–55. Reprinted in *Structure and Function in Primitive Society*. 1952. Glencoe, Illinois, Free Press.

Schneider, David H. 1961. Introduction: the distinctive features of matrilineal descent groups. In David M Schneider and Kathleen Cough (editors), *Matrilineal Kinship*. Berkeley and Los Angeles, University of California Press.

White, Harrison C. 1963. *An Anatomy of Kinship, Mathematical Models for Structures of Cumulated Roles*. New York, Prentice-Hall.

Whiting, John W.M. and I.L. Child. 1953. *Child Training and Personality*. New Haven, Yale University Press.

Whiting, John W. M., Richard Kluckhohn and Albert Anthony. 1958. The function of male initiation ceremonies at puberty. In *Readings in Social Psychology*, E. Maccoby, T. M. Newcomb and E. L Hartley (editors). New York, Holt, Rinehart and Winston.

CHAPTER 2

American Kinship: A Cultural Account

David M. Schneider

Relatives

I

What the anthropologist calls kinsmen are called "relatives," "folks," "kinfolk," "people," or "family" by Americans; the possessive pronoun may precede these terms. In different regions and dialects various words may be used, but people from different parts of the country generally understand each other and share the same fundamental definitions even when they do not use the same names for the same cultural categories. I will use the American term "relative" as the very rough equivalent for the anthropologist's term "kinsman," but this is a very rough translation indeed.

The explicit definition which Americans readily provide is that a relative is a person who is related by blood or by marriage. Those related by marriage may be called "in-laws." But the word relative can also be used by Americans in a more restricted sense for blood relatives alone and used in direct opposition to relative by marriage. Thus it may be said, "No, she is not a relative; my wife is an in-law." Or it may equally properly be said, "Yes, she is a relative; she is my wife."

One can begin to discover what a relative is in American culture by considering those terms of analysis, which are the names for the kinds of relatives—among other things—and which mark the scheme for their classification.

American kinship terms can be divided into two groups. The first group can be called the *basic* terms, the second, *derivative* terms. Derivative terms are made up of a basic term plus a modifier.[1] "Cousin" is an example of a basic term, "second" a particular modifier. "Second cousin" is an example of a derivative term. "Father" is another example of a basic term, "in-law" a modifier. "Father-in-law" is an example of a derivative term.

The basic terms are "father," "mother," "brother," "sister," "son," "daughter," "uncle," "aunt," "nephew," "niece," "cousin," "husband," and "wife." The modifiers are "step-," "-in-law," "foster," "great," "grand," "first," "second," etc., "once," "twice," etc., "removed," "half," and "ex-." The "removed" modifier is reserved to "cousin." The "half" modifier is reserved to "brother" and "sister." The "ex-" modifier is reserved to relatives by marriage. "Great" only modifies "father," "mother," "son," and "daughter" when they have first been modified by "grand," as in "great grandfather." "Great" and "grand" do not modify "cousin," "brother," "sister," "husband," or "wife." Otherwise modifiers can be used with any basic term.[2]

The modifiers in this system form two different sets with two different functions. One set of modifiers distinguishes true or blood relatives from those who are not. These are the "step-," "-in-law," and "foster" modifiers along with the "half" modifier which specifies less than a full blood sibling. Thus "father" is a blood relative, "foster brother" is not. "Daughter" is a blood relative, "step-daughter" is not.

The other set of modifiers define the range of the terms as infinite. These are the "great," "grand," "removed," "first," etc., and "ex-" modifiers. That is, the range or extent of the terms is without limit.

There are, therefore, two different kinds of modifiers. One kind, the *restrictive*, sharply divides blood relatives from those in comparable positions who are not blood relatives. The other kind of modifier, the *unrestrictive*, simply states the unrestricted or unlimited range of certain relatives.

One more important point should be noted about the modifiers. The unrestrictive modifiers mark distance, and they mark it in two ways. The first is by degrees of distance. Thus "first cousin" is closer than "second cousin," "uncle" closer than "great uncle," "great uncle" closer than "great great uncle," and so on. The second way of marking distance is on a simple "in/out" basis. Husband is "in," ex-husband is "out." (But note that "first," "second," etc. as modifiers of "husband" and "wife" do not mark closeness but only succession in time.)

---

[1] I take this distinction between basic and derivative terms from W. H. Goodenough, "Yankee Kinship Terminology: A Problem in Componential Analysis," in E. A. Hammel (ed.) "Formal Semantic Analysis," *American Anthropologist, 67:* 5, Part 2 (1965), 259–87.

[2] Compare W. H. Goodenough, op. cit. For the difference between his view and mine, see footnote, p. 99, below. It should also be noted that I do not offer this as a definitive or exhaustive list of American kinship terms. "Parent," "child," "sibling," "ancestor," "ancestress," "descendant," "pa," "pappy," "pop," "papa," "ma," "mammy," "mom," "mama," and so forth could all be considered as candidates for such a list, along with terms like "old man," "old woman," "old lady," "governor," and so forth. It is really not possible to assume that there is a finite lexicon or vocabulary of kinship terms without first providing a clear definition of just what a kinship term is and whether this definition is imposed on the data for analytic purposes or whether it is a definition inherent in the culture itself. Since I am not undertaking an analysis of either kinship terms or of terms for kinsmen here, I will reserve these questions for another time. My aim here is simply to use some terms which have kinship meanings as these are defined in American culture, as a way to begin to discover what the American cultural definition of a relative is.

This structure states a substantial part of the definition of what is and what is not a relative. The first criterion, blood or marriage, is central. The two kinds of modifiers are united in their functions; one protects the integrity of the closest blood relatives. The other places relatives in calibrated degrees of distance if they are blood relatives, but either "in" or "out" if they are relatives by marriage.

II

If a relative is a person related "by blood," what does this mean in American culture?

The blood relationship, as it is defined in American kinship, is formulated in concrete, biogenetic terms. Conception follows a single act of sexual intercourse between a man, as genitor, and a woman, as genetrix. At conception, one-half of the biogenetic substance of which the child is made is contributed by the genetrix, and one-half by the genitor. Thus each person has 100 per cent of this material, but 50 per cent comes from his mother and 50 per cent from his father at the time of his conception, and thereby is his "by birth."

Although a child takes part of the mother's makeup and part of the father's, neither mother nor father shares that makeup with each other. Since a woman is not "made up of" biogenetic material from her husband, she is not his blood relative. But she is the blood relative of her child precisely because the mother and child are both "made up of," in part, the very same material. So, too, are the father and child.

It is believed, in American kinship, that both mother and father give substantially the same kinds and amounts of material to the child, and that the child's whole biogenetic identity or any part of it comes half from the mother, half from the father. It is not believed that the father provides the bone, the mother the flesh, for instance, or that the father provides the intelligence, the mother the appearance.

In American cultural conception, kinship is defined as biogenetic. This definition says that kinship is whatever the biogenetic relationship is. If science discovers new facts about biogenetic relationship, then that is what kinship is and was all along, although it may not have been known at the time.

Hence the real, true, verifiable facts of nature are what the cultural formulation is. And the real, true, objective facts of science (these are the facts of nature too, of course) are that each parent provides one-half of his child's biogenetic constitution.[3]

The relationship which is "real" or "true" or "blood" or "by birth" can never be severed, whatever its legal position. Legal rights may be lost, but the blood relationship cannot be lost. It

---

[3] The cultural premise is that the real, true, objective facts of nature about biogenetic relationships are what kinship "is." But it does not follow that every fact of nature as established by science will automatically and unquestioningly be accepted or assimilated as part of the nature of nature. People may simply deny that a finding of science is true and therefore not accept it as a part of what kinship "is." By the same token, some items in some people's inventories of the real, true, objective facts of nature may be those which scientific authority has long ago shown to be false and untrue but which these Americans nevertheless insist are true. But this should not obscure my point here, which is simply that the cultural definition is that kinship is the biogenetic facts of nature.

is culturally defined as being an objective fact of nature, of fundamental significance and capable of having profound effects, and its nature cannot be terminated or changed. It follows that it is never possible to have an ex-father or an ex-mother, an ex-sister or an ex-brother, an ex-son or an ex-daughter. An ex-husband or ex-wife is possible, and so is an ex-mother-in-law. But an ex-mother is not.

It is significant that one may disown a son or a daughter, or one may try to disinherit a child (within the limits set by the laws of the various states). The relationship between parent and child, or between siblings, may be such that the two never see each other, never mention each other's name, never communicate in any way, each acting as if unaware of the other's existence. But to those directly concerned, as to all others who know the facts, the two remain parent and child or sibling to each other. Nothing can really terminate or change the biological relationship which exists between them, and so they remain blood relatives. It is this which makes them parent and child or sibling to each other in American culture.

Two blood relatives are "related" by the fact that they share in some degree the stuff of a particular heredity. Each has a portion of the natural, genetic substance. Their kinship consists in this common possession. If they need to prove their kinship, or to explain it to someone, they may name the intervening blood relatives and locate the ascendent whose blood they have in common. It is said that they can trace their blood *through* certain relatives, that they have "Smith blood in their veins." But their kinship to each other does not depend on intervening relatives, but only on the fact that each has some of the heredity that the other has and both got theirs from a single source.

Because blood is a "thing" and because it is subdivided with each reproductive step away from a given ancestor, the precise degree to which two persons share common heredity can be calculated, and "distance" can thus be stated in specific quantitative terms.

The unalterable nature of the blood relationship has one more aspect of significance. A blood relationship is a relationship of identity. People who are blood relatives share a common identity, they believe. This is expressed as "being of the same flesh and blood." It is a belief in common biological constitution, and aspects like temperament, build, physiognomy, and habits are noted as signs of this shared biological makeup, this special identity of relatives with each other. Children are said to look like their parents, or to "take after" one or another parent or grandparent; these are confirming signs of the common biological identity. A parent, particularly a mother, may speak of a child as "a part of me."

In sum, the definition of a relative as someone related by blood or marriage is quite explicit in American culture. People speak of it in just those terms, and do so readily when asked. The conception of a child occurs during an act of sexual intercourse, at which time one-half of the biogenetic substance of which the child is formed is contributed by the father, its genitor, and one-half by the mother, its genetrix. The blood relationship is thus a relationship of substance, of shared biogenetic material. The degree to which such material is shared can be measured and is called *distance*. The fact that the relationship of blood cannot be ended or altered and that it is a state of almost mystical commonality and identity is also quite explicit in American culture.

III

"Relative by marriage" is defined with reference to "relative by blood" in American kinship. The fundamental element which defines a relative by blood is, of course, blood, a substance, a material thing. Its constitution is whatever it is that really is in nature. It is a natural entity. It endures; it cannot be terminated.

Marriage is not a material thing in the same sense as biogenetic heredity is. It is not a "natural thing" in the sense of a material object found in nature. As a state of affairs it is, of course, natural; it has natural concomitants or aspects, but it is not in itself a natural object. It is terminable by death or divorce.

Therefore, where blood is both material and natural, marriage is neither. Where blood endures, marriage is terminable. And since there is no such "thing" as blood of which marriage consists, and since there is no such material which exists free in nature, persons related by marriage are not related "in nature."

If relatives "by marriage" are not related "in nature," how are they related?

Consider the step-, -in-law, and foster relatives. The fundamental fact about these relatives is that they have the role of close relatives without, as informants put it, being "real or blood relatives." A step-mother is a mother who is not a "real" mother, but the person who is now the father's wife. A father-in-law is a father who is not Ego's own father, but his spouse's father. And a foster son is not one's own or real son, but someone whom one is caring for as a son.

It is possible to describe a foster-child's *relationship* to his foster parents, or a step-child's *relationship* (and this is the word which informants themselves use) to his step-parent. This is, in its main outline, a parent-child relationship in the sense that it is a pattern for how interpersonal relations should proceed.

The natural and material basis for the relationship is absent, but relatives of this kind have a relationship in the sense of following a pattern for behavior, a code for conduct.

The classic tragedy of a step-child in Western European folklore, Cinderella for instance, states exactly the nature and also the problem of this relationship. A woman's relationship to her own child is one in which she has an abiding love and loyalty for it; her relationship to her husband's child by his earlier marriage is one in which that child is someone else's child, not hers. What she does for her step-child she does because of her husband's claim on her. Hence, if her husband does not protect his child, she may be cruel to it and favor her own child. This is seen as tragic because a child should have a mother who will mother it, and the parent-child relationship is quite distinct from the blood-tie which underlies it. The cruel step-mother of folklore should rise above the literal definition of her relationship to her step-child, and have the kind of *relationship*—affection, concern, care, and so forth—which a mother has for a child.

When a person is related to a blood relative he is related first by common biogenetic heredity, a *natural substance,* and second, by a *relationship,* a pattern for behavior or a code for conduct. The spouse, on one hand, and the step-, -in-law, and foster-relatives, on the other hand, are related by a *relationship* alone; there is no natural substance aspect to the relationship.

The distinctive feature which defines the order of blood relatives, then, is blood, a natural substance; blood relatives are thus "related by nature." This, I suggest, is a special instance of *the natural order* of things in American culture. The natural order is the way things are in nature. It consists in objects found free in nature. It is "the facts of life" as they really exist.

The feature which alone distinguishes relatives by marriage is their relationship, their pattern for behavior, the code for their conduct. I suggest, this is a special instance of the other general order in American culture, the *order of law.* The order of law is imposed by man and consists of rules and regulations, customs and traditions. It is law in its special sense, where a foster-parent who fails to care properly for a child can be brought to court, and it is law in its most general sense: law and order, custom, the rule of order, the government of action by morality and the self-restraint of human reason. It is a relationship in the sense of being a code or pattern for how action should proceed.

All of the step-, -in-law, and foster relatives fall under the order of law. It is in this sense that a mother-in-law is not a "real" or "true" mother—not a genetrix that is—but is in the relationship of mother—child to her child's spouse. It is in this sense that a step-mother is not a "real" mother, not the genetrix, but in a mother-child relationship to her husband's child. The crux of the Cinderella story is precisely that where the "real mother" is related to her child both by law and by nature, the step-mother lacks the "natural" basis for the relationship, and lacking this natural substance she "feels" no love except toward her "own" child and is thus able to cruelly exploit the child related to her *in law* alone.

If there is a relationship in law without a relationship in nature, as in the case of the spouse, step-, -in-law, and foster relatives, can there be a relationship in nature without a relationship in law? Indeed there can and there is. What is called a "natural child" is an example. He is a child born out of wedlock, a child, that is, whose mother and father are not married. He is a "natural child" because in his case his relationship to his parents is by nature alone and not by law as well; he is an "illegitimate" child. Similarly, the "real mother" of a child adopted in infancy, whether legitimate or not, is a relative in nature alone and not in law, and so is the genitor of such a child. Although the child is adopted and has every right and every duty of the blood child, in American belief it remains related to its "true" mother and father, its genitor and genetrix, in nature though not in law.

IV

In sum, the cultural universe of relatives in American kinship is constructed of elements from two major cultural orders, the *order of nature* and the *order of law.* Relatives in *nature* share heredity. Relatives *in law* are bound only by law or custom, by the code for conduct, by the pattern for behavior. They are relatives by virtue of their *relationship,* not their biogenetic attributes.

Three classes of relatives are constructed from these two elements. First there is the special class of relatives in nature alone. This class contains the natural or illegitimate child, the genitor or genetrix who is not the adoptive father or mother, and so on. The second class consists of relatives in law alone. This class may be called "by marriage" or it may be called "in law." It contains the husband and wife, the step-, -in-law, foster-, and other such relatives. The third class consists in relatives in nature *and* in law. This class of relatives is called "blood relatives" and contains the "father. . . daughter," "uncle . . . granddaughter" "cousin" sets, and so on.

The second and third classes of relatives can each be divided into two subclasses. The second-class, relatives in law alone, consists of the sub-class of husband and wife and the remainder, a subclass which contains the step-, -in-law, and foster- relatives and those for which there are no special lexemes. Husband and wife take basic kinship terms; the others take derivative terms. Husband and wife are the only relatives in law on a par with the closest blood relatives (the "father . . . daughter" set). Father and mother are properly also husband and wife. Finally, husband and wife are the only true relatives "by marriage" in one sense of marriage, namely, that sexual relationship between a man and a woman.

The third class also consists of two subclasses. The first consists of the "father . . . daughter" set of relatives, the second of those relatives who take the "uncle . . . granddaughter" and "cousin" terms. The modifier functions symbolize the difference between these subclasses: the first subclass is marked by the restrictive modifiers, the second by the unrestrictive modifiers. That is, the "father . . . daughter" sub-class is sharply restricted and distinguished from other kinds or degrees of "father," "mother," etc., while the "uncle . . . granddaughter" and "cousin" sets are infinitely expandable, but each expansion adds a degree of distance. Table 1 represents this summary.

Table 1

	Relatives	Nature	Law
(1)	In Nature	+	—
	(A) Natural child, illegitimate child, natural mother, natural father, etc.		
(2)	In Law	—	+
	(A) Husband, wife.		
	(B) Step-, -in-law, foster, etc.[a]		
(3)	By Blood	+	+
	(A) Father, mother, brother, sister, son, daughter.		
	(B) Uncle, aunt, nephew, niece, grandfather, grandmother, grandson, granddaughter, cousin, first cousin, etc., great grandfather, etc., great grandson, etc.		

[a] This category includes relatives for whom there are no kinship terms in the usual sense but who can nevertheless properly be counted as, or considered to be, relatives by marriage or in-law. This category of kin, therefore, contains kin without kinship terms. The cousin's spouse, the spouse of the nephew or niece of Ego's own spouse, as well as others can occur in this category in American kinship. This follows from the different application of alternate norms *within* the framework set by these categories, and may (or may not) entail the use of alternate kinship terms as well.

I have put this summary in terms of the different classes or categories of relatives in American kinship. Yet these categories are built out of two elements, *relationship as natural substance* and *relationship as code for conduct.* Each of these elements derives from or is a special instance of the two major orders which American culture posits the world to be made up of, the *order of nature,* and the *order of law.*

CHAPTER 3

Kinscripts[1]

Carol B. Stack[2] and Linda M. Burton[3]

This paper presents a framework for examining how families as multigeneration collectives, and individuals embedded within them negotiate the life course. We introduce kinscripts, a framework representing the interplay of family ideology, norms, and behaviors over the life course. Kinscripts encompasses three culturally defined family domains: kin-work, which is the labor and the tasks that families need to accomplish to survive from generation to generation; kin-time, which is the temporal and sequential ordering of family transitions; and kinscription, which is the process of assigning kin-work to family members.

The kinscripts framework is derived in part from the family life course perspective (Aldous, 1990; Elder, 1987; Hagestad, 1990; Hareven, 1982, 1986), studies of kinship (Aschenbrenner, 1975; Di Leonardo, 1986; Hinnant, 1986; Stack, 1974), and literature on family scripts (Byng-Hall, 1985, 1988; Steiner, 1974). The principal basis of kinscripts, however, is our ethnographic research conducted between 1968 and 1990 with urban and rural, low-income, multi-generational, black, extended families in the northeast, southeast, and mid-west portions of the United States. Case history data on families involved in these ethnographic studies are used to illuminate components of the kinscripts framework where appropriate.

The kinscripts framework was developed to organize and interpret qualitative observations of (a) the temporal and interdependent dimensions of family role transitions; (b) the creation and intergenerational transmission of family norms; and (c) the dynamics of negotiation, exchange, and conflict within families as they construct the life course. This framework is based on the premise that families have their own agendas, their own interpretation of cultural norms, and their own histories (Hagestad, 1986a; Reiss, 1981; Reiss & Oliveri, 1983; Tilly, 1987). Families assist individual members in constructing their personal life courses, but in the process families as collectives create a life course of their own (Watkins, 1980).

The kinscripts framework can be applied across race, ethnicity, social class, and to the range of family forms existing in contemporary American society. Typically, the conceptual frameworks used to interpret the life course of kin are derived from explorations involving white, middle class families. Kinscripts, in contrast, is an example of a framework that is derived from the study of low-income black families but offers insights for study of mainstream families as well.

The Conceptual Basis of Kinscripts

Kinscripts is grounded in a theoretical approach that weaves together the sociological perspectives on the life course and studies of kinship (Aldous, 1978; Aschenbrenner, 1975; Clausen, 1986; Elder, 1984; Fry and Keith, 1982; Glick, 1977; Nydegger, 1986a; Plath, 1980; Wilson, 1986; Zerubavel, 1981). Studies of the life course "trace individuals as social personas and their pathways along an age differentiated, socially marked sequence of transitions" (Hagestad, 1990: 151). Life course research has traditionally examined the pathways of individuals as inferred from aggregate data on the timing, duration, spacing, and ordering of role transitions in the context of family and work (Hogan, 1985; Marini, 1985). From this research, we have learned a great deal about trends and patterns in the timing and sequencing of marriage, childbearing, and entries and exits from the labor force. This research, however, tells us very little about how one individual's life course is connected to another's and how that life course, in the context of kin, is negotiated and constructed. Combining a focus on kinship with the life course perspective offers a more comprehensive view of the interlocking pathways of families as members influencing one another's life choices (Elder, 1984; Rossi & Rossi, 1990).

Two dimensions of life course perspectives and the study of kinship are central to the kinscripts framework: the temporal nature of the life course and interdependent lives. Regarding the temporal nature of the life course, Elder (1984, 1987) notes that there are four dimensions of time that influence the flow of individuals through the life course—lifetime, social time, family time, and historical time. Lifetime is delineated by chronological age and represents an individual's stage in the aging process. According to Clausen (1986) social time defines the set of norms that "specify when particular life transitions or accomplishments are expected to occur in a particular society or social milieu" (p. 2). Family time refers to the ordering of family events and roles by age—linked expectations, sanctions, and options. Historical time anchors an individual or a family in a social and cultural era. The dimensions of time most salient to the kinscripts framework is family time.

Family time has been defined by Hareven (1977, 1982) as the "timing of events such as marriage, birth of a child, leaving home, and the transition of individuals into different roles as the family moves through its life course" (1977: 58). Individual progression through these family stages are influenced by historical and social contexts and by the tensions between individual preferences for the timing of these events and familial expectations. Hagestad (1986a) offers an interpretation of family time in which families, as cultural units, devise timetables for the movement of the group through predictable phases of development and changing generational structures. Family timetables are representations of the shared understandings and interdependencies within kinship structures. They are, in essence, scripts that the entire family embraces about the flow of events in the life-cycle. The kinscripts framework is built on these premises, with the recognition that norms for transitions reflected in the broader society do not necessarily reveal the norms for timing in individual families.

In our ethnographic research, we have paid close attention to family timetables concerning the timing of childbearing. Specifically, our interests have been in the norms and sanctions families create with respect to age appropriate (on-time) and age-inappropriate (off-time) childbearing

(Burton & Bengston, 1985). Aggregate data from existing demographic studies (Hogan, 1985; Rindfuss, et al. 1988) suggests, in general, that when married couples have their first child during their 20s, it is considered normative, on-time childbearing behavior. In certain communities, however, families may establish other norms, expecting that designated adolescent females become "early" childbearers. In a recent ethnographic study conducted by Burton (1990), of a unique northeastern black community referred to as Gospel Hill, early childbearing is often considered a necessary activity. It provides grandmothers with children to raise. In these families, parenthood is normally enacted by grandmothers rather than mothers. Consequently, families believe it is important to become grandmothers as young as possible to assure women the energy to "keep up with toddlers." The following comment made by a 35-year-old potential grandmother, illustrates this desire:

> I suspect that my daughter (14 years old) will have a baby soon. If she doesn't, I'll be too old to be a grandmother and to do the things I'm supposed to do like raise my grandchild.

The second dimension of the life course perspective and studies of kinship integrated in the kinscripts framework concerns interdependent lives. Life course interdependence is described as the ways in which individual transitions and trajectories are affected by or even contingent upon the life stages of others (Elder, 1987; Hagestad & Neugarten, 1985; Kahn & Antonucci, 1980; Riley & Waring, 1976). Interdependent goals in families are witnessed in the plans that parents make about their own lives based on their assumptions of the life course progression of their children (Hagestad, 1986a). It is also observed in the transition to grandparenthood, where ascension to the role is dependent on the reproductive behaviors of one's offspring (Hagestad & Burton, 1987).

In Gospel Hill and in New Jericho, the rural black community in the Southeast recently studied by Stack (1989), the dynamics of interdependent lives are illustrated in patterns of intergenerational role responsibilities. In both communities, systems of nonadjacent generational caregiving are the norm. The primary responsibility of grandmothers in the families studied in these communities was the care of their grandchildren, and the principle duty for their daughters (the mothers of their grandchildren) was the care of the women who raised them—their own grandmothers. Mary, a 19-year-old mother, who lives in Gospel Hill, explains how this system of care across generations in a family works:

> My grandmother raised me. Now it's time for me to give her something back. It's O.K. if my mother raises my child for now. If she didn't, I wouldn't be able to take care of my grandmother.

Several aspects of the life course of kin are illustrated in these brief descriptions of dynamics in Gospel Hill and New Jericho—the timing of family role transitions (Hagestad, 1986a; Hareven, 1982), the work of kin (Bahr, 1976; di Leonardo, 1986; Finely, 1989; Rosenthal,

1985), family rituals (Lindahl & Back, 1987; Rosenthal & Marshall, 1988) and the negotiations of individual and family needs (Plath, 1980).

Building on the temporal and interdependent dimensions of the life course perspective and the study of kin, we propose the kinscripts framework for studying the lives of individuals embedded within the lives of families. The framework is based on three assumptions: (1) The life course of individuals and the life course of families are two interdependent entities; (2) The life course of families and individuals is shaped within social, cultural, and historical contexts; and (3) The life course of families involves blood and non-blood relatives who mutually share a perception of their inclusion in the family and interact accordingly (Dilworth-Anderson, et al. in press; Stack, 1974).

Kinscripts

Family Scripts

The concept of scripts as used in the family therapy literature is also an integral part of the kinscripts framework. Family scripts prescribe patterns of family interaction (Byng-Hall, 1988; Ferreira, 1963). They are mental representations that guide the role performances of family members within and across contexts.

The kinscripts framework extends the notion of scripts to the study of the family life course. Specifically, kinscripts focuses on the tensions that are produced and negotiated between individuals in families in response to scripts. These dynamics are discussed in context of three culturally defined family domains: kin-work, kin-time, and kinscription.

Kin-work

Kin-work is the collective labor expected of family-centered networks across households and within them (di Leonardo, 1986). It defines the work that families need to accomplish to endure over time. The family life course is constructed and maintained through kin-work. Kin-work regenerates families, maintains lifetime continuities, sustains intergenerational responsibilities, and reinforces shared values. It encompasses, for example, all of the following: family labor for reproduction; intergenerational care for children or dependents; economic survival including wage and nonwage labor; family migration and migratory labor designated to send home remittances; and strategic support for networks of kin extending across regions, state lines, and nations.

Kin-work is distributed in families among men, women, and children. Samuel Jenkins, a seventy-six-year-old widower in Gospel Hill, provided his own interpretation of kin-work. After Samuel's oldest daughter died, his granddaughter Elaine moved in with him along with her three children: a six-month-old baby, a two-year-old and a three-year-old. Samuel is raising these children. Elaine, he says, is running the streets and not providing care. When asked why he is parenting his grandchildren, he said:

> There ain't no other way. I have to raise these babies else the service people will take 'em away. This is my family. Family has to take care of family else we won't be no more.

Janice Perry, a thirteen-year-old pregnant woman from Gospel Hill, described her rather unique kin-work assignment. Her contribution to the family, as she understood it, was through reproduction. She states:

> I'm not having this baby for myself. The baby's grandmother wants to be a "mama" and my great-grandfather wants to see a grandchild before he goes blind from sugar. I'm just giving them something to make them happy.

Janice's mother, Helen, comments further:

> I want this baby. I want it bad. I need it. I need to raise a child. That's my job now. My mama did it. It's my turn now.

Samuel Jenkins, Janice Perry, and Helen Perry have clear notions of kin-work within families. While their individual family circumstances are different, kin-work for each one of them is tied to providing care across generations and maintaining family traditions and continuity.

Kin-work is the consequence of culturally constructed family obligations defined by economic, social, physical, and psychological family needs. Henry Evans, a 38-year-old resident of New Town (Burton & Jarrett, 1991), a northeastern black community, provided a very clear profile of his assigned kin-work. He noted that his kin-work emerged from the physical and psychological needs of his family members. Henry was the only surviving son in his family. His mother had given birth to eleven other sons all of whom were stillborn or died shortly after birth. At the time of his interview, Henry was providing care for his father, who had recently suffered a heart attack, his 36-year-old sister who was suffering from a chronic neuromuscular disease, and his 40-year-old sister and her four children. When asked about his family duties, he remarked:

> I was designated by my family as a child to provide care for all my family members. My duties read just like a job description. The job description says the following: (1) you will never marry; (2) you will have no children of your own; (3) you will take care of your sisters, their children, your mother and your father in old age; and (4) you will be happy doing it.

Henry went on to discuss how his commitment to the family life course took precedence over his personal life goals:

> Someone in my family must be at the helm. Someone has to be there to make sure that the next generation has a start. Right now, we are a family of co-dependents. We need each other. As individuals, my sisters and father are too weak to stand alone. I could never bring a wife into this. I don't have time. May be when the next generation (his sister's kids) is stronger, no one will have to do my job. We will redefine destiny.

The life situation of Henry Evans is not an unfamiliar one. Hareven (1982), in detailed historical analysis of families who worked for the Amoskeag Company in Manchester, New Hampshire, provides poignant examples of how, for many individuals, the demands of kin-work superseded personal goals (Hareven & Langenbach, 1978). Comparable evidence is noted in Plath's (1980) in-depth interview study of contemporary Japanese families. In each cultural context, across historical time, kin-work was described as self-sacrificing hard work—work designed to insure the survival of the collective.

Kin-time

(Kin-time represents the temporal scripts of families. It is the shared understanding among family members of when and in what sequence role transitions and kin-work should occur. Kin-time encompasses family norms concerning the timing of such transitions as marriage, childbearing, and grandparenthood. It includes temporal guides for the assumption of family leadership roles and caregiving responsibilities. The temporal and sequencing norms of kin-time are constructed in the context of family culture. Consequently, for some families, these norms may not be synonymous with the schedules of family life course events inferred from patterns assumed to exist in larger society.

Stack's (1993) ethnographic study of the migration of black families to and from the rural south provides an example of the relationship between kin-time and kin-work. Two aspects of kin-work are highlighted—reproduction and migration. The timing and sequencing of reproduction and migration is such that young adults first have children and then migrate to the North to secure jobs and send money back home. Their young children are left behind in the South to be reared by grandparents or older aunts and uncles. After an extended period of time, the migrating adults return to the South and, for some, their now young-adult children repeat the cycle—they bear children and migrate North.

The temporal sequencing of reproduction and migration in these families reflect a scripted family life course involving cooperative action among kin. Family members must be willing to assume economic and childcare responsibilities according to schedule. Individuals in families, however, do not always adhere to kin-time. A young adult may choose not to migrate, another may leave home but fail to send remittances, and yet others may return home sooner than expected. These individuals are considered insurgent by kin and may create unexpected burdens that challenge family resilience.

Kin-time also demarcates rites of passage or milestones within families, including the handing down of familial power and tasks following the death of family elders. For example, in the Appalachian mountains in southeastern United States, older women proclaim those few years after the death of their husbands, when they alone own the family land, as the time they have the most power in their families. The grown children and nearby community members observe, in a timely fashion, the activities of these elderly rural women. It was still common lore in the 1980s that the year these older widowed women announced plans for planting their last garden is the last year of their life. That year kin vie for their inheritances. Thus, the life course of families, which involves a scripted cycle of the relegation of power through land ownership, continues to unfold.

Kin-Scription

It is important to understand how power is brought into play within the context of kin-time and kin-work. The question this raises is summed up in the tension reflected in kin-scription. Rather than accept the attempts of individuals to set their own personal agendas, families are continually rounding up, summoning, or recruiting individuals for kin-work. Some kin, namely women and children, are easily recruited. The importance women place on maintaining kin ties and fostering family continuity has been assiduously documented (Dressel & Clark, 1990; Gilligan, 1982; Hagestad, 1989b). Placing preeminent emphasis on kin-keeping—the undertakings necessary to keep connected and family traditions transmitted—women often find it difficult to refuse kin demands.

The life course of a young woman, Yvonne Carter, who lives in Gospel Hill, offers an example of the interplay of power, kin-scription, and the role of women. When Yvonne's first love died fourteen years ago, she was twenty-one. At thirty-five, she recounted how the years had unfolded:

> When Charlie died, it seemed like everyone said since she's not getting married, we have to keep her busy. Before I knew it, I was raising kids, giving homes to long lost kin, and even helping the friends of my mother. Between doing all of this, I didn't have time to find another man. I bet they wouldn't want me and all my relatives anyway.

How relatives collude to keep particular individuals wedded to family needs—a chosen daughter in Japan (Plath, 1980), a chosen son in rural Ireland (Scheper-Hughes, 1979)—confirm Yvonne Carter's suspicion: she has been recruited for specific kin-work in her family.

Recruitment for kin-work is one dimension of power in kin-scription. Exclusion from kin-work is another, as this profile of Paul Thomas, a thirty-six-year-old resident of Gospel Hill, illustrates.

Paul Thomas, down on his luck, out of sorts with his girlfriend, and the oldest of seven children, had just moved back into his mother Mattie's home when he was interviewed. Eleven of Mattie's family members live in her two-bedroom apartment. The family members include Paul's two younger brothers (one who returned home from the service and moved in with his new wife and child) an unmarried sister, a sister and her child, and a pregnant sister with her two children. Paul reported finding his move back home, the result of repeated unemployment, particularly difficult under these living conditions.

After Paul moved back home, Mattie characterized Paul's history within the family as follows:

> Paul left this family when he was thirteen. I don't mean leave, like go away, but leave, like only do the things he wanted to do, but not pay attention to what me or his brothers and sisters wanted or needed. He took and took, and we gave and gave all the time. We never made him give nothing back.

In Mattie's view, her son Paul abandoned the family early on, claiming rights, but not assuming responsibilities. On a later visit to Mattie's apartment, family members gathered in the living room were asked a rather general question about doing things for kin. Paul stood up to speak. Addressing this question, with anger and entitlement in his voice, he said:

> I come back only for a little while. I am the outsider in the family. The black sheep. I belong, but I don't belong. Do you understand what I mean? I am only important because my mother can say, I have a son, and my sisters can say, I have a brother. But it doesn't mean anything. I can't do anything around here. I don't do anything. No one makes me. My sisters know what they have to do. They always have. They know their place! Now that I'm getting old I've been thinking that someway I'll make my place here. I want Ann (his sister) to name her baby after me. I'm begging you, Ann. Give this family something to remember that I'm part of it too.

Renegade relatives such as Paul attest to subtle dynamics that challenge their places within families. These relatives may inadvertently play havoc with family processes while simultaneously attempting to attach themselves to family legacies.

When kin act out or resist procedures to be kept in line, families have been known to use heavy-handed pressures to recruit individuals to do kin-work. However, kin may be well aware that family demands criss-cross and that it is impossible for the individual summoned to do kin-work to satisfy everyone. In particular, those family members assigned to do kin-work cannot be in two places at once. Adults, and even children under such circumstances, may be left to choose between conflicting demands. Stack's study of family responsibilities assumed by children in the rural, southeastern community of New Jericho, provides an example of competing demands placed on adolescents as they are recruited for family tasks.

In New Jericho, multiple expectations are transmitted to children whose parents migrated from the rural south to the northeast. It is not unusual for adolescents, skilled at child-care and other domestic activities, to be pulled in a tug-of-war between family households in the North and South. Kin at both locations actively recruit adolescents to move with them or join their households. Parents in the North and grandparents in the South are the main contenders. Children find themselves deeply caught in a web of family obligations. At eleven years of age, Jimmy Williams was asked to move to Brooklyn to help his parents with their new baby. But his grandmother needed his help in rural North Carolina. Jimmy responded by saying:

> I think I should stay with the one that needs my help the most. My grandmother is unable to do for herself, and I should stay with her and let my mother come to see me.

In this example, Jimmy was conscripted by two households within the family network. The decision Jimmy made to remain with his grandmother punctuates the leeway given to the children to make judgements in the context of personal and family interests. In a similar situation young Sarah Boyce said:

> I'll take to my parents and try to get them to understand that my grandparents cannot get around like they used to. I want to make an agreement to let my brother go to New York and go to school, and I'll go the school down here. In the summer, I will go and be with my parents, and my brother can come down home.

Children are conscripted to perform certain kin tasks that are tied to the survival of families as a whole. Definitions of these tasks are transmitted through direct and indirect cues from family members. Jimmy and Sarah responded to the needs of kin, taking advantage of the flexibility available to them in negotiating the tasks. That same flexibility is not always available for adults. The life situation of Sandra Smith provides an example.

Sandra Smith, married and a mother, found herself pressed between the demands of kin in her family of origin and her in-laws in Gospel Hill. She states:

> I'm always the one everybody comes to take care of children. My mother expects me to raise my sister's three kids. My mother-in-law calls upon me to mind my nieces and nephews while she takes it easy. She expects me to kiss her feet. I won't do it, none of it, everybody can go to hell.

Sandra, in fact, did refuse kin-work. When asked what impact her choice would have on her situation in the family, she said:

> It means I won't have nobody. But so what, they need me more than I need them.

Pressed between opposing set of demands and resentments that build up over the years, refusal to do kin-work is a choice some individuals opt for. Refusal, however, may be costly, particularly for those individuals who are dependent on the economic and emotional resources of kin.

Discussions

The examples of kin-work kin-time and kin-scription provided in this discussion are drawn primarily from our ethnographic studies of low-income, multigenerational black families. The examples illuminate extraordinary situations of individuals embedded in families that have scripted life courses. All families, unlike those described here, do not have such well-defined family guidelines. The family guidelines that exist for those who live in Gospel Hill, New Jericho, and New Town emerge out of extreme economic need and an intense commitment by family members to the survival of future generations.

The kinscripts framework is useful for exploring the life course of the families highlighted in this discussion, but it can also be applied to families that construct their life course under different circumstances. Kinscripts is particularly suited to exploring the effects that certain individuals within families have on the life course of kin. In all families across racial, ethnic, and socioeconomic groups there are individuals who cannot be counted on to carry out kin tasks; who leave the family fold for reasons of personal survival; who remain as dependent insiders within families making excessive emotional and economic demands on family members; and who return to the bosom of kin because of personal experiences such as unemployment, homelessness, divorce, or widowhood. From each angle, and in a diversity of family systems, the life course of kin through kin-work, kin-time, and kin-scription are affected by the personal agendas of family members.

Consider, for example, how the kinscripts framework might be used in exploring the life course of a kin network in which one of its members is experiencing divorce. Divorce is a fairly common experience in mainstream American families (Anspach, 1976; Hagestad & Smyer, 1982; Norton & Moorman, 1987). Under such circumstances, an adult child with dependent children may return to the home of his or her parents. The return home may put the scripted life course of kin in disarray, necessitating that collective family notions of kin-work, kin-time, and kin-scription be reconstructed. In terms of kin-work, grandparents, who in the past may have assumed a less active role in the rearing of their grandchildren, may now be expected to take on a more formal surrogate parent role (Johnson, 1988). With respect to kin-time, family members may delay certain transitions in response to the divorce. For example, an older parent might put off retirement for a few years to generate enough income to help their adult child reestablish themselves financially. Kin-scription may also be revised. The adult child experiencing the divorce may have been the family kin-keeper—that is, the person in the family charged with organizing family reunions, documenting family history, and negotiating conflicts between relatives. Given the change in this kin-keeper's life course, these duties may have to be reassigned to another family member.

Kinscripts can also be applied to explorations of the relationship between broader social conditions, unemployment, and the life course of kin. Under ideal conditions, unemployed family members are absorbed by kin as best they can. Given severe socioeconomic conditions, however, tensions between individual needs and kin-work, kin-time, and kin-scription may emerge. Again, the family life course may have to be redesigned. For example, low-income families attempting to absorb down and out members, or homeless mothers and children, find that sometimes in the face of economic cutbacks and emotional crisis they must, however reluctantly, "let go" of family members who cannot pull their weight. When public welfare support decreased in the 1980s, it produced a remarkable increase in families with these experiences. Stressful economic conditions decrease both individuals' and families' ability to perform effectively. Certain economic and political changes can disrupt kin-time—delaying family milestones such as childbearing and adding complexity to family timetables—and inhibit kin-work and kin-scription, thereby increasing tensions between the individual and family life course. The kinscripts framework, drawing on the life course perspective, is attentive to exploring these issues in the context of social change.

Another application of the kinscript framework is seen in the study of family members who leave the fold of kin. Under certain circumstances, particularly in the case of a dysfunctional family, an individual may temporarily disassociate himself from kin as a means of personal survival and then return to the fold having learned new family skills. Within the context of the kin scripts framework, several questions might be addressed: (a) What implications does the individual's exit from the family have on kin-work, kin-time, kin-scription? (b) How does the individual negotiate reentry to the kin network? (c) What affect does that individual's reentry have on the family's restructuring of the life course?

In summary, our contention is that kinscripts can be a useful framework for research in which the basic questions concern how families and individuals negotiate, construct, and reconstruct the life course. The utility of this framework is found in observing the interplay of three culturally defined family domains-kin-work, kin-time, and kin-scription.

Conclusion

The purpose of this paper was to suggest a way of thinking about the life course of individuals embedded within the life course of families. The kinscript framework was proposed. Kinscripts is conceptually grounded in the life course perspective, studies of kinship, and the literature on family scripts. As such many of the ideas outlined in kinscripts are not new. What is new, however, is the union of these various perspectives in the domains of kin-work, kin-time and kin-scription.

In addition to describing three domains of the family life course, kinscripts represents an attempt to use knowledge generated from the study of black multigeneration families to formulate a framework that can be useful for the study of families in general. Minority families have historically experienced issues that mainstream-families have only recently been attentive to. Examples of issues include: the juggling of work and family roles for women, single parenthood, extended family relationships, and poverty. Important lessons can be learned through exploring these issues in the context of the life course of minority families. These lessons can provide critical insights on the life course of the variety of family forms existing in contemporary American society.

Notes

1. The research reported in this paper was supported by grants from the Rockefeller Foundation to the first author, and by the National Science Foundation (R11-8613960), the Brookdale Foundation, the Center for the Study of Child and Adolescent Development, The Pennsylvania State University, a FIRST Award from the National Institute of Mental Health (No. R29MH46057-01), and a William T. Grant Faculty Scholars Award, to the second author. This paper was partially prepared while the authors were Fellows at the Center for Advanced Study in the Behavioral Sciences. We are grateful for financial support from the John D. & Catherine T. MacArthur Foundation, the Spencer Foundation, and the Guggenheim Foundation. We also wish to thank Robert Weiss, Gunhild Hagestad, Ann Crouter, Jean Lave, Blanca Silvestrini, Judy Stacey, Brad Shore, Jane Ifekwunigwe, Cindy Brache, and Caridad Souza, for their helpful comments on an earlier draft.

2. Graduate school of Education and Women's Studies, University of California, Berkeley, California 94720, U.S.A.

3. Department of Human Development and Family Studies, The Pennsylvania State University, University Park, PA 16802, U.S.A.

References

Aldous, Joan. 1978. *Family Careers: Developmental Change in Families*. New York: Wiley.

———. 1990. "Family Development and the Life Course: Two Perspectives on Family Change." *Journal of Marriage and the Family* 52(3): 571–583.

Anspach, Donald F. 1976. "Kinship and Divorce." *Journal of Marriage and the Family* 38: 323–335.

Aschenbrenner, Joyce. 1975. *Lifelines: Black Families in Chicago*. New York: Holt, Rinehart, and Winston.

Bahr, Howard M. 1976. "The Kinship Role." Pp. 61–79 in F. Ivan Nye (ed.), *Role Structures and Analysis of Family*. Beverly Hills, CA: Sage.

Beaver, Patricia D. 1986. *Rural Community in the Appalachian South*. Lexington, KY: University Press of Kentucky.

Byng-Hall, John. 1985. "The Family Script: A Useful Bridge Between Theory and Practice." *Journal of Family Therapy* 7:30 1–305.

———. 1988. "Scripts and Legends in Families and Family Therapy." *Family Process* 27: 167–179.

Burton, Linda M. 1990. "Teenage Pregnancy as An Alternative Life-Course Strategy in Multigenerational Black Families." *Human Nature* 1(2): 123–143.

Burton, Linda M. and Vern L. Bengston. 1985. "Black Grandmothers: Issues of Timing and Meaning in Roles." Pp. 61–77 in Vern L. Bengston & Joan Robertson (eds.), *Grandparenthood: Research and Policy Perspectives*. Beverly Hills, CA: Sage.

Burton, Linda M. and Robin L. Jarret. 1991. "Studying African-American Family Structure and Process in Underclass Neighborhoods: Conceptual Considerations." Unpublished Manuscript. Pennsylvania State University.

Clausen, John. 1986. *The Life Course*. Englewood Cliffs, New Jersey: Prentice-Hall.

Di Leonardo, Micaela. 1986. "The Female World of Cards and Holidays: Women, Families, and the Work of Kinship." *Signs: Journal of Women and Culture in Society* 12: 440–453.

Dilworth-Anderson, Peggye, Leanor Boulin-Johnson and Linda M. Burton. In press. "Reframing Theories for Understanding Race, Ethnicity, and Families." In Pauline Boss, William Doherty, Ralph La Rossa, Walter Schumm, and Suzanne Steinmetz (eds.), *Sourcebook of Family Theories and Methods: A Contextual Approach*. New York: Plenum Press.

Dressel, Paula L. and Ann Clark. 1990. "A Critical Look at Family Care." *Journal of Marriage and the Family* 52 (3): 769–782.

Elder, Glen H., Jr. 1978. "Family History and the Life Course." Pp. 17–64 in T. Hareven (eds.), *Transitions: The Family and the Life Course in Historical Perspective*. New York: Academic Press.

———. 1984. "Families, Kin, and the Life Course: A Sociological Perspective." Pp. 80–135 in Ross D, Parke (ed.), *Advances in Child Development Research and the Family*. Chicago: University of Chicago Press.

———. 1987. "Families and Lives: Some Developments in Life-Course Studies." *Journal of Family History* 12:179–199.

Ferreira, AJ. 1963. "Family Myth and Homeostasis." *Archives of General Psychiatry* 9: 457–463.

Finely, Nancy. 1989. "Theories of Family Labor as Applied to Gender Differences in Caregiving for Elderly Parents." *Journal of Marriage and the Family* 51: 79–86.

Fry, Christine L. and Jeannie Keith. 1982. "The Life Course as a Cultural Unit" Pp. 5–70 in Mathilda W. Riley, Ron P. Abeles, and Michael S. Teitelbaum (eds.), *Aging from Birth to Death* (Vol. 2), Boulder, CO: Westview.

Gilligan, Carol. 1982. *In a Different Voice.* Cambridge, MA: Harvard University Press.

Glick, Paul. 1977. "Updating the Family Life Cycle." *Journal of Marriage and the Family* 39: 5–13.

Hagestad, Gunhild O. 1986a. "Dimensions of Time and the Family." *American Behavioral Scientist* 29: 679–694.

———. 1986b. "The Aging Society as a Context for Family Life." *Daedalus* 115: 119–139.

———. 1990. "Social Perspectives on the Life Course." Pp. 151–168 in Robert K. Binstock and Linda K. George (eds.), *Handbook of Aging and the Social Sciences*, Third Edition. New York: Academic Press.

Hagestad, Gunhild O. and Linda Burton. 1986. "Grandparenthood, Life Context, and Family Development." *American Behavioral Scientist* 29(4):471–484.

Hagestad, Gunhild O. and Bernice Neugarten. 1985. "Age and the Life Course." Pp. 35–61 in Robert H. Binstock and Ethel Shanas (eds.), *The Handbook of Aging and the Social Sciences*, Second edition. New York: Van Nostrand and Reinhold, Co.

Hagestad, Gunhild O. and Michael S. Smyer. 1982. "Dissolving Long-Term Relationships: Patterns of Divorcing in Middle Age." Pp. 155–188 in S. Duck (ed.), *Personal Relationships*, Vol. 4: *Dissolving Personal Relationships*. London: Academic Press.

Hareven, Tamara K. 1977. "Family Time and Historical Time." *Daedalus* 107: 57–70.

———. 1982. *Family Time and Industrial Time: The Relationship Between the Family and Work in a New England Industrial Community.* New York: Cambridge University Press.

———. 1986. "Historical Changes in the Social Construction of the Life Course." *Human Development* 29 (3):17 1–180.

Hareven, Tamara K. and Randolph Langenbach. 1978. *Amoskeag.* New York: Pantheon.

Hinnant, John. 1986. "Ritualization of the Life Cycle." In C.L. Fry and J. Keith (eds.), *New Methods for Old Age Research.* South Hadley, MA: Bergin and Garvey.

Hogan, Dennis P. 1978. "The Variable Order of Events in the Life Course." *American Sociological Review* 43: 573–586.

———. 1985. "The Demography of Life-Span Transitions: Temporal and Gender Comparisons." Pp. 65–78 in Alice Rossi (ed.), *Gender and the Life Course.* New York: Aldine.

Johnson, Colleen L. 1988. "Active and Latent Functions of Grandparenting During the Divorce Process." *The Gerontologist* 28(2): 185–191.

Kahn, Robert, and Toni Antonucci. 1980. "Convoys Over the Life Course: Attachment, Roles, and Social Support." Pp. 62–93 in Paul Baltes & Orville Brim (eds.), *Life-Span Development and Behavior* (Vol 3). New York: Academic Press.

Lindahl, MW., and Kurt Back. 1987. "Lineage Identity and Generational Continuity: Family History and Family Reunions." *Comprehensive Gerontology* 1: 30–34.

Marini, Margaret M. 1984. "Age and Sequencing Norms in the Transition to Adulthood." *Social Forces* 63 (1): 229–244.

Neugarten, Bernice L., Joan Moore and John Lowe. 1965. "Age Norms, Age Constraints, and Adult Socialization." *American Journal of Sociology* 70:710–717.

Norton, A. J. and J.E. Moorman. 1987. "Current Trends in Marriage and Divorce Among American Women." *Journal of Marriage and the Family* 49: 3–14.

Nydegger, Corinne N. 1986a. "Age and Life—Course Transitions." Pp. 131–161 in C.L. Fry and J. Keith (eds.), *New Methods for Old Age Research*. MA: Bergin and Garvey.

———. 1986b. "Timetables and Implicit Theory." *American Behavioral Scientist* 29 (6): 710–729.

Plath, David. 1980. *Long Engagements*. Stanford, CA: Stanford University Press.

Reiss, David. 1981. *The Family's Construction of Reality*. Cambridge, MA: Harvard University Press.

Reiss, David and Mary Ellen Oliveri. 1983. "The Family's Construction of Social Reality and its Ties to its Kin Network: an Exploration of Causal Direction," *Journal of Marriage and the Family* 45: 81–91.

Riley, Mathilda, and Joan Waring. 1976. "Age and Aging." Pp. 89–101 in R.K. Merton & R. Nisbet (eds.), *Contemporary Social Problems*. New York: Harcourt, Brace and Jovanovich.

Rindfuss, Ronald R., S. Philip Morgan, and C. Gray Swicegood. 1988. *First Births in America: Changes in Timing of Parenthood*. Berkeley: University of California Press,

Rosenthal, Carolyn, and Victor Marshall. 1988. "Generational Transmission of Family Ritual." *American Behavioral Scientist* 31: 669–684.

Rosenthal, Carolyn J. 1985. "Kin-keeping in the Familial Division of Labor." *Journal of Marriage and the Family* 45: 509–521.

Rossi, Alice. 1980. "Aging and Parenthood in the Middle Years." Pp. 137–205 in Paul Baltes and Orville G. Brim, (eds.), *Life Span Development and Behavior*, Vol 3. New York: Academic Press:

Rossi, Alice, and Peter Rossi. 1990. *Of Human Bonding: Parent-Child Relations Across the Life Course*. New York: Aldine DeGruyter.

Scheper-Hughes, Nancy. 1979. *Saints, Scholars and Schizophrenics*. Berkeley, CA: University of California Press.

Steiner, C.M.1974. *Scripts People Live: Transactional Analysis of Life Scripts*. New York: Grove Press.

Stack, Carol. 1974. *All Our Kin*. New York: Harper Row.

———. 1993. *Call to Home: African American's Reclaim the Rural South*. New York: Basic Books,

Tilly, Charles. 1987. "Family History, Social History, and Social Change." *Journal of Family History* 12: 320–329.

Watkins, Susan C. 1980. "On Measuring Transitions and Turning Points." *Historical Methods* 13 (3): 181–186.

Wilson, Melvin. 1986. "The Black Extended Family: An Analytical Consideration." *Developmental Psychology* 22: 246–256.

Zerubavel, E. 1981. *Hidden Rhythms: Schedules and Calendars in Social Life*. Chicago: University of Chicago Press.

CHAPTER 4

The Myth of the Declining Family: Extended Family Ties Among Urban Mexican-Americans and Anglo-Americans

Susan Emley Keefe

Traditionally, it was assumed that nuclear family systems arise with urbanism due to increased geographic and socioeconomic mobility and to the extended family's loss of economic function. Substantial evidence supports the thesis that extended family ties persist among urban Mexican-Americans and Anglo-Americans in southern California. The two ethnic groups differ in reference to the geographic distribution of kin, Chicanos having local kin groups in contrast to the dispersed kin networks of Anglo-Americans, but, for members of both ethnic groups, the extended family endures and contributes in positive ways to ethnic adaptation to urban life.

It used to be thought that families living in modern cities had little contact with their relatives. This idea was suggested when people compared the apparent individualism of their own family lives with their fondly held, though often misguided, images of the "good old days." During the past two decades, there has been much careful research on kinship ties, and the general findings of these studies are (1) that kinship ties are extremely important in contemporary urban society and (2) that the existence of a vital, all-embracing extended family of the "good old days" was mostly a myth. (Caplow et al. 1982:195)

The theory that urbanization leads to extended-family breakdown has a long history in the social sciences. As Caplow et al. (1982) point out, the theory assumes that kinship organization in cities changes from an extended family system to a more isolated, nuclear family system and, furthermore, that urbanization is the cause of this change. The theory has its roots in the nineteenth century with the development of more sophisticated comparative and evolutionary social theories. For example, in his book *Ancient Law*, Henry Maine argued that, as societies become more complex, there is an evolutionary shift from kinship status to contract status:

> The movement of progressive societies has been uniform in one respect. Through all its course it has been distinguished by the gradual dissolution of family dependency and the growth of individual obligation in its place. The Individual is steadily substituted for the Family, as the unit of which civil laws take account (Maine 1861:168).

Other nineteenth-century scholars, including Émile Durkheim, Ferdinand Tönnies, and Max Weber, agreed in general that urbanism is associated with increasing individualism, growing alienation in a mass society, greater geographic and socioeconomic mobility, and the loss of a sense of community. More recent neoevolutionists, such as Elman Service (1967), continue the argument that, in comparison to primitive societies where kinship is the most significant organizing principle, urban, state-level societies have other means of organizing public life, and kinship tends to be confined to the private sphere.

Early twentieth-century sociologists and anthropologists adapted these theories to the contemporary process of urbanization and to the associated process of industrialization. Contrasting urban society with rural, preindustrial society, Talcott Parsons (1943). Robert Redfield (1941). Ralph Linton (1949), and, most especially, Louis Wirth (1938), as well as others in the *Chicago School* associated urban life with the weakening of bonds of kinship (Wirth) and the "isolation of the nuclear family" (Parsons). In addition to citing the increasing importance of individualism in urban societies as a factor in the decline of the kin group, these theorists emphasized the extended family's loss of significant economic and social functions. In urban, industrial societies, the family is no longer the unit of economic production; moreover, the labor market's demand for workforce mobility results in migration and dissolution of local kin groups. With increased socioeconomic mobility and an emphasis on individual, achieved status, the ascribed status of kinship and the associated resources of inheritance and a family name and reputation become less important. The extended family may survive, but it functions more in affective than instrumental ways (although it is generally agreed that it may remain economically functional among the poor who rely on kin for mutual aid). The extended kin group remains significant in urban societies. It is argued, primarily due to emotional bonds of attachment and to the socializing patterns they produce. Finally, according to this school of thought, due to the presumed fragility of affective, noneconomically based bonds, the frequency of visiting such kin is relatively insignificant.

The theory of the declining urban extended family continues to be perpetuated by some more contemporary social scientists (Goode 1963, 1966: Harris 1969: Smelser 1966) and is reported in textbooks read by new generations of social scientists. Moreover, as Caplow et al. (1982) note, it is a theory held, for the most part, by the general population. Perhaps this is one of the reasons why the theory persists despite the convincing evidence to the contrary amassed by researchers over the last thirty years.

Oscar Lewis (1965) is perhaps best known for proposing that urbanization and industrialization are compatible with extended family bonds when he found "urbanization without breakdown" in Mexico City. In fact, cross-cultural studies find the retention of extended family ties in urban areas around the globe: In India (Vatuk 1972), the Philippines (Jacobson 1970), West Africa (Aldous 1962), Brazil (Wagley 1964), Yugoslavia (Hammel and Yarbrough 1973), Canada (Gangue 1956), and England (Young and W1llmott 1957), as well as elsewhere. Work with many urban-American ethnic minority groups, including Italian-Americans (Palisi 1966), Jewish-Americans (Winch, Green, and Blumberg 1967). Puerto Rican-Americans (Garrison 1972), and Japanese- and Chinese-Americans (Light 1972) also indicates the existence of local kinship ties which involve significant levels of visiting and mutual exchange of goods and services. Furthermore, urban-dwelling, mainstream Anglo-Americans are by no means cut off from their extended family ties. As Sussman (1959), Sussman and Burchinal (1962), Litwak (1960a, 1960b), Adams (1968), and Greer (1956) have demonstrated, Anglo-Americans maintain a *modified extended family*, in which kin ties remain important in affective and instrumental ways despite geographic mobility. Of course, considerable variation in the precise nature of kinship organization exists among these separate cultural groups, but, clearly, urbanism does not necessarily result in the extinction of extended family networks. In Barbados, as Greenfield (1961) points out, a nuclear family system can also arise in nonurban situations, further calling into question any proposed causal relationship between urbanism and nuclear family organization.

This study examines the extended family ties of urban Mexican-Americans and Anglo-Americans in southern California. The findings are based on research conducted in three towns where Chicanos make up a large segment of the population: Santa Barbara, Santa Paula, and Oxnard. Data were collected by means of two large-scale surveys of several hundred respondents and a series of in-depth interviews with a small number of informants. In addition to the expected cultural differences between the Mexican-Americans and Anglo-Americans interviewed, significant differences in socioeconomic status are evident between the two ethnic groups: most of the Mexican-Americans come from blue-collar households and have not completed high school, while most of the Anglo-Americans live in white-collar households and have completed one or more years of college. Within the Chicano sample itself, there is considerable heterogeneity. Generation accounts for much of the variation by class and culture within the ethnic group, particularly for the contrast between immigrants from Mexico and the more acculturated and assimilated second- or third-generation Mexican-Americans.

Consistent with early social science theory, research on Mexican-Americans has more often than not asserted that the traditional Mexican-American extended family is disappearing with urbanization and acculturation (Alvirez and Bean 1976; Grebler, Moore, and Guzman 1970). Nevertheless, it is also suggested that, in comparison with the Anglo-American nuclear family system, Chicano family ties remain stronger (Gonzalez 1969; Madsen 1964); yet, few studies have actually collected kinship data on both Anglos and Chicanos. Analysis of the data on kin ties from the author's research indicates both ethnic groups retain considerable extended familism; however, there are important ethnic differences in extended family structure and the cultural values associated with familism. In the following section, the extended family systems found in these two urban ethnic groups are described, and representative case studies are presented to illustrate the differences between them.

Mexican-American and Anglo-American Extended Families

Many similarities actually exist between Mexican-American and Anglo-American kinship patterns. Both are founded on the bilateral kindred and affinal extensions. The nuclear family is the basic and most significant familial unit and normally constitutes the household. Relatives in the kindred sometimes interact as a social group and are often relied upon for assistance in times of need. Likewise, members of both ethnic groups remain in frequent contact with relatives who live nearby. Moreover, the distinction between more important, primary kin (parents, siblings, and children) and less important, secondary kin applies in both ethnic groups.

Distinctive for Chicanos is the inclusion in the extended family of fictive kin (*compadres*) ritualized through religious, and sometimes secular, ceremonies. Baptismal compadres take on special obligations, especially the willingness to assume parenthood of their godchildren, if necessary. As godparents of a child, compadres or co-parents have a special link with the real parents of the child and are typically close friends or relatives. Fictive kin often fill the same role as the real kin in the Chicano extended family; they are accorded the same attention and affection and render mutual aid when it is needed. The tendency to choose relatives as compadres increases with each generation among Mexican-Americans, however, so that the ethnic distinction of having kin who are only fictive is perhaps less significant than has sometimes been portrayed by researchers.

The analysis of family data from the author's research reveals that the distinctiveness between Anglo-Americans and Mexican-Americans emerges more in comparison of interaction and exchange with real, as opposed to fictive, kin. Moreover, there are significant differences in family organization between immigrant Mexicans and later generations of Chicanos. Finally, consideration of kin *and* non-kin social ties leads to a more comprehensive and realistic comparison of the more kin-isolated lives of Anglos versus the kin-dominated lives of Chicanos.

Turning first to a consideration of kin living in town, Mexican-Americans are much more likely to have relatives in town than are Anglos. Less than half (46 percent) of the Anglos are related by blood or marriage to other households in town, while 86 percent of the foreign-born and 94 percent of the native-born (second and third generation) Mexican-Americans have nearby relatives. Chicanos are also related to larger numbers of households in town than Anglos, although there is a significant difference between native- and foreign-born Mexican-Americans. The second and third generations have an average of seventeen and fifteen related households in town respectively, while the first generation averages only about five related households, The Anglos, in comparison, have an average of only three and a half related households in town.

Anglos and Chicanos are both likely to visit with their relatives in town, but Chicanos visit more kin and more often than the Anglos. Ninety percent or more of the Anglos and three Mexican generations with nearby relatives visit at least one related household weekly. However, Chicanos are more likely to visit households daily: 37 percent of the first generation, 52 percent of the second generation, and 54 percent of the third generation visit at least one household daily compared to 26 percent of the Anglos. Numbers of kin visited fall into a similar pattern. Anglos with kin in town visit an average of two households a week while immigrant Mexicans visit an average of three and native-born Mexican-Americans visit an average of four.

Exchange of aid with kin is characteristic of both ethnic groups, but native-born Chicanos far surpass both Anglos and immigrant Mexicans in frequency and variety of exchange. Over 40 percent of the second and third generations have given all six types of aid inquired about to relatives in town in the last year and have received three to four types of aid. In contrast, 41 percent or more of the Anglos and immigrant Mexicans have given only two types of aid and received only one type of aid.

In summary, Anglos are unlikely to have a local kin group. If they have relatives in town, they are few in number. However small the local kin group is, Anglos nevertheless visit their kin frequently and exchange goods and services with them. First generation Mexican-Americans have slightly larger local kin networks than Anglos and visit these kin somewhat more frequently; their exchange of aid, on the other hand, is somewhat less frequent than for Anglos. The native-born Chicanos, in contrast, have the largest local extended families. Moreover, they visit with more kin and exchange aid more frequently than either the Anglos or immigrant Mexicans.

Analysis of family organization by kin type rather than residence yields another perspective on ethnic differences. First, considering relations with primary kin (parents, siblings, and children), all three generations of Mexican-Americans, as well as the Anglo-Americans, maintain contact with the overwhelming majority of their primary kin. In addition, goods and services are exchanged with the majority of primary kin, although this is more characteristic of the native-born Chicanos. All three Mexican-American generations have more primary kin in town than the Anglos; however, the majority of both the Anglos' and Mexican immigrants' primary kin live outside the local area. This affects the frequency of visiting primary kin. The native-born Chicanos see the majority of their primary kin at least weekly while the Anglos and immigrant Mexicans do not.

While primary kin form the core of the individual's extended family in both ethnic groups, secondary kin tend to dominate numerically as local relatives and in the individual's network of interaction and exchange. Because native-born Chicanos recognize more secondary kin than Anglos or immigrant Mexicans and are more likely to have secondary kin nearby, their local extended families tend to be much larger. Anglos (5 percent) are least likely to have local secondary kin and have the smallest average number of secondary kin (2.1) in town. The tendency to have locally residing, secondary kin increases from generation to generation among the Mexican-Americans; while immigrant Mexicans have an average of 7.3 secondary relatives in town, the second generation averages 22.7, and the third generation averages 32.7 secondary kin in town. Interaction with secondary kin is much less common than with primary kin among all groups, but it is least common among Anglos who visit with only 12 percent of their secondary kin regardless of place of residence, compared to the three Mexican-American generations, who see 35 percent or more of their secondary kin regularly. Exchange of goods and services with secondary kin is infrequent among all groups.

In sum, the native-born Mexican-Americans have far and away the largest, most integrated extended families. The native-born Chicanos count more relatives than the Anglos or immigrants and interact and exchange aid with more relatives. While the first-generation Mexicans have much smaller kin networks, the networks are relatively well integrated through visiting and mutual aid. Anglos count a good many relatives, but the number included in interaction and exchange is comparatively small. Anglos have an average of only twelve relatives with whom they visit, less than half the number visited by first-generation Mexicans and less than one-third the number seen by the native-born. The Anglos also exchange aid with the smallest number of kin (eight) compared to between thirteen and nineteen for Mexican-Americans depending on generation. Thus, not only are Anglos less likely to have a local kin network than Chicanos, but also their full kin network is smaller and more selective than the Chicanos' kin network. Apparently. kinship as a social system is less important for Anglo-Americans.

Among Mexican-Americans, on the other hand, the kin group grows stronger and more localized with each generation. The first-generation immigrants tend to locate in urban areas where they have secondary kin, but most of their relatives remain in Mexico. Once settled, they generally establish small, but well-integrated, local extended families, primarily through their married children. Second-generation Mexican-Americans thus inherit a fairly large local kin group made up of their parents, siblings, and perhaps more distant kin, which is extended through their own spouse and offspring as well as the spouses and offspring of their siblings. The third generation, which is likely to remain residing locally, has a vast number of nearby kin, although they tend to confine the greater part of their interaction to their primary kin—parents, siblings, and children.

This process in which the later, and better-off, generations become more familistic calls into question the idea that Mexican-American extended familism is tied to poverty and the search for resources outside the nuclear family (Alvirez and Bean 1976; Grebler, Moore, and Guzman 1970). Research with other groups indicates that the urban poor are likely to have relatives who are equally as poor and have few resources to exchange. Furthermore, social agencies are designed to meet many of the needs of the poor, and, although many needs certainly go unmet, the agencies nevertheless offer tremendous resources of which a number of the poor take advantage (Jacobson 1970; Wagley 1964). Instead of the lower class, therefore, it is the urban middle and upper classes whose members have resources to spare where the tradition of extended familism flourishes.

The primary difference between the extended families of the two ethnic groups, then, involves the nature of their geographical proximity. Chicanos tend to have a *traditional* extended family. defined as a localized kin group consisting of a number of related households whose members interact together frequently and exchange mutual aid (Keefe 1979:352). Anglo-Americans, on the other hand, tend to have a *modified*, or what I have referred to as a widespread, extended family, in which ties with relatives, especially primary kin, are maintained despite geographic distances separating kin. This difference in extended family structure comes about because of a difference in geographic mobility. Anglos are more mobile than Chicanos, tend to live near few relatives, and consequently visit kin infrequently. Contact may be more frequent by mail or by telephone, however, particularly between primary kin (Keefe and Padilla 1987). Immigration, of course, affects the kin group of foreign-born Mexican-Americans, but among native-born Chicanos, residential stability is a common trait; 32 percent of the second generation and 43 percent of the third generation in the study were born in the city in which they were interviewed (compared to only 4 percent of the Anglos). This difference in geographic proximity leads to several related differences in extended family structure. While members of both ethnic groups maintain contact with most of their primary kin, Chicanos see their primary kin and exchange goods and services with them more frequently due to their proximity. Secondary kin are less important for both Mexican-Americans and Anglo-Americans, but, due to the fact that Anglos are extremely unlikely to have locally residing secondary kin, interaction and exchange with secondary kin is much less frequent for Anglos. Finally, the relative lack of local kin in general among Anglo-Americans means that most of their social network is made of non-kin (friends, neighbors, coworkers, etc.) compared to the kin-dominated social networks of Chicanos. While 89 percent of the Anglos' social contacts in town are non-kin, only about half (52 percent) of the first generations', 41 percent of the second generations', and 24 percent of the third generation Mexican-Americans' social network is made up of non-kin.

Family Case Studies

In order to fully appreciate the ethnic differences described previously, three case studies are presented in this section representing aspects of immigrant Mexican, native-born Chicano, and Anglo-American family organization, it should be emphasized that each case study represents the life of an individual whose story is unique from every other individual in their ethnic group. Yet, in these case studies we also find a pattern of family organization which, in its broad outline, fits that of the ethnic group at large. It is this pattern which is of primary interest here; the details of the individuals' lives add interest and demonstrate some of the possibilities in variation within the group.

Carmen Muñoz: A Mexican Immigrant

Carmen Muñoz is a fifty-four-year-old housewife with seven children. She was born in Hermosillo in the state of Sonora, Mexico, and has been in the United States for twenty-two years, living mostly in Santa Barbara. Carmen left most of her family in Mexico, and, since she has not traveled back since migrating to the United States, her ties with kin there are negligible. Both of her parents are dead. One of her sisters is living in San Diego and the other is in Tijuana, a Mexican border town. Her brother just recently moved back to Mexico after having lived in southern California. She sees her siblings only rarely now, as she lives in Santa Barbara, but her sister in San Diego helped Carmen when she originally migrated to the United States. Carmen cannot remember many of her other relatives and old friends that are still living in Mexico, having lost contact with them long ago. Her second husband, Miguel, has many relatives in Mexico, including his mother and siblings, and his ties are much stronger to kin in Mexico than are Carmen's. Miguel's mother came to live with them for several years but then moved back to Mexico. Carmen has met few of Miguel's other Mexican relatives and does not feel close to any of them.

Carmen and her first husband chose *padrinos* (godparents) for all of their children when they were living in Mexico, and she sees some of them occasionally on their rare visits to the United States, but, basically, she no longer has contact with those compadres. She does, however, have compadres in town, her youngest child's baptismal padrinos, and she sees them regularly.

Carmen's close social network consists primarily of her children and her children's families. She sees her five married children almost daily and has a high level of exchange of goods and services with them. For example, several times when she became critically ill, her sons or daughters would accompany her and her husband to the emergency room. When one of her daughters was hospitalized, Carmen spent most of her time at the hospital. Presently, another daughter is having financial difficulties and Carmen has taken in all four grandchildren for a while to alleviate some of the burden. Carmen's children often give her rides to the market, to church, and take her on other errands, as she does not drive and Miguel often works the night shift, sleeping during the day. This type of exchange appears to be limited to her children. Although she knows a few of her neighbors, she does not exchange favors, advice, child care, or money with them. Her exchange with her compadres in town is also minimal. There is no one in town whom Carmen considers to be a close friend.

Anna Fuentes: A Native-Born Chicana

Twenty-three-year-old Anna Fuentes is a second-generation Chicana, born in Santa Barbara. Anna and her husband, Ruben, were married immediately following her graduation from high school, and, while they are looking forward to it, they do not have children yet. As a native Santa Barbaran, Anna has a large local kinship network and very close relations with her primary kin. Specifically, Anna has her parents, one sister and one brother living in town, while a second brother lives in nearby Oxnard. Ruben has nine siblings, only one of whom does not live in town. Anna estimates that she and Ruben have about forty other relatives in town, and, of these, they see ten at least monthly. Anna usually takes her mother shopping every Saturday, and, on Sunday, she and Ruben have dinner at her parents' house, Every Monday night, Anna and Ruben have dinner at his parents' house. These immediate kin are the only individuals who Anna and Ruben are sure to see socially several times a week. Frequency of contact diminishes rapidly outside of the immediate families, as Anna sees her closest first cousin, on the average, only once a month and her aunts and other cousins perhaps two or three times each year.

Anna tends to be self-reliant and rarely asks for help from others, but, in time of trouble, she says she would rely on her primary kin. On the other hand, she recalls that she has been of service to several relatives in the past year. For example, her mother and sister confide in her about their problems, and several other relatives have also come to Anna for advice about their personal problems. Furthermore, Anna has loaned some money to one of her sisters-in-law, and she has helped her parents with household chores, as well as such tasks as preparing tamales for a party.

Anna feels very close to her family; they are the most important people in her life. She and Ruben have friends, but they are secondary to their relatives. Ruben and Anna have six good friends, all Mexican-Americans. Four of these are compadres, as Anna and Ruben are padrinos to their children. Anna sees her friends regularly and sometimes has invited them over with her relatives. For example, the one large party she had during the year of interviews was a barbecue with family and friends celebrating her and Ruben's fifth wedding anniversary. Anna does not generally exchange goods or services with friends, preferring when necessary to rely on family.

Amy Cooper: An Anglo-American

Amy Cooper is a thirty-one-year-old mother of two young children. Amy met her husband, Donald, in Santa Barbara, where they have lived for the last eleven years.

Amy has only one relative living in town—Donald's cousin, whom they see every month or so and have helped out financially on occasion. She mainly socializes with four female friends whom she has known for ten years or more. Amy not only gets together with each of her friends several times a week, but also talks to them on the telephone frequently. Most of these friends have small children as well, and they often take them to the beach or to the pool together. Amy and her girlfriends talk about shared problems concerning marital difficulties, disciplinary problems with children, worries about sick relatives, and so on. They also help each other out with baby-sitting, housecleaning, and small loans of money. Amy is also friends with a neighbor at her apartment building, and they often exchange child care or borrow small items when necessary.

Amy feels very close to her parents, but, because they live elsewhere in California (Fontana), she cannot see them as often as she would like. Still, she manages to visit with them monthly, sometimes at their home and sometimes at hers. During the interviews, Amy's mother came to stay for several days, and they talked at length about the children, Amy's grandmother's illness, her father's drinking problem, and the stress of her mother's job. Amy often takes her problems to her mother for advice, because "she cares about my life and the children." The Coopers seem to have continual financial problems due to Donald's low income in his occupation as a musician and music teacher, and Amy's parents have loaned them money several times beginning when they were first married. Amy's only brother lives in Manhattan Beach, California, and they remain in frequent contact often meeting at her parent's home. Amy worries about his wife, who has had some disturbing psychological problems. Clearly, Amy's primary kin are important to her, and she works to maintain close contact with them. Nevertheless, she has not felt it necessary to move back to the Los Angeles area, content to have her social contact with primary kin remain periodic.

Amy has several other relatives she cares about, mostly on her side of the family, including her grandparents and an aunt. Donald's mother is the only in-law she interacts with much (aside from his cousin in town), since he has no siblings and his father is dead. These relatives also live elsewhere in southern California, limiting social interaction with them, although mutual aid, especially when visiting in each other's homes, is offered.

Cultural Definitions of *Close* Family Ties

As the case studies demonstrate, familism in the traditional sense of interacting with a large, local kin group is a pervasive Mexican-American trait irrespective of level of acculturation. Those who immigrate to the United States must leave their relatives in Mexico; thus, their interaction with them obviously declines. They tend to remain emotionally close to their parents and those siblings left behind, however, and any relatives who happen to live in town become important. As the immigrants grow older, time and energy is invested in maintaining a primary kin network like Carmen's, which is based on adult children and their families. Non-kin, including friends, neighbors, and coworkers, on the other hand, never come to figure significantly in their social lives.

For the native-born, the extended kin group becomes large and cohesive. Most significant are the primary kin: parents, siblings, and adult children. Friends and other non-kin are likely to be integrated into the native-borns' social networks but never to the exclusion of relatives. For most native-borns, like Anna Fuentes, the kin group is the core of their social life. Familism as a cultural trait is thus nurtured by the first generation only to come into full bloom in later generations due to geographic stability.

As suggested elsewhere (Keefe 1984), Anglo-Americans also maintain a preference for close extended family ties; what differs is the ethnic definition of closeness. Mexican-Americans and Anglo-Americans share many interpretations of closeness, such as the expression of love and affection between kin, evidence of trust and respect among family members, sharing life experiences as a family, and knowing family members are there if needed. Chicanos differ, however, on one fundamental aspect in defining closeness: the need for the consistent presence of family members. Chicanos value the physical presence of family members while Anglos are satisfied with intermittent meetings with kin supplemented by telephone calls and letters. For Mexican-Americans, it is important to see relatives regularly face-to-face, to embrace, to touch, and to simply be with one another, sharing the minor joys and sorrows of daily life. For Anglos, these experiences are integral to nuclear family life but less important with regard to extended family ties. Anglos also feel comfortable having friends function in these roles, while Chicanos reserve them primarily for kin. As Adams (1970) has pointed out, friends and relatives can be interchangeable for Anglo-Americans with regard to social visiting and minor kinds of mutual aid.

Geographic proximity, in other words, is not the basis for the Anglo-American conception of closeness in kin ties, In fact, there are many aspects of close family relations that can be unaffected by the physical presence or absence of kin: carrying a family identity as part of a personal identity, talking or worrying about family members, and experiencing a psychological feeling of well-being stemming from family members' support. Other aspects can be fulfilled with the intermittent physical presence of kin, including being present during holidays and in times of crisis. Amy Cooper is really somewhat atypical of our sample of Anglo-Americans in that all of her primary kin live in California. Most of the Anglos in the study were born outside of California and have at least some of their primary kin living in other states, which makes them even more inaccessible.

In conclusion, early social theorists, looking at American society in general, were correct in their description of urban life as being less kin-based. This is true insofar as it concerns the face-to-face social communities of the Anglo-American majority, but it is wrong to conclude that this ethnic trait is an urban trait. In many contemporary, urban societies and urban-dwelling ethnic groups, such as Mexican-Americans, extended kinship dominates social life. Moreover, it does not follow that Anglo-Americans lack kin ties because, in fact, Anglos have significant extended-family ties which can be activated immediately and intensely in times of need (Sussman 1965). In rethinking the relationship between urbanism and kinship organization, much remains to be done in describing the extent of cross-cultural variation and potential explanations for that variation. Furthermore, it would appear that focusing on the social lives of individuals, rather than on apparent social communities, would be a better technique to use in future research on the question. In any case, it is clear that the extended family survives in cities and contributes in positive ways to ethnic adaptation to urban life.

Notes

1. The terms *Chicano* and *Mexican-American* are used interchangeably in this paper to refer to the entire ethnic group of Mexican descent in the United States. Modified versions of these terms are used to discuss sub-segments of the ethnic group (e.g., immigrant Mexicans, native-born Chicanos). The term *Anglo-American*s is used to refer to white Americans of European descent. Considerable cultural and socioeconomic diversity, which affects family organization, obviously exists within the Anglo-American ethnic group. My research, however, indicates that Chicano, versus Anglo, ethnicity is the most significant factor affecting extended family organization within the population sampled.

2. The author expresses appreciation to the National Institute of Mental Health which provided funding for this research (Center for Minority Group Mental Health Programs. Grant number MH26099. Principal Investigator: Amado M. Padilla). The first survey randomly sampled residents in three selected census tracts in each of the three cities: the final sample included 666 Chicanos and 340 Anglo-Americans. In the second survey, which produced a sample of 381 Chicanos and 163 Anglo-Americans, respondents who indicated willingness were reinterviewed. For the second set of interviews, a much longer questionnaire was used. In-depth case studies were subsequently done of twenty-four Chicanos and twenty two Anglos. Cases were selected randomly to cover a stratified range of cultural, socioeconomic, and family organization categories. Further description of the research design and findings can be found in Keefe and Padilla (1987).

References

Adams, Bert N. 1968. *Kinship in an Urban Setting*. Chicago: Markham.

Aldous, Joan. 1962. Urbanization, the Extended Family and Kinship Ties in West Africa. *Social Forces*, 41:6-12.

Alvirez, David, and Frank D. Bean. 1976. The Mexican American Family. In *Ethnic Families in America: Patterns and Variations*. Eds. Charles H. Mindel and Robert W. Habenstein, pp. 271-292. Upper Saddle River, NJ: Prentice Hall.

Caplow, Theodore, Howard M. Bahr. Bruce A. Chadwick, Reuben Hill, and Margaret Holms Williamson. 1982. *Middletown Families: Fifty Years of Change and Continuity.* Minneapolis: University of Minnesota Press.

Garigue, Philip. 1956. French Canadian Kinship and Urban Life. *American Anthropologist,* 58:1090-1101.

Garrison, Vivian. Social Networks, Social Change and Psychiatric Complaints Among Migrants in a New York City Slum. Ph.D. Dissertation. Columbia University.

Gonzalez, Nancie L. 1969. *The Spanish-Americans of New Mexico: A Heritage of Pride.* Albuquerque: University of New Mexico Press.

Goode, W. 1963. *World Revolution and Family Patterns.* Glencoe, IL: Free Press of Glencoe.

Goode. William J. 1966. Industrialization and Family Change: In *Industrialization and Society.* Eds. B. F. Hoselitz and W. E. Moore, pp. 237-255. Paris: UNESCO-Mouton.

Grebler, Leo, Joan W. Moore, and Ralph C. Guzman. 1970. *The Mexican-American People: The Nation's Second Largest Minority.* New York: The Free Press.

Greenfield, Sidney M. 1961. Industrialization and the Family in Sociological Theory. *American Journal of Sociology,* 67:312-322.

Greer, Scott. 1956. Urbanism Reconsidered: A Comparative Study of Local Areas in a Metropolis. *American Sociological Review,* 21:19-25.

Hammel, E. A., and Charles Yarbrough. 1973. Social Mobility and the Durability of Family Ties. *Journal of Anthropological Research,* 29:145-163.

Harris, C.C. 1969. *The Family: An Introduction.* London: Allen and Unwin.

Jacobson, H.E. 1970 Urbanization and Family Ties: A Problem in the Analysis of Change. *Journal of Asian and African Studies,* 5:302-307.

Keefe, Susan Emley. 1979. Urbanization, Acculturation and Extended Family Ties: Mexican-Americans in Cities. *American Ethnologist,* 6:349-365.

Lewis, Oscar. 1965 *La Vida: A Puerto Rican Family in the Culture of Poverty.* New York: Random House.

Linton, Ralph. 1949. The Natural History of the Family. In *The Family: Its Functions and Destiny.* Ed. R.N. Anshe, pp. 18-38. New York: Harper and Brothers..

Litwak, Eugene. 1960a. Occupational Mobility and Extended Family Cohesion. *American Sociological Review,* 25:9-21.

Litwak, Eugene. 1960b. Geographic Mobility and Family Cohesion. *American Sociological Review,* 25:385-394.

Madsen, William. 1964. *The Mexican-Americans of South Texas.* New York: Holt, Rinehart and Winston.

Sussman, Marvin B. 1959. The Isolated Nuclear Family. Fact or Fiction? *Social Problems,* 6:333-340.

Sussman, Marvin B., and Lee Burchinal. 1962. Parental Aid to Married Children: Implications for Family Functioning. *Marriage and Family Living,* 24:320-332.

Maine, Henry. 1861. *Ancient Law.* London: John Murray.

Parsons, Talcott. 1943. The Kinship System of the Contemporary United States. *American Anthropologist* 45:22-38.

Redfield, Robert. 1941. *The Folk Culture of Yucatan.* Chicago: University of Chicago Press.

Service, Elman R. 1967. *Primitive Social Organization.* New York: Random House.

Smelser, Neil J. 1966. The Modernization of Social Relations. In *Modernization: The Dynamics of Growth*, ed, M. Weiner, pp. 110-121. New York: Basic Books.

Wagley, Charles. 1964. Luzo-Brazilian Kinship Patterns: The Persistence of a Cultural Tradition. In *Politics of Change in Latin America*, eds. J. Maier and R. Weatherhead. New York: Frederick A. Praeger.

Wirth, L. 1938. Urbanism As a Way of Life. *American Journal of Sociology*, 44:3-24.

Vatuk, Sylvia. 1972. *Kinship and Urbanization*. Berkeley and Los Angles: University of California Press.

CHAPTER 5

Kazoku: The Kinship System of Japanese-Americans in Hawaii

Lynn Murata, San Francisco State University

Introduction

Hawaii today is still the most popular destination for Japanese tourists going abroad. Newly-weds, young couples with children, singles and even grandmothers and grandfathers flow off the jumbo jets in a never-ending wave to bask in the tropical sun of this resort. The secret to Hawaii's popularity is that they feel quite at home here, where the majority of the local population is also ethnic Japanese. The visitors can go anywhere in the Islands and be sure of a warm welcome, with no language problems. "*Furusato*—hometown? Why, Hawaii is like my furusato," they say, "It reminds me of Japan in the old days."

Ironically, while the Japanese tourist dollar is vital to Hawaii's economy, the modern Japanese visitor actually plays little part in the mainstream life of the local Japanese-American or *Nikkeijin* population. With the passage of more than a hundred years, ties of kinship to Japan are fragile. Indeed, despite the millions of Japanese tourists that visit Hawaii every year, less than one percent will actually be going there to look up relatives. With time and distance, ties to family in Japan were permanently broken, and few "local" Japanese can trace their ancestry in Japan with any certainty.

This chapter describes the transformation of the Japanese kinship system and intra-familial relations as they developed for Hawaii's Japanese American population over three generations. As immigrants, the Japanese were tied to a system different from that found in Hawaii, but not necessarily in conflict with the local society. The concepts of *kazoku* (family) and *honke* (main household) versus *bunke* (secondary households) were derived from the traditional Japanese IE (Family lineage system), but the family organization of Japanese in Hawaii has developed on a parallel yet independent path from the motherland. Perhaps it is only inevitable, that after more than a hundred years of forced separation amid a tumultuous history, the Japanese in Hawaii are

Contributed by Lynn Murata.

proud that they have made it on their own. While maintaining strong pride in their ethnic heritage, the immigrants have shown that they, as second or third sons without any material heritage, could indeed set up independent, successful bunke (secondary households), without any help from their relatives in Japan. Ironically, the IE system itself has been abolished in Japan, while traditional Japanese values and customs live on in the hearts of the Nikkeijin in Hawaii.

The Japanese in Hawaii today, as a group, are sophisticated, solidly middle-class, highly educated and respected in society. They still retain a slight majority in numbers at 22.3% (US Census Bureau 1998), but in the fast-changing demographics of the past two decades, are quickly losing ground to a new wave of immigrants from the Philippines, Korea, and even Samoa. Because of its historic majority, the Japanese-Americans (JA) have political clout—solidly Democratic—they have put several of their own into important posts, from Governor Ariyoshi, to the two State Senators, Daniel Inouye and Spark Matsunaga, to numerous City and state councilmen. The high profile of Japanese-Americans in Hawaii (JAH) is due in large part to their concept of kinship and solidarity. Having solidly left plantation manual labor and the blue-collar class behind, today the JAH ranks are filled with professionals—doctors, lawyers, teachers, nurses and administrative personnel, many of them women. The dominance of JA in Hawaii has caused animosity by other ethnic groups, particularly the Filipino, but as recent immigrants, they do not realize that the Japanese had to fight their way to success, one step at a time. Like the Chinese, Confucian family values of diligence, honesty, loyalty and endurance were all handed down through many generations. However, unlike the Chinese who place their own family lineage group before all other groups, the Japanese valued foremost group solidarity of the clan and mutual cooperation, along with respect for authority. To the Japanese, the success of one of its members reflects on the community as a whole. The ability of the Japanese community to rally around a common cause is reason for their success as a harmonious group. This cohesion based upon the concept of clan rather than lineage, was brought to Hawaii by the Issei—1st generation immigrants. The makeup of the kinship system in Hawaii has since changed, in reaction to outside pressures. Sadly, urban development has destroyed the once close-knit JA communities while American education and social values have imposed new paradigms on a heretofore traditionally Confucian-oriented society. Still, the Japanese in Hawaii recognize the value of their ethnic heritage and share a sense of brotherhood in their proud history of immigration. This chapter, then, is an analysis of the migration and assimilation[1] pattern of the Japanese in Hawaii in the twentieth century, focusing on marriage patterns and kinship organization. "Assimilation" is a term no longer accepted by Postmodernist anthropologists, but is used in this article with meanings of "successful integration into the mainstream society."

History of Asian Immigration

The Overseas Chinese and the Japanese in Hawaii are two major Asian groups who are at polar ends of a historic movement that began more than a century ago. Exhibiting different immigration and settlement patterns, largely due to historic vicissitudes, the Chinese developed different patterns of kinship ties from the Japanese in America, and serve as an important contrast study group. Due to a sudden increase in immigration in the 1980s and 1990s, the Overseas

Chinese are maintaining a major ethnic presence as a "major minority" in important urban centers around the world, such as San Francisco, New York, Vancouver, and Kobe. Through maintenance of strong kinship allegiances, the Chinese have also spread out to new areas, such as Australia and London, as part of a transnational movement. As witness to this massive new wave of immigration, new areas of Chinese settlement have expanded from the traditional downtown Chinatown in San Francisco, to new "Chinatown" enclaves in the Richmond and Sunset areas. Ironically, the Chinatown area in Honolulu, once a prosperous and bustling ethnic enclave, is today only a sad ghost of its former glory, as the newer immigrants bypass Hawaii for the US mainland.

The *Nikkeijin* (Japanese-Americans) despite their historical strength in numbers, face the future as a diminishing minority in Hawaii, with weakening kinship ties due to a definitive end of large-scale immigration.

Hawaii and Brazil were the two major destinations for Japanese migration from the late 1880s. Quickly becoming a majority ethnic group in Hawaii, the Japanese soon established a strong local community and social patterns that while deeply rooted in kinship patterns of the homeland, soon developed independently. This chapter examines the continuity and change of the Japanese kinship system in Hawaii—how concepts of clan, lineage and family honor were brought wholesale from Japan. Ironically, the majority of the Japanese immigrants—the first-generation *Issei*—were poor, uneducated farmers. That they should hold onto a kinship system that was not only repressive but offered little opportunity for women, who played an important role in the immigrants' success, is witness to the power of tradition in Japanese society in Hawaii.

Chinese and Japanese as Foreigners

Asian immigration to the United States in the 20th century was marked by contradictory trends and government policies that reflect the overall attitude, sometimes xenophobic, of WASP (white Anglo-Saxon Protestant) Americans towards "aliens"—a term used by the US Immigration and Naturalization Service—from the Far East over the course of a century. Although the Chinese and Japanese immigrants were only two of many ethnic groups to cross national boundaries, their presence was and still is, particularly visible in a country negatively sensitive to cultural and racial diversity. Besides cultural and religious practices, the obvious physical and language differences made assimilation difficult. These Asians were considered "different," strange, uneducated and scorned—an unwelcome threat to the supposed homogeneity of American society, one centered on European cultural identity.

Despite overt racism, in their escape from political and economic turmoil, *Gam san*, "The Gold Country," as the Cantonese call it, remains a magnet for those in search of real or imagined opportunities. In 1880, 87,828 or 83% of a total of 105,464 Chinese migrants to the United States were clustered in the West Coast. (Wong 1982:3) In 1882, the Chinese Exclusion Law put a virtual end to the influx of coolie migrants. The second major wave of migration came after World War II, due to several new favorable immigration laws: 1943: Chinese Exclusion Law repealed; 1945: War Brides Act; 1965: New Immigration Act, all of which opened the floodgates to relatives spanning three generations. The latest wave of Chinese migration began in the late

1980s and 1990s, in part spurred on by the normalization of relations between the U.S. and China from 1979 and the 1997 return of Hong Kong to China. Ironically, the social uncertainty fueled by such political events along with economic globalization, has fostered this latest wave of "transnational" immigration of Hong Kong and Taiwan businessmen (Wong 1982), Mainland Chinese scholars or political refugees with their families, and South East Asian refugees from Vietnam, Cambodia, or Thailand. They are diverse groups with different economic, social and political backgrounds that cannot be generalized into a single category.

Nikkeijin

The second most conspicuous Asian migration was that of the Japanese to Hawaii at the turn of the century. Following the Chinese, who proved unreliable as plantation labor, they left their homeland in search of economic wealth, but with no permanent plans for settlement in America. The first group of immigrants—the *Issei*—were a brave and hardy lot, facing monumental challenges of language, culture and racism. To this group, America was "Beikoku"—"The Land of Rice," a land rich in agricultural resources that promised much to people coming from an agricultural background themselves, perhaps the only point of reference available to these immigrants. Japan had been forcibly opened to the West in 1868—the first year of the Meiji Emperor's reign. The 150 *Gannen-mono* ("first year" migrants to Hawaii), were a mixed group of "artisans, criminals, ex-samurai, intellectuals and an occasional farmer." (Ogawa 1980:5) As with the Chinese, the Japanese faced harsh conditions and overt discrimination, despite having been invited to Hawaii by King Kalakaua under the Masters and Servants Act of 1850. On February 8, 1885, the first official wave of immigrants—944 men—arrived in Honolulu Harbor aboard the *City of Tokio*. Japanese immigration reached a peak between 1885 to 1907, dramatically increasing from 6,420 in 1888 to 61,111 in 1900 in just two years. By 1900, almost 40% of Hawaii's population was ethnic Japanese. By 1905 of the total population of 74,000 in Hawaii, the majority hailed from the three rural districts of Hiroshima, Kumamoto, and Yamaguchi. (Ogawa 1980:23). The sudden influx of the Issei was a cause for anti-Japanese legislation in Hawaii and the United States.

Although Hawaii was not declared a state until 1959, it followed the policies of the U.S. Government, having been annexed as a "territory" in 1898 after the forceful overthrow of the native Hawaiian monarchy in 1893. The "Gentlemen's Agreement" of 1907 and the Exclusion Act of 1924 stopped further Japanese immigration, but by this time, the Issei had procured "Picture Brides" and their population in Hawaii swelled. Despite the Anti-Alien Land Law of 1913 (revised 1920), which prohibited foreign-born Japanese the right to lease or own land, their unfulfilled dream of returning home as rich men soon turned to one of making it in Hawaii, their new *furusato* (hometown). The Issei worked to the bone on the sugar plantations, hard, physical labor and menial jobs that promised no future, for the sake of their children, the *Nisei*, the second generation.

Unlike their parents, the Nisei, growing up in the turbulent 1930-40s and having the advantage of local birth, were better educated and better assimilated into the American society. But they grew up in difficult times, torn between two worlds: World War II, intense racial hatred and the infamous "relocation camps," a result of anti-Japanese hostilities. Children of two cultures, they had to give up their Japanese heritage in order to prove their loyalty to America. Ironically, WWII pitted the Chinese-Americans against the Japanese-Americans in the world theatre. Who were the real Americans?

On February 19, 1942, in quick reaction to the bombing of Pearl Harbor, Franklin D. Roosevelt signed Executive Order 9066, which engendered the wholesale evacuation of 110,000 Japanese-Americans from the West Coast. The Chinese were careful to put up signs in their storefronts identifying themselves: "We are loyal Chinese." For once, the Chinese were perceived as "good" allies, while the Japanese became the hated, crafty and evil enemy to be scorned.

The importance of the relocation camps, at Manzanar, Tule Lake, Tanforan and Camp McCoy, upon the psyche of the Nisei cannot be ignored. It at once defined and displaced this generation from all other Nikkeijin for all time. The 100th Battalion and 442nd Regiment, U.S. divisions of Mainland and Hawaii GIs that fought in both Europe and the Pacific theatres, epitomized the Japanese sense of family and country. Their country was America; their kin, blue-eyed WASPs. They fought, not to preserve their ethnic heritage, but to prove that they, too, were full-blooded Americans, born of American soil, part of the American family, and willing to give their lives for the "land of the free and the brave."

The *Sansei* or third-generation JA, are Baby Boomers, born in the post-war era of prosperity. Without fear of political reprisals, the Sansei are more consciously connected to their ancestral roots. To this generation falls the duty to preserve their ethnic heritage for succeeding generations. But we are growing ever distant from the "motherland" as the memories and knowledge of our own cultural heritage fades away, in part due to the weakening of ancestral kinship ties.

Kinship and Marriage Patterns

The similarities and differences between the Chinese and Japanese kinship system were important indications of the direction of the family structure as it developed in America (Hsu 1975). Both cultures, sharing Confucian ideology, believed in and practiced filial piety, strict patrilineal authoritarianism, exogamous polygyny and lineage associations tied to ancestral worship. An importance difference was the Japanese system of unigeniture, whereby only one son, usually the eldest, inherited the house, property and family shrine for ancestors. For the Japanese, this system, along with the availability of Japanese brides, was a pivotal rationale for second and third sons to make the arduous journey to Hawaii to establish their own independent units: an extension of the honke or main household versus bunke, the secondary household concept. (Hsu, *Iemoto*:29) The extended family is another important concept that differs between the Japanese and Chinese household, as Hsu explains:

> Even though much closer relationships exist between the *honke* and *bunke* than among separate households established by brothers in the United States, the establishment of separate households by several brothers is the Japanese rule, and not, as in China, an eventuality to be avoided unless the various wives really cannot get along. In other words, living together was desirable and honorable for the Chinese married brother just as separation was the ideal for the Japanese. (Iemoto 1975:30)

In China the extended family was a precept of prosperous families: many generations, husband with First Wife, concubines and progeny, siblings, cousins and their families, all living together under one roof, usually in an urban setting, was the ideal. In Japan the reverse was the rule: the extended family seems to be more common in rural areas based on agricultural households where manpower was a daily necessity. In urban centers families tended to be nuclear, even in the large *daimyo* estates of Edo (1600-1868). The elderly parents usually resided with the eldest son, a practice that continues today both in Japan and Hawaii, and is a factor in the unpopularity of first-sons as marriage partners. In both societies, until the post-war period, marriage was foremost a contract between two families, not a relationship based upon romantic love—a concept introduced from the West. Arranged marriages are still popular in both Chinese and Japanese society. Divorce was frowned upon, and a woman's place in the family was tenuous until she bore a male child. A woman could be divorced but rarely initiated divorce as she would suffer economically and be socially ostracized with little hope for remarriage. Her children would be claimed by the husband's family as heirs to the patrilineal line.

Lineage and Kinship Terminology

The importance of surname, Wong, Ching, etc. is all-encompassing to the Chinese family system. It not only denotes one's patrilineal lineage and ancestral roots, but also determines one's rights and obligations within the family structure. Genealogical records are pivotal to Chinese society and ancestral halls remain important ideological centers for kinship relationships despite the Communist denunciation of Confucian family values. The Japanese do not construct ancestral halls, but have *butsudan* (modest Buddhist altars) within their residence, usually the eldest son's responsibility, that is maintained, on average, for no more than three generations. Both Chinese and Japanese families share a lineage system in the naming of sons. For the Chinese, the child is named according to one's generation, with each son of the same generation having the same prefix root. For instance the father's generation will all take the prefix "Wing"—Wing-On, Wing-Ling, Wing-Wah—while their sons take the prefix "Kai" to denote a different generation: Kai-Leung, Kai-Man, Kai-Wing. Hsu explains the meaning of this patrilineal name system:

> The Chinese manner of naming thus exemplifies the quality of continuity and inclusiveness within the patrilineal extended kin group. It is inclusive because all males who are members of the kin group and their spouses are bound together by the surname and all males of the kin group belonging to the same generation are identified by the common element in their personal names." (Iemoto 1975:32)

The importance of kinship terminology extends to how one addresses one's superiors or inferiors based upon genealogical ranking. With 180 terms for relationships in the Chinese family system (Wong 1999 kinship lecture), in the Chinese system, each relative is clearly addressed as "elder third uncle on father's side" or "younger 5th aunt on mother's side," etc. by birth rank order. Individuality in the Chinese family is not stressed.

This system does not carry over into Japanese terminology. There are broad generational categories of grandparents, uncles, aunts, nephews, but not as specific as with the Chinese. Matrilineal relations do not have different terminology from the patrilineal line. The only sex and age ranking is found in the immediate sibling order: *ani: older brother; ane: older sister; otooto: younger brother; imooto: younger sister.* There is also differentiation between "in-laws," who are called "*giri no . . .*" as in "*giri no haha*" (mother-in-law), or "*giri-no-otooto*" (younger brother-in-law).

The Japanese, while professing to descend from an unbroken line of emperors, do not have a long history in lineage names. Even the Emperor has no last name. The system of designating last names did not develop until the Tokugawa Period (1600 -1868) as part of the feudal *daimyo* clan ties, which were developed more by loyalty to one's local warlord than by blood ties. Japanese history is rife with blood-related feuds over succession, something not seen in Chinese history. Generations are differentiated along patrilineal father-to-son lines: for instance, my grandfather was Yoshikatsu, his son (my father) was named Yoshi-tsugi (meaning "son of Yoshi-"), his grandson could be Yoshi-hiro. However, not being in the direct patrilineal line of the first son, Yoshikatsu's younger brother will not take the "Yoshi" denoting the main family lineage, but be named entirely different: Nobu-hiro. His son will be Nobu-taka, his grandson Nobu-hide. This system most common amongst the samurai, has been discontinued in the modern era, with no relationship of name to generation. Thus while the Chinese name system is lateral, the Japanese is vertical.

Kazoku: Japanese-American Kinship in Hawaii

Probably the most successfully assimilated group of all Asian immigrants, the Japanese Nikkeijin community provides an important point of contrast to the Chinese. Exactly why the Japanese in Hawaii should be more successful in their assimilation is due to several factors, such as the immigration pattern, historical events, and the kinship system of the Japanese itself, which was flexible enough to adjust to American patterns of social interaction.

Immigration Pattern and Family Kinship

As stated, the Japanese immigrants differed from the Chinese in two important ways: the honke system and immigration policies. Chinese males were conceptually tied to the lineage system—the "Continuum of Descent" (Baker 1979:26). Any economic gain was the property of the family rather than the individual. Their loyalty was to the large clan left behind in China, thus the need for "paper sons," clan or lineage associations in Chinatown, and separated families. The Japanese migrants consisted of mostly second and third sons, expendable resources who were a burden in the unigeniture system of Japanese inheritance. They were free to make their fortunes away from the family clan. At the same time they had no lasting obligation to share their economic wealth with relatives still in Japan. Hsu explains the different kinship ties:

> The Chinese pattern exhibits pure patrilineal continuity and inclusiveness. The Japanese pattern is . . . more exclusive because it cuts off lateral relatives and lateral ancestors so that the Japanese patrilineal line becomes more narrowly defined than the Chinese

one. Lateral relatives cut off from the main line have to find some place to go. This means they must join or create groups in which they can establish their lives. (Hsu 1975:33)

With the abolishment of the samurai feudal system, drastic changes in the political and social conditions spelled uncertainty, while the farming famine that struck Western Japan, combined with the need for plantation laborers in Hawaii at the turn of the century, provided the impetus for these displaced Japanese sons to seek their fortune in America.

It is true that "Japanese-Americans are one of those rare populations in which historical events have rendered kinship-defined generations identical with birth cohorts" (Yanagisako 1992:89). But the strength of this ethnic group in Hawaii lies in the fact that traditional values, stressing close-knit cohesion of the kin-based community, based upon mutual responsibilities, rather than individual "love" or "selfish" individual-centered relations, have been firmly retained through three generations. Ogawa explains the low divorce rate among the Issei and Nisei, initiated in the Picture Bride system:

In most cases, the Issei couple had never met each other before their arranged Union; they risked their futures on a celluloid promise. The woman had not only accepted an unknown husband, but had traveled alone to a new land where life would prove, at best, to be uncertain. The man had foregone the freedom of his bachelorhood so as to support a wife and children in a dubious island environment. But both would sacrifice their personal wants, suppress their fears, and dedicate themselves to their family. As a result, a stable, moral Japanese community would flourish in Hawaii. (Ogawa 1980:77)

Concepts of family and community were maintained by the immigrants:

"The Japanese do not perceive themselves as having a contractual relationship with their spouses or families . . . they look on the family, including marriage, from the traditional standpoint of sacred bonds of blood. They sense that the family is a sacred institution, one that should not and must not be dismantled once it has been established. We Japanese tend to see ourselves not as discrete individuals, but as entities within the family. We also have a sense of ourselves as entities within other groups, such as the company we work for." (Kaji 1996:76)

The Japanese concept of kinship is tied to the overall group—the "clan" rather than the blood-relations of "lineage" so important to the Chinese. It is broadly based on the *dozoku* system as a flexible association based on common interest rather than kinship ties. For this reason, the Japanese are able to transcend individual blood interests in favor of the group, something the Chinese have not been able to overcome. Unlike the Chinese, who clearly differentiate between family and "others," the Japanese are able to incorporate "outsiders" as fictive kin in flexible relationships, as in the *dozoku* system. The strength of the loyalty inherent to the *samurai* clan system is founded upon this sense of fictive kinship. The country as one family serving one cause is an ideology innately understood by the Japanese but resisted by the Chinese. An example of this concept is the *muko yoshi* or adopted son-in-law. In families with no son or only daughters, an outside male is chosen to carry on the family line. By being adopted as a yoshi, he gives up his own heritage of "Yamada" and takes on the identity as the male progenitor of the female line, and takes her family name "Tanaka." Their children will take the name of female line—"Tanaka." This practice is openly accepted as a respectable way of transmission of the family line. While distant cousins are favored, in reality, the yoshi is usually someone already associated with the family's welfare, such as the *banto-san* (the head manager of a shop), or a *deshi*, disciple already working under the patriarch. The word *deshi* literally means "younger brother" and attests to the close familial relationship between a Japanese *sensei*, master teacher and his best pupils. My maternal grandfather, Kitahara, was a *yoshi*; a practice continued only rarely in Hawaii today, as the Nikkeijin move away from lineage identification towards the more egalitarian American methods of bilateral kinship. Not surprisingly in a strongly patrilineal society, the role of a yoshi is considered a form of emasculation, and no man goes into such a relationship without trepidation. A yoshi is subject to disrespect and ridicule, much in the manner of a "henpecked husband" in Western society.

The adoption of the banto-san is a common tradition in Japanese merchant families and is considered an honor for the banto-san, a reward in recognition of his business capabilities. While the young mistress of the household may be consulted as to this arrangement, her objections to marriage do not necessarily stop the wedding. This system is especially prevalent and important in traditional organizations such as martial arts, artisans such as carpenters, pottery-makers, textiles, etc. and the Fine Performing Arts, which operate under the *Oiemoto* system of hereditary positions, as found in Kabuki, Noh, Japanese Tea Ceremony, Japanese Dance and the like. The close sensei-deshi relationship continues for those who study the Fine Arts in Hawaii, although legal adoption to take on a school name is not normally practiced. Instead, succession to the school's head post is signified by the taking of a name that incorporates both the Sensei's name and the school's name. The incorporation of a master's name into one's own professional name is a great honor. For example, if the Sensei's name is Hanayagi Sakura (school name plus personal name = Hanayagi cherry blossom), her disciple could be named Hanayagi Ume (Hanayagi Plum); or in the case of Kendo (Japanese Swordplay): if the Sensei's name is Musashi-tomo, his successor would be named Musashi-yoshi. Most traditional schools will have special name-taking ceremonies to officially and ritualistically pass on the school's leadership.

Ethnic Identity

Due to their large number, the Nikkeijin quickly became the predominant ethnic group in Hawaii and have retained this equilibrium until the 1980s when a new wave of Filipino, Korean and somewhat smaller group of Chinese immigrants changed the social demographics. Another important result of the ethnic majority established by the Nikkeijin in Hawaii is the fact of their social, political and cultural stability and self-awareness. Not being subjected to the negative social pressures of being a "minority" group engendered a very different sense of self compared to the Nikkeijin in the 'Mainland." Partly due to the conscriptive anti-Japanese policies of WWII, and the relocation camps which psychologically and ideologically tore families apart, the self-assurance and self-worth of the Nikkeijin in Hawaii, as they identify with their ethnic heritage is lacking in the Japanese-Americans in California.

The Nikkeijin in California impress me as being on edge, in an eternal conflict, in the process of forced assimilation with the "superior" WASP culture, at once questioning yet defending the values of their ethnic heritage. To succeed in the Mainland, the Nikkeijin have to psychologically conceal their ethnic identity and don the chameleon cloak of WASP identity, or come to terms with it at some point in their lives. The reverse is true in Hawaii, where "to be Japanese" is natural and not something to hide. In fact, we in Hawaii do not refer to ourselves as "Nikkeijin." We just say we are "Japanese," without any sense of need for explanation. The rare time we use "Nikkeijin" is when a visiting Japanese national asks why we are able to speak Japanese. Then the answer is, "Because I am a Nikkeijin." Those on the mainland however, almost always qualify their ethnicity as being "American-Japanese" or "Japanese of American descent," which places an important and somewhat detrimental psychological weight on their identity.

Kinship and Assimilation

The Japanese immigrants were a mixed bag of social and education levels: illiterate farmers, educated Buddhist priests and former samurai. As such, this diverse population brought its own foundation for social infrastructure, bringing their own religious institutions, Japanese language school system and social network. The Japanese language schools, the first founded on Oahu in 1896, for the most part, were affiliated with Buddhist churches, and were an important link to the motherland's language and culture for the Nisei. Learning American ways at school in the day, the Nisei would then attend Japanese school in the late afternoon or on weekends and "return to Japan" at home.

Like the Chinese, the Japanese laborers congregated in ethnic camps, the Wailua and Haleiwa plantations, and later with the Nisei, in the urban downtown Nuuanu and Liliha areas, although a former "Japantown" was never established in Honolulu. A merchant area existed without definite borders on the fringes of Chinatown near the dock area of Honolulu Harbor, but due to the majority of their ethnic group, stores and restaurants catering to the Japanese soon spread throughout Honolulu. In this way a ghetto condition was not perpetuated as seen in the San Francisco and New York Chinatowns.

McKinley High School, which serves the Nuuanu, Liliha and Manoa districts, quickly came to be called "Little Tokyo" due to the predominance of the Nisei population there. With the GI Bill, many Nisei took advantage of education opportunities and have become the predominant group of professionals in Hawaii. Their children, the Sansei, have access to the best schools in Hawaii and the USA, with none of the discrimination that plagued their parents and grandparents.

In 1995, the Japanese community, on the celebration of 100 years of immigration to Hawaii, proudly finished reconstruction of the old Japanese Chamber of Commerce building, near the University of Hawaii. The beautiful Japanese Cultural Center is a complex of exhibition halls, martial arts and culture activity rooms and a small museum and banquet hall in lower Manoa, in the proximity of the old Makiki Japanese Language School. It serves as a much needed visible focal point for the Japanese ethnic identity in Honolulu. Still, unlike the Chinese, the JA no longer stress the necessity to learn the mother language and customs. Many Sansei cannot speak Japanese and, sadly the *Yonsei* (4th generation) have little interest in Japan. Tradition has weakened substantially in Nikkeijin third generation relations. The JA kinship connections are limited to the occasional gathering for weddings and funerals as kindred ties, in contrast to the obligatory weekly yam-cha family sessions for the San Francisco Chinese.

Death and Kinship Ties

An example of the different attitude the Japanese and Chinese have regarding kinship ties is seen in their different approaches to ancestor worship. The large ancestor hall fundamental to and typical of Chinese clan associations is not found in Japanese society, and least of all in Hawaii. Even wealthy lineages in Japan use the facilities of a Buddhist temple rather than maintaining permanent individual ancestor halls to perform periodic rituals, such as a funeral, and subsequent anniversaries, such as the 3rd year ritual. One's link to a particular Buddhist church was often due to kinship and community ties rather than whether or not one actively believed in that particular sect. As a child I remember frequently going to Buddhist rituals honoring the anniversary of a departed relative, records of such deaths being scrupulously maintained and observed. This practice has completely died out in Hawaii today and few young people have attended such an event. Buddhist funerals were the norm for Issei and Nisei, but now funerals are as diverse as the religions in Hawaii. The household butsudan, as an extension of ancestor worship, has also disappeared from Nikkeijin homes. As a child one of my duties was to carefully put rice for the daily offerings and burn incense to the ancestors enshrined in the butsudan.

Family Grave—Ohaka

Another important difference in kinship or ancestral rites is that the Japanese bury their dead individually or by patrilineal lines, all under one, simple headstone. This custom is recreated in Hawaii in the Japanese cemeteries in Nuuanu. Unlike the Chinese, to whom ancestor worship is an important family rite, there is no sense of duty or emphasis on remembrance of long-past ancestors, unless one comes from an illustrious family line, something negligible in Hawaii. Although the Nisei and Sansei dutifully "report" to their ancestor's grave rituals of passage, such as births, graduation, marriage and the like, one can expect upkeep of the "family" grave usually for only three generations, after which the memory of the deceased ancestor is forgotten, and therefore neglected.

The Chinese, on the other hand, have elaborate gravestones if their family is wealthy enough to afford one, marking not individuals, but a whole family lineage of many generations, that serves as the focus of ancestor worship rituals. In Hawaii the Chinese cemetery is forlorn, with simple graves in disrepair, a result of both neglect and the lack of kin to care for the graves of long-ago immigrants. For both groups, where the married woman is buried is important—failure to be buried in one's husband's family grave is considered proof that the woman was not legally accepted as part of the family or had been divorced.

Ancestral Ties in the OBon Festival:

Few traditional Japanese festivals are honored today in Hawaii, save the acknowledgement of the two most important, New Year's and *Obon* (the summer Buddhist ritual for honoring ancestors) which is similar to the Chinese Ching Ming. They are the only two seasonal festivals, once significant in the cyclical rhythm of the seasons for the Japanese, that are still nominally celebrated by the Nikkeijin, if only on a very superficial level. On the whole, the American holidays of Christmas, Thanksgiving, Fourth of July, and Easter take the place of traditionally celebrated festivals like Girl's Day, Boy's Day, further diluting the Japanese ethnic identity.

A recent revival of the *toro-nagashi* or "lantern floating" ritual as part of the Obon festival has gained popularity at the Haleiwa Buddhist Temple on Oahu's North Shore. Originally part of the sugarcane plantation community where Issei laborers lived, it retains much of the rural flavor of the early 20th century, including a close-knit local community. Ironically while it draws many Nisei and Sansei JA who remember the grand Obon festivals of their youth, it has also evolved into a tourist event attracting many non-Japanese participants who have little real connection with the ancestral homage due at this event. In direct response to the popularity of the Haleiwa festival, a second toro-nagashi has been organized to flow down the Ala Wai Canal bordering Waikiki by Honolulu Buddhist organizations during the Obon season that is observed from July through August. They are examples of a conscious effort by the Sansei to revive ethnic customs as part of an important cultural heritage, so that they will not be lost to the Yonsei. The fact that the OBon festivals still draws a good turnout is evidence of the strong hold that kinship ties have on the Japanese community.

Fictive Kinship Associations

Blood kinship as a system was supplanted in Hawaii by fictive kinship—*KEN* (prefectural) and *BUKKYO* (Buddhist) religious ties. Thus one belonged to the *Kumamoto-kenjin-kai (Kumamoto Prefecture Association)*, the Hiroshima Kenjinkai, Buddhist churches like the predominant Honpa Hongwanji or Soto-Zen Mission, or the Young Buddhist Association for Nisei. Tanomoshi or "Request" clubs were formed, similar to Chinese clan associations by people NOT kin-related, to deal with individual social and financial needs. Unlike the Chinese, there was never the desire or need for fictive lineage—blood-ties were not as important as ken associations. This in turn, affected marriage ties.

Ethnic Endogamy and Marriage

The Issei did not have the extended kinship relationships of the Chinese family to rely on. They did not bring in families of "paper sons," but immigrated on an individual basis. Still, because of less restrictive immigration laws, they were able to maintain ethnic endogamy, important to the Japanese, who considered maintenance of the "pure Japanese blood-line" critical. An interesting development was the early exclusion of Okinawan immigrants, who were not considered as ethnic "Japanese" by the Issei and Nisei. Disparaging comments such as "The Okinawans are hairy and have dark complexions," was a way of separating their ethnic identities, and marriage to an Okinawan was considered undesirable. Names such as Higa, Goshima or Gushiken would be immediately recognized as being an "Okinawan" name. To this day, the Okinawans remain a distinct, separate group, with their own social organizations. In 1996, the Okinawan Culture Center was recently opened in Central Oahu to commemorate Okinawan immigration and to recognize their distinct ethnic language and cultural heritage in Hawaii.

Ethnic Endogamy

The Issei brought their traditional *IE* (family) agricultural-based system of patrilineal—exogamous—patrilocal residency. Unlike the Chinese who intermarried with the native Hawaiian population, the Japanese for the most part married Japanese women due to less restrictive immigration policies and better relations between the two countries. Between 1911 and 1919, 9,500 picture brides arrived in Hawaii. The result of their fruitful unions was an explosion of Nisei: from 39,127 in 1920 to 113,289 in 1937. (Ogawa 1980:79) The importance of maintaining a "pure" ethnic bloodline, without intermarriage with other races was important to the Japanese community. Ogawa points out, "True to his family wishes, obligated to his ancestral heritage, the Issei man could marry only a Japanese woman. Interethnic marriage, though not unheard of, was inimical to the Japanese pride of race and ethnic integrity." (Ogawa 1980:79) Gladney calls this idea, "ethnic endogamy":

> (For these Hui,) ancestral heritage and ethnic identity is expressed through endogamy, which is marriage within a particular group in accordance with custom or law. Ethnic identity is often preserved and expressed through mate selection. Charles Keyes suggests that the nature of ethnic identity is shaped by the structural oppositions of interacting ethnic groups, often expressed in marriage exchange. (Gladney 1998:82)

Although the preferred bride would be Japanese, young, healthy, never-married, without any children, and from the same village or prefecture, perhaps a distant relative or sister of a good friend, in reality, the Japanese men could not afford to be so choosy. Sight unseen, they married "picture brides," setting up patrilineal, nuclear families within the close-knit compounds of plantation "camps." The larger camp population due to the close proximity of work and living quarters, became in effect the pseudo-family or a kind of loose fictive kinship. Even today ties are strong and Issei identify themselves as belonging to one or another plantation camp rather than a particular family kin lineage. The close proximity to other ethnic groups in the camps led to an increase in cross-ethnic marriages, but for the most part, the Japanese adhered to ethnic endogamy. By the third generation, ethnic exogamy is becoming more prevalent, due to the greater assimilation of the Japanese ethnic group into the larger community. Once considered a disgrace to marry a non-Japanese, such exogamous marriages are no longer frowned upon. In particular, with Hawaii's multi-ethnic community, such marriages are becoming the norm. It is important to note here, however, that the rationale for such marriages are different than from what one would find on the "mainland."

Marriage

Polygyny was practiced before the 20th century in Japan by the samurai and wealthy merchants but was not brought to Hawaii by the poor immigrants. Still the dominance of the male patriarch and the "double-standard" prevailed in local Japanese society until the 1950s and the birth of the Sansei. Extended families of three generations were common until the 1960s, when the preference for nuclear families emerged, influenced by American social standards and urban constrictions of space. However "extended families" in the Chinese sense—of lateral cousins and siblings with their wives in one household—never existed.

Dominant DYAD—Traditional Authority in the Home

While no longer maintaining close kinship relationships like the Chinese, the Japanese family was, and still is, male-dominated, a father-son dominant dyad (Hsu 1965: V67:631-661).

Marriage = Ryosai Kembo ("Good Wife, Wise Mother")

Joyce Lebra points out the concept of *ryosai kembo* or "good wives and wise mothers," the ideal image of the Japanese woman that fosters male dominance in the household. (Lebra 1981:160). Yanagisako explains this attitude brought by the Issei to Hawaii:

> Politics, community organizations, and the construction of a social world outside the household are the proper concern of men, who bear the ultimate responsibility for the security and reputation of their households in that social world. Each spouse fulfills his or her proper responsibilities without interfering in the other's domain. Men should not engage in housekeeping, and child-care activities: women should not represent the household in its relations with the community. From Issei men's point of view, the female inside sphere is encompassed by the male outside sphere and, therefore, is subject to male authority. (Yanagisako 1992:94-96)

The overt dominance of Chinese women in American society, a result of matrifocal conditions caused by immigration, is a great contrast to the deference that Japanese-American women pay to their men. Despite Ogawa's assertion to the contrary, I believe the Japanese-American woman in Hawaii is little different from her Japanese cousins in this particular trait. A Nikkeijin woman in Hawaii, by conservative training and social norm, does not openly question male authority, particularly in public. Her proper role is to support her husband, and ideally, stay at home taking care of the children and keeping the household running smoothly and "spic-and-span" clean. This attitude remains strongly ingrained in women across three generations and affects the character and function of the Nikkeijin family. Ogawa explains the dilemma of the Sansei women who are caught between two different ideologies:

> The discrepancy between independence and sexual role limitations especially affected the Sansei female. More acculturated to the American attitude of female equality than the Sansei male was acculturated to a pattern of female egalitarian treatment, the Sansei young woman was in no more secure a social position than her mother. She felt the restrictions and roles of the family—as a girl, she was expected to find a good husband and get married. (Ogawa 1980: 447)

The Japanese-American family today is characterized as being neolocal, nuclear, bilateral with neither the husband's nor the wife's side being dominant. Neolocality, as Pasternak points out, is a phenomenon of modern urban society. But in reality, marriage itself is still patrilineal, the woman taking the husband's name upon marriage and it is expected they will care for the husband's elderly parents in time. For this reason, the birth of a son has always been favored over a daughter, and celebrated more elaborately, although American values have eroded this concept for the Sansei. Still, every Japanese girl knows instinctively that her brother has more "worth" in the family, as he will carry on the family name. Boy's Day in Hawaii is still celebrated with the joyous display of large silk carp flying over the rooftop of homes that boast male children. Girl's Day is celebrated quietly, if at all, by a modest display of Japanese dolls in the home, to be enjoyed by no one in particular.

The Mother-Son Dyad = The Mother/Daughter-in-Law Conflict

"Shinbo to Gaman"—"Bear it and persevere."

The mother-daughter-in-law conflict, partly a result of the mother-son dyad, is a Japanese tradition that can divide families. Unfortunately this practice was continued by the Issei in Hawaii. Characteristic of the kinship pattern in Japanese families is the close mother-son tie, one that almost always overshadows the husband-wife relation. Hsu explains that while the Japanese kinship system is father-son dominated, it retains a mother-son bias—"the mother-son dyad is only second in importance to the father-son dyad." (Hsu:103) It subsequently affects the harmony of the mother/daughter-in-law relationship. Hsu points out the difference in Japanese relations:

> . . . the Japanese and the Chinese share the same father-son dominated kinship system. But unigeniture (one son inheritance) and mother-son subdominance are correlated with certain behavioral characteristics which differentiate the Japanese from the Chinese. (Hsu 1975:ix)

There is no doubt that the strong emotional hold a Japanese mother has on her son, particularly the first-born, has direct correlation with the traditional Japanese system of unigeniture. Pasternak explains this phenomenon:

> [In the Chinese family] Property traditionally passes in the male line, with adult sons enjoying equal rights to the family estate. Women do not share these rights and have access to productive property only through husbands and sons, a situation that pits mother-in-law against daughter-in-law, and sisters-in-law against each other. When she marries, a woman pursues the loyalty of her husband. Since she will likely outlive him, her security in old age ultimately also depends upon her sons. In that regard she has competition from her daughters-in-law. That is why, in custom and symbol, the parent-child bond takes precedence over the conjugal one. (Pasternak 1997:240)

Add to this the emotional ties that Japanese mothers have with their sons for a dangerous mix. Tales of young wives suffering from the mean-spirited actions of their mother-in-law or young men with "maza-con"—"mother-complex" is common in Japan and Hawaii, even in the modern century. The competition for the son's affection by both the mother and wife, is part of this idea that the mother-child bond is permanent. The introduction of a wife into the family is viewed on with veiled hostility by the mother, who fears that her role as provider of *amae* has been supplanted by the fresh, new presence in the household. Amae means "to depend and presume upon another's benevolence, generally used to describe a child's attitude or behavior towards his parents, particularly his mother." (Takeo Doi, in Hsu 1975:102) One cannot deny the underlying sexual tension that exists in Japanese men's attitudes towards their mother, often exhibited in literature.

Having herself suffered many years under the spiteful thumb of her own mother-in-law as part of the extended family system, the mother-in-law is now ready to move into the role she once despised. It is a way of redefining and affirming her own changed role in the family, as she is now recognized as the family's matriarch. Should the father or patriarch pass away, her role becomes pivotal in the family. Ironically, at the same time, upon the death of her husband, the elder patriarch, her son, the first-born male, succeeds to the status of patriarch, once again pitting mother against wife for his affections and power. This is the *yome* (daughter-in-law)-*shutome* (mother-in-law) conflict.

In this way, the *kafuu*, or "family traditions," is carried on by the matriarch. It is her duty to pass them on to the son's wife, who is now responsible for the daily management of household tasks, leaving the matriarch to enjoy her retirement days, albeit with an ever-watchful eye upon her daughter-in-law.

Should the daughter-in-law choose to complain against her mother-in-law, her bitter words will fall on deaf ears as the Japanese son, in essence owes his alliance first and foremost to his mother. *Haha koishii* (love and yearning for one's mother) is no small factor in conflictual spousal relations.

The matriarch wields great power over the household, and cases where the daughter-in-law was sent home or divorced because of the matriarch's dislike of her was not uncommon in the pre-war era. Today the mother-in-law wields much less power, but in rural or very strongly traditional families, especially those associated with the *Iemoto* system, the mother-in-law is a power to be feared. The strong hold that this tradition has on the Nikkeijin family is seen in one family. A Nisei woman, K married into the Otake (fictitious name), a rich and prosperous family and bore her husband, with whom she was on good terms, two children, a girl, then a son. By law, having borne an heir to the family she had all the rights of being recognized as a family member. However, her mother-in-law (Issei), taking a dislike to her, ordered K out of the household, keeping the children. For ten years, K raised a younger son R alone, R being born from her husband after she left the Otake home. With the death of the mother-in-law, K and her husband, a Nisei were re-united. Such a situation would be unthinkable in Western society. Divorce was and still is considered as "shameful" by the Japanese-Americans. To the older generation, it is often perceived as a failure of the daughter-in-law, rather than as a shortcoming of the husband. In the mother's eye, her son can do no wrong, even in cases of adultery, the typical "double-standard." A typical response by the husband's family would be, "It's the woman's fault for not keeping her husband happy, for not being a good mother or maintaining a proper household." The choices were few: either stay together in a loveless marriage or get divorced and bear social and economic ostracism, something unbearable in the close-knit Japanese community. My mother often said, "*Shoganai* (it can't be helped). You stay together for the kids' sake. *Shimbo suru shika nai* (all you can do is bear with it)." The honor of the family stood before all else. My mother recently told me that she suffered greatly under the domineering system of "mother-in-law rule."

Despite the conflicts, the practice of living with elderly parents in an extended household is still common in Hawaii. Nuclear families revert to the extended household pattern when parents become elderly. It is accepted that, "It is your duty to take care of your parents when they get old." To put them in an "old-folks home" would be unthinkable, a disgrace on the family, and is resisted by most Nikkeijin families in Hawaii. Whether this tradition of filial piety will carry on with the Yonsei generation, only time will tell.

Conclusion

Japanese immigration to Hawaii is characterized as being part of a unique time in history, one that resulted in an ethnic majority that changed the makeup of Hawaii during its formative years. The sudden influx diminished drastically after the Issei migration, resulting in a stable but somewhat static ethnic culture base. The Issei *tsunami* that hit the shores of Hawaii was a one-time phenomenon, not to be repeated within the 20th century. The Issei brought with them the values and norms of Japanese society as they knew it then— kinship systems of the Meiji Period (1868-1912)—the IE, honke and bunke organization of family resources, and the overbearing role of the mother-in-law, making for a very conservative basis. Even their language is an early 20th century form of the local dialect of their region, having exhibited no changes except for the inclusion of Hawaiian pidgin words. The Sansei or Yonsei studying *Hyojungo*, the accepted "national Tokyo dialect" taught in schools today, can barely understand their *ojiichan* (grandfathers) and *obaachan* (grandmothers).

However, immigration and a hundred years of residence has gradually changed the immigrants' kinship patterns to reflect the American social conditions. The majority of JA in Hawaii today have little connection with Japanese culture beyond the superficial, and have been touched only nominally by the post-war expansion of economic Japan. Their ties to Japan are tenuous, in contrast to the Chinese who still retain close ties with their kin in China. Unlike China, Japan has enjoyed relative stability after WWII and there is no economic impetus for further large-scale migration of the Japanese to Hawaii. Aware of their connection to ancestral Japan, the Nikkeijin nevertheless maintain a proud and separate identity. This recognition of their differences from Japanese nationals is in a large part due to their successful assimilation into American culture and positive pride in being recognized as a successful ethnic group. In contrast, the South American Nikkeijin, facing severe economic depression, have claimed their ancestral heritage and returned to Japan in droves in the 1980s and 1990s, in a pattern similar to the recent Chinese migration into Hong Kong and America, where claims of kinship become a key to economic migration. As poor relations and a burden on the already suffering Japanese economy, the South American Nikkeijin and the *Chugoku koji* (Chinese war orphans), are not welcome or recognized as "kin" by many of their Japanese relatives.

Stability vs. Change—From Here, Whence?

Japanese-Americans retain many of the values imparted by the Issei: respect for elders and authority, filial piety, and the traditional patrilineal marriage pattern, with emphasis on male authority in the home. On the other hand, today, Japanese ethnic identity is threatened. Ogawa points out that, "with the waning influences of ancestor worship, family property, the family name, and the family line, on the one hand, and with the growing influences of the ideologies, the family etiquette, and the mores of the American people, on the other, the traditional patriarch-heir relationship weakens." (1980:103) The Yonsei—4th generation JA—those born in the 1970s to 1980s and now coming to adulthood, having "assimilated" into American culture, face different conditions of kinship and ethnic identity. The Japanese-Americans in Hawaii are now facing the challenge of a changing and sometimes hostile society—one in which they will no longer be the ethnic majority. How they react and deal with this challenge to their tradition and lifestyle will determine the future of their kinship patterns in Hawaii. Long-established social norms shared by the Japanese-Americans and the general population in Hawaii, such as respect for authority and elders, politeness and diligence, solidarity and selflessness, are being challenged by the cold indifference of urbanization, new immigrants with different cultural values, and the character of modern 21st century society. Whether or not the island heritage of Aloha and the Japanese-American community as positive role models for other ethnic minorities can absorb these negative influences or fall victim to them, is intricately linked to how traditional values of kinship will hold up against a tide of negative factors. Immigration is no longer a factor in the formation of kinship ties for the Japanese in Hawaii. The Japanese-American community must now turn inward, and rely on their own strength as a close-knit ethnic family with shared values to survive in the 21st century.

Finally, while not discussed at length here, the role of gender and the rise of gender equality in American society is having an immediate influence on the development of a new role for Japanese-American women, not only in Hawaii but in California and the rest of the United States. The effect of changing gender roles will challenge traditional concepts of kinship and family for all Japanese-Americans in the coming era.

Note

1. Nikkeijin—as it is understood by the American Japanese community itself, refers to the second, third and later generations, not the Issei, who by definition, are the initial immigrants from Japan. To be a Nikkeijin, means "to have been born of Japanese parents in America and raised in America." Those of interracial marriages are technically not considered as Nikkeijin by the Japanese-American community, but are referred to as "half," or hapa—a Hawaiian word meaning their bloodline is mixed or not "pure" Japanese. These terms are used by the Japanese themselves, and I hope the reader will refrain from pointing out that they are politically incorrect terms.)

References

Baker, Hugh D. R. 1979. *Chinese Family and Kinship*. New York: Columbia University Press.

Befu, Harumi. 1971. *Japan: An Anthropological Introduction*. Tokyo: Charles Tuttle Co.

Collier, Jane and Yanagisako, Sylvia. 1987. *Gender and Kinship: Essays Towards a Unified Analysis*. Stanford: Stanford Univ. Press.

Fujimura-Fanselow, Kumiko and Kameda, Atsuko, Ed. 1995. *Japanese Women: New Feminist Perspectives on the Past, Present, and Future*. New York: The Feminist Press.

Hsu, Francis. Iemoto: 1975. *The Heart of Japan*. New York: Schenkman Publishing Company.

Jeremy, Michael and Robinson M.E. 1989. *Ceremony and Symbolism in the Japanese Home*. Honolulu: Univ. of Hawaii Press.

Keesing, Roger. 1975. *Kin Groups and Social Structure*. New York: Holt, Rinehart and Winston.

Lebra, Takie S. and Lebra, William, Ed. *Japanese Culture and Behavior*. Honolulu: The University Press of Hawaii. An East-West Center Book.

————. 1982. *Japanese Patterns of Behavior*. Honolulu: Univ. of Hawaii Press. An East-West Center Book.

————. Ed. 1992. *Japanese Social Organization*. Honolulu: Univ. of Hawaii Press.

Nakane, Chie. 1967. *Kinship and Economic Organization in Rural Japan*. New York: The Athlone Press, Univ. of London.

————. 1970. *Japanese Society*. Berkeley: Univ. of California Press.

Ogawa, Dennis M. 1978. *Kodomo no tame ni: For the Sake of the Children. The Japanese-American Experience in Hawaii*. Honolulu: University of Hawaii Press.

Pasternak et al. 1997. *Sex, Gender and Kinship: A Cross-Cultural Perspective*. New Jersey: Prentice Hall.

Rosaldo, Michelle and Lamphere, Louise. 1974. *Woman, Culture, and Society*.

Sano, Chiye. 1958. *Changing Values of the Japanese Family*. Washington, D.C.: The Catholic University of America Press.

White, Merry. 1988. *The Japanese Overseas: Can They Go Home Again?* New York: The Free Press (MacMillan, Inc.)

CHAPTER 6

The Politics of Kinship and Affection in Urban China

William Jankowiak, University of Nevada-Las Vegas

Throughout much of Chinese history, the family was organized around an ideology of filial piety that encouraged total obedience, respect and loyalty toward the father (de Groot 1982-1910; Hanan 1985; Freeman 1965). By controlling the distribution of the family inheritance, a father could effect a special, if not psychological, dependency on the part of the child. On the other hand, a mother's parenting style was seen as much a result of being considered an "outsider" as it was of a "natural" attachment fostered through child birth and early child care (Bowlby 1951; Daly and Wilson 1987). Given her lower status in her husband's family, the mother needed a friend, an ally, and what better one than in her own child (Wolf 1972). In this way, the different access to and use of economic and psychological "resources" contributed to the elaboration of the two complementary parenting styles: the father as an aloof spouse and disciplinary provider, the mother as an equally aloof spouse but, toward her children, an intimate nurturer.

Unlike their rural counterpart who often live in the same village, urban siblings and kin tend to live scattered through various neighborhoods. It is the neolocal (new) and not the patrilocal (father's) residence norm that is the most common in urban settings. Because housing units are packed so closely together, living space cannot always be expanded to embrace a new nuclear unit. When there is a shortage of available housing, any apartment is better than no apartment. This pragmatic concern contributed to the Chinese rejecting the traditional patrilocal (father's) resident rule in favor of the more flexible neolocal (or new) norm.

In the urban arena, kinship is clearly regarded as much a potential burden as a potential benefit or a familial necessity. Although an uncle, cousin or nephew is expected to have a more willing and effective relationship than a mere friend, it is unlikely that he would have access to "more doors," or favors, than anyone else with whom the lower-income or lower ranked individual deals. In fact, upwardly mobile kin often deliberately cut ties of blood which bind them to their more economically humble relatives. Parents, children, siblings and other kin tend to work at different kinds of jobs, developing individual skills and, thus, unconnected networks of job-related friends. As a result, the dependence upon one's kin is greatly reduced in favor of increasing reliance on friends in the work place.

This change requires that Chinese pursue a broad-based strategy of social interaction that includes both kin and non-kin. One insightful informant, when asked to make a distinction between kin and friends, acknowledged, "Friends are for mundane matters, family is for ritual affairs." A 28-year-old female informant poignantly observed that, "We hide from our cousins but not our friends."

The urban Chinese family is organized into three different forms: nuclear, stem and joint. While the nuclear family is the preferred form of family arrangement, most Chinese, at one time or other, will enter into some form of stem family arrangement (i.e., a family with a married couple, children and another relative, usually a parent). The rural ideal of the joint or "big family" (Cohen 1976) as the preferred family organization no longer exists in urban China or, if it does, it exists in small numbers. Within the nuclear family, relations are ideally warm and supportive and, in truth, this ideal is more often honored than breached. Still, there are examples of animosity among family members. Margery Wolf (1970) found that sibling rivalry, particularly among brothers, pervaded domestic family life. I found this to be true in Huhhot as well. Brothers close in age, like their counterparts around the globe (Sulloway 1996), privately admitted feeling resentful and not particularly close to the brother to whom they were closest in age.

Older brothers admitted to harboring deep resentment toward their younger brothers during their childhood years. Significantly, this sentiment was not symmetrical. Younger brothers tended to be bewildered by their elderly brothers' periodic bursts of anger and hostility. When there was a significant age difference of eight years or more, however, there was little demonstrable animosity. In these cases, the eldest brother consistently acted more protective and supportive than competitive. Although I did not conduct any research on relationships between sisters, I did find that cooperation between brother and sister is strong, with the closest ties being between older sister and younger brother. For these ties it appears that a wide age gap is conducive to promoting a type of mentor-apprentice relationships. It is a relationship that continues throughout an individual's life.

Unlike their rural counterparts, married couples, in setting up a household, start by forming a nuclear family. Later, upon the death of one of their parents, the family structure changes to once again incorporate the still-living parent. This re-incorporation, however, does not lead to the elderly parent becoming the head of the family. The fact is that the elderly parent is perceived to be an important but, sometimes, burdensome duty. However, this senior parent is nominally recognized, and on ceremonial occasions is usually referred to as the "head of the family," and given the seat of honor whenever a photograph is taken or a special dinner is cooked. Every elderly person I talked with lamented that, although his or her physical needs were taken care of, they still did not receive the respect they desired or felt they deserved. Some elderly even spoke as if their children had abandoned them. Significantly, fathers complained more often than mothers about the loss of their children's active attention and freely given respect. Observations of elderly parent and offspring interaction found that mothers were, in fact, treated with greater tenderness, attention and respect than fathers. (For example, they were more often asked for their opinion and their views were listened to.) Obviously, mothers, and not fathers, are able to draw upon the strong, intimate child-parent bonds previously established and maintained throughout their life. Fathers, on the other hand, those who took little or no interest in their children's development, now without property and other "resources of power," are unable to command their children's respect, and, therefore, receive only a ritualistic admission of deference and a nominal articulation of love.

Today, only at times of a major rite or life-crisis (e.g., marriage, death or serious illness) will all the siblings and their children congregate. Although the range of kinship bonds is shrinking, the value attributed to marriage and family life has never waned. People continue to think of the family as the dominant metaphor by which to assist and evaluate another's progress through life. In this and many other ways, Chinese kinship sentiments and obligations remain strong.

The Domestic Sphere: The Meaning of Marriage

Marriage and the establishment of a family remain a critical, yet truncated, marker which the urban Chinese use to sort one another out into relative degrees of social maturity, adulthood and psychological stability. There are a wide range of responses to the meaning of marriage and family life. As a rule, if a couple loved one another, they repeatedly strove to maintain mutual consideration. Thus, for example, marriage, in the words of one female, should be "a bond between equals who do not keep secrets and who enjoy one another's company. They should prefer to do everything together." Another younger female (24 years old) maintained that, "Men and women should help one another in a good marriage." Another female repeatedly insisted that in a good marriage "there should be not be any secrets between a husband and a wife." For the most part, men shared similar expectations of marriage. For example, a 42-year-old male told me that, "After marriage you should eat together, go to the movies together and always strive to be an ideal couple." He added, "It's okay to visit your best friend together. The people you don't know very well you should introduce to your wife, but this can be boring, so you might want to go yourself." Another middle-aged man, who was recently divorced, told me, "Although his wife was not a good person, in the best marriages there were no secrets." A younger uneducated man, however, felt that, "A husband should be kind to his wife, but it was okay to have small secrets" from one another. Consideration and mutual respect are values used by spouses and outsiders to evaluate the quality and success of a marriage. They are not gender specific traits.

The anthropological critique of Chinese gender relations has completely overlooked how many men, independent of the state's approval or ideological urging, are also considerate toward their spouse. A Chinese man, for example, told me, "If you want to go out at night, but notice that your wife becomes upset, you must stay home and keep her company." Another man who studied English and Esperanto in his spare time admitted that he preferred to study all day on

Sundays, but noticed that his wife became increasingly quiet and "despondent," so he gave up the practice. He noted that, "It is important to be considerate to your wife. That is why every Sunday we go to the Park for a walk." Another man told me that he enjoyed playing cards with his worker friends but stopped because his wife had become upset and missed him. Though not every man interviewed responded with similar sensitivity, a wife's wishes are given great sway in how a husband will spend his free time. Sacrifice and compromise are not constitutionally foreign to either spouse.

Still, tensions exist. Many men argued that they did other things for their wives, and it was inconvenient of their wives to demand they cease what one male worker called "having fun." Some worker families made a simple adjustment or compromise: together they visited other couples and then separated into unisexual groups to "discuss things." Other families, especially those recently married, often continued to visit their friends independently.

While it is difficult to determine the degree to which urban Chinese marriages are truly happy, it is noteworthy that the Chinese are interested in spending time assessing one another's marriages and evaluating them in terms of assumed and perceived states of happiness or unhappiness. It was not uncommon for the Chinese to speculate on the frequency with which happiness is achieved. For example, a 37-year-old female worker told me, referring to her friends and neighbors, that, "Maybe 2 percent of the marriages I know of are very happy, 80 percent are okay and the remaining 18 percent are terrible." A male cadre noted, "In America fifty percent of the marriages end in divorce. In China fifty percent of the marriages are unhappy." It is difficult to assess how representative these opinions are. Of the seventy Chinese families that I knew reasonably well, I estimate that 48 families, or 56 percent, had satisfactory marriages while 21, or 44 percent, were unsatisfactory. In short, the percentages are not always exact, but the patterns generally are. It is important to remember that marriage in China, as in America, goes through cycles of adjustment in expectations and pressures and, therefore, unsatisfactory marriages often, in time, become more satisfying and even develop into a love of deep attachment (Goode 1963).

Those couples who enjoyed one another's company and accommodated, if not actually enjoyed, their spouse's personality style and individual quirks seem to have the more satisfactory marriages. In addition to acceptance of a spouse's personality, satisfactory marriages communicated their anxiety, especially fears of losing the other's love. A common means of communicating this is for one spouse to ask the other spouse to interpret his or her dreams, a request that is treated very seriously. The request is an invitation to subjective intimacy. Typically, discussion of the dream leads to a lengthy dialogue of possible interpretation and meaning. Some spouses admit that they are never certain if their spouse had really dreamed so or made it up to elicit a detailed discussion, which was often laced with reassurances that the dream meant the opposite of what it appeared to be saying. Dreams are but one means used to convey anxieties and intimate moments.

Sexual Adventure and Familial Intimacy

In every culture, sexual access is deemed a favor women bestow upon men (Symons 1979). This is clearly the case in urban China where women generally controlled the frequency of intercourse in marriage. If a wife felt the marriage was good, she would more than amicably acquiesce to her husband's advances; if not, these advances were rejected directly or with "various excuses." This was especially true if a woman did not like her husband. A wife would focus her attention on her child rather than on her husband, and sought companionship outside the marriage with friends. In this way the parent-child sleeping arrangement is a tacit index for the intensity of a couple's emotional intimacy.

Zha Bo and Geng Wenxiu's (1992) sexual survey in southern China found that frequency of sexual intercourse decreases after a child is born (1992:17). I found similar behavioral proclivities in the north. A man, for example, who had just become a father, observed that "After the child comes, the wife plays with it, and not with the husband." Another man admitted that after a child arrives men associate with male friends, adding, "The lovers are no longer deeply committed to one another, they are committed only to the child." Even if a woman truly loves her husband, the two roles seldom are easily blended and integrated. If a woman loves her husband, she will strive to maintain his interest and involvement. A 31-year-old woman, for example, confided to me, "After I had given birth I no longer cared for him (her husband) as I had before. The only reason I continue to have sex with him is because he is a good man and I like giving him nice things." The ability of women to control sexual frequency is vividly revealed in the comment of a 37-year-old male who asserted that it is common to hear wives' teasing and even, at times, threatening "to withhold sex if their husband failed to perform some household task." When women do not like their husbands, it is common for them to reduce the frequency of sexual intercourse. A 43-year-old man admitted, for example, that, "My wife did not like sex before we had a child. Afterwards she did not like me, so we stopped having sex."

There is a Chinese folk belief that holds that too much sexual activity is unhealthy (Dikotter 1995). For example, in 1983, one 25-year-old Huhhotian intellectual told me that, "On your wedding night you can have sex a lot. But afterwards you should only have sex once a week. Otherwise you will lose your strength." In 1987 I meet him again and found that he had since been divorced and was actively seducing many women without constraints. He no longer agreed with the traditional folk belief. It is common in the local countryside for Tumote peasants to admiringly tease one another whenever they admit that they are tired. It is assumed that their tiredness is due to sexual intercourse the previous night. However, when a peasant admitted to having sex four times a week, his friends, visiting urban workers, responded that was "too much," as he would be too tired. Another worker, however, acknowledged that he "was never tired, only refreshed." The point is that, although the folk theory that posits a relationship between physical exhaustion and sexual frequency is still accepted, it is not clear whether that belief is responsible for a reduction in the frequency of sexual intercourse. A 34-year-old intellectual offered another reason for voluntarily reducing the frequency of sexual intercourse, "Too much sex is bad (that is, ethically bad) "because you will start to enjoy it, and then that will be all you want to do. You will not be able to concentrate on your work." He then added, "How then will you be able to accomplish anything?" His opinion may be representative of urbanites throughout China.

Dalin Liu's comprehensive 1988 Sexual Survey based on 20,000 questionnaires from fifteen provinces (which did not include Inner Mongolia) found that village couples had a higher frequency of sexual intercourse (5.43) verse (4.66) times a month or a little more than once a week

(9) for urban couples. Significantly the coastal cities and villages had similar rate of frequency, whereas the more northern cities have lower rates (Liu et al. 1997:251).

Chinese society in the 1980s did not sanction the pursuit of sexual variety. From most of the post-1949 Revolutionary period in Chinese history, the male identity, unlike that found in Thailand (Jiemin Bao, personal communication), Latin American culture, or pre-Communist China, was not coterminous with sexual promiscuity. Although some Huhhotian men fantasized about having love affairs, while some kept an active correspondence with women living in different cities, and a few daring married men had a "lover," everyone conducted these relationships with the utmost discretion. The cultural mores in the early 1980s simply did not sanction this kind of behavior.

The Communist party's policy of not condoning and occasionally imposing negative sanctions on anyone engaged in a sexual affair has not significantly altered male behavior. The nation-wide sex survey found that in 24 to 40 percent of all Shanghai divorce cases, women listed extramarital affairs as the primary reason for seeking a divorce (Liu et al. 1997:359). The increase in extramarital sex also corresponds with an increase in reports as to sexual disharmony among married couples. This suggests that sexual pleasure is increasingly regarded as a fundamental aspect or right of married life (Liu et al. 1997:35). It also suggests that many Chinese men are less committed to sexual monogamy than they were in the previous decade.

The Chinese sexual surveys reported that Chinese males' sexual satisfaction varied by social class (Liu et al. 1997; Zha Bo and Geng 1992). I too found that, for the most part, educated Huhhotian men were aware that women's sexual arousal differs from their own, and they stressed the importance of foreplay as the primary means for stimulating their wives to orgasm. Independent interviews with their wives found, however, that husbands were not generally successful in satisfying their wives. College-educated and non-college educated women told my female research assistant and, on a separate occasion, repeated to me, that their husbands were sexually too fast and, thus, they did not really enjoy sex. Although my sample size is small, it is consistent with Zha Bo and Geng Wenxiu's sex survey (1992) which found that, "Most females did not experience an orgasm due primarily to the short duration [of foreplay]" (1992:18). My findings are also consistent with Kinsey's finding that people with higher education tended to change sexual positions more often (Kinsey 1953).

A popular Chinese proverb from the Republican Era asserted that women's sexual appetite increases with age. The proverb says, "Women in their thirties are tigers and in their forties are wolves" (Dikotter 1995: 60). If this proverb was an accurate representation of behavior, then one explanation for contemporary women's disinterest in sexual intercourse may lie in the negative impact of the Communist revolutionary ideology that de-emphasized the body as a site of sensual enjoyment. As a consequence, many men and women were raised to regard sexual intercourse as a necessary, albeit perfunctory, activity. It may be that the return to a consumer economy will stimulate a renewed appetite for physical pleasure and erotic experimentation.

Evidence for this trend can be found among China's educated class, which tended to believe that marriage should be based on emotional and spiritual compatibility. Within this class, it was not unusual for men to become upset if their wives never experienced an orgasm. This concern was vividly revealed to me when one informant lamented that "nothing he did" aroused his wife and, hence, he felt personally responsible for his wife's inability to reach an orgasm. In exasperation, he did the unexpected: he turned to his friends for advice. They told him to kiss her breasts and to talk to her; some suggested that he show her some pornographic pictures (easily obtainable in the city's underground market). Unfortunately, their suggestions did not lead to any noticeable changes.

Unlike workers, peasants and herders, some members of the city's educated population are concerned with a new notion of eroticism, one that assumes women should also enjoy the sex act in and of itself. This is a truly new idea. In Imperial China, the primary motive behind an educated man's interest in stimulating his lover was the belief that an aroused and satisfied woman could transfer yin, the female essence, to her male lover. In Huhhot, not one informant believed this. The growing concern of some educated men with their wives' sexual satisfaction is consistent with other studies (Kinsey, et al. 1953) on human sexuality, which found the scope and intensity of a person's erotic experimentation was associated with their level of education. For example, among Huhhot's educated class, almost half of my sample of educated men admitted that their wives or lovers performed fellatio on them; however, among the city's working class, no one reported engaging in oral sex.

Marital Satisfaction and Domestic Power: Men and Women's Complaints

The *gradual* expansion of women's influence within the home has been aided by the institutionalization of neolocal residence, bilateral descent and equal work opportunity for men and women. These new realities have enabled contemporary women to achieve a sphere of power and domestic independence faster than had been the case in their mother's generation.

Huhhotian men and women are highly cognizant of the fact that domestic relations are radically different from those found in the countryside and on the grasslands. They believe then that in other times and in different social contexts, men had more power and control within the family. It is an idealization that was far from true even in Imperial China. Paterson found that the "theme of a powerful woman and the henpecked husband is an almost obsessive theme in Chinese literature" (1982:325). He adds, "Orthodox Chinese historians of the Ming dynasty refer to the entire period as the rise of the 'fearsome wives'" (1982:325), a finding that suggests, at the very least, that men were responding negatively to the strength and domination of women in a clearly tension-filled spousal relationship. Be that as it may, Chinese men believe that, in the past, husbands had an easier time controlling their wives than they do today. Furthermore, although no one in my sample believed that it is proper or correct for a wife to be dominant within the family, everyone agreed that it is typically the case. One man remarked, "In the past the mother-in-law was fearsome, now the wife is fearsome." The frequency in which this expression is invoked suggests that males are more ambivalent and less secure than in the past with their position within the family and society. Although Chinese men, particularly the uneducated, believe that female domestic power is both authentic and onerous, they have little power to effect change.

Men are keenly aware, for example, that a woman's self-presentation style shifts depending on the social context. For example, whereas a woman prefers to speak softly on a date, once married, she is just as likely to shout commands at both her child and husband. A male worker of mild temperament accustomed to listening to his wife issue pronouncements, turned to me one day and, matter of factly, said, "Women shout a lot. It's their way. We just have to accept it." Women are not sympathetic to this disappointment. It is not that uncommon for an angry wife to yell at her husband when he leaves the house, thereby communicating to her neighbors her preeminence and authority within the family. In this way, the "henpecked" jokes manifest a deeper underlying but unspoken uneasiness men have toward their position and duties in the domestic sphere.

In studies of contemporary Chinese gender, it is often asserted that spousal abuse and other forms of violence is increasingly directed toward women (Gilmartin 1990). This literature asserts that men use physical violence as one means to control women. This assertion must be qualified as we do not have very many empirical studies on spousal abuse noting regional, class, and frequency of occurrence. Until there are more indepth studies exploring how representative and valid this phenomenon is, any conclusion is suggestive and not definite.

In 1987, I conducted an exploratory survey of spousal abuse. I asked my informants to list the households of friends and neighbors where there was at least one incident of spousal abuse over the previous year. Seven of twenty-one Huhhotians noted one or two households where there had been an incident of spousal abuse. The remaining 14 Huhhotians could not name a single household. In all, I collected 10 incidents of spousal abuse in sixty households. When gender is controlled for, however, there were only seven families, or less than 12 percent, where the husband had hit his wife at least once during the previous year. Surprisingly, informants knew of three households where it was only the wife who had used physical violence.

In the few instances in which there was an instance of spousal abuse, I found that women seldom were passive in their response. For example, a 28-year-old female told me of the following incident: In 1979, my friend's husband struck her on the face, using the side of his hand. Stunned and upset, she telegraphed her husband's father that his son had unexpectedly died and that he should come to the city to bury him. Several days later, the father arrived only to discover that it was a cruel hoax. After that incident, the husband never hit his wife again. Moreover, urban Han women do not consider spousal abuse as a concern worth considering when discussing or evaluating a prospective mate. Many urban Mongolian women, however, do. In fact, it was often given as one reason why urban women would never marry a Mongol from the grasslands. Fear of spousal abuse is not an important concern among Han women and most urban-born Mongol women who want to marry a man from the city.

Men believe that, regardless of the rhetoric, it is more their responsibility, and not their wives, to achieve a promotion, increase household income and expand personal connections. It is a responsibility, an expectation, that they find demanding and take seriously. Failure to perform satisfactorily often results in their wives' complaining that their husbands "let the family down." It is a complaint that men do not want to hear because it is perceived as a stigma attacking the core of their image of manhood. For example, the only incident of spousal abuse that I personally observed took place over this very issue. A young woman, in her mid-twenties, periodically browbeat her low-keyed husband, in his late twenties, for lacking ambition and intelligence or for not knowing important people. Because he could not easily express himself verbally, he reacted by striking out with his fists. I observed this scene on two separate occasions: the wife chastising her husband for being stupid and not knowing anyone and the husband hitting her.

Although most Huhhotian wives do not habitually lament and describe their husbands' overall shortcomings, a husband's under-achievements are noted and commented upon. Typically, Chinese women expect that men demonstrate clear competence in their work and provide some demonstration or evidence of worldly ambition and the likelihood of future success. In this way women continuously assess men's and, in particular, their husband's, performance, achievement and relative social standing vis-a-vis other men in the prevailing social hierarchy.

In turn, men feel compelled to maintain a posture that most will never actually achieve: becoming an important and influential person. Not surprisingly, the striving for "success," with its accompanying emphasis on symbolically indicating that it is within one's grasp, can promote an uncertainty that is sometimes acute. Ambitious women, in particular, expect and demand more things from their husbands and often become extremely disappointed with their failure to deliver. Both men and women are equally demanding but, because they desire different things from one another, they often become disinterested, critical or unresponsive when their demands are not recognized or, at least, partially met.

Daughter-in-Law, Mother-in-Law and the New Natal Reality

The frequency with which Huhhotian couples see their mothers is an important index of urban women's ability to manage their personal affairs. It is also suggestive of the continuing importance that the mother exerts in their lives. The special attachment of younger wives to their mothers is reflected in the frequency of their contacts. Young wives, particularly after the birth of their first child, see their own mothers regularly, daily if possible, and weekly at a minimum. Significantly, however, fatherhood seems to gradually sever the link between mothers and sons. In the past, it was expected that a daughter-in-law would work closely with her husband's family. She was constantly tested to see if she would put her new family's interest above all others. If she did not pass this test, she was thought to be unreliable and disloyal. In traditional China, a mother's greatest fear was that she would lose her son to his wife (Wolf 1972). This fear appears to have become a commonplace reality today in Huhhot and throughout China (Honig and Hershatter 1988:168-173; Whyte and Parish 1984). After marriage, men and women are expected to continue to visit each other's family. I found that if the marriage was more or less satisfactory to both parties, then the spouses strove to maintain satisfactory relations with both parents. If the marriage was not satisfactory, the spouses often spent Sunday dinner with their own family. Even if the marriage is deemed satisfactory but one of the in-laws is excessively demanding which, given the patrilineal ideological bias, is usually the husband's mother, then the couple will naturally gravitate toward the family which is kind and respectful to both partners. In this situation it was not unknown for a husband who loves his wife to spend more time associating with his wife's family.

The factors that contribute to a wife's success in shifting their husbands allegiance, at least in the early years of the marriage, are the absence of a patrilocal residence rule, women's new-found financial independence, and a husband's emotional dependency on his wife. The most significant factor behind the shift, however, is childbirth. It is an event that fundamentally alters the social roles which form the nuclear family. Young wives, who dutifully had followed the patrilineal custom of regularly visiting her husband's family, will, after the birth of the child, look to their own mother for advice, emotional support and free childcare. If the mother is retired or has remained a full-time housewife, she will in turn assist her daughter and help raise the grandchild.

In an effort to prevent the loss of their sons, Huhhotian mothers today, in a dramatic break with traditional norms, tend to cater to their daughter-in-law. Indeed, most mother-in-laws treat their daughter-in-law as honored guests whenever they visit. One fifty-four year old mother pointed out to me that she treated her daughter-in-law with extra special attention because she did not want to lose her son and become a forgotten mother. She added:

> Whenever she drops over, I give her special things and even if she wants to help out, I always praise her and thank her. You see China has changed. I'm afraid if she doesn't feel comfortable in her husband's home, she will stop accompanying him and, in time, I will lose my son to her family. [long pause] Do you know that in China daughters follow their mothers; husbands follow their wives?

Other mother-in-laws were not so enlightened, to their own dismay. A seventy-three year old woman shouted:

> When I was young, I obeyed my mother-in-law. Not so today. Everything has changed. My daughter-in-law is not afraid of me. In fact, she rarely listens. She worries more about her own mother than me, her husband's mother!

Another elderly woman bitterly and continually complained that her son loved his wife more than his own mother because, "Men love sex more than their own mothers."

Further evidence that the dwindling homage paid to mothers-in-laws extends beyond Huhhot can be found in television programs that focus on the plight of the "ill-treated mother-in-law." I saw three such television programs between 1981 and 1983. It is becoming a common sour chord in Chinese culture today.

Women's present-day ability to shift their family's Sunday visiting schedule away from their husband's family toward their own natal family is representative, within the domestic sphere, of women's new-found confidence and their ability and power to successfully assert themselves. This phenomena cuts across every social class. In this way, family politics is grounded in the rhetoric of folk axioms, socialist ideology, and personal guile.

Parent-Child Relations

The Mother-Child Bond

One of the primary means whereby women attempt to secure and protect themselves from a hostile mother-in-law and often unsympathetic husband, is to foster an intense emotional dependency on her children so that, once grown, they will take care of her (Wolf 1972). In Margery Wolf's study of contemporary urban life in the PRC, she observed that recent socialist changes no longer make it necessary for women to foster this type of parent-child dependency. She adds:

> The uterine family has disappeared because the need for it has disappeared. Urban women do not express the same degree of anxiety about their old age that they used to. Young women work and expect pensions, older women who do not have pensions are assured by the government that they are cared for (1985:207).

I found that in Huhhot, the parent-child dependency had not disappeared. It is persistent, however, for a different reason: the continuing preference and habit of cultivating bonds of intense emotional dependency. Mothers continue to exercise tremendous psychological control over their offspring. In fact, the mother-child relationship is the most admired and revered parent-child dyad. It is the mother who is the primary educator of very young children. Of all family dyads, the mother-child bond is by far the most emotional, enduring and psychologically pleasing. For example, in all 58 cases that I collected of parental intervention in an offspring's mate selection, it was, inevitably, the mother who was the deciding force. Middle-aged informants frequently confided to me that their emotional involvement with their mothers remained remarkably strong after their marriage and throughout their adult lives.

Although the Chinese respect their fathers, they adore their mothers. It is culturally understood and accepted that a son or daughter will exchange, at some point, harsh words with one's father, but it is considered bad and regrettable form should this happen with one's mother. The intensity of the emotional adoration was expressed to me by several college students in their twenties, who allowed me to read sections of their diaries. One twenty year-old young man wrote that:

> In the evening I write to my mother. I miss her very much, and I can imagine how much she misses me. I've just received a letter from my mother. She told me she is very healthy and pleased. She said she misses me and hopes I can go back home on the holidays.

An extremely articulate twenty-three year-old female worker from Nanjing told me that:

> Since I came to this city, I've missed my family, especially my mother. I cried while I read my mother's letter. I often dream of my family and getting together to eat dinner

and watch television or go to the movies. I often say to myself: "You aren't a child; you're a grown-up." I do not know why I can not overcome my weakness. Maybe my mother gave me too much love.

A nineteen-year-old student who was suffering from a cold acknowledged that, "I think of my dear mother. If she was here, she could cook delicious food for me and comfort me. But here 5,000 miles away from home, who could be as dear as my mother?" Finally, a twenty-one year-old male student recorded rather bleakly in his diary, "Another Sunday of loneliness and restlessness. I'd rather be a bird, then I could fly back home and see my mother."

Adoration is probably not too strong a word to describe such emotional connections above. When I asked my informants to respond to the following hypothetical situation, the extent to which Chinese symbolically extend this connection was vividly and dramatically revealed to me. I asked them to imagine walking across a bridge with their mother and father. Suddenly the bridge collapses and everyone is thrown into the water. If they could save only one person, who would it be? Of the twenty-nine informants (nineteen males and ten females), twenty selected their mother for saving while the remaining nine refused to answer. In this respect and many others, the Chinese mother is the glue that binds the family together. She is the center of the communication network. Through visits she becomes the focal point for news and a pivot for influencing various kin opinions and actions.

For reasons other than simple fear of a vengeful mother-in-law or hostile spouse, the emotional bonds between mother-child formed during infancy and the early childhood years are never relinquished. These bonds are sustained, in large part, through a Chinese tradition which promotes and legitimizes intense life-long emotional dependency between mother and child (Solomon 1971). It is a bond that is idealized in literature and in conversation as a celebration of harmony, remembrance and enduring love. Moreover, the intensity of its expression signifies to every Huhhotian the continued importance, influence and power of the Chinese woman.

The Father-Child Bond

Throughout Chinese history fathers believed that their role, as a counterpoint to the role of mothers, was to *not* encourage or tolerate emotional indulgence which promoted dependency. Fathers instead assumed the role of a stern disciplinarian (Fei 1939; Ho 1987; Wilson 1974). Chinese fathers were not, however, without compassion or love for their children. Although the articulation of that sentiment was restrained by their traditional parenting role and its expectations (Solomon 1971) most Chinese fathers, in fact, felt a warm deep sentiment toward their children. In some cases, a father supplied strict discipline as a compliment to the mother's overindulgence. Or, at least, a balance was to be reached between a mother's understanding and a father's demands. Solomon quotes a Qing dynasty scholar-official who wrote that a "father loved his child with all his heart, but he would not express it" (Solomon 1971:60). It was a posture that sometimes produced resentment and acute anxiety for the child in later life (Solomon 1971:39-61). Nonetheless, a cultural ethos emerged which justified different parenting postures: the father facilitated a child's entry into the outside world, whereas the mother provided a secure and loving environment within the home. It was assumed that these roles were inevitable and unchangeable. Moreover, it also was assumed this sexual division in parenting roles contributed to producing a more responsible and ethical person overall.

The sex-linked roles were traditionally sustained, if not developed, because men and women occupied different positions within the social structure. In addition, by controlling the distribution of the family inheritance, a father could effect a special, if not psychological, dependency on the part of the child. On the other hand, a mother's parenting style was seen as much a result of being considered an "outsider" as it was of a "natural" attachment fostered through child birth and early child care (Bowlby 1951; Daly and Wilson 1987). Given her reduced importance and status in her husband's family, the mother needed a friend, an ally, and what better one than her own child (Wolf 1972). In this way, the different access to and use of economic and psychological "resources" contributed to the establishment and elaboration of the two complementary parenting styles: the father as a disciplinary provider, the mother as a intimate nurturer.

The Emergent Urban Father-Child Relationship

The "traditional" Chinese conception of the parenting process is similar to Parsons and Bales' (1955) typology which posits that, within the domestic sphere, men perform an instrumental or competence-directed role, whereas women perform the more expressive or empathetic role. The typology is an accurate representation of how the Chinese peasant views parent-child relations. It is also strikingly similar to the parenting style found in Taiwan (Ho 1987). However, in Huhhot, the emergence of a new urban infrastructure has fostered a supportive environment for the expression of warmer sentiments and closer interaction between father and child. This expression is a result of a new attitude readily found in casual conversation and reflective comments, and stresses the importance of intimate father-child interaction. As such, it challenges the traditional father-child role, a role and style of interaction that was, in fact, seen by the previous generations' fathers as no longer satisfying or necessary.

There are three factors that contribute to the increasing intimacy of father-child interaction in both public and private settings. First, over 80% of women between 26 and 46 years old work—a fact that compels even the most reluctant father to become more involved in caretaking activities. Second, the economy of domestic space, or the typically small one-room apartment, places the father in constant and close proximity to his child, thereby enabling more intimate parent-child interaction. Third, a new folk notion promoting fatherly involvement has emerged within many households. Although it has yet to receive official endorsement in state publications (Honig and Hershatter 1988:181), this notion nevertheless is repeatedly articulated in conversations across Huhhot.

Father-Daughter Love

The core of Chinese kinship has been the father-son relationship (Hsu 1967). The homage to that relationship and the patrilineal tradition which spawned it, continues to be expressed in a variety of social settings. One example is the many *ad hoc* folk theories of conception.

Throughout Chinese history the mother was considered primarily responsible for determining the sex of the child. Thus whenever a child was born, it was not the man's but rather the woman's doing or, in the case of a girl, her "fault." (The word "fault" is used to indicate the traditional preference for a male child.)

Publicly Huhhotians speak continually about the importance of "having a son," an obsession so acute that relatives and friends closely watch a pregnant woman's every step whenever she enters a door. It is believed that if the mother-to-be enters with her left foot first, she will give birth to a girl, if with the right foot, then it will be a boy. Moreover, whenever people ask a pregnant woman about the expected delivery date, they seldom use the gender-neutral word "child" but, instead, use the word "son" as the generic term for the fetus. Hence, they ask, "When are you going to have your son?" The obsession is so complete that everyone interviewed on the topic publicly hoped for a son. However, my research assistant found in private interviews with the college-educated women that half of them wanted a daughter, a fact which suggests that women's public comments are more a social form than an accurate expression of personal conviction. At least among the college-educated, it also suggests that the linguistic terminology used to speak of pregnancy might be more a residue of tradition than true evidence of a continued preference for a son.

Although Huhhotians, as elsewhere in urban China, continue to publicly value sons over daughters, I found that parents were also very happy with the birth of daughters. In fact, even in those families that unreservedly wished for a son, parents rapidly adjusted and came to value their daughter. As previously shown in the section on mother-in-law and daughter-in-law relationships, sons are increasingly regarded as unreliable in fulfilling family obligations. They are seen as easily lost to their wives and her family, while daughters are thought of as more considerate and faithful in continuing to visit their natal home. Whenever fathers discussed their children, it was common to stress "how wonderful little girls are." This is a new occurrence and as such, it constitutes an enormous shift in a patrilineal tradition that valued sons and grandsons over daughters and granddaughters.

The socialist transformation of cultural meanings has had a corresponding impact on men's conception of themselves as husbands and fathers. Young fathers continue to assume a firm and somewhat formal posture toward their sons, while paradoxically insisting they did not want to be as formal and reserved as their fathers had been with them. In Huhhot, I often heard a man insist (much as in traditional China) that, while he "loved his father, he did not like him." Younger male Huhhotians felt strongly that it was improper for a child to grow up and not like his or her father. Although contemporary Huhhotian fathers wish to become a close friend with their child, as opposed to striking the more traditional note of a stern moral authority ever ready to criticize shortcomings, they remain uncertain and confused as how to express this wish. Warmth and immediacy of affection are not easily achieved. It is easier for them to accomplish this with a daughter than with a son. Significantly, fathers are more ambivalent than mothers in balancing their obligations as both spouse and parent. This ambivalence was profoundly articulated by many college-educated fathers voicing concern that their child loved their mothers more than them. Although the male desires to become more emotionally involved and though it is far from achieved, it is a desire frequently heard in intimate conversation among close friends. As such, it has enormous implications for the quality of future parent-child relations and the development of a new Chinese person.

Conclusion

Not only has the socialist transformation of China's urban infrastructure stimulated the re-evaluation of customary kinship obligations, it has also resulted in an re-evaluation of the conjugal expectations and parenting duties. The transformation has not, however, eliminated gender antagonism—only the style in which it is expressed. Previously muted through habit and the pragmatics of patrilocal politics, women's yearnings, opinions and demands have forcefully emerged to reshape the politics of family management.

The new "resources of power" have empowered urban women. They now are able to initiate divorce, organize the Sunday visiting schedule to favor their natal family over their husband's, control the frequency of sexual intercourse, participate in romantic affairs, effectively ignore an overbearing mother-in-law or husband and, at the same time, retain a greater hold than their husband over their children's love and loyalty. They are also now better able to balance their spouse's expectation and demand for greater intimacy with the desires and obligations necessitated by child rearing. Given access to these new found "resources of power," women have achieved, within the domestic sphere, a greater degree of female independence and autonomy than in any previous time in Chinese history.

On the other hand, the shift in China's economy away from collectivism toward a more open market economy has resulted in heightening men's anxiety and confusion. Men are confused by the transformation of the social organization, one that has undermined their place within the Chinese social order. Among intellectuals, self-doubt has been further experienced regarding the father's role in the parenting process. Exacerbating this uncertainty is the re-evaluation of the importance and value of daughters. This shift in public sentiment—that a daughter makes just as good and, in many instances, a better child than a son—cuts across every social class and constitutes the emergence of a new urban consensus. It carries enormous implications for the meaning of marriage, family, and gender relations within modern urban Chinese society.

Notes

1. The material that forms much of this research was collected in Huhhot, the capital of Inner Mongolia Autonomous Region, People's Republic of China between 1981-83 and, again in 1987 for a period of 2½ years. Partial funding for the research was provided by the University of California General Research Grant, Sigma Xi, and CSCPRC, National Academy of Sciences. I am grateful to the following scholars for their advice, encouragement and thoughtful suggestions: Chris Atwood, Jim Bell, Lisa Cushing, George Gmelch, Tom Paladino, Elizabeth Whitt, Walter Zenner.

References

Bowlby, J. 1951. *Maternal care and Mental Health*. WHO, Geneva.

Cao, J. 1987. Single women and men over 30 in China. In *New Trends in Chinese Marriage and the Family*. Beijing, China: Women of China.

Cohen, M. 1976. *House Divided House United*. New York: Columbia University Press.

Daly, M., and Wilson, M. 1987. *Homicide*. Hawthorne, NY: Aldine De Gruyter.

DeGroot, J. 1882-1910. *The Religious System of China*, 6 Vols. Leiden: Brill.

Dikotter, F. 1995. *Sex, Culture and Modernity in China*. London: Hurst and Company.

Fei, X. 1935. *Peasant Life in Rural China*. Shanghai: Shanghai Press.

Freeman, M. 1965. *Lineage in Southeastern China*. London: University of London Press.

Gallin, B. 1966. *Hsin Hxing, Taiwan, a Chinese Village in Change*. Berkeley: University of California Press.

Gilmore, F. 1986. *Manhood in the Making*. New Haven: Yale University Press.

Gilmartin, C. 1990. Violence against women in contemporary China. In J. Lipman and S. Harrell, eds. *Violence in China*. Albany: SUNY Press.

Goode, W. 1963. *World Revolution and Family Patterns*. New Haven: Free Press,

Ho, D. 1987. Fatherhood in Chinese society. In *The Father's Role: Cross-Cultural Perspective*. M.E. Lamb (Ed.). Hillsdale, NJ: Erlbaum.

Honig, E., and Hershatter, G. 1988. *Personal Voices Chinese Women in the 1980s*. Palo Alto, CA: Stanford University Press.

Hsu, F. 1967. *Under the Ancestors' Shadow*. New York: Doubleday Anchor Book.

Jankowiak, W. 1993. *Sex, Death and Hierarchy in a Chinese City*. New York: Columbia University Press.

———. (ed.). 1996. *Romantic Passion*. New York: Columbia University Press.

———. 1999. Sexuality, gender, and Chinese society: recent trends in the study of Chinese gender. *Bulletin of Concerned Asian Scholars*. Vol. 31.

Kinsey, A.C., W.B. Pomeroy, and C. E. Martin. 1953. *Sexual Behavior in the Human Female*. Philadelphia: W.B. Saunders.

Lamb, M.E. 1987. *Father's Role: Cross-Cultural Perspective*. Hillsdale, NJ: Erlbaum.

Levinson, D. and M. Malone 1982. *Toward Explaining Human Nature*. New Haven: Yale University Press.

Levy, M. 1968. *The Family Revolution in Modern China*. New York: Atheneum.

Liu, Dalin, Man Lun Ng, Li Ping Zhou, and Erwin Haeberle. 1997. *Sexual Behavior in Modern China*. New York: Continuum.

Paterson, O. 1982. *Slavery and Social Death*. Cambridge: Harvard University Press.

Potter, Sulasmith and Jack Potter. 1990. *China's Peasants: The Anthropology of a Revolution*. Cambridge: Cambridge University Press.

Solomon, R. 1971. *Mao's Revolution and the Chinese Political Culture*. Berkeley: University of California Press.

Sulloway, F. 1996. *Born to Rebel*. New York: Crown Books.

Wolf, M. 1968. *The House of Lim*. Englewood Cliffs, NJ: Prentice-Hall.

———. 1970. *Child training and the Chinese family*. In *Family and Kinship in Chinese Society*. M. Freeman (Ed.). Palo Alto: Stanford University Press.

———. 1972. Uterine families and the women's community. In *Women and the Family in Rural Taiwan*. M. Wolf (Ed.). Palo Alto: Stanford University Press.

———. 1985. *Revolution Postponed*. Palo Alto: Stanford University Press.

Whyte, M. 1988. Changes in mate choice in Chengdu. In *Center for Research on Social Organization*, the Working Paper Series. Ann Arbor: University of Michigan.

Whyte, M., and Parish, W. 1984. *Urban Life in Contemporary China*. Chicago: University of Chicago Press.

Wu, R. 1987. The urban family in flux. In *New Trends in Chinese Marriage and the Family*. Beijing: China International Book Trading.

Yang, M. 1945. *Chinese Village*. New York: Columbia University Press.

Zha Bo and Geng Wenxiu. 1992. Sexuality in urban China. *The Australian Journal of Chinese Affairs*, No 28, July: 1-20.

CHAPTER 7

Enculturating the Self: Person, Relation, and the Discourse of Child-Rearing in the American Family

Diane M. Hoffman, University of Virginia

Introduction

In recent years, anthropologists have considered ideas of self as important influences on many domains of culture, from cognition and emotion to morality and practices of formal education. In this chapter, I explore the cultural meanings and value of self in the context of the American family, focusing in particular on cultural models or scripts for the self as they are embedded in the practices and discourses of child-rearing in American families. I thus seek to elaborate on the process whereby parents and children through their interactions participate in the construction and learning of cultural models and scripts, relying upon a view of enculturation as an active process of meaning-creation and learning and not merely as a passive process of meaning transfer across generations.

Normative cultural models or scripts for selves are at the same time models for self-other relation; and, as much anthropological work has pointed out, the self cannot be understood or constructed apart from its relationality with others. In some sense, then, notions of self are also fundamental to the study and understanding of kinship, for they provide basic orientations to person and relation that ground the meanings, values, and organizational patterns present in kinship systems. While the link between cultural psychologies of personhood and kinship is not often made, in my view the study of kinship has much to gain from deeper attention to the cultural psychological domain of self and, in particular, to the ways in which narrative, discourse, and practice shape the kinds of selves that are learned through early social experiences in families. In at least

---

Contributed by Diane M. Hoffman.

one sense, then parent-child interactions can be taken as sites for discursive formulations of self that provide one window on what may be the psychocultural foundations of kinship systems.

The focus of my discussion will therefore be upon elucidating the nature of the cultural scripts that guide the practice of raising children in American families, attempting to define the key values or meanings that constitute an implicit frame for what it means to be a person in the American sense, and focusing in particular on those ideas that concern the child's developing self and its relations to others. A number of existing studies on family socialization/child-rearing in America will be explored for the ways in which the findings reflect culturally normative visions of the self. The insights gained from these sources will then be used alongside some analyses of contemporary views of parent-child relations and child-development/child-rearing present in popular magazines and texts, in order to present a more complete view of parent-child interactions as sites for the enculturation of the self.[1]

One difficulty in this discussion relates to the obvious problems of defining just what is meant by "American" or "American middle class." A popular argument is that there is no "American culture" because America is so diverse; yet I side with Herve Varenne (1994), Ruskin & Varenne (1983), and Spinder (1994) on the issue, all of whom argue that there is an overarching American culture variously defined through modes of discourse and participation in American life. For some of these anthropologists, this American culture co-exists with the variety of minority cultures on a different level of abstraction; for others, it is present in the very ways in which minority cultural, racial or ethnic identities are themselves constituted. In the sense that I use the term, "American culture" refers to a body of meaning and values that constitute scripts or discourses that govern the meanings and structures of self-other relations and civic participation in American life. These discourses represent normative visions of the self and person (including moral orientations, fairness, democratic participation, individualism) most readily identified with the anglo, white middle-class but also present and recognized as structures of access to or for participation in American society by culturally and ethnically diverse groups (as well as being contested by these groups). However, as Spindler (1994) points out, it is in these very debates and contests that a definably American culture emerges.

Background: Theoretical Perspectives on Family, Culture, and Child-Rearing

Anthropological studies of child socialization have been in many ways central to anthropology in its development as a discipline for children and childhood were, of course, central concerns for some of the major anthropologists of the earlier part of the century, notably Margaret Mead and Ruth Benedict. In their studies of child socialization, the notion of cultural patterning in child-rearing was prominent, as were its links to personality formation. Dissatisfaction with the pattern approach, however, led John M. Whiting and colleagues to elaborate a different view emphasizing the influence of larger cultural and social systemic factors on child-rearing practices. Their statistical approach permitted a fair degree of reliable cross-cultural generalization about the effects of various social and environmental factors on a wide variety of child-rearing behaviors. In sum, it is now generally accepted that the cultural contexts in which children are reared have a strong and formative influence on children's enculturation and development (Bornstein, 1991:3).

The ecological theme was later picked up and taken in a slightly different theoretical and methodological direction by LeVine (1974) and LeVine, Miller, and West (1988) and LeVine et al. (1994). LeVine and colleagues argued that child care practices embody assumptions and tacit knowledge as well as idealized goals or representations that guide parental behavior toward children. Comparison of child-rearing practices across societies reveals both differences and similarities in goals of child-rearing. As one approach to studying the cultural niche for child-development, determining how different cultures define parental goals for child-rearing remains influential, according to Harkness (1996:42).

More recently, the concept of cultural and environmental influence on child enculturation has been elaborated by Super & Harkness (1986), who considered childhood to be a culturally constructed "developmental niche" consisting of three components: the physical environment or social setting, the customs or behaviors of childcare and child-rearing, and the caretakers' own beliefs and values (Harkness, 1996:41). The emphasis in the developmental niche framework is on interactions between the environment and mental representations or cultural models. Enculturation, in this view, requires the acquisition of mental representations (schemas or models) from the environment that are internalized and subsequently guide the process of development. Against earlier "passive" views of enculturation and cultural transmission, the cultural model is an active construction that results from guided participation in activity or apprenticeship (Rogoff, 1989; 1990). Cultural models may or may not be explicit within given groups or particular cultural domains, yet they have directive force regardless of how much participants may be subjectively aware of them. At the same time, because they are constructions of learners in interaction with environments, they are not carbon copy replications and they can and do change over time (D'Andrade and Strauss, 1992).

Indeed, all theories of culture acquisition must deal with the reality of cultural change and in particular with the reality of change in the structures, functions, and salience of families in individual development. While it is still probable that the family is a primary site for child socialization, the relative strength of parental and family influence, particularly in societies with high levels of media saturation and organized institutional child care, cannot be presumed in advance. Similarly, in societies where the nuclear family is not dominant, "family influence" may mean something quite different from what it does in the contemporary United States. In the U.S., because of the predominance of the nuclear family, family socialization is closely identified with parental influence and control over children (this may be especially true for the urban, white middle class.)

At the same time however, all families—including nuclear families— are part of larger societies and therefore children are socialized at the same time into structures that extend beyond the family, as Talcott Parsons (1955) reminds us:

> We must not forget that the nuclear family is *never*, most certainly not in the American case, an independent society, but a small and highly differentiated subsystem of a society. . . . First, the parents, as socializing agents, occupy not merely their familial roles, but these articulate, i.e., interpenetrate, with their roles in other structures of the society, and this fact is a necessary condition . . . of their functioning effectively as socializing agents, i.e., as parents, at all. Secondly, the child is never socialized only for and into his family of orientation, but into structures which extend beyond the family, through interpenetrating with it. (p. 35)

Parson's emphasis on seeing family socialization as interconnected with larger social and cultural structures is, in fact, one that closely recalls the contemporary emphasis on cultural models and discourses or scripts in parental socialization of children. The idea is that these discourses embody values and meanings that are in fact available in the culture at large and are widely shared across families; the family socialization process is, therefore, not a unique, idiosyncratic one but a culturally situated and contextualized one. While there may well be idiosyncratic patterns or meanings in individual families (one often hears of unique "family traditions" or ways of being and behaving seen by family members themselves as quite different and distinct aspects of their identity as family members) these are embedded in and shaped by the cultural scripts and models available in the society at large. It may even be the case that the discourse on uniqueness is a particularly American cultural tradition, mirroring the prevalence of discourses on personal and individual uniqueness found in American cultural notions of self (see Hoffman, 1996; 1998).

Perhaps the most important theme in contemporary work on enculturation in the context of children's development in families is the notion that parental images of how children should be—the kinds of persons they ought to become—constitute a formative and as yet under-researched dimension of our understandings of child development.

The goal in the remainder of this chapter will be to set out some of the assumptions governing American middle-class notions of child-rearing and child-development, paying attention to values and beliefs that appear relevant to the formation of children's selves: ideologies of developmental stages, individuality, emotion and emotional management, power and control, and consumer orientation. I will draw principally from popular child-rearing magazines for illustration of normative beliefs, and secondarily from studies concerned with parenting and childcare in a variety of American and cross-cultural settings.

Scripts for the Self: Cross-Cultural Comparisons

As Harkness, Super, and Keefer (1992) point out in their study of American families, cultural models for parenting and children's behavior allow parents to make sense of their children's behavior and to impose a meaningful structure on the disparate experiences of everyday life. Two particularly salient models emerging from their research were "stage" and "independence." Calling these concepts "pervasive themes in the way Americans think about themselves and the larger social entities of which they are a part" (p. 165), the authors show how much parental ideas about children's behavior as occurring in stages and as expressions of a child's growing "independence" are part of normative American cultural models for personal growth and development.

Additional suggestions for domains of particular salience in the development of American children's selves come from comparative research conducted by Dunn & Brown (1991). Dunn and Brown focused on talk between mothers and children in the United States and England, and they found that while discussions of rules, transgressions, and prescriptions and discussion of feelings/emotions were salient domains for construction of children's selves in both the United States and England, there were marked differences that can be read as reflections of differences in ecological factors as well as cultural goals and models for growth of the person. In the U.S., there was much more talk about individual actions and negative emotion in discussions of feelings than in England, and in England more emphasis on politeness, appropriate behavior, and avoidance of doing harm to others.

A large literature in fact exists on differences in child-rearing beliefs and practices across cultures, and it points to a number of interesting domains for consideration of how differing cultural scripts or cultural models for the self affect child rearing practice. One of the more developed areas in this literature compares American and Japanese child-rearing beliefs and practices. While this literature is too large to summarize here, a number of themes are worth noting in terms of cultural expectations regarding the self. The first is the area of dependency. American families see infants as dependent and their goal for socialization is to promote early self-reliance and independence. Japanese, on the other hand, see infants as socially unconnected or independent, and believe that they need to be taught dependency—especially in relation to the mother, in an enactment of the cultural valued notion of *amae*—warm indulgence and presumption upon another's goodwill. According to Takeo Doi (1973), *amae* is the fundamental characteristic of self among the Japanese. While its expression must come under strict social controls as the child matures, the on-going ability to depend upon others even in adulthood is a normative aspect of the Japanese self, possibly related to the oft-noted "sociocentrism" of the Japanese. It should be stressed that for the Japanese, the experience of *amae* is linked to very positive emotions, especially those of warmth and emotional security.

Interpersonal dependency as a culturally valued goal for the self is also reflected in Japanese patterns of discipline. Japanese parents do not attempt to get the infant or young child to conform to parental will so much as they encourage the child to empathize with others and internalize desires to be "a good child." (Lewis, 1995). Similarly there is little appeal to adult authority or to power in adult-child relations, but much reliance on emotional attunement and getting a child to "understand" rather than getting a child to "behave." Indeed, as Machida (1996:250) notes, Japanese mothers avoid direct instruction and overt control so as not to damage their affective relationship with the child. In contrast, American parents emphasize the need for external (adult) controls of children's behavior and the use of such controls so as to obtain compliance with adult will as well as to direct children toward "optimal" performances (Fogel, Stevenson, &

Messinger, 1992:36). Furthermore, there is early encouragement toward self-direction among American children, particularly in the domain of making choices; in Japanese child-care, however, personal choice is not deemed particularly important as a domain for the exercise of the child's will (see Fujita and Sano, 1988).

Another particularly salient domain for the comparative socialization of self concerns the degree to which a culture normatizes the practice of social shifting of self, or shifts in social self-presentation. In Japan the practice of social shifting is culturally marked (*kejime*) and valued as a developmental goal: children need to learn to shift between formal, *omote*, *tatemae*, or "front" behavior, and informal, *ura*, *honne*, or "back" behavior. The culturally normative self is, thus, a layered one, as Takie Lebra has illustrated (1992). While mature adults also engage in social shifting in the United States, this is not regarded as a particularly desirable behavior, nor is it a culturally well-marked one. Indeed, among Americans, the cultural ideal is the person who does *not* hide his or her true feelings—who is frank, forthright, who doesn't "beat around the bush." There is much less value attached to being able to deflect or hide one's true feelings, and much more on expressing oneself and experiencing subjective consistency of the self across social situations. It is important to note, however, that this is a cultural ideal from which real experiences may and often do diverge considerably. Perhaps the extent to which there is a divergence between culturally normative ideals for the self and the real experiences is itself an important aspect of the socialization of self and behavior cross-culturally.

Cultural Practices, Themes and Values in American Child-Rearing

While it is almost a truism to say that American families promote autonomy, individualism, and independence in the self, the values and goals for formation of children's selves are much more complex than these terms convey. While "individualism" is a much valued goal in American families, we need to consider in what ways discourses about individualism may in fact mask cultural practices that diverge considerably from this goal and even, perhaps, reflect deep-seated psycho-cultural anxieties and insecurities regarding what it means to be "individual" and what may be lost, perhaps, in the pursuit of this goal. In this section I consider a number of self-themes drawn from the analysis of articles on child rearing published in two popular American "parenting" magazines: *Parents and Child*.[2] While we cannot assume that parents behave toward their children in the ways experts tell them to, or that they follow the advice given in such magazines, such publications are excellent sources for accessing normative beliefs and meanings, for finding out what "experts" recommend, and for accessing common parental concerns about raising children. They are, in sum, texts or discourses embodying cultural norms and values available in middle-class American culture for raising children and, ultimately, enculturating selves.

1. Developmental Stages and "The Individual Child"

Ages 3 to 4: Power struggles. "Four year-olds are particularly fascinated by superheroes and other larger-than-life forces," says Wilford [director of the Early Childhood Center at Sarah Lawrence College]. Kids this age are trying to get a sense of how much they can influence their environment and the people around them.

Ages 5 to 6: Grasping Individuality. "By the time kids are age 5 or 6, they can understand more of the complexities of a character's personality," Wilford explains. As they learn to appreciate the individuality of characters, they want to add more realistic details to their play.

Ages 7 to 8: Acting out scenes. By this stage, kids are fascinated by miniature worlds and may be very interested in collecting . . . action figures. . . . "Seven year olds may be less likely to pretend to be a character and will instead use toys to act out scenarios that they've created," says Wilford. Essentially, a child has gone from being the "actor" to being the "director."[3]

A central frame for viewing the child as a developing person in American culture is the stage-orientation. The child is assumed to move through developmental stages on the road to adult competencies, with each age range characterized by particular kinds of behaviors. While stages are explicitly defined by what a child actually does, they are also implicitly defined in American discourse by notions of what a child can*not* do; the presence of such implicit negative competencies is a large part of defining and thinking about "stages." For example, in the text above, the phrasing of what a child is able to do ("By the time kids are age 5 or 6, they can understand more of the complexities of a character's personality") implicitly assumes that children younger than 5 "cannot understand the complexities of a character's personality."[4] Each stage is, in fact, defined by behaviors—both those of which the child is assumed capable as well as by those he or she is assumed incapable of.

Indeed, the stage perspective encourages parents to see children through a lens emphasizing their skills, competencies or abilities, rather than a lens that sees the "whole child" or the child as a complete person with a self created in and through relations with others. Stage-orientation places the focus entirely on the individual child as the unit of analysis, with individuality defined in terms of manifest skills/abilities/behaviors. Almost paradoxically, however, at the same time as the individual child is the unit of analysis, children are seen far less as individual persons than as exemplars of a particular "stage." In the end the focus is not on understanding a child's individuality or the child's self taken as a whole, but on how well the child's behavior reflects a particular optimal or normal "stage" of development. Implicitly, parents are encouraged to understand their children less as complete persons than as exemplars of "stages" on the path to personhood. Their individuality is less a part of the entirety of self and of affective relations with others than with the particular constellation of abilities and behaviors each demonstrates.

At the same time, much lip service is paid to understanding children as "individuals" in contemporary discourse on childrearing. Indeed, a few pages later, one reads about the importance of "connecting to your child as an individual."[5] This article is critical of those parents who "try too hard to get the details of parenting right," and who as a result "put their babies under a spotlight instead of sharing the sunshine [of unconditional love] with them,"[6] suggesting that much contemporary childcare advice and practice (from the need to stimulate children constantly "for the sake of future abilities" to the need to "control everything [the child] does) has a reductionistic ring to it, as if one could, by changing the parenting "formula," turn out children who had exactly the right amount of desired abilities or qualities. While parents cannot determine everything, the author also argues against the idea that parents don't matter, for the unconditionality of love that parents show children is most important. The article points to and is explicitly critical of strong trends in the culture of American parenting toward a behavioral/performance perspective on relations with children (the notion of the child's individuality defined by particular constellations of abilities/skills). It suggests greater emphasis on the ways parental love functions to support children's development—implicitly emphasizing the relational side to the development of the self that the obsessive focus on abilities and skills neglects.

At a more abstract level, one might say that the actual practices that shape personhood in American families, while occurring as part of an ostensible ideology of individuality, in fact undermine the cultivation of the "whole person" by focusing on performances, behaviors, or other externalized attributes of the self while ignoring the more fundamental conditions of affective relationality with parents and others. That is to say, the kind of "self" that is produced by the American discourse of developmentalism is one that is exteriorized and fragmented in terms of discrete behaviors, performances, abilities, and skills, rather than one that is socially embodied or constructed through experiences of affective identification with others or understood in terms of an inner self that remains separate from its manifestations in social interactions.

2. Power/Control

What is most interesting in this discourse about stages is perhaps not that parents use stages to understand their children, but the characteristics of the child's self that are assumed to be displayed at each stage and what interpretations adults place on such behavioral displays. One of these primary interpretations concerns power. Throughout the discourse on American parent-child relations power and control are regarded as essential and fundamental themes in the child's relationship to parents and to the world at large. In the text above, for example, we find that the age range from three to four is described as the stage of "power struggles." At this stage children are supposedly "trying to get a sense of how much they can influence their environment and the people around them." The power/control theme again emerges in the age seven to eight bracket: children go from being "actors" to "directors"—a role shift involving increased sense of power and control.

Parent-child relations are frequently characterized as a "contest of wills" or as a "test of parental authority" in American childrearing discourse, as in the following:

>At every stage of development, children are going to challenge a parent's authority and push against your limits. . . . But when a conversation becomes a battle of wills, it begs the question, 'Who's really in charge here?' Usually, parents get trapped in this type of tug-of-war because they've failed to understand the subtext of a child's defiance. . . . Four- and five-year-olds test to see if the rule you set yesterday still holds today. . . . Once you enter a verbal sparring match, you're actually sending the message that your rules are open to discussion.[7]

Note that in this text, the *adult* is assumed to "make the rules" and—perhaps more profoundly—that rules are simply assumed to be "natural" parts of the relationship between parents and child. Parental authority as embodied in rules is simply assumed, along with children's efforts to "push against" rule-based authority.

Yet the lens of power/control through which adult-child interactions are seen is a culturally particular one, as cross-cultural work on childrearing in other cultures—particularly Japan—as shown. The very concept of "parental control strategies" in relation to children has been found to be based on Western assumptions (see Machida, 1996). For example, Machida writes: "As a construct, parental control strategies fit well within a unidirectional model of parenting wherein, as scholars have presumed until recently, mothers control children. Children were perceived by many in the West as needing direct instruction on how to behave, talk, and think." The explicitness of direct control and appeals to parental authority among American mothers, in contrast to Japanese mothers, is highly marked in cross-cultural work in this area. American mothers are much more likely to appeal to their own authority as mothers in demanding obedience, whereas Japanese mothers are likely to resort to reasoning or to getting the child to empathize with others' feelings or views (Lewis, 1995).

Aside from its grounding in cultural assumptions, what effects does the lens of power/control have to do with the normative constructions of self in American families? One of the characteristics of self implicit in the power/control lens is subjective sense of separation or differentiation: that is to say, there is perceived to be a great gap between parent and child, or expert and novice, grounded in their respective positions of power/knowledge. As Chen (1996:125) notes, to Westerners, the gap between the child and the adult is an insuperable fact of life. Indeed, power or control over others or over the environment are only possible when the other is defined as "separate" from self, as having boundaries that make it "external" to self and thereby potentially subject to self's "control." (See Hoffman, in press). In contrast, when the other is experienced as contingent on or continuous with self, direct appeals to control/power are far less likely; rather, the stress is on positive affect and empathic emotional identification. Chen (1996) continues:

>In contrast [to Western views of socialization], the Japanese socialization process can be better depicted by using the cobathing metaphor. Here the folk emphasis is on the creation of an atmosphere believed to be most conducive to the transference of skills and knowledge. This is achieved as adults come as close as possible to the children through

reducing perceptual strangeness. In other words, the Japanese approach emphasizes the quality of intersubjective feelings of the dyad by creating an atmosphere in which the child will feel little psychological discrepancy or discontinuity (p. 125).

In the Japanese model, the adult and child are not conceptualized as separate or distant from each other, each occupying a separate universe where issues of power dominate their interactions, but rather as occupying the same emotional space, and adults make great efforts to reduce the perceptual as well as emotional disparities between themselves and children so as to foster a sense of empathic closeness and oneness viewed as conducive to enculturation or learning of desired cultural traits. This theme has also been noted in ethnographic studies of teacher's interactions with young children in Japan, where great efforts are made not to assert adult or authority over children, but to understand children, to be close to them and have close emotional bonding with them (*kizuna*; *kakawari*).[8]

A second effect of the power/control lens in the American context is that, given the separation of selves, the source of power/control is perceived as "external" to self: children obey because they are constrained to do so, not because they have internalized a desire to obey or because they "identify" or empathize with others. (This point has been amply demonstrated in cross-cultural comparative studies and in studies of early childhood education: for American children, when the external constraint is removed, the child disobeys; Japanese children are far more likely to conform to adult expectations even in the absence of direct adult supervision: thus, there is no need for "substitute teachers" in Japanese elementary classrooms; see Hoffman [1995].)

A third potential effect in terms of self concerns the role of affect: where power and control are present as a dominant lens on parent-child relations, direct displays of negative emotion and resistance become expected parts of self-development. Indeed, they are assumed necessary as marks of "becoming independent," as the following American expert assures his readers: "The egocentric toddler truly believes he's the center of the world. If he shouts, 'You can't make me!' when asked to pick up his blocks, he's making a declaration of independence—a critical developmental move for him."[9] In this passage a link between displays of behavioral resistance, negative emotion (anger), and becoming an "independent" self is clear, suggesting that negative emotion and the ability to express it is a critical value of "independence" our autonomy in the American self. Cross-cultural research on the self suggests, again, that this is a culturally particular formation not shared in other cultural contexts (see Briggs, 1998) for a very different perspective on the relationship between autonomy, resistance, and anger in child socialization among the Inuit.) Also, among the Japanese, the overall concern is with a developing self that is *not* perceived as emotionally discrete and individual, but that is emotionally tied to others and indeed achieves its development by experiences of positive emotional bonding—quite opposite to the American assumption that it is negative experiences of resistance that lead to self-development.

3. Emotions and Emotional Management

Variations in emotional socialization have been recognized as a primary arena for exploration of the cultural factors shaping child development across cultures (see Lewis & Saarni, 1985). In this light, the American discourse on parent-child relations is particularly marked by strong emphasis on negative emotion—both on the part of children as well as parents. Even a cursory glance at American parenting magazines reveals much space devoted to issues related to the understanding and management of negative emotions. Dunn & Brown also found in their comparative research that there was much more discussion of negative emotions in American families than in English ones (1991). That so much attention is paid to the topic suggests that negative emotion—and perhaps emotion more generally—is a problematic area for American families, requiring "strategies" for management and control that may have formative effects on the enculturation of the self along normative American middle-class lines.

Intrusive Attribution

The first of the characteristic American approaches to emotional management lies in what I call intrusive attribution: the practice of adult "labeling" a child's emotion *for* the child and directing the child to attend to the *adult's interpretation* of the emotion rather than the subjective state itself (rather than allowing the child to label it him or her self or even to avoid putting a label on it). Consider the following passage, where parents are advised how to handle a child's expression of negative emotions toward the parent, such as in "I hate you!" "You're a mean mommy!"or "I don't want you. I want Daddy!":[10]

> Don't retaliate in kind. ("Well, I hate you, too, right now! . . .) Instead, acknowledge his right to feel the way he does, try to identify the emotion troubling him (sadness, disappointment, confusion, nervousness) and *label it for him*. [italics added] . . . You might say, "You sound pretty angry at me; tell me why."[11]

In this example, parents are encouraged to apply their own interpretations of a child's emotional state and to assume a certain expertise and neutrality in this process, regardless of whether the child in fact has used any explicit reference to an identified emotional state or feeling, and—more importantly, perhaps—in the absence of any emphasis on or assumption of emotional empathy or identification. Almost along a therapeutic model, the parent acts as the emotionally neutral "analyst" of the situation who suggests labels and courses of action based on this stance of neutrality. The contrast with the empathic model of emotional sharing present in Japanese approaches to emotional socialization is striking.

Similarly, Harkness and Super (1985) in their comparative study of emotional socialization among Americans and the Kipsigis of Kenya, noted that American mothers and Kipsigis mothers responded very differently to their child's crying. The Kipsigis mother "chatted" to her child and distracted him by talking about other things and providing a different activity. In contrast, the American mother first "labels the emotion that produced the crying ('I know you're angry'). Next, she offers an explanation of what made him feel that way and indicates that this is a natural way to feel ('It's frustrating trying to build such a tall tower.') Finally, . . . the mother . . . directs her son to return to the activity that led to his crying." (p. 31). They stress the verbal labeling and interpreting that the American mother imposes on her son's experience.

In their study of emotional socialization in day care centers in the United States, Leavitt and Power (1989) also found that the theme of emotional labeling was very prominent: caretakers repeatedly applied labels and interpretations to children's supposed emotional states, many times in ways that directly contradicted the children's own behaviors and/or statements, such as "Oh, you're not angry, you're just tired." Children's own emotional interpretations and subjective experiences were repeatedly denied or re-interpreted along adult models, so that they could be more effectively managed. In the long run, Leavitt and Power raise serious questions about the effects of such emotional management on children's senses of self (including denial of one's own perceptions about oneself and the world as well as sense of competency or ability to manage one's own emotional life and to have it respected/understood by others).

Inauthenticity

Selections from American parent guidance magazines suggest quite strongly that not only are adult attributions and interpretations concerning children's emotions based on adult perspectives (not children's) and intrusively imposed on situations to guide behavior, but that frequently adults are encouraged to mask, deny, or otherwise misrepresent their own genuine emotions or the nature of the emotional tenor in a situation in their interactions with their children. There is thus an explicit encouragement toward inauthenticity in parent-child emotional relations. Consider the following citations from an article advising parents how to do time-outs properly with misbehaving children.[12]

> Describe time-out in positive terms . . . tell your child a time-out will be an opportunity for her to calm down. Don't say "This is what happens when you're bad." [Even though, indeed, this is what happens when the child is bad.] (p.114)

> Watch your tone of voice. . . . Your goal should be to sound neutral and matter-of-fact, no matter how frustrated you're feeling inside. (p. 116)

> State a request once. If your child protests or continues the misbehavior, start the count in a *nonemotional* way [italics added] with no additional talking. (p. 116)

> If your child leaves the time-out chair, put her back with an *incredulous* (but not *angry*) look. You can also say sternly but calmly, "Never get out of the chair without permission" or "You don't have to like this, but you do have to do it." [Italics added] (p. 116)

Aside from treating children in a very mechanistic and demeaning fashion,[13] the overarching theme is one of emotional inauthenticity: even while angry or frustrated, the parent is not supposed to show anger or frustration—instead these emotions are to be masked, denied, or manipulated toward the goal of nonemotionality or neutrality.[14] One may well question, first of all, whether children can be "fooled" by this emotional pretense in the first place and, in the long run, what the cultural lessons are and their impacts on the child's self (not to speak of the adult's). There is, first of all, the lesson of the desirability of emotional disengagement in one's relations with intimates(the very opposite, one might add, of Japanese emphasis on emotional sharing and empathy). Second, the self is compartmentalized or fragmented in such a way that "emotion" is allowed expression only if it is positive; anger is to be masked or denied under the guise of "neutrality." Third, exerting control or power over others ought to be done in an emotionally disengaged manner, so that basic empathy and connectivity of self to other is denied. In sum, close analysis of the contemporary discourse concerning emotion in American child-rearing suggests the troubling idea that in the long run, children's selves may well be shaped by the lessons of disengagement and dissimulation in emotional relations with others.

4. The Child as Product: Consumerist Ideologies of Child-Rearing

Discourses on child-rearing in American families can also be characterized by a marked consumerist orientation that pervades the entirety of the relationship between parent and child. In the consumerist ideology, children are "products" of parental efforts and "investments" of parental energy and work. Indeed, Americans have gone from simply being *parents of children to parenting children*: and in the conversion from noun to verb, the child becomes the passive object—the product of a parent's skills or efforts.

> One perfect spring day as I sat on my deck, I looked up from the book I was reading to see my daughter, then 2½, nose-to-nose with the daffodils in our garden. Bending from one flower to another, she gave each of them a gentle kiss. Swamped with love and pride that *I had produced* such a sweet and tender child, [italics added] I rushed to sit beside her. That's when she calmly turned, looked me straight in the eye, and said, "Go away, I don't want you here. I want Daddy." I was devastated.[15]

Note that the mother describes her daughter as her production, and one that she felt *pride* in. This child was far more astute than her parent gave her credit for: not only had she learned the lesson of delivering hurt with emotional neutrality, she sensed her mother's intrusiveness—the attitude that led her mother to consider her a "product." The child is not a person with a naturally sweet and tender personality; rather, the child's self is seen as the achievement of the adult—the result of the mother's efforts or work—and therefore as something that gives the mother a sense of pride in her *own* accomplishment.

Further evidence for the child as parental achievement or product is found in the extent to which the text emphasizes how much rejection from the child makes us "lose confidence, feel guilty, and doubt our ability to parent. . . . Whenever you have such a personal *investment* in someone, you're acutely vulnerable to what that person says or does."[16] The use of the term *investment* in this context is revealing, for it again emphasizes the commercial or consumerist theme that dominates recent middle-class American thinking about their children. If the child doesn't "produce" dividends in the way the parent intends, the parent interprets this as an assault on his or her *parenting skills* that represents a failure of parental *investment*. That the parent's sense of self-worth is so shaken by the child who shouts "I don't love you!" reveals much about the extent to which the child is viewed as a product or creation of the parent's skills or efforts.

Moreover, the discourse of consumer options abounds in contemporary American child-rearing. In an article on getting children to sleep through the night, the author debates the pros and cons of two divergent approaches—one of which advocates letting the child cry it out alone in his room and the other known as "the family bed." These are presented as choices or options to be made by parents, and are debated almost exclusively from the perspective of adult needs and desires. The main factor, according to one expert, is "flexibility and *choice*. What do you and your partner *want*? What makes you comfortable?" (Note that the question is not, "what makes the baby comfortable?") . . . You have to ask yourself and your partner honestly, "Where do we want our baby to spend the night?" . . . It's critical to consider w*hat you and your partner like and don't like* at night."[17] This discourse of parental likes and desires entirely ignores the question of children's welfare; it turns child-rearing practice into a set of consumer choices or options to be made on the basis of parental likes and dislikes. In sum, "getting your baby to sleep is a personal decision."[18] The market mentality based on "personal decision" or choice becomes the dominant lens through which to frame relations between parent and child.

Whatever method is chosen, at some point parents are told they need to "teach children that they have rules at night." The existence of "rules" that limit children's closeness or interaction with parents at night (just like the "rules" that govern daytime behavior) is also interesting. Rules are a major part of the parenting culture for middle-class Americans:

> To those who consider it barbaric to leave a baby to cry at night, Dr. Ferber points out that all parents, from time to time, need to let a child cry. "When a youngster wants to play with something dangerous, we say no and set limits that he may balk at," he observes. "Teaching him that you have rules at night [e.g., not coming to the parents' bed] is the same thing. It's in his best interest to get a good night's sleep."[19]

In this text, rules are generalized as a cultural good or value, such that playing with something dangerous and sleeping with parents—as rule transgressions—are both regarded as equally "damaging" or "dangerous." Under the umbrella of rules, what is in fact primarily the self-interest of the parent can be translated into the child's "best interest."

In another passage regarding young children's assumed "defiance," the author writes that the defiant child is really asking is, "'Who am I? What are the rules? And how far can I go?' By around 18 months, a toddler begins to understand the concept of rules. Now that he knows there are rules, he wants to break them."[20] Rules have a paradoxical function in the American enculturative system: on the one hand, it is assumed that having rules is essential to family life, and that at the same time it is assumed that they are naturally challenged and/or broken. What are the implicit messages regarding the relationship between parents and child, and more generally, between self and other, contained in this discourse? Rules seem to assist in the attainment of self-other differentiation or opposition; they set the limits whereby one self can impinge or impose upon another. Indeed, in the absence of emotional empathy and sharing, they are almost the sole source for the regulation of self. However, when a strong cultural emphasis on emotional symbiosis, empathy, or identification is present in child socialization (as in Japan), we find that "rules" are almost entirely absent in parental discourse on child-rearing. It would thus seem that rules and empathy are partial substitutes for each other in the socialization of the self, and also that they produce, in the end, different kinds of selves: a socially embedded and emotionally relational self, versus a separate and emotionally autonomous self. Indeed, American parents are told that, "When a child contradicts her parents, she's making the statement, 'I'm not part of you—I can be myself.'"[21] The "autonomy" of the American self is thus predicated on a condition of separation from others in which abstractions of rule provide the fundamental boundaries or conditions for relatedness/separateness against which the self struggles. Emotional identification or empathy is therefore to be controlled, masked, or if need be denied, because it threatens the condition of autonomy that is regulated by hierarchies of power and control.

Conclusion:
Producing American Selves and the Question of Relationality

As Weisner (1999) points out in his large-scale longitudinal study of American families, there does exist a definable middle-class American practice of child-rearing that transcends both conventional and non-conventional American families and furthermore persists across generations. Significantly, the child-rearing practices and values Weisner identifies are closely connected with children's selves, as I have suggested above. They are, in fact, programs for the production of selves along culturally normative lines.

Although what is defined as middle class changes constantly, there are two general characteristics of middle class parenting and child development that have persisted for the last three generations and longer, and which most families in our sample (nonconventional and comparison sample alike) by and large reproduced.

First is the "pedagogical" cultural model for child development . . . characterized by . . . emphasis on individual child stimulation and active engagement of the child with others, exploratory behavior, cognitive and verbal signs of intelligence, verbal communication (such as treating the child as a presumptive co-equal interlocutor), and question-response exchanges.

Second middle class parents—certainly compared to parents in other cultures—place an emphasis on individualism, autonomy, self-reliance and self-expression in their children . . . esteem of the self, and use of praise and encouragement. . . . Conventional and nonconventional families . . . were more similar to each other in their relatively high rates of stimulating behaviors, or autonomy-encouraging practices, compared to much lower rates for those parental and child behaviors found in many cultures around the world. (p. 4)

Support for both the "pedagogical model" as well as for autonomy is present in the texts analyzed here; but what is more interesting is that both of these themes implicitly contain formulations or normative cultural understandings for the nature of self's relations to others, as well as understandings of who directs or "achieves" the selves that ultimately are produced. I have argued that there is evidence for what might be called "negative autonomy," or autonomy achieved through active resistance or defiance against others as well as by emotional disidentification with others. In this model, much lip service is paid to cultural goals of "individuality" and "individualism," but in fact there is much more emphasis on the external domain of action and choice (individualism) than on the development of the inner self (individuality) that may not be expressed in action (See Hoffman, 1999). Indeed, as I have suggested, there is evidence that the individuality of children as persons is, in fact, often overlooked, especially in the light of dominance of stage theories for understanding children and in the context of the consumerist ideology of childrearing dominated by ideologies of parental production and personal choice. Furthermore, the practices of emotional silencing and negation that seem to characterize expert advice on childrearing reflect a cultural modality of self in which emotions remain a problematic and to some extent threatening domain—perhaps because to recognize the reality of their power and influence would be to abandon some cherished cultural values of autonomy, rationality, and free choice.

To the extent that parenting discourse embodies assumptions and values concerning what kind of selves children ought to have, it also reflects on how those selves are related to others, both intimates and strangers. Even more, perhaps, this kind of analysis allows us to see how intimates become strangers, and strangers become intimates, and in the end who qualifies as one or the other. And implicit in such understandings of intimacy and otherness is a more general and far-reaching account of the ways in which middle-class American families envision their place in the world.

Notes

1. Of course, no necessary connection is made or assumed here between the values and meanings present in discourse and behavior and what, in the end, gets "learned" by the child. The latter is a totally different question in at least one sense, and its answers lie in close study of children and their development that is beyond the scope of this paper.
2. The present article is based on articles from only two issues; yet the themes identified have much broader currency and can be found across the popular literature on child-rearing in the United States.
3. "What Kids Learn From Playing Star Wars." *Child* (May, 1999), 19.
4. This is an assumption that reflects much more adult thinking about the child than the reality of children's perceptions, I believe. I've seen much younger children very well aware of personality differences and extremely observant of individual idiosyncracies.
5. Penelope Leach, "How Much You Matter," *Child* (May, 1999), p. 44.
6. *Ibid.*
7. Margery Rosen, "Pushing Your Buttons," *Child* (May, 1999), p. 55-56.
8. See Shimahara and Sakai (1995).
9. Eugene Beresin, quoted in Margery Rosen, "Pushing Your Buttons," *Child* (May, 1999), p. 55.
10. That these things are considered "normal" for children to say to their parents in the first place is itself fertile ground for cross-cultural comparison.
11. Rosen, "Pushing Your Buttons," p. 55
12. See Marie Faust Evitt, "3 Tested Time-Out Tactics," *Parents* (May 1999): 113-116. Time-out is a very popular method of disciplining children in the American middle-class, described in this article as "the discipline technique that most modern parents view as the humane alternative to spanking. Time-out has become one of the most ubiquitous buzzwords of discipline." (p. 113)

13. One expert recommends the one-two-three method: e.g.:
    Parent: "Time to turn the TV off."
    Child: "But this is my favorite show."
    Parent: "That's one."
    Child. "You're the meanest mother in the whole world."
    Parent: "That's two."
    Child: "Danny gets to watch as much TV as he wants."
    Parent: "That's three. Take five."
    Notice that the mother does not empathize or reason with the child; she merely enforces the count, treating the child not as a person, but as an object of disciplinary control.

14. In U.S. childrearing discourses the same theme of emotional disengagement/neutrality is strongly advised as well by advocates of spanking as a disciplinary method: one should not spank in anger, but with emotional neutrality. First of all, is it humanly possible to spank a child when one is *not* feeling anger? One may very well argue that to spank in a condition of unfeelingness or neutrality is the ultimate process of dehumanization: it turns the parent into an automaton who is capable of causing physical pain to others *without having any feelings or emotional reaction*. The dangers of such de-emotionalization have hardly been recognized.

15. Margery D. Rosen, "Pushing Your Buttons," *Child* (May 1999), 54.

16. *Ibid.*

17. Margery D. Rosen, "Getting your baby to sleep," *Child* (May 1999), 25-28.

18. Ibid., p. 26, 28.

19. Ibid., p. 28.

20. Meg F. Schneider, "The Age of No." *Parents* (May 1999), 197.

21. Ibid., p. 197.

References

Bornstein, Marc H. 1991. Approaches to parenting in culture. In *Cultural Approaches to Parenting*, Marc H. Bornstein, Ed., pp. 3-19. Hillsdale, NJ: Lawrence Erlbaum Associates.

Briggs, Jean. 1998. *Inuit Morality Play*. New Haven: Yale University Press.

Chen, Shing-Jen. 1996. Positive Childishness: Images of Childhood in Japan. In *Images of childhood*, C. Philip Hwang, Michael E. Lamb, and Irving E. Sigel, Eds., pp. 113-127. Mahwah, NJ: Lawrence Erlbaum Associates.

D'Andrade, Roy G., and Strauss, Claudia. 1992. *Human motives and cultural models*. Cambridge: Cambridge University Press.

Doi, Takeo. 1973. *The anatomy of dependence*. (J. Bester, trans.) Tokyo: Kodansha International.

Dunn, Judy, and Brown, Jane. 1991. Becoming American or English? Talking about the social world in England and the United States. In *Cultural Approaches to Parenting*, Marc H. Bornstein, Ed. (pp. 155-172). Hillsdale, NJ: Lawrence Erlbaum Associates.

Fogel, Alan, Stevenson Barratt, Marguerite, and Messinger, Daniel. 1992. A comparison of the parent-child relationship in Japan and the United States. In *Parent-child socialization in diverse cultures*, Jaipaul L. Roopnarine and D. Bruce Carter, Eds., pp. 35-52. Norwood, NJ: Ablex Publishing Corporation.

Fujita, Mariko, and Sano, Toshiyuki. 1988. Children in American and Japanese Day-care centers: Ethnography and reflective cross-cultural interviewing. In *School and Society: Learning content through culture.* Henry T. Trueba and Concha Delgado-Gaitan, Eds., pp. 73-98. Westport, CT: Praeger.

Harkness, Sara. 1996. Anthropological images of childhood. In *Images of childhood,* C. Philip Hwang, Michael E. Lamb, and Irving E. Sigel, Eds., pp. 36-46. Mahwah, NJ: Lawrence Erlbaum Associates.

Harkness, Sara, and Super, Charles M. 1985. Child-environment interactions in the socialization of affect. In *The Socialization of Emotions,* Michael Lewis and Carolyn Saarni, Eds., pp. 21-36. New York: Plenum Press.

Harkness, Sara, Super, Charles M., and Keefer, Christine. 1992. Learning to be an American parent: how cultural models gain directive force. In Roy G. D'Andrade and Claudia Strauss, *Human motives and cultural models.* Pp. 163-178. Cambridge: Cambridge University Press.

Hoffman, Diane M. 1995. Models of self and culture in teaching and learning: an anthropological perspective on Japanese and American education. *Educational Foundations,* 9(3): 19-42.

———. 1996. Culture, Self, and Multicultural Education: Reflections on Discourse, Text and Practice. *American Educational Research Journal* 33(3): 545-569.

———. 1998. A Therapeutic Moment? Identity, Self, and Culture in the Anthropology of Education. *Anthropology and Education Quarterly,* 29 (3): 324-346.

———. 1999. Spirit, self, and culture: Individualism and individuality in the Japanese educational tradition. Paper presented at the annual meeting of the Comparative and International Education Society, Toronto, Canada, April.

———. (In press). Turning power inside out: Reflections on resistance from the anthropological field. *International Journal of Qualitative Studies in Education.*

LeVine, Robert A. 1974. Parental Goals: A cross-cultural view. *Teachers College Record. 76(2),* 226-239.

LeVine, Robert A., Miller, P. M., & West, M. M. 1988. *Parental behavior in diverse societies.* San Francisco: Jossey-Bass.

LeVine, Robert A., Dixon, Suzanne, LeVine, Sarah, Richman, Amy, Leiderman, P. Herbert, Keefer, Constance H., and Brazelton, T. Berry, 1994. *Child Care and Culture: Lessons from Africa.* New York: Cambridge University Press.

Leavitt, Robin, and Martha B. Power. 1989. Emotional Socialization in the Postmodern Era: Children in Day Care. *Social Psychology Quarterly* 52 (1):

Lebra, Takie S. 1992. Self in Japanese culture. In *Japanese sense of self.* Nancy R. Rosenberger, Ed., pp. 105-120. Cambridge: Cambridge University Press.

Lewis, Catherine. 1995. *Educating hearts and minds.* Cambridge: Cambridge University Press.

Lewis, Michael, and Saarni, Carolyn.1985. Culture and emotions. In *The Socialization of Emotions,* Michael Lewis and Carolyn Saarni, eds., pp.1-20. New York: Plenum Press.

Machida, Sandra. 1996. Maternal and cultural socialization for schooling: lessons learned and prospects ahead. In *Japanese Childrearing, two generations of scholarship.* David W. Shwalb and Barbara J. Shwalb, eds., pp. 241-259. New York: The Guilford Press.

Parsons, Talcott. 1955. Family structure and the socialization of the child. In *Family, Socialization, and Interaction Process,* Talcott Parsons and Robert Bales, eds., pp. 35-131. Glencoe, IL: The Free Press.

Rogoff, Barbara. 1989. Toddler's guided participation in cultural activity. *Cultural Dynamics,* 2, 209-237.

Rogoff, Barbara 1990. *Apprenticeship in thinking: Cognitive development in social context.* New York: Oxford University Press.

Ruskin, Frances, and Varenne, Herve. 1983. The production of ethnic discourse: American and Puerto Rican patterns. In *The sociogenesis of language and human conduct.* B. Bain, Ed. pp. 553-568. New York: Plenum.

Shimahara, Nobuo, and Sakai, Akira. 1995. *Learning to teach in two cultures: Japan and the United States.* New York: Garland Publishing.

Spindler, George, and Spinder, Louise. 1987. Cultural dialogue and schooling in Schoenhausen and Roseville: A comparative analysis. *Anthropology and Education Quarterly,* 18, 3-16.

Varenne, Herve. 1984. Collective representation in American anthropological conversations: Individual and culture. *Current Anthropology* 25(3): 281-300.

Weisner, Thomas. 1999. Vales that matter. *Anthropology Newsletter,* 40, 5 (May), 1; *4-5.*

Part Two

The Use of Kinship in Contemporary Life

Introduction

Despite ideas to the contrary, kinship in modern society is far from dead. In fact, kinship still plays a pivotal role in many aspects of contemporary life. Part Two gives examples of such systems. Robert Ibarra shows how ethnicity and kinship define both identity and structure within the social life of Norwegians living in Wisconsin. Ibarra even went on to argue that many of the social values, kinship behavior and the ideology of the family firm of Norwegian-Americans continue to influence the larger community and the state of Wisconsin.

Ramu used his data from India to show that kinship plays an important role in the economic activities of the Third World. The article also discusses the concepts of family, kin, lineage, and clan, showing how the principles of kinship are used for social as well as economic activities.

Similarly, Bernard Wong demonstrates how Chinese kinship has contributed to the entrepreneurial activities of the Chinese in the Philippines. He shows how family, clanship, kinship, marriage, friendship and *compadrazgo* relationships are used for the organization of family firms and other entrepreneurial pursuit. The Chinese kinship organizations in Manila, on the other hand, are also changed as a consequence of entrepreneurial activities.

Carol Delany's chapter is about gender, kinship and nationalism. It gives us a glimpse into political power and its connection with kinship.

In the Anglo-American world, kinship and friendship have not been abandoned as predicted by some urban sociologists. On the contrary, Graham Allan shows us that friendship and kinship networks are treasured in contemporary Britain. Many contemporary values and ideologies are effectively communicated through the idiom of kinship and enculturated through the family systems.

Issues such as whether kinship is an impediment for economic development, if kinship has any role to play in state-organized societies, and if kinship is still instrumental in the development of self, community and society, are relevant to the lives of students. These readings can be used to stimulate discussions on the use of kinship in politics, economics, enculturation, social organizations and social activities. Students should be encouraged to explore these issues in their research papers or class discussions.

CHAPTER 8

Kinship Structure and Entrepreneurship: An Indian Case[1]

G.N. Ramu[2]

Socio-economic development is contingent upon the cultural, human, and material resources, and political structure of a given society and, therefore, it is fallacious to assume that it occurs in neat, uniform, and universally predictable stages as some modernization theorists would have us believe (c.f. Rowstow, 1962, Werner, 1966, Levy, 1966). The challenges of development are not met everywhere with the same institutional responses as in Western societies. Instead, the responses to developmental strains are shaped by structural and historical conditions unique to a given society. Institutional conditions which historically proved to be antithetical to economic development in one social setting may serve as facilitators in another (Singer, 1968, 1973). Moreover, economic development, although welcomed by most societies, is a painful process because it entails institutional adaptations and strains. Various social institutions such as the extended family and kinship system, lineage, caste, or community often mitigate the stresses of change not only by offering refuge and security but also by assimilating new structures. In such a situation, individual autonomy, entrepreneurship, economic rationality and other concomitants of economic development become adjuncts, not alternatives, to existing value systems.

In the context of the foregoing, the central thesis of this paper is that in developing societies such as India, extended family and kinship ties facilitate rather than hinder the process of development, taken here to include entrepreneurship, commercialization, industrialization, and other correlates of modernization. I propose to demonstrate the way in which a traditional kinship group has (a) responded to the development of a particular industrial and urban setting in India and (b) adjusted to the necessities of modern business in terms of economic rationality, mobilization of capital, manipulation of credit, and socialization of the younger generation for entrepreneurial roles. Essentially, the following is intended to illustrate the general relationship between kinship structure and entrepreneurship in the context of a developing society.

The Setting

The study was conducted in the Kolar Gold Field (hereafter KGF) of South India in 1971. At the time, KGF was an industrial city with a population of about 125,000 of which approximately 17,000 worked for two federally owned industries-gold mining and earthmoving. In addition, an estimated 5000 persons were in occupations which are urban in character (for details see Ramu, 1977:13-22). During its 96-year history, KGF experienced a steady growth of population until 1951 (to about 150,000) and then a gradual decline for about 15 years, leveling off in 1971. Because of its valuable resource—gold—KGF attracted persons from various races, nationalities, religion, languages, casts and classes.

With such a heterogeneous population, KGF epitomizes the cultural pluralism, continuity, and change that observers have noted in other Indian urban contexts (Pocock, 1960; Lynch, 1967).

Marwaris in KGF

Marwaris (referring to those whose origins are from Marwar in Rajasthan) are a money-lending caste, who at the turn of the century migrated to KOF in small numbers seeking new opportunities and higher profits for their capital (for a general account of Marwaris see Timberg, 1979). Relative to other caste and ethnic groups, the Marwari migration to KGF has been small; e.g., in 1971, of the 1908 KGF households, only 408 were Marwaris. Their minority status, however, has not detracted from their economic dominance. Thus in 1979, ninety percent of noninstitutional money-lending, as well as trade and commerce, was in the hands of these households.

Alexander (1967:148) suggests that in certain periods of the history of a given society, socially marginal groups that are conservative in nature tend to produce entrepreneurs. Farber's (1972) study of the role of the family in economic development in Puritan New England indicates that entrepreneurship could emerge even in the most traditional settings (also see Bailyn, 1955). Comparable evidence emerges from the history of entrepreneurship among the KGF Marwaris In the initial phases of development of KGF as an industrial city, most Marwaris, who are a conservative and educationally backward minority relative to other elite groups in this setting, chose to be money-lenders and pawnbrokers. This vocation seldom involved risks because collateral was almost always required for loans and thus assured secure returns within a short period of time. Nevertheless, by 1931 the burgeoning mining town was in desperate need of a variety of commercial establishments, such as jewelry and hardware stores. In addition, the growing mining industry was in need of contractors and suppliers. The Marwaris, with their mercantile heritage and capital, were best placed to seize this opportunity, although this meant a deviation from their traditional occupations and institutional reorganization. Their adaptation was also stimulated by the stiff competition of various banks and cooperative credit firms.

The Marwaris were not alone in responding to the demands of the new economic milieu; other merchant castes, such as the Setty, Chettiar, and Mapilla, also participated. Few of these groups, however, could match the entrepreneurial success and sustained economic dominance of the Marwaris. In this sense, entrepreneurship among the KGF Marwaris is best understood as a "set of actions resulting in the establishment of business and industrial enterprise which have not existed before in that setting" (Papanel, 1976:69-70). Entrepreneurship for Marwaris was facilitated by their ability to assess profitable opportunities in various sectors of the economy and by utilizing their own resources (e.g., skills, capital and manpower) to exploit such opportunities successfully. Few of the KGF Marwaris were innovators in the strictest sense of the term, and fewer may be credited with any significant technological break-through. But in a developing. context, even a shift from traditional money-lending to trade or commerce and small scale industries will have a catalytic influence on regional development.

The role of the joint family and kinship ties was crucial for the entrepreneurial ventures and economic adaptations of the KGF Marwaris. Historically and ideal—typically, joint family referred to a household including all agnates of a patriliny with common hearth, worship and property, and with a hierarchical power structure based on age and kinship status (for details see Madan, 1961, 1976; Shah, 1964). Joint family ties involve "mutual expectations of support and amity, and the associated affective dimension of kinship, which are most intensely experienced and explicitly acknowledged among primary kin, whether residing in the same household or not, [and they] become gradually diluted with the stretching of degrees of kinship; but they never cease at the boundaries of the household" (Madan, 1976:215). Despite the normative significance of agnate solidarity, self-interest and conflict often lead to the formation of nuclear households and division of ancestral property. But the argument in this paper is that groups such as the Marwaris, who managed to maintain joint ownership of ancestral property and solidarity, also succeeded as entrepreneurs in at least one urban setting—KGF.

Of the 408 Marwari households, 225 (55 percent) were either collateral or lineal joint families, 124 (30.5 percent) were joint family variations (e.g., unmarried siblings living with ego) and 59 (14.5 percent) were nuclear families. Although nuclear households are formed for a variety of reasons (Ramu, 1973), two important criteria determine whether joint family ties are maintained: (1) the joint maintenance of right in family property by male agnates and their dependence on it for their subsistence and (2) maintenance of kinship ties with all customary rituals, rights, and obligations. By these standards, only 24 KGF Marwari households could be defined as nuclear.

The basic unit of kinship among the KGF Marwaris was the joint family or agnatically (i.e., through males only) interrelated nuclear families. Thus in this paper, the terms "joint family" and "kinship" are used interchangeably. The "fit" between kinship networks and migration, urbanization, industrialization and entrepreneurship during various phases of economic development in culturally diverse societies has been amply documented (Ames, 1973; Benedict, 1968; Bennett and Despres, 1960; Clignet, 1966; Comhaire, 1956; Farber, 1972; Hall, 1978; Ito, 1966; Kasdan, 1965; Khalaf and Shawayri, 1966; Landes, 1975; Madan, 1976; Marcus, 1980; Nafziger, 1969, 1978; Owens, 1971, 1973; Singer, 1968, 1973). Although there are differences in the degree of "fit," what has been established by these studies is that kinship ties have not only been generally adaptive, but have also fostered economic changes in most cases. From this point of view, kinship among the KGF Marwaris is the medium through which the group's economic interests are advanced. As I shall show in the next section, it is common among the Marwaris for agnates to form business partnerships and for the joint family to provide the required training and capital for fledgling entrepreneurs.

Kinship Structure and Entrepreneurship

In my effort to establish the relationship between kinship structure and entrepreneurship, I focused on ten family firms that were owned and managed by ten joint family groups. It should also be noted that these groups differed with respect to the number of coparceners, the size of their assets, and the nature of their businesses. For reasons of space, I have chosen mainly to deal with patterns, commonly found among these ten groups.

The most successful entrepreneurs were those who were able to restructure their family and kinship networks effectively and use them as resources for economic success. Table 1 presents data on the ten most successful business firms owned by Marwari joint families. These are the same firms studied in 1971 (Ramu, 1973). It is important to note that the working capital of all the firms expanded enormously during the intervening years. The main reason for this growth was that, after a period of recession concomitant with an unprofitable and stagnant mining industry, KGF's economy was revived by the establishment of an earthmoving machinery factory. This created the demand for the expansion of business operations.

Table 1: Chacteristics of the Ten Most Successful KGF Marwari Business Firms, 1971 and 1979

Type of firms	No.	No. of families which own the firms[a]	No. of salaried employees 1971	No. of salaried employees 1979	Working capital[b] 1971	Working capital[b] 1979
					(000's rupees)[c]	
1. Industry	1	1	53	96	1,000	5,000
2. Retail textile stores	4	4	21	35	250	750
3. Banker	1	1	4	4	300	500
4. Hardware store	1	1	10	16	200	600
5. Drug store	2	2	8	10	200	450
6. Jewelry store	1	1	0	2	200	500

[a] The term family is a reference to joint family.

[b] Working capital refers only to cash transactions in a financial year and does not include assets such as real estate, gold, and other forms of property (car, silver utensils, etc.).

[c] While there are serious problems in stating these figures in U.S. dollars, for a rough comparison 1 $ U.S.=6.50 rupees in 1979.

In view of its setting (Ramu, 1977), KGF offered limited scope for further entrepreneurial endeavours not only for Marwaris but for other merchant groups as well. Obviously, the kinds of opportunity structures generated by urbanization and industrialization depend upon wider contexts. Large industrial centers such as Bombay or Calcutta provide ample opportunities for entrepreneurs not available in relatively small settings such as KGF. Given restricted opportunities, different merchant groups have responded in ways determined by (and favorable to) their family, caste, and economic conditions. For example, in one KGF Chettiar family, of the three sons, only the first was designated to take over the family business while the other two were sent to professional schools (engineering and law), with the expectation that upon graduation they would pursue careers independent of the family business. In some cases "surplus" sons were trained in engineering, commerce, or law, so that their expertise could be employed in the expansion and efficient management of family firms (Singer, 1968). The KGF Marwaris did not take this path; instead, they chose to diversify their business interests and establish branches out of town. The Marwari kinship norm emphasizing that all-male adults be placed within the family business firm is responsible for such diversification and expansion. For example, the KGF Marwaris have large families—an average of six children, two more than the average KGF family in 1971. There was a need to seek additional economic opportunities for young men. Consequently, the ten family firms served as bases for new enterprises elsewhere for which the initial capital was provided by the parent firms in KGF (see Table 2). (The branches were legal subsidiaries of the parent firms in KGF but managed independently by male agnates.)

Table 2: The Nature of Diversification of Business and Creation of Branches by the Ten Parent Marwari Firms in KGF, 1979.

Parent firms in KGF	Diverse enterprise outside JCGF	No. of Branches	No. of Employees	Working capital[a] (000's rupees)
1. Industry	Automotive distribution, trucking & cooking oil factory	3	55	3,000
2. Retail textile store	Wholesale textiles, financiers, record store, printshop, and warehousing	6	22	900
3. Banker	Contractor	1	4	400
4. Hardware store	Printshop (poster) and contractor	3	16	600
5. Drug store	Drug store	1	2	200
6. Jewelry	Chewing gum factory	1	22	450

[a] The working capital of the branch firm is independent of the working capital of the parent firm.

Kinship and Business Partnership

All ten firms were owned by coparcenary groups that formed business partnerships based on investments derived from the joint family. Three main factors encouraged business ties among agnates: inheritance patterns, the tax structure, and kinship amity.

The *Mitakshara* law which governs the inheritance patterns among Marwaris stipulates that

> each son acquires at his birth an equal interest with his father and on the death of the father the son takes the property, not as his heir but by survivorship. The position of the son or grandson in the *Mitakshara* is somewhat similar to that of *sui heredes*, who, under Roman law, regarded as having a sort of dormant ownership in the estate of their father even during his lifetime. Their succession was not so much a succession as coming into enjoyment of what in a sense had already belonged to them (Mulla, 1970:45).

Because the father's interest in the joint family assets passes to the surviving son(s) who, at birth, acquires an interest equal to his father's (unlike the pattern in 19th century New England (Farber, 1973; Hall, 1978) and Europe (Habakkuk, 1955), the power of the father to dispose the ancestral property in his will is severely limited. Ideally, such an inheritance pattern serves as a buffer against fragmentation of the capital resources necessary for economic development. Furthermore, "since no member of a *Mitakshara* family is entitled to any definite share of the joint property, it follows that no member is entitled to any definite share of the income of the joint property. But all coparceners are entitled to joint possession and enjoyment of the family property" (Gulati and Gulati, 1962:3).

In addition to the inheritance laws, business partnership among the Marwari coparceners were encouraged by the tax structure. Indian income tax laws clearly recognize the joint family as a distinct, taxable corporation. Individual members, however, are exempted from personal income tax as long as their income is derived from the corporation. In this regard, Gulati and Gulati (1962:6-7) note,

> Since income of the Hindu undivided family (HUF) is liable to tax separately, a member of the HUF is not taxable at all in respect of any such member, out of income of the family, even though the family may not have paid the tax on its income. But income from separate and self-acquired property of a Hindu which has not been thrown into the common stock is assessable as the income of the individual and not as the income of the HUF even though the Hindu is a member of joint family. Thus a member of a trading HUF carrying on business for his personal account is assessed to income tax on his profits as an individual even though he had borrowed the capital out of the family funds.

In their detailed analysis of the tax privileges of the joint family, Gulati and Gulati (1962) demonstrated the economic advantage to the coparceners of maintaining the corporate character of the joint family and concluded that "it should be evident that although the HUF is treated as a separate taxable entity *apparently* on the same footing as the individual, it enjoys a number of advantages over the latter by virtue mainly of the peculiar rules of the Hindu Law on the subjects and succession to joint family property" (1962: 11-12).

The crucial aspect of the tax law for the present discussion is that its emphasis is on the joint family, not as an integrated kinship unit or household but as an economic corporation. This is "because for the purpose of tax assessment, a family continues to be joint even when its members (or groups of members) live and eat separately. *Joint living and common kitchen are not essential to the recognition of the HUF for purposes of tax*" (Gulati and Gulati, 1961: 22; italics mine). Such a tax structure appears regressive, given the conspicuous inequalities of wealth and income in India. Taxing individual coparceners for the income derived from the joint family property would undoubtedly yield additional revenues, but in the long run it would inhibit the entrepreneurial function of the family and kinship and thus hinder the process of development.

Other than pragmatic reasons, business partnerships with kin were considered by Marwaris as an expression of solidarity and amity. As Benedict (1968) has shown in the context of east Africa, family and kin networks are valuable for training, for infusing the trust and confidence essential for risk-taking, and for providing links for trade and credit. Moreover, partnership with kin serves as a hedge against failures in entrepreneurial ventures.

Kinship and Capital

To accumulate capital for expansion, families need to exercise social skills in favorable legal and market institutional setting as well as in kinship relations. While the major source of capital for the ten coparcenary groups was domestic assets, credit appeared to be a key element in Marwari entrepreneurship. Timberg's (1979:29) remark that "the genius of a trading community lies in its manipulation of credit" essentially captures a significant aspect of Marwari success: an astute entrepreneur takes risks not with his own capital but with the capital of others. Nearly all of the ten coparcenary groups relied on credit when they shifted from money-lending to other ventures, including those who had domestic wealth.

Unlike the 19th century New England entreprenuers (Farber, 1973; Hall, 1978) who, in the absence of lending institutions, formed family partnerships and trusts, the KGF Marwaris did have access to credit institutions at the beginning of this century (Kolar District Gazetteer, 1968: 230-262). Yet the general tendency among the Marwaris was not to depend on banks or other institutional sources for credit because they felt that these agencies demanded excessive collateral for loans as well as causing costly delays by their inefficient procedures. Of the ten groups, only two reported heavy dependence on banks. As an alternative, there existed an informal preferential scheme with regard to creditor debtor relationships among kin. Most Marwaris preferred to borrow from their patrilateral kin and only when they could not raise the required funds from this group would they approach matrilateral kin.

The preference for obtaining credit from kin was based on several pragmatic and affective considerations. First, the process was simple and direct, and it required minimal documentation Second, there was no tangible collateral demanded. Other than trust, the past record of promptness, the value of family assets, and the nature of enterprise for which credit was sought served as direct, collateral. Third, credit transactions reinforced kinship ties by serving as occasions for mutual visits and interaction. In general, there were two ways in which credit was arranged depending, of course, in the amount of money, the degree of kinship, and duration for which credit was given or received. First, there was overnight borrowing, usually to meet "cash flow" problems, at nominal interest or what Hazelhurst (1966: 20) calls "social concessional" credit. The second form of credit transaction involved large sums given or received on the basis of written promissory notes (IOU) with no collateral. Almost all groups studied used both types of credit in their business dealings.

Kinship and Training

Although most Marwaris expect their children, especially males, to complete high school, few depend upon college education to provide skills necessary to run family business. As it is the responsibility of the joint family to provide economic means to the males (and practically no Marwari in KGF had a salaried job outside the family business), young males were systematically trained for business ventures. A Marwari boy of 14 or 15 years typically spent two or three hours a day as an apprentice in the family business in addition to attending school. Further, it was common for male teenagers to engage in minor trading activities independent of the family business using capital provided by the family.

Upon completion of high school, young men were inducted into the family business as apprentices. Their positions and training were contingent upon the elders' assessment of their capacities and character. Although the kinship group trained individuals in various aspects of management of the family business, one was deemed "graduated" only after mastering the art of maintaining the *vahi*. The *vahi* is a ledger of accounts written in *Mundi* Hindi, a script different from the *Devanagari* script, of Hindi. The *vahis*, which tended to be unique to each family firm, were written in such a way as to disguise the actual transactions, and they served as a confidential second set of books not available to outsiders, especially tax officials.

All ten groups maintained two sets of accounts: one for tax purposes and the other for coparceners. The ledger of accounts for tax purposes seldom provided an accurate financial profile of a coparcenary group but reflected, rather, an exercise in creative accounting. The *vahi* in contrast, contained not only business accounts, but details of income and expenditures related to marriage, household maintenance, credits, gold reserves, and even the personal expenditures of each coparcener. The apprentice had to learn the technique of maintaining such a register in order to obtain intimate knowledge of the economic affairs of the coparcenary group. In at least four of the ten groups, some individuals were not successful in acquiring the competence to maintain the Vahi. Nevertheless, the elders were generally tolerant of such incompetence and hoped to train them eventually.

Conclusion

The Marwari entrepreneurs exploited opportunities afforded by the developing situation by moving from moneylending to retail trade to banking and, finally, to ownership and management of factories. While it is true that the ten cases discussed in this paper are small relative to many large private industrial and business corporations in India, the history of each unit is a clear illustration of risk-taking and rational response to changing economic conditions. The magnitude of risk and success depends on the initial available capital, the ability of the group to raise credit, and the size of the kinship group. Furthermore, the relation between the Indian inheritance law and income tax structure clearly favored family partnerships and economic development allowing the joint family to maintain solidarity with limited amity despite geographic mobility, smaller households, and a century of social and political change.

Notes

1. The study reported is part of an ongoing research project titled "Structure and Process in an Indian City." Using participant observation, questionnaires, interviews, and family histories, various aspects of the social life of KGF have been studied over a period of fifteen years beginning in 1964. The data on Marwaris, however, were collected during two field trips—the first in 1971 and the second in 1979. In 1971 general information on all 408 Marwari households was collected, including the composition of the household, the nature of their economic activities, family life, and migration histories. In 1979 specific data concerning kinship structure and economic activities of the ten most successful joint families were collected and provide the basis for this paper.

   The 1971 research was funded by the University of Illinois Geisert Fellowship in sociology, research grants from the Department of Sociology, Research Board, and Center for International Comparative Studies at the University of Illinois. The 1979 research was partially supported by Social Science and Humanities Research Council of Canada sabbatical fellowship and from a grant from the Shastri Indo-Canadian Institute, Canada. The author is indebted to these agencies.

2. Department of Sociology, University of Manitoba, Winnipeg, Manitoba R3T 2N2, Canada

References

Alexander, Alec P. 1967. "The Supply of Industrial Entrepreneurship," *Explorations in Entrepreneurial History*. Second Series. IV, Winter.

Ames, Michael. 1973. "Structural Dimensions of Family Life in the Steel City of Jamshedpur," in *Entrepreneurship and Modernization of Occupational Cultures in South Asia*. Ed. Milton Singer. Monograph. 12. Program in Comparative Studies in Southern Asia, Duke University.

Bailyn, Bernard. 1955. *The New England Merchants in the Seventeenth Century*. Cambridge: Harvard University Press.

Benedict, Burton. "Family Firms and Economic Development," *Southwestern Journal of Anthropology* 24 (1):1-19.

Bennett, John W. and Leo A. Despres. 1960. "Kinship and Instrumental Activities: "A Theoretical Inquiry," *American Anthropologist* 62 (2):254-267.

Clignet, Remi. 1966. "Urbanization and Family Structure in the Ivory Coast," *Comparative Studies in History and Society* 8(4):385–401.

Comhaire, Jean L. 1956. "Economic Change and the Extended Family," *The Annals of the American Academy of Social and Political Sciences* 305:45–52.

Farber, Bernard. 1972. *Guardians of Virtue: Salem Families in 1800*. New York: Basic Books.

Gulati, I.S. and K.S. Gulati. 1962. *The Undivided Hindu Family: A Study of its Tax Privileges*. New York: Asia Publishing House.

Habakkuk, H.J. 1955. "Family Structure and Economic Change in Nineteenth Century Europe," *Journal of Economic History* 15:1–12.

Hall, Peter D. 1978. "Marital Selection and Business in Massachusetts Merchant Families, 1700-1900," in Michael Gordon, Ed., *The American Family in Socio-Historical Perspective*. 2nd ed. New York: St. Martin's Press.

Hazelhurst Leighton W. 1966. *Entrepreneurship and the Merchant Castes in a Punjabi City*. Monograph 1. Program in Comparative Studies on Southern Asia, Duke University.

Ito, Shoji A. 1966. "A Note on the Business Combines in India—With Special Reference to Nattukottai Chettiars," *The Developing Economies* 4(3).

Kasdan, Leonard. 1965. Family Structure Migration and the Entrepreneurship Comparative Studies in *Society and History* 7 (2);345–357.

Khalaf, Samir and E. Shawayri. 1966. "Family-Firms and Industrial Development: The Lebanese Case," *Economic Development and Cultural Change* 15(1):59–69.

Landes, David. 1975. "Bleichroeders and Rothschilds: The Problem of Continuity in the Family Firm." in Charles E. Rosenberg, Ed., *The Family in History*. Philadelphia: University of Pennsylvania Press.

Levy, Marion, J. 1966. *Modernization and the Structure of Societies*. Princeton, New Jersey: Princeton University Press.

Lynch, Owen M. 1967. "Rural cities in India: Continuities and Discontinuities," in Philip Mason, Ed., *India and Ceylon: Unity and Diversity*, New York: Oxford University Press.

Madan, T.N. 1962. "The Joint Family: A Terminological Clarification," *International Journal of Comparative Sociology* 2 (1): 7-16.

———. 1976. "The Hindu Family and Development," *Journal of Social and Economic Studies* 4(2).

Marcus, G. 1980. "Law in the Development of Dynastic Families Among American Business Elites: The Domestication of Capital and Capitalization of the Family." *Law and Society Review*, Vol. 14, (4). Summer.

Mulla, D.F. 1970. *Principles of Hindu Law*. Bombay: Tripathi & Co.

Nafziger, Wayne. 1969. "The Effect of the Nigerian Extended Family on Entrepreneurial Activity," *Economic Development and Cultural Change* 18(1): 25–33.

———. 1978. *Caste, Class, and Entrepreneurship*. Honolulu: University of Hawaii Press.

Owens, Raymond. 1971. "Industrialization and the Indian Joint Family," *Ethnology* 10:223–250.

———. 1973. "Peasant Entrepreneurs in a North Indian Industrial City," in *Entrepreneurship and Modernization of Occupational Cultures in South Asia*. Ed:, Milton Singer. Monograph 12. Program in Comparative Studies on Southern Asia, Duke University.

Papanek, Hanna. 1973. "Pakistan's New Industrialists and Businessmen: Focus on the Memons," in *Entrepreneurship and Modernization of Occupational Cultures in South Asia*. Ed., Milton Singer. Monograph 12. Program in Comparative Studies in Southern Asia Duke University.

Pocock, D.F. 1960. "Sociologies: Urban and Rural," *Contributions to Indian Sociology*.

Ramu. G.N. 1973. "Family Structure and Entrepreneurship: An Indian Case," *Journal of Comparative Family Studies* 4 (2) :239-256.

———. 1977. *Family and Caste in Urban India*. New Delhi: Vikas Publishing House.

Rostow, W.W. 1962. *The Stages of Economic Growth*. New York: Cambridge University Press.

Shah, A.M. 1964. "Basic Terms and Concepts in the Study of Family in India." *The Indian Economic and Social History Review*, 1 (3): 1–36.

Singer, A.M. 1968. "The Indian Joint Family in Modern Industry," in *Structure and Change in Indian Society*. Eds., M. Singer and B.S. Cohn. Chicago: Aldine Publishing Co.

————. 1973. Ed. *Entrepreneurship and Modernization of Occupational Cultures of South Asia*, Monograph 12. Program in Comparative Studies on Southern Asia, Duke University.

Timberg, Thomas A. *The Marwaris: From Traders to Industrialists*. New Delhi: Vikas Publishing House.

Weber, Max. 1958. *The Religion of India*. Glencoe, Illinois: The Free Press.

Weiner, Myron. 1966. *Modernization: The Dynamics of Growth*. Bangalore: Higginbothams Ltd.

CHAPTER 9

Father State, Motherland, and the Birth of Modern Turkey

Carol Delaney

Introduction

This paper will analyze the familiar and familial images of Father State (*Devlet Baba*) and Motherland (*Anavatan*) through which Turkish national identity is conveyed. The language of kinship is so commonplace that most people hardly ever pay any serious attention to it. And anthropologists, for whom kinship has been a major focus of study, often dismiss as merely metaphor its use outside the context of kinship. However, it could also be argued that, because family and kinship relationships are felt to be natural, the imagery of the family used in other contexts helps to naturalize them as well. Anderson seems to have been thinking of something like that when he suggested that nationalism might be more productively treated "as if it belonged with 'kinship' and 'religion' rather than with 'liberalism' or 'fascism'" (1983:15). That is, nationalism should be understood not in terms of explicit political ideologies, as is conventional, but in terms of larger cultural systems (kinship and religion) from which Anderson thought it derived (ibid.: 19). Anderson's intuition had already been preceded by David Schneider (1969), whose article noted the *conceptual* similarity between the categories of kinship, nationality, and religion.

One becomes a member of a family (or kinship unit), a nation, and a religion in remarkably similar ways: either by being born into it or in some cases by being naturalized. Schneider suggested that perhaps the boundaries between nationality, religion, and kinship were not so well marked, at least in cultures influenced by Judaism and Christianity, and, I would add, Islam—in other words, the Abrahamic religions. All three terms—family, nation, and religion—are usually felt to demarcate separate domains or areas of human experience but, at the same time, "they all seem to say one thing. They are all concerned with unity of some kind," which Schneider defined as "diffuse and enduring solidarity" (1977:67). Although Schneider did not use the word, he appeared to be talking about identity and the *similar* ways in which *different* sorts of identity are constructed. Alternatively, one might say that the same rhetoric is used in different contexts, contexts that tend to become concretized as distinct, and even natural, domains. Yet, while Schneider raised the question of the blurred boundaries between the seemingly distinct social domains of family, nation, and religious community, he did not ask: Why is the head of the family, the nation, and the church symbolically, as well as normatively, male? In other words, he did not ask who is on top!

The fact that the family, nation, and church are each spoken of, and imagined as a unit obscures both the internal stratifications and the gendered hierarchies in these institutions. For example, the conceptualization of the family as a "natural" unit has been a staple not just of kinship theory but also of political theory going back at least as far as Aristotle.[1] The notion of family as a natural unit not only naturalizes (and thus universalizes) western notions of kinship as derived from (i.e., constituted by) blood relations resulting from sexual intercourse, but it also naturalizes power as it submerges asymmetries of age and gender as well as differing interests.[2] In Turkish, the word commonly translated as "family" is *aile*, but this has different meaning for women and men. *Aile* refers to wife and children; thus only men really *have* families; women are part of one.[3]

The fusion of gender, sexuality, and kinship and the "forgetting" of the different structural places each person occupies within the image of the unified family is comparable on the personal level to that required of different groups by the inclusive rhetoric of nationalism. "Forgetting," said Renan more than a century ago, "is a crucial factor in the creation of a nation" (1990:11).

My goal in this paper is not just to highlight the differential placement of men and women in and to the nation—an issue that has been addressed by some feminist scholars,[4] but notably not by Anderson, Gellner, or Hobsbawn—but more importantly to show the role that the symbolism of mother and father play in the conception of the nation. By attending to these procreative images and meanings of gender, I hope to extend the theoretical import of Schneider's argument as I contextualize it with material from Turkey. The implications of the material suggest that the concept of the nation-state is itself gendered and therefore that gender inequality vis-a-vis the nation is not an accidental feature but is inherent in the notion of the nation as it has been historically conceived in the West. The geographical and temporal origin does not, of course, preclude its being exported to and adopted by peoples elsewhere.

Conceiving the Nation

Father State (*Devlet Baba*) and Motherland (*Anavatan*) are concepts familiar to all Turks and were well known to peoples living under Ottoman rule. Thus, although they were not newly invented with the Republic of Turkey in 1923, they were used in a new way. In shaping the nationalism that would help to create the new nation, Mustafa Kemal, later known as Atatürk, drew upon these familiar concepts but changed the referents.

Father State epitomized Ottoman rule. The state was both patriarchal and paternalistic, and the people, organized into *millet* ("nations"), were dependent on its benevolence and its protection. Confessional groups, whether Muslim, Jewish, or one of various forms of Christianity such as Greek Orthodox, Armenian, or Syrian, were the basis of the *millet* system. Religious identity most often coincided with ethnic and linguistic identities and membership was a matter of birth. Within the Ottoman Empire were many nations.

The land was owned by the state and imagined both as the vast amorphous expanse of state patrimony and as the small area of the earth one was reared on. But in either case, *Anavatan* ("Motherland") was a generalized medium of nurture, under the control of the state but without specific boundaries or identity.

People were familiar with the concepts of nation and state, but these did not go together naturally; indeed, in certain circumstances they could be seen as opposed. The notion of a circumscribed body of land isomorphic with the body politic was absent. In order to bring the nation-state into being, the conceptual ground first had to be laid. The power and success of the nationalist movement was due, I believe, not only to Mustafa Kemal's military strategy but also to his rhetorical strategy. He *refigured the imaginative terrain as he sought to redefine the physical.*

The transformation from the sprawling Ottoman Empire to a European-type, territorially based nation-state of Turkey did not occur in a vacuum, nor was it inevitable. Even before the collapse of the Ottoman Empire at the end of World War I, two other powerful ideologies for fostering solidarity were competing for peoples' allegiance: pan-Islam and pan-Turkism. The same two options have once again come to the forefront of political consciousness: on the one hand, the rise and spread of militant Islam calls for an extended Muslim brotherhood; and on the other, the end of the Cold War has made porous the boundaries separating Turkey from other Turkic-speaking groups in the former Soviet Union.[6] As people's allegiances are pulled in different directions, Turkey is being divided and, in the process, its future is being charted.

Pan-Islam as its name implies, is based on the unity or brotherhood provided by Islam. This was the most accessible ideology, since Islam was the source of identity and the primary cultural context in which the majority of people lived their lives. A great many Turks still continue to identify primarily as Muslims and as people from a particular area in Turkey—Konyah (of Konya), Ankarah (of Ankara), etc.—rather than primarily as Turks. Pan-Islamic identity would include most of the various Arab peoples in the empire but would exclude the Christians and Jews living in their midst.

Pan-Turkism, in contrast, was a nationalist theory based on linguistic affinities with other Turkic-speaking peoples in Central Asia, Russia, and even as far as China, some of whom were at least nominally Muslim, while others practiced local varieties of shamanism. Since many of these peoples were not at that time within the empire, this theory had quite definite expansionist aspects. Drawing on notions of a glorious pre-Islamic past, pan-Turkism could easily be seen to be in conflict with Islam. For this reason, it would hardly appeal to the Ottomans of the ruling class or to the majority of the people who were villagers. It did, however, captivate the imaginations of a number of the urban intelligentsia.

Pan-Turkism was a romantic and mystical ideology that drew a compelling portrait of an "imagined community" (Anderson 1983) called "Turan." The notion of Turan had become widely known through a famous poem by Huseyinzade Ali in the late nineteenth century—a poem that, according to Ziya Gökalp, "heralded the beginning of a new revolution in Turkish life" (Gökalp 1968:6). It supposedly provided the inspiration of the Young Turk movement of

1908—1909 to unite all Turkic-speaking peoples. The notion of Turan was further immortalized in another poem, this time by Gökalp himself (1876–1924), who is often credited with laying the foundations of Turkish nationalism; he promulgated his ideas in short essays and poetry that were printed in journals, newspapers, and pamphlets and widely disseminated. In a 1911 poem, he wrote: "The fatherland of the Turks is neither Turkey nor Turkestan; their fatherland is the vast and eternal Turan" (Landau 1984). It is more than a curious footnote to mention that a number of U.S. & European historians and political scientists have exposed their biases by translating *vatan* and even *anavatan* as "fatherland" rather than "motherland," which is how Turks understand the words.[7] Such an oversight on the part of the analysts reveals that they have not fully comprehended the gendered significance of the terms and the sentiments they can arouse.

Nationalist ideas on the European model had also been discussed in Turkey since the late nineteenth century among the intellectual elites, some of whom had even been educated in Europe, but such ideas had not captured the popular imagination. Mustafa Kemal was well aware that in order to capture the imagination as well as the allegiance of the majority of the people, he would have to communicate his ideas and plans for the country in a language and genre with which they were familiar. The language of the people was not the language of the Ottoman court, and the language of the Ottoman court was hardly Turkish. According to Gökalp,

> there were two languages side by side in Turkey. The first, known as Ottoman, was recognized officially and had a virtual monopoly on writing. The second, which was limited almost entirely to speech among the people, was referred to contemptuously as Turkish and was considered as the argot of the common people. Nevertheless, it was our real and natural language, whereas Ottoman was an artificial amalgam created out of the grammar, syntax, and vocabulary of three languages: Turkish, Arabic, and Persian. (1968:24)

He goes on to say how there were two prosodic systems and two musical forms, and that a similar dichotomy existed in literature, comprising myths, tales, proverbs, ballads, legends, epics, anecdotes, and folk plays (ibid.:24). Another intellectual at the turn of the century ruefully reflected that Ottoman "was not the language of one nation. It is not Persian, Arabic or Turkish. The masterpieces of our literature cannot be understood by an Arab or a Persian . . . [and] we do not understand it either. Are we getting to be a nation without a language?" (Ahmet Midhat Efendi, 1884—1913, quoted in Başgöz 1978:124).

Both men encouraged the modernizing, nationalistically inclined intellectuals to turn to the "common people" and to folklore for inspiration. It was in folklore—tales, proverbs, and especially folk poetry, often communicated by traveling minstrels—that the sentiments and values of the *Turkish* people could be found. This was the language and the genres that the people understood, enjoyed, and preserved. "The language of this poetry had served as a viable means of communication for centuries among uneducated peasants, a means which the new intellectuals had been searching for to bridge the gap between the rulers and ruled" (Başgöz 1978:128). While much of the folk poetry and song contained religious ideas, these were, nevertheless, often cast in terms of secular images and themes, especially of nature and romantic love.

A large part of the appeal of Mustafa Kemal was his ability to utilize this vast store of familiar folklore and poetry as a catalyst for change. Social scientists, especially in the United States, have failed to understand or take account of the political role of poetry in other cultures because it is so devalued in their own.[8] The focus on folk traditions helped to enhance the self-perception of Turks, to bring out the uniqueness of their language and customs, their culture. It was also meant to help fashion a notion of the integrity of their culture and institutions, to foster a notion of the nation-state as one integrated entity unlike the Ottoman regime in which state and nation were split. Here Mustafa Kemal drew upon not just familiar imagery but also imagery of the family. In order to understand the power of that imagery and how it figured in the conception and creation of the Republic of Turkey, it is important to explore in more detail the meanings (if the gendered images of *baba* ("father") and *ana* ("mother").

The creation of a modern, secular, western-type of nation-state was the goal of Mustafa Kemal; ironically, as will become clear shortly, something of the power of religion gets built into the structure by means of those very things felt to be most natural, namely reproduction and gender. Images configure the imagination; not only is gender utilized in the conceptualization of the nation, but that conception has the potential to affect the way people think about men and women (cf. Helmreich, 1992). What is emphasized, however, is not just gender, but gender in the context of reproduction.

It is easy, even natural, to discuss the creation and existence of a nation in terms of procreation and birth: "a nation in travail," "the birth of a nation," a "nation reborn." Each concept has been used in the title of a book about the emergence of modern Turkey, but they all could apply to any number of other nations.[9]

Notions of Conception

If it is easy to use the language of procreation and birth to discuss the nation, it is even easier to assume that procreation and birth are natural givens in human existence. While not denying that certain physiological processes do occur, most of us do not entertain the theoretical possibility that the processes of coming into being are constructed and interpreted within specific cultural frameworks of meaning and value in which the very meaning of "nature" derives from its place in a specific cosmological/religious system. While it is common in the West to figure nature as symbolically female[10] there is nothing natural about that designation; instead, "nature" and "the natural" come imbued with gender associations that are embedded in a particular religious or cosmological system.

The system that has been dominant in the West for millennia construes nature as created by God, who is figured symbolically as masculine; nature, that which is created by God, is both inferior to and dependent upon God, and is symbolically construed as female. The laws that govern nature were implanted by God, and early modern scientists thought they were exploring these God-given laws and regularities. "Nature," therefore, could not possibility have the same meanings and associations in different cosmological systems, in different views of how things came to be. Something is lost when God drops out of the picture, as has happened in modern science, and it is not just God. What has also been lost is the awareness that our notion of "nature" has been constructed within a culturally specific cosmology, and therefore our understanding of "nature" is neither natural nor universal. Even when women are associated with the "natural world" elsewhere, one must consider the cosmological context in which that world has a place and the meanings of gender in that context. Today, most of us think of procreation as a natural phenomenon; yet in other contexts, as will become clear shortly, only one aspect of it, namely the woman's role or contribution, is considered natural, the other is associated with the divine.

Much of what I say will be familiar because the symbols and theory are not confined to Turkey. These were the terms in which I first learned about procreation; they are widely known, and still taught to children in much of the United States and Europe as well as Turkey. Despite scientific theory, these images still continue to operate in less explicit contexts such as poetry and song as well as nationalist discourse, and thus assumptions about gender are seamlessly incorporated and reinforced in the construction of the nation.

Baba and *ana* are defined by their culturally perceived roles in procreation. These words, I argue, are not merely labels attached to male and female parents but are also meaningful terms that are differentially coded and hierarchically ordered as is clear when used in the phrases "to father" vs. "to mother." Thus, understanding their meaning and role may help to understand their significance when they are deployed as *Devlet Baba* and *Anavatan*.

In the theory of procreation I have been investigating,[11] men are believed to be the generative agents; they provide the "seed." Women, in contrast, are imagined as "soil," which can be either barren or fertile. They receive the seed-child and, if fertile, provide the generalized medium of nurture that helps to make it grow. Villagers used to cite the *Qur'an* in order to legitimate their view. In Sura 2:223 it is stated, ["Women are given to you as fields; Go therein and sow (your seed) as you wish."] Note also in this passage how God speaks *to* men *about* women; God and men are in an I-Thou communicating relationship, women are objectified. This is hardly a unique example in the *Qur'an*; it is also a common form in the Bible.

Through "seed," men provide the spiritual identity that distinguishes one person from all others. In a non-Turkish religious context, this rhetoric and imagery was made explicit by Elijah Muhammad in relation to the creation of the nation of Islam, and more recently by David Koresh, the Waco cult leader who saw his mission as increasing the "seed" of the House of David.[12] And in a nationalist context, I can recall reading that Herder, the German theorist of cultural nationalism, said something to the effect that neither the land nor the climate is the source of the national spirit, which comes from the seeds of the fathers.

Women are symbolically associated with the earth—what was created by God. And women come to be defined by their physical and nurturing, rather than generative, qualities, which come to define their social role. The differences between men and women are seen as both natural and in the order of things. These ideas are embraced by many Turkish-Muslim women. According to Nükhet Sirman (1989:24), such women applaud the challenge that feminists have made against the objectification and commoditization of the female body and sexuality, but they conclude that the solution is for women to embrace their true nature as wives but more especially as mothers.

In order to do that women must work for the "restoration of the original Islamic community . . . which requires a total submission to their nature as the only possible form of true existence. Motherhood constitutes a crucial element of this essential nature" (Sirman 1989:25). What they do not realize is that the "essential nature" they esteem has itself been constructed within a specific theory of procreation.

This *theory* of procreation, hardly the "facts" open to observation, is what I have called a "monogenetic" theory of procreation, for there is only one principle of creation. Although women are necessary for procreation and are valued for their contribution to the process, men, in their pro*creative* function, are associated with divine creativity and partake of its power and authority. There could have been a variety of conceptual possibilities for the male role: that (1) in sexual intercourse he merely opened the way for the fetus, (2) he merely was feeding it, (3) that he contributed something to its substance. But none of these are equivalent to what has been meant by paternity. The paternal role has been conceptualized as the generative, creative role; the father is the one who bestows life as well as essential identity via the soul; thus he is the means for the divine entering into human society. This ability is what has allied him, symbolically at least, with God.[13] Procreation, then, has hardly been viewed as merely a natural process; instead it has become a highly charged arena for naturalizing divine power.

This is captured succinctly, but perhaps unwittingly, by Seyyed Hossein Nasr, a well-known Muslim scholar: "The Muslim family is the miniature of the whole Muslim society. . . . The father and his authority symbolizes that of God in world" (Nasr 1985:110). God, the Head of State, and the father form a devolving but unilineal structure of authority. During the Ottoman period, the Sultan or Padishah was not only the Head of State, he was also "the direct representative or shadow of God in the world" (Berkes, cited in Tachau 1984:59). The only legitimate order was that decreed by God. Binnaz Toprak, a Turkish political scientist, notes that for Muslims, "political *legitimacy* is primarily a theocratic question rather than a political one" (Toprak 1981:25). Theoretically, at least, "there is one God in heaven, who gave one law to mankind and established one ruler to maintain and enforce that law in his one community" (B. Lewis 1988:46).

The reality, of course, is not and was not so simple. There was an Ottoman Empire and an Ottoman state but no Ottoman nation; Ottomans were part of the Muslim nation. More importantly, perhaps, there was no Turkish nation; Europeans may have referred to the Ottomans as Turks, but that was not a term of self-reference. Indeed, not all Ottomans were Turkish.[14] In fact, it has been said that the greatest sufferers of Ottomanism were the Turks!

"Turk" was a derogatory term that referred to the Anatolian peasants. It was a great achievement of Mustafa Kemal to turn that derogatory term into *the* defining term of national identity. Not until the birth of the republic was announced did Mustafa Kemal make the claim "How happy is the person who can say 'I am a Turk'" But how did he do that, and what or who is a Turk? This is an important question, but the answer is not so simple. The people who today call themselves "Turks" have "Turkic, Kurdish, Albanian, Bosnian, Armenian, Bulgarian, Greek, Circassian, Georgian, Laz, Abkhazian, Arab, and Iranian origins" (Meeker 1992:413); they can hardly be seen to be the direct descendants of the ancient Turkic tribes from central Asia. Therefore, any answer to the question "Who is a Turk?" involves a specific narrative of origin.[15] Despite Mustafa

Kemal's belief that national identity was primarily a matter of language and culture, there was always slippage into an ethnically based notion of Turkishness. Some have suggested that the Republic of Turkey ought to have been named Anatolia or the Ottoman Republic in order to avoid the conflation of language with ethnicity. Indeed, these did become conflated by Atatürk's researches into history and language whereby he promulgated the theory that Turkish was the Ur Language and Turks the original people (see G. Lewis 1984). His theory was given institutional legitimacy by the establishment in 1932 of the Türk Tarihi Kurumu (Turkish History Association) and, in the same year, the Türk Dil Kurumu (Turkish Language Association).

The Birth of Turkey

The task of Mustafa Kemal was to create a national consciousness and to instill sentiments of "diffuse, enduring solidarity." But the inclusive rhetoric of nationalist beliefs and strategies was diametrically opposed to the policy of the Ottoman Empire. That policy was to preserve the distinctiveness of the various nations rather than to assimilate them—a policy that in a benign mode could be seen as the essence of multiculturalism, but given a more sinister cast could be seen as an expression of a kind of "divide-and-conquer" strategy. At the conclusion of World War I, the latter strategy prevailed when the Allied powers agreed to divide and distribute the territory among the British, French, Italians, and Greeks. The breakup of the Empire may have stirred the hopes of other groups to take advantage of the situation to stake claims (or autonomy, but at the time, it seems, their best hopes were with the nationalists, who sought liberation from the Allied powers.

Mustafa Kemal wanted not to conquer but to regain possession of the land about to be dismembered. At the capitulation of the Ottomans to the Allied powers, Kemal, distinguished in the Battle of Gallipoli, was ordered to relinquish his commission and demobilize his troops. He refused, and for his disobedience was condemned to death by a military court.

Eluding the military police, he made a whirlwind tour of the country and rallied the people to resist the partition and claim the country as their own. The appeal was made to their sense of honor; they must come to the defense of the *Motherland* that, he claimed, had been prostituted under the capitulation and was about to be mutilated by the partition.

The power of his plea was immediate. According to two of his biographers, the emotional appeal may have been the result of the fact that he identified his own mother with the motherland and felt injuries to the latter as if they were to the former (cf. Volkan and Itzkowitz 1984).[16] He used a popular poem by Namik Kemal (no relation) that very clearly drew an analogy between land and mother. Mustafa Kemal changed the last sentence and thus also drew attention to his vision of his own role. The last two lines of Namik Kemal's poem read "the foe thrusts his knife into the heart of the land/there was none to save our ill-fated mother." Mustafa Kemal who imagined himself as the land's savior changed the last line to read "but yes, one is found to save our ill-fated mother." Peasants did not have to understand the idea of a nation-state to be motivated to protect their own threatened soil if it was understood as their mother who was being raped and sold into captivity. Once their sense of honor was called upon, they rose up against the intruders and ejected them from their soil.[17]

Fixing the boundaries was equivalent, I suggest, to restoring the integrity or virtue of the motherland:[18] this land would henceforth be the *physical basis* for the nation. All those born upon and nurtured by her soil were henceforth to be related like siblings. *Vatandaş*, the word coined to mean "citizen," is literally "fellow of the motherland"; it is like the word *kardeş*, which means both brother and sibling, literally "fellow of the womb." The physical substance (consubstantiality) of siblings is from the mother, but their essential, eternal identity comes from the father. Although both men and women can be citizens, it remains the male's prerogative to transmit it.

Political Procreation

The transformation of political structures was paralleled by a transformation in the structure of personal life. The change from the Empire with its many nations, like the Sultan and his harem, to a modern nation-state was accompanied by a transformation in marriage laws—from the polygamy permitted in Islam to monogamy as practiced in the western nation-states. This was not to suggest that monogamy was the ideal and/or that women were not also oppressed in monogamy but that the relationship was changed. In Turkey, divorce could no longer be unilaterally declared by the man.

The nation-state was imagined as an inviolable union—a wedding—that presupposed a notion of differentially sexed, valued, and situated people; but in this case, the union was of Father State and Motherland—now the vast Anatolian heartland. In Turkish this is called *Anadolu*, which in folk etymology means "mother filled" or "filled with mothers." These mothers, identified with the rich, fertile soil of Anatolia, are nevertheless represented by the state, which is symbolically masculine. In her fine analysis of Güntekin's famous *Çalikuşu* (the first "nationalist" novel set in Anatolia), Sibel Erol (1991), argues that the family was the central image through which national identity was communicated. At the same time, she did not fully examine the gendered and heterosexual implications.

Mustafa Kemal, the founder of the Republic, was renamed Atatürk—Father Turk or Father of the Turks. If the land of Anatolia was symbolically the Mother, Mustafa Kemal surely was the Father, not so much Father State but Father of it. And while he would have rejected the dependency encouraged by the image of Father State as the primary benefactor, it could also be argued that his personal style in relation to the people was paternal, if not patronizing. A law passed in 1934 "forbade the use of Atatürk by anyone else. Thus, he became the *one and only* Father Turk" (Volkan and Itzkowitz 1984:302) (emphasis added), though most people referred to him simply as "Ata," which is another word for father or ancestor, he became the symbolic progenitor of the people as well as Father of the State that he ruled with one party.

Scholars both inside and outside Turkey (e.g., F. Ahmad 1977; Yerasimos 1987) have called this a "monoparty" rather than a single party rule. By this they mean to show that there was a conflation of party and state during the early years of the Republic. The difficulties encountered with the shift to multiparty politics have been discussed in terms of legitimacy, specifically about the problem of "dual legitimacy" (Hotham 1972:63).[19] Although the discussion is about *political* legitimacy, the language and theory of procreation in which there can be only one principle of legitimacy, that which comes from the father, are helpful in grasping the nature of some of the problems.

The rhetoric of kinship and descent that provides for a person's identity and legitimacy was deployed to give national identity and legitimacy to the new citizens. They could claim legitimacy from the *ata* ("ancestor-father") Atatürk who bestowed it, and recognize their common substance by being born and nurtured from the same soil, *Anavatan*. Building upon familiar concepts and meanings, Atatürk used them symbolically to bind a people to a land and to provide a more general and more inclusive identity.

Notions about procreation seem to be implicitly behind considerations about who is a citizen. The new Turkish constitution of 1982, drafted over several years following the military coup of 1980, makes it clear that the child of a Turkish father or a Turkish mother is a Turk (Dodd 1990:172). But only a child with a Turkish father is a citizen; thus, nationality and citizenship do not necessarily coincide.[20] Children with foreign fathers but Turkish mothers are not automatically citizens, nor can a Turkish woman married to a foreign man acquire property in Turkey. Clearly, citizenship is not gender neutral.[21]

Lessons in Nationalism

As soon as the boundaries of the new nation were drawn, the major problem confronting the victors of the war of independence was that of forming a national consciousness and sentiments of solidarity. While nationalism had been discussed among the intelligentsia, it needed to be taught to the majority of the people whose notion of nation was *millet*, i.e., a concept of nation that meant group of people, not territory. Ziya Gökalp, whose ideas greatly influenced Atatürk, rejected all definitions of the nation based on ethnic or racial identities and stressed instead common culture. His inclusion of religion in common culture made Atatürk nervous, even though Gökalp's ideas about religion, influenced by Durkheim, were hardly traditional. Atatürk felt that Islam would compete with the new nation for people's loyalty, for he knew that "the primary loyalty of individuals is to the *umma* rather than to the state" (Toprak 1981:25). In order to create a modern, secular, westernized nation-state in a Muslim context, religion had not to be so much separated from the state as subsumed by the state. Atatürk, like Gökalp, stressed the moral superiority of ancient Turkish culture, a move that Meeker (n.d.) suggests was "a prescription for loosening the ties of the people of Asia Minor with their Ottoman and Islamic past and thereby easing the way for a program of secularizing and Westernizing reforms."[22]

Atatürk's idea of nation, incorporated into his party's program, "is a political and social body composed of citizens who are bound together by language, culture, and ideals" Heyd 1950:63). In order to bring a western-type nation-state into being, a national identity had to be created. Since culture is not a natural but an acquired characteristic, it can be learned, and education was to play a key role in creating a national consciousness. Not surprisingly, Atatürk often presented himself as the quintessential teacher with blackboard and chalk as he went around the country giving lessons in nationalism. Two subjects were especially important—the position of women, and language.

The Position of Women

The position of women in society, for both Gökalp and Atatürk, was an issue of major importance. Both argued that among the ancient Turks women were much more highly regarded than in Islam, and both believed that a modern nation could not come about without the elevation of women.

"Is it possible," asked Atatürk, "that one-half of the nation can be developed and the other half neglected? Is it possible that one-half of the nation can be uplifted while the other half remains rooted to the ground?" (Taşkiran 1976:62). Although he believed that women should be emancipated, educated, and uncovered, he also said "(They must be virtuous, dignified, and capable of gaining respect" (ibid.:63). His explicit discourse on the liberation of women was, however, undermined by his view that "the highest duty of women is motherhood" (ibid.:56). "Their duty is to bring up and educate a strong new generation of people who will defend the country with determination and courage and pass on the spirit of our nation to future generations" (ibid.:62—63). In this way, Atatürk reinscribed Muslim notions of womanhood in the modern state. Kandiyoti goes further and suggests that despite the fact that "the woman question became a privileged site for debates concerning questions of modernization vs. cultural conservatism" (1989:127), women were actually pawns in the process.[23]

Regardless, Atatürk initiated revolutionary reforms affecting personal status, usually the last bastion of religious conservatism. In place of the *Sharia* (Islamic law), Atatürk substituted the Swiss Civil Code and thereby instituted changes in laws dealing with marriage, divorce, property, education, and enfranchisement. Ironically, Turkish women were given the vote years *before* their Swiss sisters! Although women can vote and stand for office, there has been a steady decline in the number and the enthusiasm since the beginning of the Republic, which suggests, to me, that something else continues to interfere with these efforts. Clearly, one part of the problem has to do with the lack of theorization and implementation of what is necessary to make women's full participation possible, for example, education and day care. But another part of the problem is related to the way the imagery and symbolic associations of the nation and citizenship continue to undermine the democratic intentions. As Nükhet Sirman noted: "Representation thus becomes primarily a gender specific relationship: it is men, and not just any men but household heads, who by virtue of their position become representatives and women, [who become] the represented, *par excellence*" (1990:45).

Women do not represent, they are what is represented. Perhaps this was behind the statement I heard Kenan Evren make on television a few months after the 1980 coup: "Turkey is a nation of men, not women." He meant to express the feeling that the virility of the nation had been restored (why virility?); but he also implied that men defend as well as represent the Motherland. His choice of words perpetuates the indigenous symbolism, as it also reinforces traditional meanings of gender. This observation opens theoretical space to think about the differences between symbolization and representation, often held to be the same. In many countries, not just Turkey, *women may symbolize the nation, but men represent it.*

Women's symbolic function operates in a number of ways. In common speech, the nation is often referred to as "she." She is also often fashioned into a generalized statue to embody and display the special virtues and honor of a particular nation, for example, France, America, or Germany (cf. Mosse 1985).[24]

Language Reform

Another important reform had to do with language. The language of the Ottoman court was Osmanlici, It was written in Arabic script and many of the words and expressions, as well as some of the flowery sentence structures, were considered foreign. Atatürk wanted to purge the language, as he had the land, of foreign influences that he felt were defiling and polluting the *anadil*, the mother tongue. While the *anadil* was the generalized medium of expression, it was the sayings of the fathers, *atasöz*, that gave shape and distinctiveness to it.

In his desire to foster literacy among the people, Atatürk ordered that Turkish be written in Latin letters, which were able to represent the vowel harmony of Turkish far better than Arabic. At the same time, however, Turkish was no longer written in God's script but in that of the infidels. This shift was felt by some religious people as a terrible affront, and even today it continues to irritate some of them.

The changes have been enormous; indeed, Osmanlici is about as different from modern Turkish as Chaucerian English is from contemporary English (Henze 1982:108). But the change has occurred within sixty years and is an ongoing process. Every year, the Turkish Language Association creates new words from Turkish roots and publishes them; these new words are referred to as Öztürkçe (real, true Turkish). Turkish national identity, therefore, can hardly be seen as based on linguistic or scriptural *continuity*, as Anderson supposes. Instead, the people were given a new identity and a new language with which to express it, but they were also cut off from their past. While nationalism may have been fostered in the late nineteenth century by the emergence of several Turkish (as opposed to Ottoman) language newspapers, the language was still written in Arabic script and was, of course, incomprehensible to all but the educated elite. Anderson bemoans the fate of the various Turkic-speaking peoples of Turkey, Iran, Iraq, and the USSR. He assumes that this "family of spoken languages [was] once everywhere assemblable, thus *comprehensible*, within an Arabic orthography" (1983:48) (emphasis added) and thus that Atatürk destroyed their unity when he imposed compulsory romanization. What Anderson fails to note is that these languages were incomprehensible to the majority of the people and that Atatürk's language reform made literacy attainable for them. Furthermore, the vernacular Turkish that Atatürk wished to emphasize was far more comprehensible to the far-flung Turkic speaking peoples than was the artificial creation, Osmanlici.

Additionally, Anderson never addresses, nor considers, the gendered components of language—that the transnational use of Arabic orthography, like Latin of an earlier time, was accessible only to educated men (Ong 1982). Nor does he consider the fact that even when the vernacular became the standard written language, women were not automatically educated to read, and that gender disparity in literacy continues today.

Atatürk's belief that national identity was a matter of language and culture also, of course, posed problems for groups who persisted in their own ethnic and/or religious definition of nationality. The familial rhetoric undergirding the construction of Turkish nationalism and the nation-state is pervasive and tends to undermine the democratic intentions. It is easier to see how it obscures the interests of the various ethnic groups who did not accept Atatürk's inclusive notion of nationality and descent and persisted in their own ethnic and/or religious definition of nationality. It is usually much more difficult to see that *the differential implications for men and women are not natural.*

Gendered Nation

Although the imagery I have been discussing is specific to Turkey, much of it has a familiar ring. It suggests, I believe, that the very conception of the nation and the discourse of nationalism is itself an inherently gendered discourse. Because of their symbolic association with land, women are, in a sense, the ground over which national identity is played out. This becomes quite clear in war and was commented upon during the recent Gulf War, where all sides used the language of penetration, attack, "scoring," and conquest that clearly drew upon notions not so much of heterosexual intercourse but more significantly of rape.[25] In a less explicit way, national identity is also played out in the civilian context of national sport (cf. Appadurai 1990; Archeti 1991; Maurer 1992), the national "ground" in this case having shrunk to the size of the playing field. Yet the scholars who have begun to explore this phenomenon have rarely attended to the gender implications, namely that it is still men who represent the nation on this field and "fight" for its honor.

The discourse of nationalism is not only a gendered discourse, it has been historically, at least, also a western discourse. "The roots of nationalism spring from the same soil as Western civilization" says Hans Kohn (1960:41). While the nation-state is a modern political formation associated with events of the American and French Revolutions, its conception goes back to ancient Greek and especially Hebrew culture: "Three essential traits of modern nationalism originated with the Hebrews: the idea of the chosen people, the emphasis on a common stock of memory of the past and of hopes for the future, and finally national messianism" (ibid:41).[26] He is hardly the first or the only person to have called attention to this. In a series of lectures given at Harvard in 1987 and published in *God Land: Reflections on Religion and Nationalism,* Conor Cruise O'Brien noted:

> Nationalism, as a collective emotional force in our culture, makes its first appearance, with explosive impact, in the Hebrew Bible. And nationalism, at this stage, is altogether indistinguishable from religion; the two are one and the same thing. God chose a particular people and promised them a particular land. (1988:2)

When nationalism and religion coalesce, there is always a danger of deifying the nation, making it almost a sacred entity. Although Atatürk wished to subsume Islam under the state, the nation-state did take on some of the aura of the sacred. In addition to being called Ata, he was also called the "Gazi," a word that usually referred to a "defender of the faith"; clearly in this context the meanings were transferred to the "sacred" nation. The first sentence of the new constitution justifies the military intervention of 1980 because of the threat to "the integrity of the eternal Turkish nation and motherland and the existence of the *sacred* Turkish state" (Dodd 1990:154) (emphasis added).

O'Brien's focus was religion and nationality; yet implicit in the idea of "one people" is the element that is the focus of David Schneider's paper, namely kinship. Schneider notes that "in the tradition of Judaism nation, state, and kinship group are one" (1977:69). At the same time, neither Schneider, Kohn, nor O'Brien consider the way the age-old but pervasive imagery of procreation and gender is incorporated into the discourse of nationalism and is thus intimately involved with the very conception of the nation.

The words nation, native, natal, and nature are all derived from the Latin roots for birth or being born, as Vico, an Italian philosopher, pointed out long ago. He talked about the way a "nation is etymologically a birth or a being born and hence a race, a kin or kind having a common origin or more loosely a common language and other institutions" (1986:xx). But he was even more specific: nations developed out of Chaos which he "defined as the confusion of human *seeds* in the state of the infamous promiscuity of women" (Vico 1986:260) (emphasis added). Certainty of offspring was thought to bring Order out of Chaos and civil society out of barbarism. Like Aristotle before him and Engels after him, Vico saw the beginnings of civil society as coincident with the so-called discovery of paternity, which "just naturally" demanded the control of women and the institution of heterosexual and monogamous (for the woman) marriage so that the paternity and legitimacy of children could be established.

Paternity was taken as a natural fact rather than as a cultural construction within a particular theory of procreation. It is not, of course, the same theory we hold today, in which, at the very least, "seed" would have to be imagined as the *combined* entity created from the contribution of both male and female. But in the earlier idea, the father as contributor of "seed" was imagined as the "author" of the children; because of that authority, he became the ruler in the family; and this, according to Vico, was felt to be not just a reflection of nature but also a reflection of the Divine order (Vico 1986:420) as it is inscribed in the Bible, in other words, the "natural" and the "divine" converged in this most important example of naturalizing power.

The interrelation between kinship, nationality, and religion has been integral since the beginning when God promised Abraham: "I will make of thee a great nation and give to you and your seed all the land of your wandering"[27]—the land flowing with milk and honey; images often used to symbolize woman in western European and other nations influenced by Judaism, Christianity, and Islam. Kinship, nationality, and religion are interrelated, but the means of their integration is a specific theory of procreation in which specific definitions of gender are absolutely central.

Notes

This paper has been through several versions. An abbreviated version was first presented in March 1991 at the meetings of the American Ethnological Society in Charleston, NC, on an invited panel on "Nationalism and Gender." It was later presented at a workshop on "Gender, Islam and Democratization" at UCLA in January 1992, and in February 1992 to a faculty seminar on "The State and the Construction of Citizenship" at the University of California, San Diego. Most recently, a version was presented at the AAA, November 1992 in an Invited Session in honor of David Schneider. Over time, a number of people have offered helpful comments, some of which I hope have found their way into this version.

1. See especially *Politics*. However, the theoretical basis for his ideas about the "natural" gender roles can be found in *Generation of Animals*. See also Locke's *Two Treatises on Government*, Filmer's *Patriarcha*, and Pateman's *The Sexual Contract* for an excellent discussion of the gender assumptions in political theory about the family.

2. David Schneider (1965, 1968, 1972, 1984) has been in the vanguard of showing how anthropological concepts and theory about kinship have derived from and reinforce western notions of kinship. Picking up from there, Sylvia Yanagisako and Jane Collier (1987) have shown how kinship theory incorporates notions of gender and that they are both part of the same system. My own work (Delaney 1986, 1991) shows how our notions of kinship and gender are not just about biology but incorporate cosmological or religious ideas as well.

3. This notion is not unique to Turkey. Engels reminds us than the very word family derives from the Latin *famulus*, which "means a household slave and *familia* signifies the totality of slaves belonging to one individual." It came to "describe a new social organism; the head of which had under him wife and children and a number of slaves, under Roman paternal power, with power of life and death over them all" (Engels 1972: 68).

4. See especially Pateman (1988), Stolcke (n.d.), and Yuval-Davis (1987). The male scholars of nationalism seem to assume a generic individual without recognition that the generic image is male.

5. From my own observations and those of other scholars of Turkey (cf. Jenny White 1994; Nükhet Sirman 1990), this attitude of dependence is still very much a part of Turkish culture. For example, in the village she studied, Sirman notes: "the dominant image of the state is that of a paternalistic provider" (24) and "The state, *devlet*, is in the same structural position to the villagers as a father is to his sons" (44).

6. In the summer of 1992, I revisited the village I had lived and worked in from 1980 to 1982 and found to my surprise that the daily television news included a map and weather reports from towns such as Alma Ana and Tashkent—places the villagers had previously little knowledge of or interest in. Bringing them into the homes by way of television seemed to be a way of bringing them closer, into the extended Turkish family.

7. Despite the fact that *vatan* is the Turkish form of *watan* (an Arabic word), which I have been told does mean "fatherland," it does not necessarily follow that it will have that meaning in Turkish. Similarly, the fact that some peoples do use "fatherland" or *patrie* rather than "motherland" does not mean that the labels are interchangeable; they convey different images and emphasize different qualities. And even in those countries which use "fatherland," I believe that the land as a physical entity is still imagined symbolically as female. "Fatherland" may have more to do with spiritual identity than with material substance.

8. Redressing this bias, several recent anthropological works have drawn attention to the political importance of poetry, especially in a Middle Eastern context. See Abu-Lughod (1986), Caton (1990).

9. *Turkey in Travail: The Birth of a New Nation* (Armstrong 1925); *Turkey Reborn* (Bigelow 1941). *The Rebirth of a Nation* (Kinross 1964); *Turkey: Rebirth of a Nation* (Ahmed 1961); *Turkey—Decadence and Rebirth* (Paneth 1943); *The Rebirth of Turkey* (Price 1923). No doubt there are others.

10. See Bacon (1964), MacCormack and Strathern (1980) and Easlea (1983); and from a different culture an alternative view, Strathern's "No Nature, No Culture" (1980).

11. It was the subject of my anthropological research in Turkey from 9/79–7/82, twenty months of which were spent in an Anatolian village. The results of that work have been published in a number of articles and in *The Seed and the Soil: Gender and Cosmology in Turkish Village Society* (1991).

12. Elijah Muhammad is quoted in the recent film, *Malcolm X*, and David Koresh's statements were cited in numerous newspapers, news magazines, and on television. Both men used this rhetoric as the rationale for legitimizing their taking of many girls and women as "wives." The notion that the identity of a child is given by the man also became clear in the rape of Bosnian Muslim women, who said they did not want to have a "Serbian" baby. The rape might have been reason enough not to want the child; their statement, however, reinforces the logic that men give identity.

13. These ideas have been presented in greater detail in Delaney (1986, 1991).

14. Wives and concubines of the Sultan (and other elite Ottomans) often came from different racial and ethnic groups and different areas of the world, and Sultans too were ethnically mixed. In addition, the elite Janissary Guard was composed of men taken as boys from Christian families and adopted by the court. They were provided with the best food and clothes and brought up and educated along with the Sultan's sons.

15. Levent Soysal (n.d.) in "The Origins of the Ottoman Empire: Narratives of (Dis)Continuity" argues that modern histories are constructed around a number of different and even mutually exclusive origin stories. In stressing the Ottomans and Islam, one must naturally suppress Turks and pre-Islamic origins; yet in another scenario, the reemergence of the Turks is equated with the authenticity of pre-Islamic practices.

16. The associations are well known among Turkish men, since all are familiar with "duelling rhymes"—taunts in which one man can humiliate another by sexual slurs against his mother (Dundes, Leach, and Özkök 1972), Clearly, the use of such imagery on a grand scale touched a sensitive nerve.

17. In one of the most mismatched battles in the history of war, the tattered "nationalist" army defeated the Allied powers. An especially interesting article is that by Gawrych (1988). But see also Kinross (1965); B. Lewis (1968); and Volkan and Itzkoswitz (1984).

18. It is not surprising that during the turbulent decade of the 1970s, when the country was again seen as divided against itself and in danger of splitting apart, these familial images were again evoked. After the period of military rule, it was a political coup on the part of Türgüt Ozal and his supporters to use the comforting image of *Anavatan* as the name of the party. Despite predictions to the contrary, it won by an overwhelming majority.

19. What they refer to by this term is the conflict about the basis of the nation, especially secularism and democracy, both principles advocated by Atatürk. But what happens, they ask, when the will of the people (the democratic principle) acts against the principle of secularism in an effort to reestablish Islam?

20. Despite universalistic claims of citizenship, I would agree with Pateman (1988) and Stolcke (n.d.) that women in a number of European nations do not really have a nationality of their own; it comes

from descent and marriage, that is, a woman's nationality follows that of her father or her husband. Nor can she pass her own nationality down to her children except in the case of illegitimacy. While nationality laws are concerned with the control of reproduction, that is, who shall reproduce the nation, they also incorporate and restate much older conceptions of gender.

21. Nira Yuval-Davis (1987) discusses the Jewish notion that it is the mother who bestows nationality—that is, only the child of a Jewish mother is a Jew. She states that this practice came about among a persecuted minority population that was often subject to pogroms and rape. She goes on to say that it does not in any way diminish the importance of paternity. The child takes the name of the father, and all laws pertaining to family matters of marriage, divorce, child support, legitimacy are in the hands of Orthodox religious leaders, all male. She also discusses the way nationalist policies to "increase" the nation often conscript women into reproductive labor.

22. At the same time, Meeker draws attention to the fact that such a move eclipsed notions of descent and cultural heritage of other groups in the Empire.

23. Today, when there is resistance against the West, it is women who are called upon to display loyalty to Turkey and to Islam—by becoming covered. Again, I would say they are pawns (see Olson 1985; Mandel 1989; Delaney 1994).

24. At the same time, real women in Turkey must also often display national symbols on or with their bodies, for example by female circumcision or by the less violent form of female enclosure, namely veiling.

25. G. Lakoff (1990–91) gave a talk about the metaphors of war at Stanford during the Gulf War; he had also circulated a paper on that topic over the computer networks. I, too, spoke about the sexual metaphors of war during the crisis.

26. Conor Cruise O'Brien (1988), also notes the way in which these elements figured in conceptions of the nation among Americans, French, and Germans, and I would add, Zionists. The image of "the promised land" and the notion of "manifest destiny" of the Americans draw heavily upon biblical stories.

27. This is a paraphrase of Gen. 17:2–8, but similar notions occur in numerous passages in Genesis (12:2–3; 14:14–16; 15:5, 18; 18:18; 22:17–18).

References

Abu-Lughod, L. 1986. *Veiled Sentiments*. Berkeley: Univ. of California Press.

Ahmad, F. 1977. *The Turkish Experiment in Democracy, 1950–1975*. Boulder, CO: Westview.

Ahmed, G. 1961. *Turkey: Rebirth, of a Nation*. Karachi, Pakistan: Ma Aref.

Anderson, B. 1983. *Imagined Communities: Reflections on the Origin and Spread of Nationalism*. London: Verso.

Appadurai, A. 1990. "Nations and Passions." Talk given in October to Dept. of Anthropology at Stanford University, Stanford, California.

Archeti, E. 1991. "Masculinity and Soccer: The Formation of National Identity in Argentia," paper presented at the AES meetings.

Aristotle. 1932. *Politics*. Loch Classics. Cambridge, MA: Harvard Univ. Press.

———. 1942. *Generation of Animals*. Loch Classics Cambridge, MA: Harvard Univ. Press.

Armstrong, H. 1925. *Turkey in Travail: The Birth of a New Nation*. London: John Lane.

Bacon, F. 1964. "The Masculine Birth of Time or the Great Instauration of the Dominion of Man Over the Universe." In *The Philosophy of Francis Bacon*, edited by Benjamin Farrington, 61–72. Chicago: Univ. of Chicago Press.

Başgöz, I. 1978. "Folklore Studies and Nationalism in Turkey." In *Folklore, Nationalism and Politics*, edited by Felix J. Oinas, 123–37. Columbia, OH: Slavica.

Bhabha, H., ed. 1990. *Nation and Narration*. New York: Routledge.

Bigelow, R., ed. 1941. *Turkey Reborn*. Scotch Plains, NJ: Flanders Hall.

Caton. S. 1990. *Peaks of Yemen I Summon: Poetry as Cultural Practice in a North Yemeni Tribe*. Berkeley: Univ. of California Press.

Delaney, C. 1986. "The Meaning of Paternity and the Virgin Birth Debate." *Man* 21(3): 494–513.

———. 1991. *The Seed and the Soil: Gender and Cosmology in Turkish Village Society*. Berkeley: Univ. of California Press.

———. 1994. "Untangling the Meaning of Flair in Turkish Society." *Anthropological Quarterly* 67(4).

Dodd, C. H. 1990. *The Crisis of Turkish Democracy*. 2d ed. Cambridge, UK: Eothen.

Dumont, Paul, 1984. "The Origins of Kemalist Ideology." In *Atatürk and the Modernization of Turkey*, edited by Jacob M. Landau. Boulder, CO: Westview.

Dundes, A., Leach, J., and B. Özkök. 1972. "The Strategy of Turkish Duelling Rhymes." In *Directions in Sociolinguistics*, edited by J. Gumperz and Dell Hymes, 130–60. New York: Holt, Rinehart and Winston.

Easlea, B. 1983. *Fathering the Unthinkable: Masculinity, Scientists and the Nuclear Arms Race*. London: Pluto.

Eickelman, D. 1978. "The Art of Memory: Islamic Education and Its Social Reproduction." *Comparative Studies in Society and History* 20(4): 485–516.

Engels, F. Zurich. 1884. 1972. *The Origin of the Family, Private Property and the State*. Reprint, New York: Pathfinder.

Erol, S. 1991. "Güntekin's *Çalikuşu*: A Search for Personal and National Identity." *The Turkish Studies Association Bulletin* 15(1): 65–8 2.

Filmer, Sir R. 1887. *Patriarcha; or, the Natural Power of Kings*. Included with J. Locke's *Two Treatises on Civil Government*. London: George Routledge.

Gawrych, G. 1988. "Kemal Atatürk's Politico-Military Strategy in the Turkish War of Independence, 1919–22." *Journal of Strategic Studies* 11(3): 318–41.

Gellner, E. 1983. *Nations and Nationalism*. Ithaca, NY: Cornell Univ. Press.

Gökalp, Z. 1968. *The Principles of Turkish*. Translated from the Turkish by R. Devereux. Leiden: E. J. Brill.

Güntekin, R. N. 1949. *The Autobiography of a Turkish Girl*. Translated from the Turkish by Wyndham Deeds. London: Allen and Unwin.

Helmreich, S. 1992. "Kinship, Nation, and Paul Gilroy's Concept of Diaspora." *Diaspora* 2(2): 243–249.

Henze, P. 1982. "Turkey: On the Rebound." *The Wilson Quarterly* 6(5): 108–35.

Heyd, Uriel. (1950) *Foundations of Turkish Nationalism*. London: Luzac.

Hobsbawn, E. J. 1990. *Nations and Nationalism Since 1780*. Cambridge, UK: Cambridge Univ. Press.

Hotham, D. 1972. *The Turks*. London: John Murray.

Kandiyoti, D. 1989. "Women and the Turkish State: Political Actors or Symbolic Pawns," In Woman-Nation-State, edited by Yuval-Davis and F. Anthias, 126–149. London: Macmillan.

Kinross, L. 1965. *Atatürk: The Rebirth of a Nation*. London: Weidenfeld and Nicolson.

Kohn, H. 1960. "Hebrew and Greek Roots of Modern Nationalism." In *Conflict and Cooperation Among Nations*, edited by Ivo Duchacek, 39–41. New York: Holt, Rinehart and Winston.

Lakoff, G. 1990–91. "Metaphor and War." Paper circulated on computer networks, December 1990, and presented at Stanford University, January 1991, during the Gulf War.

Landau, Jacob M., ed. 1984. *Atatürk and the Modernization of Turkey*. Boulder, CO: Westview.

Lewis, B. 1968. *The Emergence of Modern Turkey*. Oxford: Oxford Univ. Press.

———. 1988. *The Political Language of Islam*, Chicago: Univ. of Chicago Press.

Lewis, G. I. 1984. "Atatürk's Language Reform as an Aspect of Modernization in the Republic of Turkey." In *Atatürk and the Modernization of Turkey*, edited by Jacob Landau, 295–320. Boulder, CO: Westview.

Locke, J. 1 887. *Two Treatises on Civil Government*. London: George Routledge.

MacCormack, C., and M. Strathern, eds. 1980. *Nature, Culture and Gender*. Cambridge, UK: Cambridge Univ. Press.

Mandel, R. 1989. "Turkish Headscarves and the Foreigner Problem." *The New German Critique* 46:27–46.

Maurer, B. 1992. "Striking Out Gender: Getting to First Base with Bill Brown." *Public Culture* 4(2): 24.

Meeker, M. n.d. "Turkish National Identity and the Ancient Oghuz: How Basat Killed Tepegoz." (Personal copy on file with author.)

———. 1992. "The Dede Korkut Ethic." *International Journal of Middle East Studies* 24(3): 395–417.

Mosse, G. 1985. *Nationalism and Sexuality*. New York: Howard Fertig.

Nasr, S. H. 1985. [1966] *Ideals and Realities of Islam*. London: Allen and Unwin.

O'Brien, Conor C. 1988. *God Land: Reflections on Religion and Nationalism*. Cambridge, MA: Harvard Univ. Press.

Olson, Emelie 1985. "Muslim Identity and Secularism in Contemporary Turkey: The Headscarf Dispute." *Anthropological Quarterly* 58(4): 161–171.

Ong, W. 1982. *Orality and Literacy: The Technologizing of the Word*. London: Methuen.

Pateman, C. 1988. *The Sexual Contract*. Stanford, CA: Stanford Univ. Press.

Paneth, P. 1943. *Turkey—Decadence and Rebirth*. London: Alliance.

Price, C. 1923. The Rebirth of Turkey. New York: Seltzer.

Renan, F. 1990. "What Is a Nation?" In *Nation and Narration*, translated and edited by H. Bhabha, New York: Routledge. Given originally as a lecture, 1882.

Schick, I., and F. A. Tonak, eds. 1987. *Turkey in Transition*. Oxford: Oxford Univ. Press.

Schneider, D. 1965. "Kinship and Biology." In *Aspects of the Analysis of Family Structure*, edited by A. Coale, et al., 83–101. Princeton: Princeton Univ. Press.

———. 1968. *American Kinship: A Cultural Account*. Englewood Cliffs, NJ: Prentice-Hall.

————. 1977. "Kinship, Nationality and Religion: Toward a Definition of Kinship." In *Symbolic Anthropology*, edited by J. Dolgin, D. Kemnitzer, and D. Schneider, 63–71. New York: Columbia Univ. Press. Originally published in *Forms of Symbolic Action*, edited by Victor Turner (1969).

————. 1972. "What Is Kinship All About?" In *Kinship Studies in the Morgan Centennial Year*, edited by P. Reining, 32–63. Washington, DC: Anthropological Society of Washington.

————. 1984. *A Critique of the Study of Kinship*. Ann Arbor: Univ. of Michigan Press.

Seni, Nora. 1984. "Ville Ottoman et Representation du corps Feminin." *Les Temps Modernes* 456–457 (July–August): 65–95.

Sirman, N. 1989. "Feminism in Turkey." *New Perspectives in Turkey* 3(1): 1–34.

————. 1990. "State, Village and Gender in Western Turkey." In *Turkish State, Turkish Society*, edited by Andrew Finkel and Nukhet Sirman, 21–51. London: Routledge.

Soysal, L. n.d. "Origins of the Ottoman Empire: Narratives of (Dis)Continuity." (Unpublished paper on file with author.)

Stolcke, V. n.d. "The Individual between Culture and Nature: The Nature of Nationality." (Personal copy on file with author.)

Strathern, M. 1980. "No Nature, No Culture." In *Nature, Culture and Gender*, edited by C. MacCormack and M. Strathern, 174–222. Cambridge, UK: Cambridge Univ. Press.

Tachau, F. 1984. "The Political Culture of Kemalist Turkey." In *Atatürk and the Modernization of Turkey*, edited by J. Landau, 57–76. Boulder, CO: Westview.

Taşkiran, T. 1976. *Women in Turkey*. Istanbul: Redhouse.

Toprak, B. 1981. *Islam and Political Development: Turkey*. Leiden: E. J. Brill.

Vico, G. 1986. *The New Science of Giambattista Vico*. Translated from the Italian by Bergin and M. Fisch. Naples: 1744. Ithaca, NY: Cornell Univ. Press.

Volkan, V. D., and N. Itzkowitz. 1984. *The Immortal Atatürk: A Psychobiography*. Chicago: Univ. of Chicago Press.

White, J. 1994. *Money Makes Us Relatives: Women's Labor in Urban Turkey*. Austin, TX: Univ. of Texas Press.

Yanagisako, S., and J. Collier, eds. 1987. *Gender and Kinship: Essays toward a Unified Analysis*. Stanford, CA: Stanford Univ. Press.

Yerasimos, S. 1987. "The Monoparty Period." In *Turkey in Transition*, edited by I. Schick and A. Tonak, 66–100. Oxford: Oxford Univ. Press.

Yuval-Davis, N. 1987. "The Jewish Collectivity and National Reproduction in Israel." In *Women in the Middle East*, 60–98. London: Zed Books.

CHAPTER 10

Social Networks and Informal Ties

Graham Allan

Most of this book has been concerned with examining the character of kinship and friendship as separate types of relationship. In many ways this is sensible, because kinship and friendship are based on different principles and do occupy different social realms. Yet at another level, treating kin ties and friend ties as totally discrete and separate is itself questionable. Without getting into issues of the extent to which kin and friend relationships can be substituted for one another, it does seem worth while considering informal relationships in unison if we are to understand their role in modern society. That is, without ignoring the significant differences there are between various categories of relationship, a sociology of informal relationships needs to take a more global perspective than one which treats each form of relationship individually (Morgan, 1975; Allan, 1979).

There have been various attempts to do this. The theoretical perspectives discussed in Chapter 2 are amongst the most influential. In particular, those theories that claimed a decline in communal and familial solidarity had a vision of the ways in which industrialization had altered the significance of informal relationships in social life. Yet the empirical evidence, both contemporary and historical, relevant to these theories is not entirely persuasive. We know primary kin ties remain significant to people, both in practical and emotional terms, even if they are not as central in the organization of daily life as they once were. And we know that friendships are important for people too, again in terms of both practical support and emotional meaning. Virtually all the studies which have focused on these issues, in Britain and in the United States, have come to the same general conclusions.

And yet clearly it would be curious if the role of informal relationships in everyday life did not alter as the economic and social bases of society were transformed with the development of modernity in its different guises. Industrialization affected every facet of life; it inevitably altered kinship and other informal relationships. So too, the changes occurring more recently with the emergence of what Giddens (1991) terms "late modernity" have also had an impact on the social organization of informal ties. A major premise of this book has been that informal relationships, be they ties of kinship or friendship, often have the appearance of being removed and separate from the main business of social and economic life but in reality are integral to it. If this is so, then it obviously follows that such relationships will be modified as the social and economic structure of society is transformed. This insight lies at the heart of a sociological appreciation of informal relationships.

In this chapter, then, the aim is to look at informal relationships generally and consider how best the part they play in contemporary life can be understood. In doing this, the chapter will draw on an approach which has been referred to in various chapters but not developed in any depth. This is the approach known as social network analysis. Although the idea of social networks was originally developed in Britain, there have been relatively few studies in this country which have utilized the approach in a full fashion for examining people's informal relationships. Consequently this chapter will rely for much of its material on research carried out in North America. Having discussed the potential of a social network perspective, the chapter will conclude by revisiting the discussion of privatization developed in Chapter 2.

Social Network Analysis

Network analysis gained popularity in sociology through the work of two British social anthropologists, John Barnes and Elizabeth Bott. Barnes introduced the idea of examining informal relationships in terms of a network in reporting on a study of a small fishing village in Norway (Barnes, 1954). In the course of his fieldwork, he realized that what held social life together was what he later called "the ever-ramifying web of cognatic kinship, affinity and friendship" (Barnes, 1969: 72). In more simple language, what needed to be understood was the ways in which informal relationships were used by members of the village to achieve their aims and to provide a framework of order.

Appropriately enough for a study of a fishing village, this led Barnes to think of informal relationships as a net The lines of the net were the individual relationships which people maintained, while the places where the lines joined one another—the nodes in the net—were the individuals involved. Thus the network provided a visual analogy of the total set of informal ties maintained in the village, each link within the network representing a different relationship. This idea of representing informal relationships as a net attracted wide attention and was developed further by Elizabeth Bott in her study of twenty London families, *Family and Social Networks* (1957; 2nd ed. 1971), one of the most influential studies of family issues ever produced. What Bott did as the result of extensive informal interviews with these families was plot out the networks which each family maintained, based on who they knew, and on the relationships these others maintained independently with one another.

On the basis of the analysis of these networks, Bott argued that there was a link between the structure of the networks married couples maintained and the organization of their domestic lives. Specifically, she hypothesized that the "degree of segregation in the role-relationship of husband and wife varies directly with the connectedness of the family's social network" (Bott, 1971:60). Whether or not Bott's analysis is correct (and there has been much research and debate generated by it; see Milardo and Allan, 1996 for a review) is not really relevant here. What matters is the impact it had on the use of a network approach for understanding the significance of the set or informal ties in which individuals were embedded. More than any other study, Bott's opened up the way for fresh appreciations of the part such relationships played in shaping people's lives.

There were a number of reasons why Bott's work attracted so much attention. Two are particularly relevant here. First, it appeared to offer a solution to the vexed question of "community." In contrast to the definitional wrangles and the normative assumptions which the idea of community contained, network analysis offered a far more rigorous way of recording the patterns of informal relationships which actually existed. It allowed the set of relationships to which individuals were party to be laid out in diagrammatic form, and in turn this mapping allowed a far fuller appreciation of the interconnections involved. In addition, unlike traditional notions of "community," network analysis was not restricted to relationships which occurred in the same locality. It could readily incorporate all informal relationships irrespective of whether they were local, This was important given the reduced significance of the "local" in most people's lives with the development of mass transport and communication systems.

Second, network analysis attracted much support because, at least in the way Bott had used it, it offered the prospect of explaining social actions in a form which was anything but trivial. If the connectedness (or density as it later became known) of people's social networks was strongly linked to marital organization, then in theory at least network configuration might also help to explain a range of other social activities. Thus the idea of network became much more than a metaphor or even a mode of description. With the publication of Bott's study, it had become, in Barnes's later phrase, an "orienting statement" with a central theme that "the configuration of cross-cutting inter-personal bonds is in some unspecified way causally connected with the actions of these persons and with the social institutions of their society" (1972: 2). The details would need to be specified, but the promise that network analysis held out to those interested in community and informal relationships was apparent.

In fact, it is questionable whether this particular promise has really been fulfilled with regard to community sociology. Bott's results have not been replicated despite a number of attempts to do so, and other causal explanations of a similar character to hers have not been advanced, at least not in so elegant a form (Milardo and Allan, 1996). At the same time, though, there has been an explosion of interest in network analysis among sociologists of different sorts. (See Wellman and Berkowitz, 1988, and Scott, 1991 for reviews.) Here we will only consider those approaches which are directly concerned with examining the field of personal relationships. As we will see, the language of network has become common currency, but quite frequently the concepts have been used in a fashion that makes the approach appear less innovative and less satisfactory.

Personal Networks and Personal Stars

In order to understand the direction that network analysis has taken in this field, it is first necessary to understand what exactly networks are. As Figure 1 Illustrates, the initial conception of social networks was that they would be full depictions of not only the individuals known to a person (or as in Bott's research, a couple), but also of the relationships there were between these others. Methodologically, collecting such information is an extremely complex (and expensive) task, except where you are only interested in a relatively small group, like that found, for instance, in a particular workplace or other bounded social setting. To do it properly would involve collecting data from person A about their contacts and then interviewing the other people mentioned about the people they know to see if the others named by person A are also directly linked to the other interviewees. Indeed, one could extend this further by then going on to interview the people identified by interviewees B, C, D, etc. to see what relationships they maintain. This could be continued *ad infinitum*, and of course would need to be if a genuinely full network were to be collected. This, though, is obviously impractical.

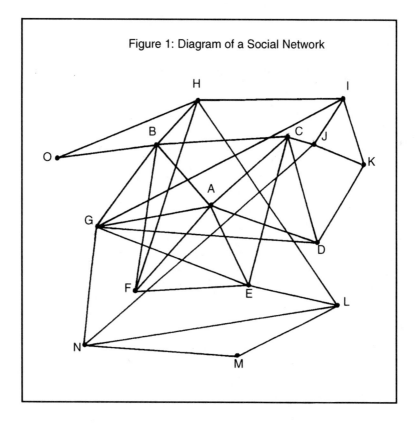

Figure 1: Diagram of a Social Network

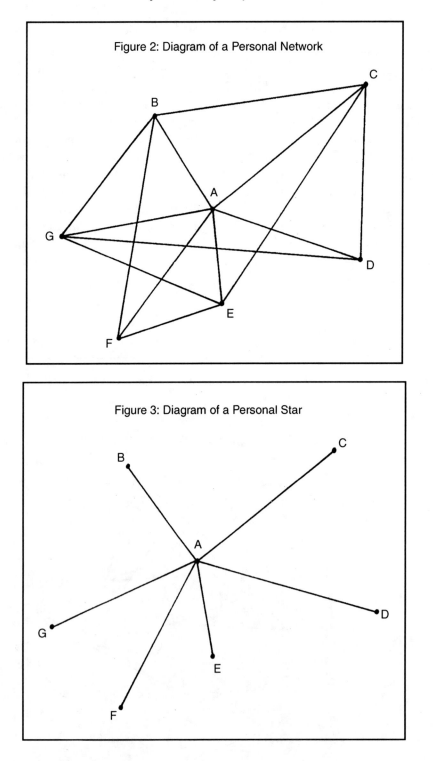

Figure 2: Diagram of a Personal Network

Figure 3: Diagram of a Personal Star

Instead of doing this, most researchers have merely asked their respondents about those they know, sometimes without gathering additional information about the further relationships between those named. Thus in Barnes's terms, the information being collected is at best about personal (or "ego-centred") networks or just personal stars. As illustrated in Figure 2, a personal network is essentially one in which data are limited to the relationships between the known contacts of a given individual (usually the respondent), while a personal star consists solely of those others an individual knows, irrespective of any further ties which exist between them (see Figure 3). This of course simplifies data collection but does generate a different level of information than proponents of a network perspective first envisaged. There is another problem here too. It is that quite often researchers who want to ensure that they have a reasonably representative (and therefore usually quite large) sample of respondents are forced, because of cost factors, to limit the range of relationships about which they can ask their respondents for information. Thus they might, for example, only ask people about their four or six closest or most frequently seen contacts outside the household.

A further difficulty with constructing social networks lies in deciding which relationships should be included. Bott's original formulation was deceptively simple: It relied on specifying all those known to her respondents. But what exactly do we mean here by "known?" Various people have tried to estimate how many others people on average know. The numbers estimated are surprisingly large, in the range of 1,000 to 1,500 (Boissevain, 1974; Pool and Kochen, 1978). While contemporary computers may have the power to deal with these sorts of number, ascertaining information about the relationships maintained with all these people, and then with all the other 1,000 to 1,500 others they all know, is some task.

Now if you try out Activity 1, it should be clear to you that at the boundaries you have to make decisions about who you "know." There are some people who you have met and who may recognize you but do not have anything very much to do with you or know anything about you. These are, in a sense, equivalent to the kin who were unnamed in Firth's characterization discussed in Chapter 4. This issue is actually more significant than it first appears, just as you have

---

Activity 1

See how many people you know. Start off with the genealogy you constructed in Chapter 3. Now add all those people you know through school and college. What other friends and contacts have you got, for example, through clubs you belong to, sports activities, church, etc.? Now think of all those people who you know through your parents, brothers, and sisters. And what about people like your doctor, local shopkeepers, and the like? Once you have listed all those you know, see whether you can construct a personal star. Can you transform this into a personal network? As you should be able to tell from this, interviewing other people to construct their personal networks is not as simple as it sounds!

to decide which people to include and which to exclude, so too the same applies to any construction of social networks. Some relationships are sufficiently significant to warrant inclusion while others are deemed to be of lesser consequence. But on what criteria should it be decided to include people? And how does the decision about criteria relate to the theoretical concerns which drive the network analysis in the first place? For example, should the collection of network members concentrate on those people who are known best? Or those who are seen most frequently (which might include, for example, colleagues who you interact with little outside of the context of work)? Or should it be restricted to those who provide you with most support and practical help? The answers given to these types of question are important because they govern the shape and configuration of the network which is generated.

In other words, personal networks are not simply portrayals of an external reality. They are not straightforward representations of an empirical world. Rather, they are analytical constructions generated by the researcher, which certainly aim to reflect the real circumstances of respondents but which nonetheless operate with an analytical filter. That is, the network which is constructed by the researcher reflects the criteria which she or he chose about which ties should be included and which should not. Thus, and this is the important point, the shape or configuration of the network is actually a consequence of these analytical decisions. In other words, the configurational properties of a personal (or any other sort of) network, which are those characteristics like network density which network analysts focus on, are not fixed but depend on what the analyst takes to constitute a link. As Mitchell emphasized a good while ago, "any statement we may wish to make about the morphological features of a social network must be premised upon what links constituting the framework of the network are assumed to be" (1974: 22).

In recent years the significance of this has been recognized more widely and efforts have been made to specify more tightly the different dimensions of network links. Milardo (1992), for instance, has recently distinguished between two different personal networks based on separate criteria for the inclusion of relationships. The first of these he terms "psychological networks." These are composed of people who the respondent considers important or significant In their lives. In terms of the kinship categories discussed in Chapter 4, they are closest to the intimate kin set. These people have developed strong relationships with the individual over time but, depending on circumstances, may not now be interacted with very frequently. The second type of network Milardo delineates is "interactive networks." These consist of people with whom there is frequent interaction—family, colleagues, friends and with whom we exchange advice, support, and aid. Note how even here the boundary problem remains: how much advice or whatever do we need to exchange to warrant including the other person in the network? While this and other classifications help bring greater rigour to network construction, remember that the networks created remain analytical constructions, and consequently so too are the network properties they embody (Scott, 1991).

The Use of Personal Networks

As discussed earlier, Bott (1971) attempted to use network properties, in particular network density, to explain marital organization. In more recent work, the emphasis on explanation has not been so pronounced. Instead, what researchers have concentrated on rather more is using network approaches as a means of depicting people's social worlds, that is, the overall sets of informal relationships in which they are involved. What this allows is for comparison to be made between the personal networks which people with different social and economic characteristics have, and also for changes in people's networks to be plotted as their own personal circumstances change.

One of the most important contributions to personal-network analysis has been made by Barry Wellman in his studies of informal relationships in East York, Toronto (Wellman, 1979, 1985, 1992; Wellman et al. 1988; Wellman and Wortley, 1990). Wellman's aim was to examine whether it was true that people had become more isolated and less involved in local social relationships in the manner suggested by "loss of community" theories. He initially undertook a large-scale survey of over 800 residents of East York. As with other large-scale studies, he asked each respondent about a relatively small number— in his case, six—of their most significant relationships instead of trying to plot their full personal networks (Wellman, 1979). The results of the survey showed that while the locality was a source of few close relationships, people were not as a consequence socially isolated. The majority did maintain significant personal relationships, both with kin and non-kin, but not in most instances with others living nearby. Modern technologies, in particular cars and phones, allowed these non-local relationships to be kept alive without much difficulty.

Yet while this survey, like others of its kind, provided useful data on the major personal relationships of those involved, and in particular, data that demonstrated the weakness of some theorizing about the nature of community in the later twentieth century, it also became evident that the shallowness of the material gathered in this sort of large-scale survey limited the understanding of the networks that could develop. As a result, Wellman extended his study by conducting far more extensive research on a subsample of 33 of the original respondents ten years later (Wellman et al., 1988). While this is a very small number from which to generalize about contemporary personal networks, It did allow information on the relationships people maintained to be examined in far greater depth. As a result of this Wellman has been able to add considerably to our knowledge of how personal networks differ and what types of factor influence these differences.

Wellman's 33 respondents reported over 400 "significant" ties, that is "relationships they actively think about and maintain (although not necessarily through frequent contact)" (ibid. 137). These included 164 "intimate" relationships, which were ones identified by the respondents as socially close, and 96 "routine" ties, In which there was contact, in person or by phone, at least 3 times a week. On average the respondents In this study had at least 11 active ties in their personal networks. Most had at least 4 intimate contacts and 3 people with whom they were in contact 3 or more times a week (ibid. 140).

Only 4 of the 33 respondents were judged to be socially isolated, 2 having fewer than 6 members in their active networks. In contrast, 9 had more than 20 significant members in their networks. For all but one person, immediate kin were important others, making up almost half of all active and intimate ties. The other significant members of these people's personal networks consisted in the main of a combination of friends, co-workers, and, especially for women, neighbours. The ties themselves had lasted a surprisingly long time. Their average duration was 1.9 years, though clearly this is a consequence of the inclusion of kin as part of their active networks. However, Wellman et al. reported that even the non-kin relationships had lasted for 8 years on average (ibid. 146).

So it is clear that most of the respondents in this study were not socially isolated. They maintained a range of informal relationships that were important to them, in terms of both personal attachment and mundane support. Aside from the kinship links though, the networks in which people were incorporated tended not to have particularly high densities. That is, the close friends which the respondents had did not necessarily know one another particularly well. Collectively these ties provided Wellman's respondents with a good deal of support, even though the tendency was for individual ties to be restricted to specific types of help. As Wellman et al. (ibid. 174-5) note, the various informal relationships their respondents maintained provided them with "*havens*: a sense of being wanted and belonging, and readily available companionship . . . "*band-aids*": emotional aid and small services . . . *ladders* to change their situations . . . and *levers*, to change the world." These ties "are important to the routine operations of households, crucial to the management of crises, and sometimes instrumental in helping respondents change their situations" (Wellman and Wortley, 1990: 583; Wellman, 1992).

In ways like this, thinking of the various relationships which people maintain within their personal network can help generate a fuller understanding of the part that informal ties play in everyday life. Certainly the language of network has had a big impact on the way in which these relationships are conceptualized and reported. Indeed, it is noticeable in Britain how this approach has now become common currency. In particular, those concerned with analysing the care provided to people, especially elderly people in need of support, often write about "networks of carers," though they rarely explore the full meanings of this notion. On the other hand, some studies have tried to understand patterns of care provision through looking systematically at the different personal-care networks available to elderly people.

Wenger's longitudinal study of the support received by elderly people in rural north Wales (1984, 1989, 1995) is particularly important. Wenger found that on average her elderly respondents had between five and seven members in their support networks, i.e., not their overall personal networks but those people available to provide care and support on a regular basis. This figure is in line with that found elsewhere (Wenger, 1989). As might be expected from the research discussed in Chapter 6, the majority of the people in the support network were kin. Like Wellman, Wenger first conducted a large-scale survey investigating the supportive relationships maintained by a sample of elderly people (Wenger, 1984). She then followed this up with a far more intensive, three-year study of 30 of the respondents aged 75 or over included in the first phase (Wenger, 1989). She has also been involved in other studies of the support networks of older people (Wenger, 1995). However, Wenger took a different stance to Wellman and his colleagues in analysing the support networks. Rather than examining the configurational properties like density or clique structure, she focused on the variation there was in overall network composition. She was able to identify five different types of network based on three criteria: (1) the availability of close kin; (2) the level of involvement of family, friends, and neighbours; and (3) the level of interaction with voluntary and community groups (Wenger, 1989, 1995: 61–2). The five types were:

1. *the local family-dependent support network*: mainly relying on close kin, who often shared a household or lived locally;
2. *the locally integrated support network*: typically consisting of local family, friends, and neighbours;
3. *the local self-contained support network*: usually restricted in scale and containing mainly neighbours, with comparatively little kin involvement;
4. *the wider community-focused support network*: typically involving a high level of community activities, and a high number of friends and kin;
5. *the private restricted support network*: characterized by an absence of close kin aside from a spouse in some cases and with few friends or neighbours.

The commonest form of support network appears to be the locally integrated one, followed by the local family-dependent one. Interestingly, these two were also the most "robust" in terms of providing elderly people with informal support. The particular form which support networks take is influenced by factors like the size of the individual's primary kin group, her or his level of geographical mobility, and her or his class position (Wenger, 1995).

Networks: Kinship and Other Ties

There can be no doubt that the concept of network has come to play a significant part in the study of informal relationships. Rather than just focusing on one type of tie—say, kinship, or neighbourship, or friendship—it provides a framework for appreciating the interplay of all these different relationships. Moreover this framework is structural. Instead of simply allowing the characteristics of individual relationships to be assessed and compared, it allows for comparisons to be made between some of the collective properties of the set of relationships any individual (or family or other social unit) maintains. While this is generally in terms of the configurational patterns within a network, subtlety can be added by making the network models more complex and differentiating within them relationships which have different qualities. This certainly allows for comparisons to be made quite readily between different people, between the types of relationships people are committed to at different times, and between the dominant forms of networks in different societies.

Whether or not this framework of itself generates explanations of social action in the Bott form can be left aside for now. What matters is that the approach has opened up new and interesting questions about personal ties, replacing older formulations which, if not redundant, appeared at the time to be offering few new insights. At the same time, it is worth recognizing that the network approach does not offer all the answers. Examining the part which different personal relationships play in people's lives is a crucial task within the sociology of kinship and other personal ties. There is much to be gained from seeing kinship as part of a wider set of ties (Allan, 1979). Yet network perspectives are just that: perspectives, ways of seeing and interpreting some of the patterns which occur. They cannot provide a complete picture. Other types of question which the approach is less well equipped to answer are also important.

Thus social network analysis cannot fully answer questions about the sense of obligation and commitment we feel towards particular ties, even though it can indicate some of the ways in which we are embedded in cliques or highly dense sets of relationships and so constrained by the costs to our other relationships of behaving in ways defined as inappropriate in any one. Equally, network analysis cannot of itself explain why some friendships matter more than others, why kinship plays a larger part in some people's lives than in other people's, or indeed often why we construct the particular social networks we do. It allows us to see these patterns more clearly, but it does not explain them solely in its own terms.

Yet this is no mean achievement. Done properly, and one can argue that certainly in Britain but also elsewhere few have managed to collect data on personal networks with the same thoroughness as Bott back in the 1950s, the relative significance of different personal relationships in people's lives can be appreciated more fully. The great achievement of social network analysis for the study of personal relationships is that it encourages a rigour in the conceptualization of research problems that is often missing in other perspectives and also provides a framework for the systematic collection of information. It may not have generated in full the explanatory advances once heralded, but it has certainly led to new and interesting questions being asked. In particular, the concepts of personal stars but, more significantly, personal networks have quietly revolutionized the ways in which people's informal relationships are thought about in sociology and social science more broadly

Conclusion: Privatization and Social Networks

By way of conclusion, let us briefly return to some of the issues which were raised in Chapter 2, in particular those concerning the extent to which contemporary social life is becoming privatized. Leaving aside questions about social participation in the past, what we can recognize is that the idea of privatization contains in it a number of themes which are analytically distinct Three are worth considering in this conclusion. They are, first, the idea that most people's social life does not revolve around communal sociability in public settings; second, the idea that the home and domestic relations are given priority over their other relationships; and third, the idea that people lead relatively isolated social lives. Let us consider each in turn.

From the different studies that have been discussed throughout this book, it is evident that the majority of sociability is not communal in the way simpler notions of the privatization thesis suggest it was in the past. Thus, for example, the neighbourhood is not significant as a source of social solidarity for the majority of people. Nor do most people interact with others principally in settings which are, in some sense, "collective." Certainly informal relationships are often developed and activated in "public" or "semi-public" settings, like social clubs, pubs, and other activity-based contexts. And equally, individuals can experience satisfaction from the solidarity which such collective settings encourage. However, for most people, such settings are places for developing and sustaining particular relationships with a few individual others, rather than being places of communal involvement per se. As noted in Chapter 7, there appear to be class and gender variations in the extent of this form of communal involvement, but overall the majority of personal networks contain strong individual ties rather than being more amorphously "communal."

Second, it can be recognized that the home and the domestic relationships entailed in it are highly significant for the majority of people throughout most life-course phases. As discussed in earlier chapters, marriage, children, and the construction of a satisfactory home life are high on the list of people's priorities. To this extent, social life in the late twentieth century can be described quite accurately as "home-centred." Within this, the home is used by many as a suitable location for socializing with others (Wellman, 1992). Primary kin relationships, in particular, are normally activated and serviced within the home. Indeed, familialism and domesticity are central concerns of these relationships. But for friends and other non-kin too, the home is often a key setting for sociability. A range of factors influence this, including in particular class position and marital organization. But generally, as people commit more resources to their home, so it appears the home becomes a place to which people can be invited rather than excluded (Franklin, 1989).

Finally, there is the question of whether people lead socially isolated lives. The answer to this should be clear. It is, of course, that most people do not. Most of us have personal networks which contain large numbers of others, and within which a smaller number are particularly important to us. Some of these important relationships are with kin and some are with non-kin. The patterns here do vary depending on a wide range of circumstances. And equally, some people do lead quite restricted lives and are socially isolated. The point, though, is that this is relatively unusual rather than the normal state of affairs in contemporary society. As we have seen in this chapter, even those elderly people who might be expected to be most isolated have active support networks with an average of five to seven members in them.

Yet in a sense Wellman is right to argue that the individual relationships to which people are party have themselves become "privatized." This, though, does not mean that life-styles under contemporary social and economic conditions are privatized in a fuller sense. What it means is, first, that sociable relationships are frequently enacted away from public gaze and scrutiny. This certainly applies to most primary kin ties. However, many friendships are also organized in this fashion, with the private sphere being one of the key arenas in which friends engage with each other. Second, it means that social networks overall often have lower densities than would otherwise be the case. Although the subset of kin ties within the personal network will be highly connected, friendships are often more individual. An individual's different friends are quite likely to have met each other through that individual, but they are not themselves necessarily friends or involved with each other in any other way. Thus these parts of the personal network will have relatively low densities.

Overall it can be recognized that social life under conditions of contemporary modernity is more complex than the idea of privatization initially implies. However, drawing on the idea of social and personal networks in the manner different analysts have is an extremely useful tool for capturing some of the variations which occur, though, as the earlier part of this chapter made clear, the concept of "network" is not a panacea for all the problems of accurately representing the character of people's social participation and involvement. Nonetheless, the network approach does offer a useful aid for understanding and interpreting the range of informal relationships in which people are involved. Although adequate network studies are quite expensive to conduct, it would certainly be valuable to have more research, especially in Britain, which explored systematically the patterning of the social networks people maintain and the ways these change over time as their circumstances alter. It would then be possible to explore more fully the various ways in which social life is affected by changes in social and economic conditions.

Further Reading

Analysing social networks quickly becomes technical. John Scott's *Social Network Analysis: A Handbook* (1991) provides a very clear introduction to the topic, though the treatment of the material in later chapters is necessarily quite advanced. *Social Structures: A Network Approach* (1968) by Barry Wellman and S. D. Berkowitz includes a number of chapters which explore the development and utility of network analysis for a range of issues in sociology, including those discussed in this chapter.

References

Adams, R. G. 1987. "Patterns of network change: a longitudinal study of friendships of elderly women," *The Gerontologist*, 27: 222–7.

———. 1989. "Conceptual and methodological issues in studying friendships of older adults," in Adams and Blieszner (eds.) (1989).

Adams, R.G. and Blieszner, R. (eds.) 1989. *Older Adult Friendships: Structure and Process*, Newbury Park, Sage.

Allan, G. 1979. A Sociology of Friendship and Kinship, London, Allen and Unwin.

———. 1982. "Property and family solidarity," in Hollowell, P. (ed.), *Property and Social Relations*, London, Heinemann.

———. 1985. *Family Life: Domestic Roles and Social Organization*, Oxford, Blackwell.

———. 1986. "Friendship and care for elderly people," *Ageing and Society*, 6: 1–12.

———. 1989. Friendship: *Developing a Sociological Perspective*, Hemel Hempstead, Harvester Wheatsheaf.

———. 1991. "Social work, community care and informal networks," In Davies, M. (ed.), *The Sociology of Social Work London*, Routledge.

Allan, G. and Adams, R. G. 1989. "Aging and the structure of friendship," in Adams and Blieszner (eds.) (1989).

Allan, G. and Crow, G. 1991. "Privatization, home-centredness and leisure," *Leisure Studies*, 10: 19–32.

Allatt, P., and Yeandle, S. 1991. *Youth Unemployment and the Family: Voices of Disordered Times*, London, Routledge.

Anderson, M. 1971. *Family Structure in Nineteenth Century Lancashire*, Cambridge, Cambridge University Press.

Arber, S., and Gilbert, N. 1989. "Men: the forgotten carers," Sociology, 23: 111–18.

Arber, S., and Ginn, J. 1992. "In sickness and in health": care-giving, gender and the independence of elderly people," In Marsh, C., and Arber, S. (eds.), *Families and Households: Divisions and Change*, London, Macmillan.

Arensberg, C., and Kimball, S. 1940. *Family and Community in Ireland*. London, Peter Smith.

Ballard, R. (ed.) 1994. *Desh Pardesh: The South Asian Presence in Britain*, London, Hurst.

Bankoff, E. 1981. "Effects of friendship support on the psychological well-being of widows," in Lopata, H. Z., and Maines, P. (eds.), *Research in the Interweave of Social Roles: Friendship*, Greenwich, Conn., Jai Press.

Barclay Report 1982. *Social Workers: Their Role and Tasks*, London, Bedford Square Press.

Barnes, J. A. 1954. "Class and committees in a Norwegian island parish," *Human Relations*, 7: 39–58.

Barnes, J.A. 1969. "Networks and political process," In Mitchell, J. C. (ed.), *Social Networks in Urban Situations*. Manchester: Manchester University Press.

———. 1972. "Social Networks," *Module in Anthropology*, No. 26, Reading: Mass., Addison-Wesley.

Bell, C. 1968. *Middle Class Families*. London: Routledge and Kegan Paul.

Bell, R. 1981. *Worlds of Friendship*, Beverly Hills, Calif., Sage.

Bhachu, P. 1985. *Twice Migrants: East African Sikh Settlers in Britain*. London: Tavistock.

Binns, D., and Mars, G. 1984. "Family, community and unemployment: a study in change." *Sociological Review*, 32:662-95.

Blau, L. 1961. "Structural constraints on friendship in old age." *American Sociological Review*, 26:429–39.

Bliesner, R., and Adams, R. G. 1992. *Adult Friendship*. Newbury Park, Sage.

Boissvain, J. 1974. *Friends of Friends*. Oxford, Blackwell.

Bott, E. 1957, 2nd edn. 1971. *Family and Social Networks*. London: Tavistock.

Briggs, A., and Oliver, J. (eds.) 1985. *Caring: Experiences of Looking After Disabled Relatives*. London: Routledge and Kegan Paul.

Bulmer, M. 1986. *Neighbours: The Work of Philip Abrams*. Cambridge: Cambridge University Press.

Cancian, F. 1987. *Love in America: Gender and Social Development*. Cambridge: Cambridge University Press.

Cohen, T. 1992. "Men's families, men's friendships: a structural analysis of constraints on men's social ties." in Nardi (ed.) 1992.

Cotterill, P. 1994. *Friendly Relations: Mothers and their Daughters-in-Law*. London: Taylor and Francis.

Crow, G., and Allan, G. 990. "Constructing the domestic sphere: the emergence of the modern home in post-war Britain," in Corr, H., and Jamieson, L. (eds.), *Politics of Everyday Life: Continuity and Change in Work and the Family*. London: Macmillan.

———. 1994. *Community Life: An Introduction to Local Social Relationships*. Hemel Hempstead: Harvester Wheatsheaf.

Cunningham-Burley, S. 1985. "Constructing grandparenthood: anticipating appropriate action." *Sociology*, 19:421–36.

Deem, R. 1982. "Women, leisure and inequality." *Leisure Studies*, 1: 229-46.

Dennis, N., Henriques, F., and Slaughter, C. 1956. *Coal is our Life: An Analysis of a Yorkshire Mining Community*. London: Tavistock.

Devine, F. 1992. *Affluent Workers Revisited: Privatism and the Working Class*. Edinburgh, Edinburgh University Press.

Dickens, W.J. and Perlman, D. 1981. "Friendship over the Life Cycle', in Duck, S. W., and Gilmour, R. (eds.), *Personal Relationships: 2. Developing Personal Relationships*. New York, Academic Press.

di Leonardo, M. 1987. "The female world of cards and holidays: women, families and the work of kinship." *Signs*, 12: 440-58.

Duck, S. 1990. "Relationships as unfinished business: out of the frying pan and into the 1990s." *Journal of Social and Personal Relationships*, 7:5-28.

Edgell, S. 1980. *Middle Class Couples*. London: Allen and Unwin.

Finch, J. 1987. "The vignette technique in survey research." *Sociology*, 21: 105–14.

———. 1989. *Family Obligations and Social Change*. Cambridge, Polity Press.

Finch, J. and Groves, B. (eds.) 1983. *A Labour of Love*. London: Routledge and Kegan Paul.

Finch, J. and Mason, J. 1990. "Divorce, remarriage and family obligations." *Sociological Review*, 38: 219–46.

———. 1993. *Negotiating Family Responsibilities*, London: Routledge.

Firth, R. 1956), *Two Studies of Kinship in London*. London: Athlone.

Firth, R. Hubert, J., and Forge, A. 1970. *Families and their Relatives*, London: Routledge and Kegan Paul.

Fischer, C., and Oliker S. 1983. "A research note on friendship, gender and the life cycle." *Social Forces*, 62: 124–33.

Forrest, R. Murr, A. and Williams, P. 1990. *Home Ownership: Differentiation and Fragmentation*. London: Unwin Hyman.

Frakenbgerg, R. 1957. *Village on the Border: A Social Study of Religion, Politics and Football in a North Wales Community*. London, Cohen and West.

Franklin, A. 1989. "Working class privatism: an historical case study of Bedminster, Bristol." *Environment and Planning D: Society and Space*, 7: 93–113.

Gallie, D., Gershuny, J. and Vogler, C. 1994. "Unemployment, the household, and social networks." in Gallie et al. (1994).

Gallie, D. Marsh, C. and Vogler, C. (eds). 1994. *Social Change and the Experience of Unemployment*, Oxford: Oxford University Press.

Gans, H. 1962. *The Urban Villagers*. New York: Free Press.

Giddons. A. 1991. *Modernity and Self-Identity*. Cambridge: Polity.

———. 1992. *The Transformation of Intimacy*. Cambridge: Polity.

Gitens, D. 1993). *The Family in Question*. London: Macmillan.

Goffman, E. 1959. *The Presentation of Self in Everyday Life*. Garden City, NY: Doubleday Anchor.

Goldthorpe, J. H., Lockwood, D., Bechhofer, F., and Platt, J. 1969. *The Affluent Worker in the Class Structure*. Cambridge: Cambridge University Press.

Grieco, M. 1987. *Keeping it in the Family: Social Networks and Employment Chance*. London: Tavistock.

Harris, C. C. 1969. *The Family: An Introduction. London: Allen and Unwin.*

———. 1990. *Kinship*. Milton Keynes: Open University Press.

Hart, N. 1976. *When Marriage Ends*. London: Tavistock.

Hess, B. 1972. "Friendship," in Riley, M. W., Johnson, M., and Foner, A. (eds.), *Aging and Society. Vol 3: A Sociology of Age Stratification*. New York: Russell Sage.

———. 1979. "Sex roles, friendship and the life course." *Research on Aging* 1:494–515.

Hobson, D. 1978. "Housewives: isolation as oppression," in Women's Study Group, Centre for Contemporary Cultural Studies, *Women Take Issue*. London: Hutchinson.

Hunt, G., and Satterlee, S. 1986. "Cohesion and division: drinking in an English village." *Man*, 21:521–37.

———. 1987. "Darts, drinks and the pub: the culture of female drinking." *Sociological Review*, 35: 575–601.

Hutson, S., and Jenkins, R. 1989. *Taking the Strain: Families, Unemployment and the Transition to Adulthood*. Milton Keynes: Open University Press.

Jerrome, D. 1981. "The significance of friendship for women in later life." *Ageing and Society*, 1:175–97.

———. 1984. "Good company: The sociological implications of friendship." *Sociological Review*, 32: 696–718.

———. 1992. *Good Company: An Anthropological Study of Old People in Groups*. Edinburgh: Edinburgh University Press.

Jones, G. 1995. *Leaving Home*. Milton Keynes: Open University Press.

Leonard, D. 1980. *Sex and Generation: A Study of Courtship and Weddings*. London: Tavistock.

Lewis, J., and Meredith, B. 1988. *Daughters Who Care: Daughters Caring for Mothers at Home*. London: Routledge.

Litwak, E. 1985. *Helping the Elderly: The Complementary Roles of Informal Networks and Formal Systems*. New York: Guilford.

———. 1989. "Forms of friendships among older people in an industrial society," in Adams and Blieszner (eds.) (1989).

Lund, M. 1987. "The non-custodial father: common challenges in parenting after divorce," in Lewis, C., and O'Brien, M. (eds.), *Reassessing Fatherhood: New Observations on Fathers and the Modern Family*. London: Sage.

Lupton, T., and Wilson, C. S. 1959. "The social background and connections of 'top decision-makers.'" *The Manchester School*, 27: 30-51.

McKee, L. 1987. "Households during unemployment: the resourcefulness of the unemployed," in Brannen, J., and Wilson, G. (eds,), *Give and Take in Families: Studies in Resource Distribution*. London: Allen and Unwin.

McKee, L. and Bell, C. 1986. "His unemployment, her problem: The domestic and marital consequences of male unemployment," in Allen, S., Waton, A., Purcell, K., and Wood, S. (eds.), *The Experience of Unemployment*. London: Macmillan.

Mansfield, P., and Collard, J. 1987. *The Beginning of the Rest of Your Life? A Portrait of Newly-Wed Marriage*. London: Macmillan.

Marks, S. 1994. "Intimacy in the public realm: The case of coworkers." *Social Forces*, 72:843–58.

Mason, D. 1995. *Race and Ethnicity in Modern Britain*. Oxford: Oxford University Press.

Milardo, R. 1987. "Changes in social networks of women and men following divorce: A review." *Journal of Family Issues*, 8: 78–96.

———. 1992. "Comparative methods for delineating social networks." *Journal of Social and Personal Relationships*, 9:447–61.

Milardo, R. and Allan, G. 1996. "Social networks and marital relationships," in Duck, S., Dindia, K., Milardo, R., Mills, R., and Sarason, B. (eds.), *Handbook of Personal Relationships*. London: Wiley.

Mitchell, J. C. 1974. "Social Networks." *Annual Review of Anthropology*, 3:279–99.

Mogey, J. 1956. *Family and Neighbourhood*. London: Oxford University Press.

Morgan, D. 1975. *Social Theory and the Family*. London: Routledge and Kegan Paul.

Morris, L. 1990. *The Workings of the Household*. Cambridge: Polity.

Nardi, P. (ed.) 1992. *Men's Friendships*. Newbury Park: Sage.

Nissel, M., and Bonnerjea, L. 1982. *Family Care for the Handicapped Elderly: Who Pays?* London: Policy Studies Institute.

Oakley, A. 1974. *The Sociology of Housework*. London: Martin Robertson.

O'Brien, M, 1987. "Patterns of kinship and friendship among lone fathers, in Lewis, C., and O'Brien, M. (eds.), *Reassessing Fatherhood: New Observations on Fathers and the Modern Family*. London: Sage.

O'Connor, P. 1990. "The adult mother-daughter relationship: a uniquely and universally close relationship?" *Sociological Review*, 38: 293–323.

———. 1992. *Friendships between Women*. Hemel Hempstead: Harvester Wheatsheaf.

Oliker, S. 1989. *Best Friends and Marriage: Exchange among Women*. Berkeley, CA.: University of California Press.

Oxley, H. G. 1974. *Mateship in Local Organization*. Queensland: University of Queensland Press.

Pahl, R.E. 1965. *Urbs in Rure: The Metropolitan Fringe in Hertfordshire*. Papers in Geography, No. 2. London: London School of Economics.

———. 1984. *Divisions of Labour*. Oxford: Blackwell.

———. and Wallace, C. D. 1988. "Neither angels in marble nor rebels in red: privatization and working class consciousness," in Rose D. (ed) *Social Stratification and Economic Change*. London: Hutchinson.

Parker, R. 1981. "Tending and social policy," in Goldberg, E.M., and Hatch, S. (eds.), *A New Look at the Personal Social Services*. London: Policy Studies Institute.

Parsons, T. 1943. "The kinship system of the contemporary United States." *American Anthropologist*, 45:22-38.

———. 1956. "The American family: its relations to personality and to the social structure," in Parsons, T., and Bales, B. (eds.), *Family: Socialisation and Interaction Process*. London: Routledge and Kegan Paul.

Peristiany, J. 1976. *Mediterranean Family Structures*. Cambridge: Cambridge University Press.

Pleck, J. H. 1976. "Man to man: is brotherhood possible?" in Glazer-Malbin, N. (ed.), *Old Family/New Family: Interpersonal Relationships*, New York, Van Nostrand.

Pool, I., and Kochen, M. 1978. "Contacts and influence." *Social Networks*, 1: 5–51.

Procter, I. 1990. "The privatisation of working-class life." *British Journal of Sociology*, 41: 157–80.

Querishi, H., and Walker, A. 1989. *The Caring Relationship: Elderly People and their Families*. London: Macmillan.

Rees, A. D. 1950. *Life in a Welsh Countryside*. Cardiff: University of Wales Press.

Reid, H., and Fine, G. 1992. "Self-disclosure in men's friendships: variations associated with intimate relations," in Nardi (ed.) (1992).

Robinson, M., and Smith, D. 1993. *Step by Step: Focus on Stepfamilies*. Hemel Hempstead: Harvester Wheatsheaf.

Rosenthal, C. 1985. "Kinkeeping in the familial division of labor." *Journal of Marriage and the Family*, 47: 965–74.

Rosser, C., and Harris, C. C. 1965, 1983. *The Family and Social Change: A Study of Family and Kinship in a South Wales Town*. London: Routledge and Kegan Paul.

Rubin, L.B. 1985. *Just Friends: The Role of Friendship in Our Lives*. New York: Harper and Row.

Saunders, P. 1990. *A Nation of Home Owners*. London: Unwin Hyman.

Schneider, D. 1968. *American Kinship: A Cultural Account*. Englewood Cliffs, NJ: Prentice-Hall.

Scott, J. 1991. *Social Network Analysis: A Handbook*. London: Sage.

St. Leger, F., and Gillespie, N. 1991. *Informal Welfare in Belfast: Caring Communities?* Aldershot: Avebury.

Strathern, M. 1981. *Kinship at the Core: An Anthropology of Elmdon, a Village in North-West Essex in the Nineteen-Sixties*. Cambridge: Cambridge University Press.

Suitor, J. 1987. "Friendship networks in transitions: married mothers' return to school." *Journal of Social and Personal Relationships* 4:445–61.

Tiger, L. 1969. *Men in Groups*. New York: Random House.

Tönnies, F. 1955. *Community and Association*. London: Routledge and Kegan Paul.

Towsend, P. 1963. *The Family Life of Old People*. Harmondsworth: Penguin.

Ungerson, C. 1987. *Policy is Personal: Sex, Gender and Informal Care*. London: Tavistock.

Wallace, C. 1987. *For Richer, For Poorer: Growing Up In and Out of Work*. London: Tavistock.

Warrier, S. 1994. "Gujarati Prajapatis in London: family roles and sociability networks," in Ballard (ed.) (1994).

Wellman, B. 1979. "The community question." *American Journal of Sociology*, 84:1201–31.

———. 1985. "Domestic work, paid work and net work," in Duck, S., and Penman, D. (eds.), *Understanding Personal Relationships*. London: Sage.

———. 1988. "Structural analysis: from method and metaphor to theory and substance," in Wellman and Berkowitz (eds.) (1988).

———. 1992. "Men in networks: private communities, domestic friendships," in Nardi (ed.) (1992).

Wellman, B. and Berkowitz, S. D. (eds.) 1988. *Social Structures: A Network Approach*. Cambridge: Cambridge University Press.

Wellman, B. and Worthley, S. 1990. "Different strokes from different folks: community ties and social support." *American Journal of Sociology*, 96:558–88.

Wellman, B., Carrington, P. J., and Hall, A. 1988. "Networks as personal communities," in Wellman and Berkowitz (eds.) (1988).

Wenger, G. C. 1984. *The Supportive Network*. London: Allen and Unwin.

———. 1989. "Support networks in old age—constructing a typology," in Jefferys, M. (ed.), *Growing Old in the Twentieth Century*. London: Routledge.

———. 1995. "A comparison of urban with rural support networks: Liverpool and North Wales." *Ageing and Society*, 15: 59–81.

Werbner, P. 1981. "Manchester Pakistanis: lifestyles, ritual and the making of social distinctions." *New Community*, 9:216–28.

Westwood, S., and Bhachu, P. 1988. *Enterprising Women: Ethnicity, Economy and Gender Relations*. London: Routledge.

Williams, R.G.A. 1983. "Kinship and migration strategies among settled Londoners: two responses to population pressure." *British Journal of Sociology*, 34:386–415.

Williams, W.M. 1956. *The Sociology of an English Village: Gosforth*. London: Routledge and Kegan Paul.

———. 1963. *A West Country Village: Ashworthy*. London: Routledge and Kegan Paul.

Willmot, P. 1963. *The Evolution of a Community*. London: Routledge and Kegan Paul.

———. 1986. *Social Networks, Informal Care and Public Policy*. London: Policy Studies Institute.

———. 1987. *Friendship Networks and Social Support*. London: Policy Studies Institute.

Willmot, P. and Young, M. 1960. *Family and Class in a London Suburb*. London: Routledge and Kegan Paul.

Wilson, P., and Pahl, R. E. 1988. "The changing sociological construct of the family." *Sociological Review*, 36:223–66.

Wirth, L. 1938. "Urbanism as a way of life." *American Journal of Sociology*, 44: 1-24.

Wright, P. 1982. "Men's friendships, women's friendships and the alleged inferiority of the latter," *Sex Roles*, 8: 1-20.

Young, M., and Willmot, P. 1957. *Family and Kinship in East London*. London: Routledge and Kegan Paul.

CHAPTER 11

Shaping American Values: The Legacy of Social Organization in a Norwegian American Farm Community

Robert A. Ibarra, The University of Wisconsin-Madison

Historian, William Cronon, once remarked to state commissioners that Wisconsin was "neighborly enough to be viewed as one large community." The people there held Middle West values toward clean government, a strong tradition of service and cooperation—"a deep commitment to democracy, [and] an egalitarian respect for all people." He declared that "the next great reform movement in America must embrace some version of this communitarian ideal" (Cronon n.d.).

These ideals emerged from a great social experiment that originally forged the state— the European immigration of the 1800s. Drawn by economic opportunities in this region, legions of northern, western and southern Europeans, primarily Germans, Scandinavians and various groups from Great Britain, launched a series of mass immigrations that ultimately populated the state of Wisconsin and much of the upper midwest. This demographic shift imprinted a communitarian ethic and left a legacy of ethnicity and culture that shaped many social values in this country (Nelson and Ibarra 1999).

Communities with egalitarian values like these gave birth to the progressive era of American politics and the venerated "Wisconsin Idea"—a compact forged between public and private institutions, and the University of Wisconsin—for which the state became famous during this last century. University partnerships with agriculturists from the Old World, for instance, invented breakthrough ideas in agriculture, food production and nutrition (e.g., patenting vitamin D)

Contributed by Robert A. Ibarra.

that have literally changed the world. Such forward thinking ideas linking government, politics, education and industry are attributed to fostering the establishment of land-grant institutions.

The cultural mosaic of Wisconsin, USA, today is decidedly old-world European. The predominant ethnic groups are still the German Americans followed by the Scandinavians, especially Norwegian Americans. As demonstrated by the variety of folk festivals and ethnic activity in the region, these communities maintain a mixture of genuine immigrant, rural American and commercialized ethnic cultures and values (see Ibarra 1976; Ibarra and Strickon 1989; Strickon and Ibarra 1983). But these patterns reflect more than just a century of acculturation; they represent adaptive strategies for cultural survival generated by strong communal bonds—an ethnic communitarian ideal.

This chapter is a study of one of these old-world Norwegian American farm communities in Vernon County, Wisconsin. By adopting a mixture of historical and contemporary perspectives on patterns of kinship and social organization, this study explores the social/cultural dynamics that model communitarian ideals found throughout Wisconsin and the Midwest. The focus is on systems of social organization that gave rise to traditional American democratic values—egalitarian, cooperative ideals—now embodied in the Wisconsin Idea.

Agriculture and religion make up the essence of rural Norwegian life. Norwegian farmers in Vernon County adopted their own particular agricultural practices that combined dairy farming and various cash crops such as tobacco to create a successful economic strategy. In this context, ethnicity plays a vital role in determining the pattern of rural social organization and community identity. The rural Norwegian farm community is a tightly knit social system in which the family, or series of extended families, form the central core. This intense system is manifest in the inter-personal relationships, in kinship and social structures within the community and is solidified by social interaction with non-Norwegians at the community's boundary.

The Community

Norwegian immigrants began settling in Southwestern Wisconsin between the late 1840s to the 1870s. In 1850, Vernon County, located just south of the city of LaCrosse, became one of the first Wisconsin counties established along the Mississippi River. At the time, it had the largest concentration of approximately 135 Norwegian settlers. By 1870, close to 23,000 Norwegians were living within seventeen western counties situated mainly along the river (see map). Vernon County eventually grew to become one of the most densely settled Norwegian areas and townships in western Wisconsin (Ibarra 1976). Immigrants mainly from Gudbransdal, Norway established the primary settlement in Vernon County and chose to live on Coon Prairie and in the adjacent Coon Valley area. It is this settlement, begun in 1848, that was the focus of ethnographic research used in this study (Ibarra 1976).

Today, the Norwegian community in Vernon County is centered around two communities; the city of Westby on Coon Prairie, with a population during the field study of close to 2,000 people, and Coon Valley Village, with a population of well over 1,000 and growing rapidly. Although both communities were involved in the research, the discussion here will concentrate

ETHNIC BOUNDARIES IN VERNON COUNTY FROM THE NORWEGIAN PERSPECTIVE
1976

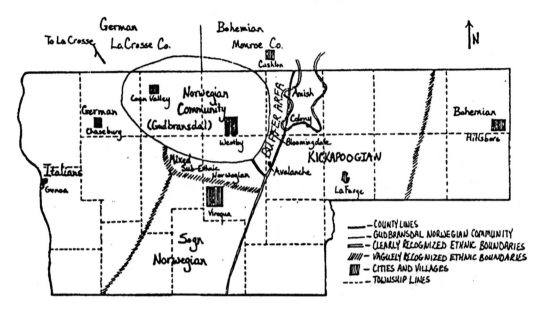

(Map 8, from Ibarra, 1976:148)

mainly on the Norwegians living near Westby. Since rural Norwegians tend to locate in homogeneous clusters, one can easily and with some accuracy locate the seven or eight townships that comprise the Gudbransdal Norwegian community. In Vernon County place names like Bohemian Valley, Irish Ridge, German Coulee and Skogdalen are identifiable with these rural ethnic clusters and further demarcate ethnic areas (see Hill 1941, 1942).

Outsiders can soon learn to detect visual clues that differentiate Norwegian areas from other ethnic clusters. For instance, Norwegian farmyards are characteristically neat with numerous freshly painted buildings and well-manicured lawns. The unusual number of building clusters is characteristic of Norwegian farms, a custom which may be associated with older farm patterns found in Norway (Wingate 1975, personal communication 1974; Munch 1947). Occasionally, one sees *rosemaling* (Norwegian flower designs) painted on mailboxes or building fronts to indicate Norwegian affiliations.

Although accurate, these visual distinctions are only the outward aspects of social organization and community boundaries. A more profound boundary lies within the realm of social interactions. Communities, to paraphrase Arensberg's definition, "are the basic units of organization and transmission within a culture providing a minimum of cultural adaptation to nature and the kind of inter-personal relations necessary to assure survival and cultural transmissions to future generations" (Arensberg 1955:1143).

A critical factor in studying ethnic populations is to understand the nature of the social boundaries that form and define the ethnic community. Though these boundaries may have territorial counterparts, such as the Norwegian and German communities, ethnic groups are not merely or necessarily based on the occupation of exclusive territories (Barth 1969). The nature of ethnic continuity, therefore, depends on the maintenance of social and, at times, territorial boundaries. If a group maintains its identity when members interact with others, this both determines and signals membership and exclusion (Barth 1969:15). Boundary maintenance, in effect, reinforces ethnic identity, and is crucial to the continuance of the complex social organization, behaviors and relationships that make up the ethnic community.

Ethnic Identity: The Norwegians

Norwegians in the community have almost always been intensely aware of their own ethnic identity. Sub-ethnic identities, Gudbransdal, Sogning, Flekkefjording, and so on, no doubt stem from regional distinctions (*bygds*) developed in Norway, which was then carried over to the settlement period in America and still continue today in Vernon County. Most locals identify themselves as "Norwegians," according to one informant, "and not Norwegian-American. You're either a Norwegian or you aren't. I don't know what you'd say with only one Norwegian parent." This distinction is crucial since descent is derived equally from both sides of the family among Norwegians. A "full Norwegian" by local definition is also "100% Norwegian," and it helps if both one's mother's and father's families can trace their ancestry back to the immigrants.

Most community members are aware of these degrees of "Norwegianess" since many different families in the community are closely related to each other. The knowledge of one another's genealogy is often well-known. Even if one marries a Norwegian of a different sub-ethnic heritage, which usually means a different community, personal background remains an identifying factor. For a non-Norwegian, the intensity of ethnic identity in the community is sometimes overwhelming. As one participant put it, "Out here among the Norwegians I feel less aware of my German heritage and more aware that I'm a non-Norwegian."

Other Ethnic Groups

Aside from the Norwegians there are Italians, Bohemians (mainly Czechoslovakians), Germans, Yankees (English), Kickapoogian, and a flourishing Amish colony living in Vernon County. The Italians, recognized mainly as Catholics clustered near the Mississippi River, were the least well-known to the Norwegian community on the central prairie. Bohemians living in eastern Vernon County were also known to be Catholics, but most Norwegians in Westby were simply unsure of the ethnicity of that community.

Norwegians in Westby characterized Germans in the area as being exceptional farmers with larger farms and different crops. Unlike Norwegian farmers, the Germans did not usually grow tobacco (a favored cash crop grown primarily among Norwegians, see Ibarra 1976) but they did grow more wheat, barley, and other grains for a cash crop. Cultural differences, dietary preferences (e.g., sauerkraut, potato salad), and church-related customs (e.g., card parties, wedding dances), were the most obvious ethnic variations mentioned by the Norwegians.

People, who are known as "Old Americans" in the county, because of their predominance both numerically and culturally, are the best known among Norwegians. But because of certain unique characteristics about this group, Norwegians have learned to distinguish and sub-divide them into at least two, perhaps three categories: English, Yankee and Kickapoogian. The term "English," is specifically associated with educated professionals (e.g., doctors, lawyers) whose families had emigrated to the county seat of Viroqua from eastern cities on the Atlantic seaboard in the 1800s. Since the term is not used by many, it is unlikely a major distinction among Norwegians, and may be incorporated in the term Yankee.

The terms "Yankee" and "Kickapoogian" are both used by Norwegians to refer to people of Old American background. The terms, however, reflect an important ethnic distinction. The most commonly used term among Norwegians is "Yankee," which is used to identify all English-speaking people who are not Norwegians. Irish, Welsh, Scots and those of British heritage fall into this category and are generally associated with the Yankee ethnic group if their ethnic heritage is unknown or unobservable.

The term "Kickapoogian" holds a totally different, sometimes derogatory, ethnic connotation among Norwegians. In general, it refers to people of Old American heritage, both farmer and townspeople alike, that live along the Kickapoo River and watershed in central Vernon County. Its negative connotation implies socio-economic distinctions not unlike those associated with the term "Hillbilly" given to populations living a backwoods existence in Appalachian areas in the United States (see Caudill 1963)

Finally, members of the Amish colony in Vernon County are viewed by the Norwegians as a strict German religious sect that shuns modern conveniences, electricity and mechanization to live an isolated existence as 19th century farmers according to their religious beliefs.

On the basis of attitudes and inter-ethnic relationships as perceived by the Norwegians, one could formulate a generalized pattern of ethnic status or rank. Excluding the Amish colony, Norwegians view Kickapoogians as having the lowest status and place themselves above them in rank. Germans, Bohemians and Italians carry equal status with Norwegians, though undoubtedly the Norwegians would place themselves slightly above the others. Begrudgingly, Norwegians still feel subordinate to Yankees in the area. But due to their agricultural successes, Norwegians are aware that their farming abilities can match those of the nearby Yankees.

Status, Class and Social Differentiation

The Norwegian Gudbransdal community does not have a stratified social system in terms of the traditional sociological categories of upper, middle and lower classes. According to one rural sociologist, social class can be defined as "groups of people who have like occupations, economic status, prestige and lifestyle, and who consciously recognize that they have a community of interests with others similarly situated" (Slocum 1962:342). According to Slocum, most American farmers do not fit the traditional urban concepts of class stratification (1962:343), although there is reason to believe that in many mixed Yankee communities nearby there is a greater feeling of class stratification (Strickon 1976, personal communication).

But Norwegian communities like Westby characteristically seem to lack a class structure. In Port Haven, Washington, which appears as homogeneously Norwegian as Westby, "a strong egalitarian ethic and stress on individual worth tend to permeate social relations" (Anastasio 1960:13). Thus, instead of exhibiting tight and impenetrable distinctions, Westby, like other rural Norwegian communities, tends to be socially differentiated by individual characteristics. This holds true for making distinctions even between ethnic groups.

It is by a complex system of overlapping and fusing of various characteristics that people differentiate others, and are themselves differentiated. For example, individuals with prominence in the community may not have the same attributes as others of equal prominence. Being wealthy may not in itself bring status or prominence. But a combination of characteristics, such as club membership, occupation, education or ethnic background, may bring prominence to others where having money could not. The permutations are numerous and not always predictable. One may appear to have the qualifications of prominence and high status, but due to some character flaw (e.g., excessive drinking, an uncooperative personality, etc.) the individual may lack high standing in the community, despite his or her occupation or wealth. Within the system of social differentiation it is possible to identify various groups: church, family, business people and professionals, clubs, etc. But many of these groups and their spheres overlap and there is a notable shifting of positions by individuals within them. Thus, the attributes of status, prominence or rank in the community do not create a fixed social structure.

Residents outside of the community can mistake group solidarity and social interactions as a type of class system. One Yankee outsider visualized Westby as class stratified with a certain group of elite business individuals or "Old Guard," forming the upper ruling strata. On closer examination, these individuals were indeed prominent citizens but were not the most influential people in the community. Located in political positions or established business enterprises, the Old Guard was only one of several informal groups whose influence was not as all pervading as the Yankee informant imagined.

There is a serious question as to whether the lack of a class-stratified society is specifically closely associated with Norwegian communities, or whether it is a phenomenon found in rural communities in general. However, observing, interviewing and conversing with people in the community leads one to believe that their claims of an egalitarian, independent society is not a facade many communities present to outsiders. Although people were aware of "differences" among individuals and groups in the community, few were able to give consistent reasons for these differences or even to attribute them to class phenomena.

Perhaps the lack of class stratification may have been an early reaction to the social system at the time of immigration in Norway. Skardal (1974) and Munch (1975) report that one of the central motives for immigration was to escape from an oppressive class system in the home country. The privileged class in Norway consisted of educated professionals, clergy and landed individuals. In America, as Munch points out, much of the controversy in establishing the Lutheran Church centered on the high church that was the embodiment of the upper class system for the early immigrants. Thus, in the New World, immigrants abhorred and rejected measures to establish the hated class system. Despite the establishment of the high church, the institution never became a class-stratified organization among Norwegians in America.

The system of social differentiation found in Westby can be described as a status rank system. The rank system is based on social prestige, ascribed or achieved, and defined as having social value (i.e., social status). Status rank is never permanent. That is, within the assigned status role, individuals are not fixed in their social position but may be socially mobile within the continuum. Hence, they are not rigidly "class" ranked. The status rank and social differentiation systems in Westby are guided and influenced primarily by ethnic cultural patterns. The ethnic and economic continuity of Westby since the 1940s has made it a fairly stable community in terms of its characteristics of social differentiation. If indeed, other rural communities have similar social systems, then I believe that Westby's ethnic dimension has at least helped to keep it from stratifying.

Social differentiation in Westby is divided among a number of characteristics: family prominence, club membership, education, business or profession, church affiliation, wealth, ethnicity, and personal attributes. These, in turn, are shaped by the social organizations of rural farm life: work groups, voluntary groups, social clubs, and other community organizations. In terms of the larger community, ethnicity is one of the major characteristics of social differentiation as well as social organization. Thus, to understand how Norwegian American social organization has shaped American values, one must also understand the dynamics of marriage, kinship and the family in a rural Norwegian community.

The Norwegian Community: Social Organization and Rural Farm Life

As ethnic identity determines the community boundaries, it also influences the inner organization, social activity and other farm-related phenomena among Norwegians. It was not unusual for Norwegian pioneer settlers to give Norwegian names to the various locations in their settlement. But what is unusual is that the Norwegians generated an extensive and complex place-name taxonomy that is still in use today. In many Norwegian American communities, neighborhood names were derived from larger natural features of the landscape, social groupings (i.e., family clusters) and individual farm names, all of which were a means of identifying the activities of the neighborhood (Haugen 1953). The names which referred to specific valleys and ridges tended to define a "loosely organized neighborhood, less extensive than the 'settlement' as a whole" (1953:225).

The Norwegian immigrant custom of naming and nicknaming people and locations has deep roots within the Norwegian culture. It has been well documented that Norwegians had a complex naming system which confused the Yankees when they first arrived (Kimmerle 1941). Unlike the English system where one's offspring carried the patrilineal surname, Norwegians had a confusingly complex system of naming, which often included farm and locality names in Norway. Norwegian immigrants compromised with a consistent surname system in America, but the sources for these family names came from a multitude of patronymics, farm names, nicknames and their permutations (1941:22-26).

Farm names in Norway, for example, were the most common family identification since farms were generally held in the family. But if the family moved away, they did not take the farm name with them (Kimmerle 1941; Munch 1947). In Vernon County, there is some evidence that old farm names are still attached to some families in the community. One Westby citizen generated a list of twelve families with associated farm or nicknames. Other individuals verified that these names were indeed names of previous Norwegian farm owners that had become attached and identified with the present farm owners' family. Although this system is now falling into disuse, farm names are occasionally associated with families, not unlike the old farm name system in Norway.

Rural Neighborhoods

Most Norwegians in the community organize themselves much like the rest of rural America. Social participation patterns revolve around kin and friendship groups that have been subject to change over the years. These changes are due to technological developments in transportation and mass media communications. Informal social participation patterns that involve the social interaction of people on a voluntary basis are commonplace in rural areas (Taylor and Jones 1964). Rural neighborhoods in the Norwegian community, for instance, are like neighborhoods in other rural areas, except that neighborhood interaction patterns in Norwegian townships are also shaped by Norwegian cultural patterns.

The rural neighborhood concept has been well-documented in sociological literature (Slocum 1962; Melvin 1954; Taylor and Jones 1964; Munch and Campbell 1963). A neighborhood, according to Slocum, "can be defined as an interacting group of families and individuals residing in a particular locality, most of whom consider themselves to be members of a distinctive neighborhood group which comprises all or most of the families within a definite and contiguous geographic area" (1960:375). Debate over the concept has centered on the problem of whether or not neighborhoods are meaningful social groups and whether or not to redefine them as locality groups (Munch and Campbell 1963; Slocum and Case 1953).

Observing Norwegian communities in southern Wisconsin, Munch and Campbell (1963) discovered collective units that were recognized as distinctive entities by members and non-members alike. These entities, or "symbolic groups," were determined by ethnic group, "clan" ("family" in the broadest popular sense of the word), and neighborhood (1963:22). "Symbolic group" interaction patterns were categorized by exchange-work, participation in local co-op dairy operations, trade and service center preferences, visiting patterns, church membership and school district affiliation (Munch and Campbell 1963:23).

Among a number of significant conclusions, the authors found that neighborhood interaction patterns varied according to the nature of the association. Exchange-work rings, for example, were composed primarily of adjoining neighborhood farms as a matter of convenience and proximity. But deviations in such neighborhood patterns were often the result of "existing positive and negative social relations derived from collective identifications other than neighborhoods, such as, particularly clan, ethnic group and status level" (Munch and Campbell 1963:30). Ethnic selectivity, therefore, functioned not only on the larger inter-community level, but effectively manifested itself in highly selective cliques within their respective neighborhoods and kin groups, which they tend to call "clans." "Clannish" here does not have the usual anthropological significance but instead means, "to be stand-offish, removed, turned-inward and not really friendly" (Strickon 1976:11). Thus, ethnic group identification and kinship affiliations were the major factors in establishing interaction patterns (Munch and Campbell 1963:30).

Even though local townships contain predominantly Norwegian populations, symbolic group and selective interaction behavior was also evident among established rural neighborhoods. These established neighborhoods often showed up on the Norwegian place name system as topographically determined units or unincorporated communities (e.g., Lovass Ridge, Lindvig Ridge, Rongstad Ridge, Newry, Bloomingdale, Esofea). Local and regional newspapers set aside specific neighborhood news columns in recognition of their existence as cohesive social units.

The solidarity and persistence of such rural neighborhoods is determined by the nature of the "symbolic group" (Munch and Campbell 1963), and interaction such as family and kin relations, farm inheritance patterns, inter- and intra-ethnic marriage patterns or church membership and friendship networks. A number of neighborhood groupings, which have lost much of their significance today, such as threshing groups and Luther Leagues, etc., were at one time the backbone of neighborhood interaction behavior.

Agricultural Work Groups

Threshing groups, a form of exchange-work, were one of the few ethnically mixed voluntary associations within the Norwegian community. Eight to twelve farmers, usually from adjoining farms, would work as a grain harvesting team on each other's farms in the fall season. Memberships were generally continuous and there was a clear understanding of trade work. Silo filling groups and corn-shredding groups were also formed out of threshing groups, and group size depended on the amount of work needed. The advent of new labor-saving farm machinery (e.g., combines, forage harvesters) brought about the decline of these neighborhood groups and increased dependency on agriculturally specialized work and combine teams outside the neighborhood.

Rural Schools

Before the recent consolidation into one large school district, small rural neighborhood school districts were important centers for neighborhood activity and social life. The local school district, numbering around thirty families, was part of the neighborhood regardless of whether one had children or not. All families would gather together for school functions, picnics, and Christmas, Thanksgiving or Halloween programs where gift and card exchanges frequently took place. The school district not only supplemented rural social life, it also determined the school tax and regulated school board elections. It became a meaningful political division within the neighborhood. Although school districts near community boundaries incorporated ethnically mixed areas, certain functions were ethnically selective. Among the Norwegians and Germans, for example, the public schools were used as parochial schools in the summer to teach the Lutheran catechism in the Norwegian or German language, depending on the church.

Rural Social Clubs

As a result of school district activities, a number of social groups and clubs were formed in the neighborhoods. School districts and social clubs are inherently formal organizations, but much of their activities were informal or voluntary in the beginning. Luther Leagues, a forerunner of present day 4H clubs, were always family affairs and closely associated with the church and school district. At least one rural church in the Norwegian community is reported as still having a league during the 1970s. The gradual decline of family participation and the formation of youth oriented 4H clubs at the county level brought an end to the neighborhood Luther Leagues.

Among adult organizations, Ladies Aids, a precursor of the church circles of today, were important functions among rural women. Like church circles, aid groups were primarily occasions for visiting and gossiping among friends, but unlike circles, aid groups were not necessarily tied closely to the church. Each neighborhood had its own Aid that met either in member's homes or neighborhood school buildings.

Homemakers' Clubs are women's groups that have been created and organized at the county level. Although the clubs are intended to be open to anyone interested in homemaking activities, ethnic and rural neighborhood selectivity seems to play a large part in-group membership. In Christiania Township near Westby, for example, one non-Norwegian newcomer was directed by county officials to join a local homemakers club. The club, however, complained, and rejected her on the grounds that she did not fit in with the other members. It was later discovered that the club, which was organized under county extension services, was in fact a closed Norwegian gossip circle whose membership consisted of close neighborhood friends, most of whom were related through kinship.

Club membership within the city of Westby adds another important differentiation in the community and is even subject to a loose system of ranking. Most social activity revolves around membership in one or more of the voluntary associations or clubs found in the community. Nearly everyone belongs to some form of organized group, whether it is church related, a national organization, or a local private club. In Westby, these clubs and organizations demonstrate two important patterns: one, that of rural American culture (e.g., The Lions; Kiwanis; the Rod and Gun Club) and Norwegian immigrant culture (e.g., the Ski [jumping] Club; the Sons of Norway), and two, the extent of social differentiation in the community. Most organizations can be categorized under male and female or service and private association labels. But in Westby, these can be further divided between rural American and Norwegian immigrant distinctions.

Marriage, Kinship and Farm Inheritance

One of the most salient factors among Norwegian rural neighborhoods is the system and pattern of marriage, intermarriage and family-kin relationships. Closely tied with the patterns of farm succession and inheritance, these customs are one of the major forces working for ethnic persistence and Norwegian homogeneity in the community. Ethnic persistence may be related to the degree of intermarriage, that is, non-incestuous intra-family linkages within the ethnic group. "If marriage partners are chosen exclusively, or even predominantly, from the same ethnic group, the mother tongue and various cultural traditions are more likely to be preserved" (Nelson 1960: 45). According to a study by Lowry Nelson in a number of Minnesota counties, the author found that out of eleven ethnic groups analyzed, "A marked preference for in-group marriage was evidenced among people of German and Norwegian descent." (1960:47). The only way to account for such phenomenon was the numerical predominance and intense homogeneity among German and Norwegian farmers in rural Minnesota.

In discussing families and marriage among the Norwegian farmers in Vernon County, there was always one reoccurring phrase, "Everybody is married to everybody. You're afraid to say something bad about someone for fear the person you're talking to may be related to them." The extensiveness of kinship relations in the community may be somewhat exaggerated, but there is some truth to these statements. One community member stated that she had a total of fifty-five first cousins, only a few of whom she had never met. Another Norwegian, who was also interested in his family genealogy, calculated that he was related to at least forty-five different families within the Norwegian community and had not yet completed his search. It became clear in talking with locals that there was an extensive system of overlapping and linked networks of relatives. The value of the family-kin relations cannot be overestimated among Norwegians.

The family and kinship system forms a strong bond among Norwegians, and families of Norwegian descent tend "to be egalitarian in the treatment of members of the same generation" regardless of age or sex, (Anastasio 1960:9). This tendency for generational unity among siblings is extended to cousins as well. In his study of the Norwegian community of Port Haven, Anastasio reports similar kinship characteristics, including the use of special Norwegian terminology to distinguish the unusually close sibling-first cousin relationship (1960:8). The value put on kinship relations, combined with a preference for in-group marriages and unique sibling-cousin relationships, may have some bearing on the nature of intermarriage among rural Norwegians.

Intermarriage in the Westby community is perceived in a number of ways: marriage with a person from a different ethnic group, marriage with a person from a different religious background, or marriage with someone who is a relative or close family relationship. The latter, apparently, was a common occurrence at one time in the neighborhood. Many attribute this proclivity to the tight kindred networks that make up the core of many rural neighborhoods. The attitudes according to one informant, "Were so clannish that marriage outside the Norwegian area or to even a half Norwegian was frowned upon." Since social relationships and interaction were determined and structured by one's kinship relations, marriage to non-Norwegians or outsiders would severely limit one's social network. A number of informants reported instances of second and third cousin marriages among Norwegian families resulting from such endogamous constraints. Though marriages of this nature are rare today, incidences of "double cousin" relationships are still quite common in the community.

"Clan" families, according to local definitions, are families which have exchanged siblings in marriages. Although there was one reported case of a widower marrying his former wife's sister in an established "clan" family relationship, there is no evidence to show that this practice was customary. A clan family would often have been one and the same with a rural neighborhood, which occasionally bore the family name. Since post-nuptial residence was rarely neolocal, (a new location) a number of "clan neighborhoods" were described as clusters of closely interrelated families located within an average radius of three miles. These residence bonds are extremely close. The threat of outsiders breaking them up was so intense that many resorted to playing nasty tricks or ignoring newcomers in an effort to make them leave. In general, many rural Norwegian neighborhoods were, and still are, highly endogamous kin communities.

According to Raitz, Norwegians in Wisconsin have had an eighty-percent in-group marriage rate (1970:48). Data gathered from church and county marriage records and from knowledgeable informants support the hypothesis that rural Norwegians in Vernon County are intensely endogamous, although exact figures in the community are difficult to determine. The data further support local claims that Norwegian endogamy is being eroded by an increasing number of inter-ethnic and inter-religious marriages during the 1970s. Among younger generations, "mixed marriages" today are more frequent, although religion is still more of a barrier than ethnic background. Dating German Lutherans, for example, causes much less consternation today among Norwegian parents than it did in the past.

Incidences of Norwegians marrying Catholics have also increased with apparently little social consequence. Although Catholic marriages occur primarily with outsiders, during the mid-1970s, a Catholic-Lutheran ceremony between locals in the Norwegian Church was considered a milestone in the community. Marriages with German Lutherans occur more frequently, although synodical and perhaps ethnic differences between German and Norwegian Lutheran Churches have been attributed to keeping this frequency quite low. Reasons for German-Norwegian marriages could not be determined concretely. However, Raitz found that in general, Norwegian wives were very popular with all ethnic groups that grew tobacco (1970:48). Locals agreed that German Lutherans residing near the Norwegian community often sought Norwegian women for marriage because they "were considered good cooks, milked cows, had experience with tobacco." As Raitz points out, the most effective way German men learned to grow tobacco was to marry a Norwegian woman who either had tobacco experience or inherited a tobacco allotment (1970:166-176).[1]

Within the community there is an unusual phenomenon peculiar to Norwegian culture and marriage patterns: bachelor and spinster siblings farming the homestead together. Norwegian marriage goals explain this phenomenon in part. As one Minnesota Norwegian put it, the ideal marriage mate among farm families was a Norwegian with an equal or better financial standing. Since Norwegians have generally large families (Marshall 1950), and not every son could inherit the homestead, a number of sons would not have the financial future which a home farm could bring. A good marriage was very important for daughters too, so families would occasionally try to influence, if not arrange "good" marriages for their offspring. Those who could not find such a marriage were said to relegate themselves to bachelorhood or spinsterhood.

Others in the community would argue that isolation or invalid parents caused them not to marry. But in Norway, bachelors and spinsters apparently exist in farm areas also. At the time of farm succession there may be children in the family who had not as yet found a spouse. "Two unmarried brothers may inherit a farm, or a man and his sister; there is little likelihood then that either will later feel free to marry, since a single farm calls for a single household" (Park 1962:420). In Vernon County, there are an unusually large number of unmarried brothers and sisters living and working the home farm together. Being elderly, most have friends and relatives near by. Thus, as in Port Haven, "They are part of a larger kinship group and are not socially isolated" (Anastasio 1960:7). Whether it is a failure to find the right marriage partner, or simply a matter of circumstances, bachelor-spinster households are a phenomenon that holds little stigma in the Norwegian community.

Farm Inheritance

A crucial factor in maintaining Norwegian homogeneity is the ability to keep the farm or home place within one's ethnic group. In a Norwegian culture whose prerequisite is an agricultural life style, the farm holds a great deal of importance. As one perceptive resident pointed out, "Selling the farm into the family or to relatives is good for the farm. It is also good for the community because it tends to stabilize it."

American farmers, like Norwegian farmers, are equally proud if the sons take over the farm. Incentives like wage-share or income sharing agreements, renting to offspring and transfer agreement are just a few of the ways to coax a son to stay on (Nelson 1954:73). Nearly all farmers face the problem of losing their sons to the metropolitan areas, so Norwegians have adapted ways of coping with the situation. Apparently they have been successful since the area is still largely Norwegian and the number of Century Farms (farms owned by the same family for one hundred years) is increasing every year.

Early accounts of Norwegian-Americans warned of the dangers of children leaving their homesteads, but in fact, were more concerned about parents allowing their sons to stay on as renters (Fonkalsrud 1915:91-92). This break with traditional Norwegian patterns was felt to cause undo friction in Norwegian homes where, "Innate craving for a home impels the son to break the old ties." (1915:92)

Unlike the large commercial agri-business farms in America, the classic Norwegian farm, or *gard*, was an inseparable unit of people, animals, house and land. Not unlike a feudal village, the gard was economically self-supporting, had a definite structural-ecological set-up, was cooperative in function and was strongly associated with extended family groups (Munch 1947:356). The gard concept shows strikingly similar patterns with the rural neighborhood "clan families" in Vernon County. The gard farm, however, was essentially a patrilateral stem group or *aett*. Yet it carried a name usually referring to the person who first cleared and settled the gard. This name remained with the gard regardless of turnover. Succession was strictly by primogeniture. If the eldest son did not want the farm, it would be passed to the next eldest and so on. But if the owner wanted to sell, the nearest of kin had the right of preemption, even if the land had already been sold out of the descent group (Munch 1947:360-363). The joint family gard no longer exists in Norway and the pattern did not follow the Norwegians to America. But certain patterns of inheritance did find their way into the community in Vernon County.

According to local farmers, a primogeniture system was an ideal inheritance pattern that was seldom attained in the community. Most acknowledged that middle or youngest sons often took over the farm. Eldest sons were usually forced to seek other farms or job opportunities since fathers were still active in farming. But a number of Norwegian farmers in Vernon County either purchased or helped finance farms near the home place for eldest sons if they were interested. If the father planned to retire, the remaining son would theoretically buy the farm from the father. In most cases this meant paying $1.00 and transferring the deed. The retiring couple could choose to stay on the farm, which many preferred, or face the alternative of living in Westby or Coon Valley, which many did.

In a number of cases, however, parents would transfer farms under certain stipulations which have been called by locals the "Norwegian Deed." One informant reported, "Our deed on this place has a rider that allows my mother to live here as long as she lives and that we will take care of her." The Norwegian Deed was a parental strategy to set up their own social security, but it also created a moral obligation for their children to remain on the farm and keep it in the family. According to Holmes (1944) the legality of the Norwegian Deed has been upheld by the Wisconsin Supreme Court in protecting the rights and interests of parents.

In situations where the father dies before the farm is transferred to one of the sons, a good number of wills have provisions which enable the children to purchase the farm at a very reasonable price. Often the child most interested in remaining to farm the homestead would be specifically designated in the will. All the children are given equal consideration, but not all obviously are interested in farming. Through informal agreements among the heirs, the interested sibling is given the right to purchase or inherit the farm in return for payment to the others. The Norwegian Deed system is still in effect and the farm remains in the family. In instances where there are no heirs or children interested in staying on, relatives are given first choice of purchase.

Some farmers remarked that many of them were unsure whether their families or relatives would want to hold onto the farm after their deaths. These farmers, according to informants, were willing to take an earlier retirement in order to sell the farm to a neighbor, or at least another Norwegian. However, their attempts to keep these farms in the hands of other Norwegians in the community have been threatened since the early 1960s by an increasing number of outside buyers from the metropolitan areas of Chicago or Minneapolis. As local realtors point out, Norwegian farmers have been hard-pressed to sell to locals, or even family members, when extremely high prices are offered by city people looking for isolated recreational farms. The ethnic homogeneity of the community, however, is not in immediate danger. Although exact figures are unavailable, local informants report that over the years a great number of the younger generation have tended to move back into the community after finishing their education or tiring of city life.

"Norwegian-Lutheran-Agriculturalism"[2]

In summary, the family farm is an important part of rural Norwegian identity and value systems. Close ties to the land are intertwined with close familial, community and ethnic associations. Inheritance patterns, Norwegian Deeds, even the structural layout of farms reflect old patterns from the homeland adapted to the rural American environment and lifestyle. In many ways Norwegians have changed little since their ancestors first came to Vernon County. Like their immigrant kinsmen, Norwegian farmers devote their way of life to agriculture, the family and the Lutheran Church (see Legried 1997). Though little has been mentioned here of the Lutheran Church, one can hardly describe Norwegian rural society without considering the influence of its religious tenets. It regulates moral and social values as it segregates along ethnic and religious lines in marriage. The concept, one of intense homogeneity and cultural persistence, has been termed "Norwegian-Lutheran-Agriculturialism" by one former resident, and validated by several local individuals. The term conveys the essential characteristics which make up local Norwegian society (Vogel 1974).

It is a complex relationship that binds the family, the farm, ethnic identity and the rural value system into a unified whole. According to locals, agriculture, for example, is so intertwined with Norwegian mores that farmers feel alienated when they retire to the city. Thus, many retire only to the Norwegian towns of Westby and near by Coon Valley. Friendships and kin-groups are not lost, but only re-allocated into a farm-town perspective. The church, which has become closely associated with the towns, is still the vital force in the Norwegian ethos. Throughout the farmer's life, the city has represented the antithesis of "Norwegianness" and in a farmer-townsman dichotomy, even animosity has been a problem to contend with.

Yet Norwegian-Lutheran-Agriculturalism lives on in a modified form within these market centers and has even thrived in ethnic renaissance. With respect to social structure and organization, ethnic homogeneity is maintained by a relatively exclusive social system dependent on closed networks of inter-family relations, bonded by ethnic and religious affiliation. The solidarity of rural kin groups and the strong intermarriage patterns remain a part of town-life as they have in the rural neighborhoods. Thus, town life is but an extension of the rural Norwegian farm community. Ethnic identity is vivid and seeks outlets in these market centers, as if compensating for the loss of agricultural values. The city of Westby, and its surrounding farm neighborhoods become theaters where Norwegian ethnicity can be viewed in its most intense form.

The Legacy of Egalitarian Ideals

Just as the family farm strengthens rural Norwegian identity, the strength of familial ties is the backbone of Norwegian character. Social activity, projects and hobbies are usually family-oriented and a great deal of time is spent in doing things together as a unit. According to locals, apparently the Norwegian propensity for homogeneity is also evident in patterns of collective behavior. Yet these collective behavioral patterns were not always as readily observable as the egalitarian values noted throughout the social structure of the community.

For example, rather than adopt a rigid class structure, social differentiation among Norwegians in Vernon County was derived from a status rank system of personal attributes that seems flexible and amenable to change. Norwegian farm life is also inter-dependent not only on the strong cultural bonds of kinship and marriage, but also on the social values of cooperative exchange-work between neighbors and community members. The relatively large number of agriculturally oriented cooperative enterprises, thriving in the community today represents the permeability of these values in Norwegian society.

Many locals claim that Norwegians are particularly receptive to the socialistic philosophy of brotherhood and cooperation inherent in these membership-driven associations, or co-ops.

However, co-ops that offer members reduced prices on goods and services have a firm foothold in many ethnic communities throughout the state. The result is that Wisconsin is noted as one of the few states with the largest concentration of co-op enterprises in the country (Ibarra 1976).

The various forms of egalitarianism found in the Norwegian communities of Vernon County ultimately translate into values that elevate the concept of "commonness" into the highest individual attribute one should strive for and achieve. Being "common," according to one Norwegian, describes, "A person who does not reach beyond his level in society. One does not strive for higher status or position of authority openly." (Ibarra 1976:288). Others described it as being humble and open to others. Hypothetically, one could make a lot of money or hold prominent positions or status in the community, but as long as he or she stays Lutheran and follows the necessary expected behavior patterns, they are still considered "common." As an example, persons leaving the community for work or school may still have the attribute of commonness as long as the social prerequisites and cultural conditions are maintained when they return. Thus, social constraints not only tend to reinforce community values, but also tend to function as a leveling mechanism within the Norwegian social system.

Sometimes these social dynamics transfer into larger social systems beyond the community. The best illustration of egalitarianism functioning as a social leveling mechanism is found in the American myth of the ethnic "melting pot." This metaphor came to symbolize the "American Dream" of success for newly arrived immigrants at the turn of the last century. It implied that all ethnic cultures will or should eventually melt into an amalgamation of American culture and values. In principle everyone in a community should be treated equally, and no one should be viewed differently than anyone else. It was assumed that with time, the differences and disagreements should disappear. During the early 20th century, many believed that the best way to achieve this transformation was to encourage ethnic groups to acculturate quickly into the mainstream of an emerging American culture and society.

Rural ethnic groups in the Midwest also valued education as a positive attribute for social status. Despite their reservations towards urban life, many European ethnic groups perceived higher education as facilitating the acculturation process, or at best, that it would benefit their offspring. From these new American values came a concept embedded with egalitarian ideals in which the state and its flagship university take great pride—the "Wisconsin Idea." At its inception 150 years ago, the university strove to implement the civic mission of a public land-grant institution—to build rural democracy and help develop local communities. This mission grew out of the early days of the university, concurrent with the era of European immigration and its egalitarian and communitarian ideals. Thus, it was a time when university research invented breakthrough ideas that offered better agricultural practices to farmers throughout the state and the nation (Nelson and Ibarra 1999). The phrase, "The boundaries of the University are the boundaries of the State," became a common refrain for describing it. To many, this refers to the transfer of research knowledge toward application in state government, businesses, farms, schools, citizens' lives, and now, throughout the world.

Egalitarian ideals, first developed in immigrant communities like Westby, were critical to the growth and development of the university model, but their legacy also tended to encourage academic conformity. Back then, scholars and students were developing relatively new scientific ideas and methodology. Based on a German research model imported to America about that time, scientists were trained to think consistently in a rigorous new scientific context. That made all the difference for changing higher education from the model of small private liberal arts colleges circa the mid-1800s into the research-driven public universities we see today. But there was a price to pay for this growth. The methods of teaching and learning became formulated and highly structured, and despite breakthrough innovations, academic traditions placed greater value on maintaining these structures and ideals than changing them (Nelson and Ibarra 1999).

In contemporary social terms, the legacy of egalitarianism in these forms favors an archetypical color-blind society in which no one is viewed differently. In theory this sounds like a positive goal, but in reality neither the egalitarian ideals nor the American melting pot were ever achieved. Today, images of an ethnic melting pot are being replaced by values that celebrate ethnic or gender differences, not homogenize them. Despite these changes, one can still find Old World ethnic community values advocating that success is dependent upon becoming an "American." To culturally adapt and become accepted by mainstream society has been perceived throughout the 20th century as a primary pathway toward advancement and success. In light of rapidly increasing technological and demographic changes in the country today, those values and strategies are becoming harder to defend.

One challenge before us is to determine whether or not the cultural legacy of Mid-American values will serve this nation well into the next millennium. Quite simply, it is a question of choosing to build a society that is "color-blind" or "color-full." In his concluding remarks, Historian, William Cronon (n.d.) expressed the issue succinctly, "Much of the challenge of communitarianism is to reinvent the 'we' that defines our sense of community to make room for the many people who have not felt themselves a part of that American 'we." This too is a legacy of Norwegian American farm communities in the upper Midwest.

Notes

1. An important cash crop for Norwegians in Wisconsin, and specifically Vernon County, is Type 55 tobacco used for cigar wrappers and chewing tobacco. This labor-intensive crop was well suited for the large Norwegian families in the late 1800s and was soon adopted into the seasonal cycles of their small dairy farms as a reliable source of extra income. When the Great Depression hit Wisconsin farm communities in the 1930s, the federal government began restricting tobacco farming by assigning acreage allotments to only those farms with existing plots in an attempt to stave off further economic disaster. Because Norwegians in Wisconsin almost exclusively grew tobacco, it immediately became identified as an ethnic crop. Consequently, the value of farms with tobacco allotments and the labor-value of individuals with expertise in growing it rose with the steadily increasing price of tobacco. Over time, a tobacco-dairy strategy emerged that helped keep small family farms intact while raising the premium on access to tobacco plots (see Ibarra and Strickon 1989).

2. I first encountered the term in an unpublished paper by an undergraduate at the University of Wisconsin-Janesville. The author was originally from the city of Cashton near Westby (Vogel 1974).

References

Anastasio, Angelo. 1960. Port Haven: A Changing Northwestern Community. Washington Agricultural Experiment Station, Bulletin 616, Pullman: Washington State University.

Arensberg, Conrad M. 1954. The Community Study Method. *The American Journal of Sociology* 60:109-124.

———. 1955. American Communities. *American Anthropologist* 57:1143-1162.

Barth, Fredrik, ed. 1969. *Ethnic Groups and Boundaries.* Boston: Little Brown and Company.

Caudill, Harry M. 1963. *Night Comes to the Cumberlands: A Biography of a Depressed Area.* Boston: Little Brown and Company.

Cronon, William. n.d. Planning Another Century of Good Government: The Wisconsin Idea in the Twenty-First Century. Remarks Before the Wisconsin SAVE Commission (Study of Administrative Value and Efficiency), University of Wisconsin-Madison, unpublished MS.

Fonkalsrud, Alfred O. in collaboration with Beatrice Stevenson. 1915. *The Scandinavian-American.* Minneapolis: K.C. Holter Publishing Company.

Haugen, Einar. 1953. *The Norwegian Language in America: A Study in Bilingual Behavior* (2 Volumes.), Philadelphia: University of Pennsylvania Press.

Hill, George W. 1941. The Use of the Culture-Area Concept in Social Research. *American Journal of Sociology*, No. 1, 47:39-47.

———. 1942 Wisconsin's Changing Population. *Science Inquiry*, Publication IX, No. 2642, General Series No. 2426, Madison: Bulletin of the University of Wisconsin.

Holmes, Fred L. 1944. [1974] *Old World Wisconsin: Around Europe in the Badger State.* Madison: Wisconsin House, Ltd.

Ibarra, Robert A. 1976. Ethnicity Genuine and Spurious: A Study of A Norwegian Community In Rural Wisconsin. Ph.D. dissertation, University of Wisconsin-Madison.

Ibarra, Robert A. and Arnold Strickon. 1989. The Norwegian-American Dairy Tobacco Strategy in Southwestern Wisconsin. *Norwegian American Studies*, 32:3-30.

Kimmerle, Marjorie M. 1941. Norwegian-American Surnames. Norwegian-American Studies and Records, Norwegian-American Historical Association, 12:1-32.

Legreid, Ann Marie. 1997. Community Building, Conflict, and Change: Geographic Perspectives on the Norwegian-American Experience in Frontier Wisconsin. In *Wisconsin Land and Life*, Robert C. Ostergren and Thomas R. Vale, eds. Pp. 300-319. Madison: University of Wisconsin Press.

Marshall, Douglas G. 1950. The Decline in Farm Family Fertility and Its Relationship to Nationality and Religious Background. *Rural Sociology*, No. 1, 15:42-49.

Melvin, Bruce L. 1954. The Rural Neighborhood Concept. *Rural Sociology*, No. 4, 19:371-376.

Munch, Peter A. 1947. GARD: The Norwegian Farm. *Rural Sociology*, Vol. 12:356-357.

———. 1975. Social Conflict in Pioneer Communities of the Middle West: Norwegians in Wisconsin During the Mid-Nineteenth Century. Paper presented at the Annual Meeting of the Midwest Sociological Society, Chicago, April 9.

Munch, Peter A. and Robert B. Campbell. 1963. Interaction and Collective Identification in a Rural Locality. *Rural Sociology*, No. 1, 28:18-34.

Nelson, Helene and Robert A. Ibarra. 1999. Forward Wisconsin: Demographic Changes and Wisconsin Choices. The La Follette Institute's Sesquicentennial Paper Series, July1999, University of Wisconsin-Madison.

Nelson, Lowry. 1954. *American Farm Life.* Cambridge: Harvard University Press.

———. 1960. *The Minnesota Community: Country and Town in Transition.* Minneapolis: University of Minnesota Press.

Park, George K. 1962. Sons and Lovers: Characterological Requisites of the Roles in a Peasant Society. *Ethnology,* 4:412-425.

Raitz, Karl B. 1970. The Location of Tobacco Production in Wisconsin. Ph.D. dissertation, University of Minnesota.

Skardal, Dorothy Burton. 1974. *The Divided Heart: Scandinavian Immigrant Experience through Literary Sources.* Oslo, Norway, Universitetsforlaget.

Slocum, Walter L. 1962. *Agricultural Sociology: A Study of Sociological Aspects of American Farm Life.* New York: Harper and Brothers.

Slocum, Walter L. and Herman M. Case. 1953. Are Neighborhoods Meaningful Social Groups Throughout Rural America? *Rural Sociology,* No.1,18:52-59.

Strickon, Arnold. 1975. Ethnicity and Social Class in Rural Wisconsin. Paper presented at the Annual Meeting of the American Anthropological Association, San Francisco, December.

———. 1976. The Structure of Ethnicity: Ethnic Boundaries and the Boundaries of Ethnicity. Paper presented at the Annual Meeting of the Central States Sociological Association, Quebec, May.

Strickon, Arnold and Robert A. Ibarra. 1983. The Changing Dynamics of Ethnicity: Norwegians and Tobacco in Wisconsin. *Journal of Ethnic and Racial Studies,* No. 2, 6:174-197.

Taylor, Lee M. and Arthur R. Jones. 1964. *Rural Life and Urbanized Society.* New York: Oxford University Press.

Vogel, Lois. 1974. A Generation Study of a Norwegian Family. University of Wisconsin-Janesville, unpublished MS.

Wingate, Robert G. 1975. *Settlement Patterns in LaCrosse County Wisconsin, 1850-1875.* Ph.D. dissertation, University of Minnesota.

CHAPTER 12

The Role of Kinship in the Economic Activities of the Chinese in the Philippines

Bernard P. Wong

Introduction

Kinship plays an important role in the entrepreneurial activities of the Overseas Chinese in general, and in the Philippine Chinese in particular. This paper is dedicated to an examination of the relationship between entrepreneurship and kinship. Of this particular group, the term "entrepreneur" in this paper denotes a person who exercises wholly or partly the functions of 1) initiating, maintaining or aggrandizing a profit-oriented business unit for the production or the distribution of economic goods and services and 2) bearing the risks of its operation (Schumpeter 1934; Greenfield, Strickon and Aubey 1979; Wadinger, Aldrich and Ward 1990).

The term 'kinship' in this paper denotes the relations between 'kin' i.e., persons related by real, putative or fictive consanguinity (R. Fox 1984). Thus, in dealing with kinship, we must take into consideration the three concentric circles of relatives in Chinese life: *family, kin* and *lineage*. These three circles are recruited on the basis of blood ties and affinal ties. The term "family" is used in this paper in accordance with the current Chinese concept of the family (*Chia* in Chinese) which refers to the economic family, i.e., a unit consisting of members related to each other by blood, marriage, or adoption, and having a common budget or common property (Lang 1985; Baker 1980). The *kin* (*chin-chi* in Chinese) of the Chinese are those relatives for whom one has to wear a symbol of mourning, such as a black ribbon during the mourning cycles. Kinsmen are divided into three groups: paternal relatives, maternal relatives and the relatives of the wife. The paternal relatives includes all brothers and their wives; sisters; paternal uncles and their wives, cousins and their wives. This group of paternal kinsmen constitutes the traditional "extended family." Historically, many stayed under one roof. This is particularly the case among the rich (Hsu 1971; 1981). The maternal relatives include only one's grandparents, uncles, aunts and first cousins. The wife's relatives are her parents, grandparents, uncles, sisters and brothers. The lineage is an exogamous group of the same surname, whose members were related to one another by descent to a traceable common ancestor. In the provinces of Guangdong and Fujian, it is now uncommon to have a single lineage inhabiting a village. Some villages are composed of multi-lineages, while others are single-surname villages, i.e., single lineage villages (Freedman 1966).

In the Overseas Chinese communities, the concept of clan is quite important (Wong 1998). A Chinese clan is composed of members who are supposedly related to each other by blood but whose consanguineal descent, however, cannot be demonstrated. Members of a clan assume that they are related to each other by descent from a common ancestor. Thus, a Wang may assume that he is related to another Wang and call each other as 'clan brothers.' They *pretend* that they are descendents of the common ancestor Wang. This assumed consanquinity, as will be demonstrated in this paper, is significant in the Philippine Chinese community.

Lineage and clans are also ritual groups. Ancestor worship in pre-revolutionary China (before 1949) was conducted collectively. Both in the Philippines and China, the lineage groups make use of their descent from a common ancestor as a principle to render political and economic help. Politically, the lineage management in pre-1949 China had the obligation to defend the lineage interest and to settle conflicts between the different families. Economically, the lineage members were obligated to favor each other in all economic endeavors: employment, loans, etc. Clan mimics lineage, except that there is no natural intimacy between the members. Family, kin and lineage were the three circles of relatives that played important roles in the economic pursuits of the Chinese in traditional China. The relations within the family are the most intimate; in the kin rather external and in the lineage most external. The relations within the clan are even more artificial and were to be cultivated.

The central problem of this paper is: What is the relationship between entrepreneurship and Chinese kinship? It is frequently asserted in the literature on economic development that kinship ties which include a big circle of relatives and the accompanying obligations and constraints will be detrimental to entrepreneurial activities. This view implies that influences of kinship ties on economic development are necessarily inhibiting. On the other hand, some economists and anthropologists contend that economic factors can harm kinship. They argue that capitalistic development and the urban economy cause the demise of kinship. This one-sided assertion of the economy over kinship or vice versa is not a realistic proposition. The relationship between kinship and entrepreneurship is a reciprocal one, both are mutually influencing each other. The present study is set forth to investigate the interactive aspect of kinship and entrepreneurship. It attempts to show the contribution of kinship to the modern economy of the Chinese in the Philippines. Family members, kinsmen, lineage and clan members bring numerous advantages to the Chinese entrepreneurs. In particular, the present study asks three questions:

1. What are the functions of the Chinese family and kinship in the entrepreneurial activities of the Chinese in the Philippines?
2. What is the changed nature of the Chinese kinship organization in the Philippines?
3. What are the factors contributing to the success of the Chinese entrepreneurs in the Philippines?

In analyzing the activities of the Chinese entrepreneurs in the Philippines, it is imperative to have a comprehensive knowledge about their historical backgrounds, economic environment and occupational role (Glade 1967; Aubey 1969; Wong 1988). This knowledge is further necessary for an understanding of their success. In the next section is a brief review of the historical background and the opportunity structure of the Chinese in the Philippines.

Historical Background of Chinese Entrepreneurs in the Philippines

The total number of the Chinese in the Philippines is estimated to be around one million, which is about 2 percent of the country's total population. Half of the Chinese population live in Metro Manila.

The Chinese in the Philippines originally migrated from the Fujian and Guangdong provinces of China (T. Chen 1940; Purcell 1951). However, Hokkienese or Fujianese outnumber the Cantonese from Guangdong at a ratio of 9:1. The Chinese presence in the Philippines is traceable to the Spanish colonial period. Thus the development of the Chinese community was shaped by Spanish colonialism. The Philippine Chinese, in fact, is a perfect example of how public policies could affect the social formation and identity of an ethnic group.

Much of the present day anti-Chinese feelings in the Philippines could be understood in historical context (C. Chen 1962). The colonial legacy of Spain was responsible for the development of the community as well as the inter-ethnic relations between the Chinese and the Filipinos. In 1571, Spanish colonizers occupied the area around Manila and organized Manila into a city and the capital of the Philippines (Alip 1959). The Spanish colonizers needed the Chinese as laborers, artisans and traders. Further, the Spanish merchant class began utilizing the Chinese traders for their commercial enterprises. Encouraged by the fair treatment of the Spanish government and pressed by economic difficulties at home, the Chinese flocked to the Philippines. During the early years of the Spanish era, the Chinese were allowed to settle freely in Manila and its suburbs (Alip 1959). The Chinese set up bakeries, foundries, repair shops, laundry houses and tailoring stores (Felix 1966). They were also traders and suppliers for the Spaniards. However, in order to control the Chinese, in 1584 the Spanish colonizers set up the first Chinese quarters, *parian*, in Manila (Liao 1964). It was a buffer zone between the Spaniards and the natives. All the Chinese were required to live in the *Parian* (Settlement) which was ruled by a Spanish *alcademayer* (Liao1964:23). This was the beginning of the Chinatown in Manila and was also the start of antagonism between the Chinese, the Spaniards and the Filipinos (Guerrero 1966).

1. The Formation of the Chinese Community by Transnational Power: Colonialism and Nationalism

The Spanish Era 1571–1898

Between 1854 and 1762, there were four incidents of the Spanish colonialists massacre of the Chinese ethnic population (Wu 1959; Santamaria 1966; Liao 1964). The reasons for the massacres were both economic and political. The Chinese were seen to have posed a constant political and economic threat to the small Spanish colonial administration, whose control of the Philippines was often quite weak. There was also the fear the Chinese Empire would interfere with the affairs of the colony. Any unusual activities related to the Chinese were viewed with suspicions. In 1574, the first incident occurred when Lim-Ah-Hong, a Chinese pirate, arrived with an expedition of 62 war junks, 2000 soldiers, 2000 seamen, 1500 women and artisans as well as a large supply of seeds, tools and domestic animals. Lim began harassing the Spaniards in 1574 (Liao 1964:2). Historians believed that he had come in search of a kingdom and intended to expel the Spaniards from the Philippines. This invasion was repelled but at great cost to the Spanish. In 1603, three mandarins came from China to investigate Chin San (mountains of Gold) in Cavite (Liao 1964:25). They found none and sailed for home but the visit left the Spaniards suspicious. Their activities were considered hostile and were interpreted as espionage activities against the city's defenses. On October 3, 1603, the Spanish government initiated its first massacre. With the cooperation of the Filipinos, the Spanish massacred more than 23,000 Chinese in the years of 1639, 1662 and 1792 (Liao 1964; Wickberg 1965; Lynn Pan 1996). The seeds of antagonism between the Chinese and the Filipinos were sown during these years and as a result, thousand of Chinese were expelled from the Philippines.

Toward the end of the Spanish Era, Filipino nationalism was in fermentation. A nationalistic movement was generated by Filipino intellectuals in the 1880s. Mostly trained in the European tradition, they demanded the expulsion of all aliens, including the Chinese. By the end of this era, the Chinese were not only viewed with suspicion because they were traders and "infidels" by their colonial administration, they were also viewed as non-citizens, non-natives and non-patriots of the Philippines. During the end of Spanish Era, there was a stratum of well-established Chinese *mestizos* (offsprings of marriages between the Chinese and the natives) which was well accepted and distinguishable from the Chinese immigrants (Wickberg 1964).

American Era: 1898–1946

During the American Era, the new colonial administration from the United States conveniently applied their American laws to deal with the Chinese in the Philippines. These included the "Chinese Exclusion Act" of 1882 and the "Chinese Expulsion Act" of 1902, enacted in the United States (Coller 1960:49). These laws provided for the exclusion of all Chinese except for students, teachers, clergymen, traders, and dependents of resident Chinese. So, in actuality, the only ones who were really excluded were the unskilled laborers. The application of the Expulsion Act had two significant impacts on the community. The first was the formation of a relatively pure mercantile community due to the exclusion of a massive influx of unskilled labor (Amyot 1973). The second result was the establishment of a community that was homogeneous in linguistic and regional composition since the dependents of the residents had priority rights to enter the country (Weightman 1964:91). The present population of the Chinese community in the Philippines is still very homogeneous. In terms of origin, they are either from Fujian or Guangdong; in terms of occupation, they are mostly merchants. They are the entrepreneurs of Philippine society. However, many of their descendants tend to be highly educated professionals.

During the American era (1898-1946), the Chinese continued to fill the needs of the expanding economy by maintaining or initiating profit-oriented business units for the production of economic goods and services. Most of the Chinese were merchants or owners of bakeries, department stores, grocery stores, restaurants and repair shops. Some had branched out into other fields: mining, metal manufacturing, sugar processing and lumbering (Castillo 1964).

The Republican Revolution of 1911 in the homeland of the Chinese also played a role in the social formation of the ethnic community. There was growing Chinese nationalism as a result of the revolution in China. Nationalistic Chinese schools began to teach the superiority of Chinese culture and tried to instill loyalty to China among the Overseas Chinese in the Philippines (Applaton 1960).

After the independence of the country, Philippine nationalism came into play. It followed the policy of "Filipino first." There were legislation and judicial rulings, which were adverse to the Chinese. According to the Philippine constitution, no alien, except for Americans, could buy agricultural land, mineral claims, or timber rights. In 1949, the Philippine government began to make Chinese naturalization difficult, lengthy and ultimately so expensive that only the wealthy Chinese could be eligible. In 1950 (Republican Act No. 1180), the Government forbade the Chinese from engaging in retail trade. They were not allowed to participate in the exploitation of the country's natural resources either. There has been restriction of dollar allocation for the Chinese importers. The government favored the Filipino retailers over the Chinese by the establishment of NAMARCO (National Marketing Corporation), an agency to procure, purchase, and distribute commodities at reasonable prices to Filipino retailers (Castillo1964:173). The economic environment surrounding the Chinese from the 1940s to 1970s had not been a friendly one. Paradoxically enough, it was during those years that the Chinese attained high economic success in the Philippines (Castillo 1964). During those years of national building, the Philippines not only needed skilled laborers for many services essential to daily living, but also the participation of the Chinese entrepreneurs in production and manufacturing industries. According to many of my informants and written sources, the prohibition against the Chinese from participating in retail trade actually propelled them into some other lucrative businesses, namely, manufacturing and production activities. There has been great demand in the food processing business, automobile assembly plants, textile plants, tobacco and garment manufacture, steel mills, banking, insurance and transportation sectors. Some of the Chinese have become quite wealthy. This was also a source of envy among the natives. Many Filipino kidnappers target the Chinese as their victims. There is this pervasive kind of uneasiness between the natives and the Chinese. Colonialism, nationalism and class relations have influenced the nature of ethnic relations (Tan 1988; McPhelin 1966)). In the past, they were viewed as the "infidels," "the aliens" and "exploiters of the Philippine economy." Today, they are seen as "rich" businessmen who can afford and are willing to pay ransom to kidnappers

2. Naturalization Laws and the Chinese in the Philippines

The Chinese ethnic identity has undergone drastic changes since the 1970s. Today, 90 percent of the Chinese in the Philippines are citizens. Before 1975, very few qualified for citizenship. The reason for this progress in civil equality for the Chinese was President E. Marcos' change in naturalization policies on the eve of his trip to China. By 1975—before his visit to China—Marcos had granted amnesty and made naturalization possible for the Chinese in the

Philippines, so that it would not be a troublesome issue during his trip. Thus due to the relaxed naturalization laws, the majority of the Philippines Chinese took advantage of the new climate of cooperation. It was a political move to prevent the Chinese from falling under the influence of the PRC. Furthermore, before 1975, no ownership of land was allowed by Chinese nationals in the Philippines. However, after 1975, the ownership of land has become possible—due to citizenship status.

The change of "Naturalization Laws" also led to a change in business activities and the political scenery. First, there was the switch in the recognition of Taiwan over China. Second, there was the Filipinization of all Chinese schools. Third, there was the change in the naturalization process for the Chinese. The last one was highly significant as local-born Chinese could obtain citizenship. The descendants of citizens are also recognized as citizens. In general, the majority of the Chinese could apply and become citizens of the Philippines. According to the law, the Chinese are recognized as equal to other native groups in the Philippines. As citizens, they are entitled to have the same civil and economic rights. This has a beneficial effect for the Chinese in their participation in the global economy. As an example, in a bid for the purchase of the prestigious Manila Hotel, the Chinese-Filipinos made the same offer as that of the Malaysian Chinese. Using their citizenship as a leverage, they were able to secure the purchase and rebuff the foreigners' competition. This is a case in point of how the nationalistic laws of the Philippines worked in their favor.

As citizens of the Philippines, the Chinese can now enter all trades and participate in all economic activities. In fact, recently, the so-called "Seven Taipans" of the Philippines (Lucio Tan, John Gokongwei, Henry Sy, Young Kong Yan, Gotesco, Gobenhuy, Yao Ka Pho) proposed to the government to rebuild the congested International Manila Airport. The Seven Taipans are well-known entrepreneurs in the Philippines who are active in international trade and participate enthusiastically in the global economy. In addition to commerce, the Philippine Chinese engage in restaurants, banking, insurance, transportation, mining, electronic and garment manufacturing, food and tobacco processing.

It is said that 85 percent of the Philippine economy is controlled by 2 percent of the population. Will this invite any backlash? According to my informants in the Philippines, the Chinese in the Philippines today are integrated to a greater degree than the Chinese in other Asian countries. It is therefore unlikely that there will be any anti-Chinese riots like those found in Indonesia. However, on the negative side, the Chinese are often targets for Philippine kidnappers. Reasons for their becoming targets is attributed to social inequality and the conspicuous consumption of the Chinese. Their wealth is the object of envy. Hence, experts argue that it is more a "class" rather than "ethnic" phenomenon. However, some informants argue that rich or well-to-do natives are targets as well. It is not just the ethnic Chinese who are targeted.

3. Contributions of the Philippine Chinese to the Economy of the Philippines

The Philippine Chinese use their connections with China, Taiwan, Hong Kong and other overseas Chinese communities to facilitate international trade. They are important importers of products from the United States, Japan and Europe. They are manufacturers of clothing for domestic and international markets. American cars and Japanese electronic goods are often produced in factories run by the Philippine Chinese. Many of the mega shopping malls and merchandise chain stores with items produced all over the worlds are owned and operated by Chinese Filipinos. Thus they play an indispensable role in the globalization of the economy.

In this history of the Chinese entrepreneurs in the Philippines, we have seen the high adaptability of these businessmen to the economic niche in the Philippines. This ability to make use of opportunities in the Philippines brings them great financial success. As early as 1609, the Spanish intelligentsia acknowledged the value of the Chinese contribution to the economic life of the Philippines. Antonio de Morga, a jurist and historian, wrote in 1609:

> They are excellent workmen, and skillful in all arts and trade. It is true that the colony cannot exist without the Chinese as they are workers in all trades and business and very industrious and worked for small wages (In: Liao 1964:31).

Another historian, Juan de la Concepcion wrote at the end of the 18th century, "without the trade and commerce of the Chinese these dominions could not have subsisted" (In Liao 1964:31). In 1900 the Philippine Commission had this to say:

> They (the Chinese) succeeded everywhere in obtaining a monopoly of wholesale and retail trade, becoming, by the unit of purpose which they possess, the proprietors of mechanical arts and trades in the country. They lend each other cooperative aid, and all work together for the same end, thus forming a vast commercial society with which it is impossible for other merchants, who work separately, to compete (Report of the Philippine Commission 1900 I:158).

Amyot (1973) found virtually no poverty in the Manila Chinese population. The majority of the Filipinos today think that the Chinese are well-off and that they control the Philippine economy. Why are they so successful? Is this due to ethnic solidarity in a minority situation? Analyzing the economic behavior of the Chinese entrepreneurs, we shall soon discover that the success of the Chinese is due to a complex interweaving of several factors. Kinship is one of them. The Philippine Chinese adaptability mechanism will also be revealed in this study. The economic behavior of the Chinese will be examined in terms of the role of family, kinship, clanship, friendship and the community's collective efforts.

The Role of Family in the Entrepreneurial Pursuit

In the homelands of the Chinese, kinship was structured along the lines of land ownership. Only family and lineage were able to own land. A kin group was mainly a mourning circle and owned no common property. Due to the change of environment, the Chinese kinship system is modified in the Philippines. The urban setting, the capitalistic economy, and the minority situation do not permit transplantation of the Chinese kinship system without changes. Significant changes are found on the level of the lineage rather than on the level of the family.

International migration made the transplantation of lineage impossible. First, a lineage group is too large to migrate together. Second, the life of an immigrant is such that it is impossible for a lone immigrant in a strange place to economically support a large collection of lineage members. However, the family is still the most basic economic unit among the Philippine Chinese. Why is family important for the entrepreneurial activities of the Chinese? The answer is simple. It maximizes **gain**. The Chinese family firm has several major contributions to the success of Chinese business activity: generating the maximal use of liquid resources, providing efficient training for family members and encouraging the spirit of risk taking and frugality among the members. A family owns common property under the name of the family head who is usually the father or oldest effect male member of the family. The resources of the family are no longer land alone; they are mainly capital. In addition to the three types of traditional families: nuclear, stem and residential extended family, there exists a new type—the non-residential extended family.

Co-existing with the four types of Chinese families, there are four types of Chinese family firms. The smallest Chinese family firm is that run by a conjugal or nuclear family which is composed of a husband, wife, and their unmarried children, occupying a single residence. It is not uncommon to find the residence at the back of the shop or on the floors above. In the Binondo district of Manila and many small towns in the Philippines, one can find this kind of firm family. The second type of Chinese family firm is that run by the stem family, composed of two conjugal families, that of the father and one of his married sons, usually the eldest. The stem family occupies a single household in which the eldest son marries and continues to live with the parents, while the other sons and daughters marry and leave the family unit. The father assists those sons who marry out of the household in establishing new, independent households. In some instances, these sons will have their own individual small business firms established for them by their father. In most of the cases, these sons will be assisting the father and the eldest brother to run the family firm. Examples of this kind of firm are the Equitable Banking Corp. of Lu Do & Lu Ym, and the China Banking Corp. run by the Go Family and his son (Yoshihara 1988:186-187).

The third type of family firm is that run by the residential extended family. The residential extended family is that of the classical Chinese patrilineal, patrilocal and patriarchal family occupying what is known in Manila as the "big house" type of residence. They normally live in a compound in cities like Manila, Quezon City, Davao, Iloilo, and Bacolod. This type of family includes a father and a mother, all their sons, their unmarried daughters, their sons's wives and children, the sons of their sons, and so on, for as many generations as possible. In traditional China, married daughters normally moved out of their father's household. In the Philippines, married daughters with their families may also live in the father's big house. This reflects a change in the patrilineal kinship ideology and patrilocal residence of traditional China.

The fourth type of family firm is that run by the non-residential extended family. The composition of the family is the same as that of the residential joint, or extended family. Although the members of the extended family have their individual households, kinship ties are not broken and they still function as a family unit. The individual residences are usually in the same section of the city and are near each other. In some cases, these households are scattered in the city mainly due to the impossibility of acquiring satisfactory housing. Recently, some of these non-residential extended families have become globalized, having members of the families living in different parts of the world participating in the new global economy (Appadurai 1996; Basch, Glick and Blanc 1994; Wong 1992, 1998; Ong and Nonini 1997). They do so because of the globalized nature of their family business. Thus, for instance, a family may have an import-export business in the U.S. and the Philippines. It is convenient to have some family members living in the two countries to oversee their business.

The third and fourth types of Chinese family businesses are sometimes so big that they do not own all the business. Nevertheless, the family has a substantial share and administers the business in a significant way. Examples of such firms are: Yutivo Sons Hardware Co., Cham Samco and Sons, Inc., La Perla Cigar and Cigarette Factory, Inc. and Philippine Blooming Mills.

The above description of the four types of family firms with their corresponding family types is a synopsis of the general situation. There are some firms that do not fall into the above categories. For example, Austin Hardware is run by an uncle and nephew. The nephew owns nearly the whole firm, while the uncle assists and owns a portion of the business. Some firms were run by brothers like the trading company of Ang Tuan Kai & Co (Yoshihara 1988:184). However, these variations are only individual cases and by nature, they cannot be put into any typological scheme. What should be remembered here is that the family, whether they be nuclear, stem or extended families, play an important part in the entrepreneurial activities of the Chinese in the Philippines. Amyot (1973), Reynolds (1963, 1966), Weightman (1964), Yoshihara (1988), Redding (1990) and Brown (1996) have pointed out that most of the Chinese firms started as family concerns.

The foundation of the Chinese family firm is usually the conjugal or nuclear family. The decision-maker is the head of the household. As the founder's family expanded, the firm also often grew into a large corporation which remained in the family. At times, uncles and nephews may be recruited from China to assist the family enterprises (Palanca 1995) Thus, the economic institution of the Philippine Chinese is shaped by their *Chia* or household (Brown 1996; Palanca 1995; Weightman 1964).

1. Family Firm as Training Center

Most of the Chinese families are effective in enculturating the importance of the following values to the young generation: *filial piety (shau—respect and obligation toward the parents)* and the family firm as a *means for survival*. Further, Chinese without Philippine citizenship were barred from many professions by the Philippine Laws. Chinese nationals were not allowed to practice law, medicine and engineering. A person born of Chinese parentage is always Chinese, even though he may be a fourth-generation Chinese born in the Philippines. Philippine citizenship is based on *Jus Sanguinis*, or Law of Blood, which limits the possibility for the Chinese to become Filipino citizens (Espina 1957). This situation was changed in the 1980s by President Marcos, but legal citizenship does not necessarily mean cultural citizenship. Many Chinese are now legally citizens of the Philippines but are still not accepted as full-fledged members of

Philippine society. This is exemplified by discrimination as well as the kidnapping of Filipinos of Chinese descent. Chinese children learn very quickly that money is particularly important for the survival of the Chinese in Philippine society. They are told to work hard to accumulate money and often the only avenue to accumulate wealth is via the family firm. The hostility of the environment and the traditional emphasis on filial piety have compelled Chinese teenagers to work in the family firm during their spare time. Furthermore, the family firm is successful in transmitting the Chinese values of filial piety and hard work, as well as being a source of knowledge, often trade secrets, special information relating to dealing with government officials and outsiders or insider knowledge of the Chinese business culture. This kind of invaluable information is transmitted in the informal atmosphere of the firm, over dining table conversations or sometimes by whispering to each other. Children learn about survival and business information within the confines of the family.

The family firm is also a school for transmission of basic business skills such as accounting, skills in dealing with customers and practical know-how of the family trade. The relationship between the parent and children in the Chinese firms could be understood in terms of the transactional behavior model advanced by Fredrik Barth (1960). In the environment of the family firm, transactional behavior between the father and sons begins as early as when the young children can carry out chores in the firm. The father is constantly making *prestations* or trust in the son's relationship to him. The children receive no payment, their rewards are the words of praise from the father or the confidence shown on the part of the father. By the time they are in college, the sons are entrusted to handle business matters that are of real importance. For example, one son may be sent on a business trip to check a branch shop in Davao (a city in Visayas). One of the sons may be sent to the wholesaler to negotiate some business contracts, while another will be sent to bring gifts to some *compadre* (god-father). Thus the system of *Compadrazgo* (Mintz and Wolf 1950) plays also an important role among the Philippine Chinese.

Occasionally, the family head will send his sons abroad for special training. But the sons are expected to reciprocate the *prestation* of their father by returning to the family firm to apply their expertise as well as by working harder to reciprocate the trust shown by the father. The transactional behavior between father and sons in the Chinese family firm is similar to that in the African family firms described by Benedict (1968). If the sons fail to come back, they will be considered to be lacking in *filial piety*. They are considered disobedient and disrespectful not only to the father but also to their ancestors. They cause the loss of "face" of the family (or the loss of family honor). Further, failing to return also brings injury to the family's reputation. For the outsiders or relatives, it could be an indication of conflict between father and sons and the failure of the family education. Usually, a son will find that these strong family ties and family value bring him back. Many times the son will succeed to the family business, even though his inclination is not in this line. He makes it a point of *filial piety* to continue the family business, not to allow the hard work of several generations to go to waste.

Most of the Chinese children receive their business initiation within the family firm environment. However, in the modern-day Philippines, many families also send their children to business schools to receive additional training. This is particularly so in the large family-managed corporations.

One of my informants, Mr. Y., started to work with his father informally when he was still a teenager. He said that he worked formally in the firm since the age of twenty-two, after graduating from college. All four brothers cooperating in the business have now become independent and occupy separate residences. It is no longer one family under one roof. But the business continues as a family firm. The firm is owned, according to the Chinese tradition, under Y's name, because he is the eldest son. All the brothers finished their college training and knew the business very well. After the death of the father, the brothers decided to live in separate households. However, there was never any intention of dividing the family firm. A younger brother acts as manager; he is the most capable one because of his experience and capacity for work. He makes the routine decisions. In case of disagreement among the brothers, the informant, as eldest brother of the family, will decide what course is to be taken and his decision is viewed as the final word. He prefers this partnership with brothers rather than outsiders because he can *trust* them. In his words, it is not possible for them to swindle him and get away with it because they are "tied" to him. The word "tied" here has social significance. First, it means that a break in the relationship resulting from dishonesty is not an ordinary one between business associates but also brothers. Secondly, the principle of trust is a primary rule in this community. If the rumor goes around saying that "so and so is not even trusted by his own family" then his reputation would be ruined. No one dares to violate this rule. Should he be found untrustworthy, the result would be that he is cut off completely from all Chinese business associates.

My informants all agreed that family firms transmit not only business know-how, they also pass on Chinese cultural values, family traditions, and family fortune. The well being and survival of the family firms are often thought to be pivotal for the survival of the family.

2. Family Firms and Risk-Taking

It is said that the success of the Chinese entrepreneurs in the Philippines is due primarily to their risk-taking. This is true. They are quick to seize upon economic opportunities when they arise. They were among the first to come down from the provinces into the urban area after World War II to rebuild their businesses. For example, much of Quiapo—the downtown area of Manila—was rebuilt by the King family. Many fortunes were made from the sale of army surplus goods. When dollar restrictions made importing difficult, the Chinese were among the first to manufacture the commodities locally whenever possible. In the past twenty years, the Philippine society has experienced an emerging new social class—a middle class that aspires to reach modern living standards. The Chinese were quick to respond to the needs of the situation. Many electronic and computer assembly plants were established. First class night-clubs and restaurants were opened. Movie houses were built. Because of the large remittance from the Philippine Overseas workers and the enlargement of the consumer base, many "mega" shopping malls and large-scale retail businesses were established. Henry Sy's Shoe Mart Inc., Young Kong Yan family's Fair Mart Inc., John Gokongwei's Robinson's Department Store, Gotesco family's Ever

Emporium and Gobenghuy's Isetann are just some examples. Children of these family firms are thus constantly exposed to the risk taking habits of the family. This will, presumably, give them advantages over those who have no such opportunity.

This tradition of risk-taking did not start after the Second World War. The Chinese pioneering spirit was manifested at the time they first set foot in the Philippines. During the Spanish Era, the Chinese were the first ones to open small stores, bakeries, etc. (Liao 1964). The Sy Soo family was the first one to start the production of macaroni in Manila (Liao 1964). The Feng family was among those who turned to the utilization of native clay and other materials for the production of enamel and glazing material, enamel ware, chinaware, and other ceramic goods. These are only a few examples. A review of the literature will show constant evidence of this risk taking habit of the Chinese. Jose Campos (Jose C. Yao) took advantage of the government's incentives for drug production in 1953 to launch United Laboratories, which became the largest pharmaceutical company in the Philippines. Yu Khe Thai started to assemble GM cars in the post-war period.

The pioneering spirit and the acceptance of business risk contribute greatly to the success of the Chinese. In the family firm environment, this spirit of risk-taking is effectively enculturated amongst the younger generations. Some of these family businesses are now fourth-generation family business. This differs from the American Chinese (B. Wong 1998) family firms and those discussed by S.L. Wong (1985). Both B. Wong and S.L. Wong found in common the problem of continuity among the Chinese family firms (Wong, McReynolds and Wong 1991). Apparently, the data from the Philippines indicates that Chinese family firms could last for many generations. The success in ensuring the continuity of the family business may be due to two major factors. The first is due to the success of the Chinese family firms in the Philippines. The emotional and financial investment that led to their success may be thought to be a venture too good to waste. The family makes special efforts to keep their business empire going. Second is the size of the Chinese family business. These big family firms have more resources to sustain loss or financial misfortune and hence, have more durability. However, not all the Chinese family firms are successful in overcoming the problem of discontinuity. As will be pointed out in the next section, leadership is a pivotal consideration.

3. The Maintenance of the Family Firms

The maintenance methods of family firms is a function of size. The small Chinese family firm often is run by the entire family. Every family member who can help works in the firm and contributes to the common resources. A hardware store, which I observed, had all the sons working there. Married sons draw just enough salary for the maintenance of their individual family units. Unmarried sons usually get only what is needed for their education and other necessities. Some of these small family firms are production and consumption units. They live together and take their meals together. In some small firms, lunches are provided from a common kitchen. Wealth is gradually accumulated through savings both from free labor supplied by the family members and from joint expenditure. Topley (1961) and Amyot (1973) also pointed out that saving on labor costs and minimizing expenditures are more crucial than profits to small shops in their growth and expansion.

Aside from frugality, Chinese entrepreneurs are known for their habit of industry. They are willing to work tirelessly for long hours and to live humbly. Even when they become successful, they continue to live frugally and reinvest their profits in the business. Over a period of time, a shopkeeper may accumulate a great deal of wealth without showing it. Extra money is used in the following ways: 1) to buy American dollars or gold bars; 2) to buy land; 3) to invest in the education of offspring; 4) to use the money to purchase a large store or 5) to move into a beautiful house in the suburbs and live a life of elegant retirement.

In the Chinese family firm, authority is structured by generation, birth order and sex. In principle, this goes from the oldest male of the senior generation to the youngest of the last generation. The position of unmarried females is rather ill-defined but it is generally inferior to that of males of their own generation. The father is the absolute authority in the family firm. He is responsible for decision-making. During the absence of the father, the eldest son will be responsible for the administration of the family firm. In the small family firm run by the nuclear family, the eldest son alone will succeed to the family business, while the rest of the sons will assist their eldest brother in continuing the family business. In the medium and large-sized family firms run by the stem or extended family, all the sons will share in the family wealth. The daughters have no share in the business, but usually receive a certain amount of the family wealth in the form of dowry. In case the family is split, the eldest brother will always get an extra share of the family inheritance. For instance, four brothers will divide the family wealth into equal shares and the eldest brother will get two shares, in addition to the father's initial residence.

Medium and large-sized family enterprises in the Philippines, upon the death of the father, may find themselves in crisis. The important factor for continuity is leadership. The family usually stays together as long as a strong leader maintains it. Usually, if the eldest brother is capable of forming new management with sufficient authority at this transitional period, the family business can continue and even expand. Ellen Palanca (1995) hypothesized that due to modern management techniques, some of the large family-owned corporations may survive after the death of the founder-entrepreneur. Palanca comments on the survivability of these big corporations:

> Most of the present Chinese businesses, though still family-based, follow the structure and organization of modern businesses. Such organizational structure may define better the role and control of the children, ensuring fairness for all members as well as a smooth transition when the founder-patriarch should not longer be in control. The size of the conglomerate may enable it to service the expansion of the family (Palanca 1995:212).

Decision-making in the Chinese firms is more hierarchical and action can be taken immediately without much consultation. This is particularly the case for small family firms. The family head decides how the family enterprise is to be conducted, what merchandise it to be bought, whom will be hired, what market sought. He decides whether property is to be bought or sold, from whom money has to be borrowed or to be distributed. His decision is final in all matters concerning the family. However, routine decisions are delegated to the sons. Trust between family members provides security and support for the possible consequences of such decisions (Palmier 1961:84). A mistake by a son is tolerated and he will be given another chance. He learns from mistakes. This is why a family firm is a better organization for business training (Benedict 1968: 3-6).

Increasingly, the large Chinese family-controlled/owned corporations have to hire middle managers from outside of the family. Financial experts and MBAs are recruited from outside of the families. There is a genuine concern on the part of the family head to modernize his business organization in the global economy. However, the authoritarian aspect of the leadership can still be detected. Many outsiders who work for these big family corporations told me that this is indeed the case and tried to justify this pattern as a cultural feature in the Philippines, among both the Chinese and the Filipino firms.

The Role of Kin

Larger kin-centered economic corporate groups, including affinal kinsmen and collateral kinsmen, exist among the Chinese in the Philippines. However, these kinds of firms are not always successful They last as long as partners need each other. There is always the suspicion of corruption between partners. Partnerships can dissolve as a consequence of loss or gain in the business. Sometimes, partnerships split with prosperity, because the increase of assets will enable the individual partners to separate and set up their own firms.

Larger kin-centered corporations are more generally found than partnerships. In the Philippines, the circle of kinsmen contribute to the entrepreneurial activities in three general ways: 1) by providing credit, 2) by supplying labors, 3) by sharing useful information.

At the initial stage, the Chinese could get credit from his kinsmen to start his business. A Chinese feels more secure lending money to his kinsmen than to outsiders. Both sides found advantages in this practice. A kinsmen is not required to repay with interest. However, he will try to be grateful, rewarding the lender in many different ways—by recommending friends and customers to the kinsman's shop, by giving information relevant to the business and by giving discounts. Interaction between the kinsmen is always characterized by the principle of reciprocity. Investing in one another's enterprise is also a common practice. This is not only a gesture of good will, but will bring the kinsmen closer, eventually bringing advantages to the entrepreneurial pursuit. Breach of contact or refusal to lend or repay will have serious consequence. Not only will it alter business relations but will also harm kinship relations.

In employment, kinsmen are always preferred. In the past, Chinese employees were imported by their kinsmen from China. One of my informants told me that his grandfather had sponsored five kinsmen from China and that when these people came in they rendered their services to the firm for years. They did not get much salary. But they made no demands either, knowing that the host family had spent quite a large sum for their trip. These kinsmen reciprocate to the kindness of the family by working very hard. After a period of years of service in which they thought they had finally paid back the family's investment in bringing them to the Philippines, they would leave the company. They were subsequently employed in other firms, receiving regular salaries. They now have shops of their own. The host family is always proud of the success of the kinsmen and has more prestige in the community because of the fact that these kinsmen were brought into the country by the family.

This practice of bringing in kinsmen from China is advantageous for both the employers and employees. The employers always feel that these members are trustworthy and loyal to the family. They are expected to work hard and put in more hours. In fact, these kinsmen-employees always worked hard and voiced no complaints. As family members, they do not mind the long working hours. Some medium-sized stores I visited in Manila have no specific time for closing. They remain on call, available to the customers even after closing. When customers come, the employee will go out to receive them and serve them. These kinsmen-employees also have invaluable experiences during time of service. Being very close to the administration of the firm, they receive much informal but practical education about business practices in the Philippines. Thus, when they start an enterprise in the future, they will have a sound knowledge of basic business practices. Furthermore, even though they work without much pay for the sponsor families, they are still much better off than they were in China. They now have enough to wear and eat quite well. The poverty in the rural areas in traditional China was so deeply entrenched that many could not afford three square meals a day and rarely had enough to wear, the people eking out a meager existence. The kinsmen-employee situation thus offers a distinct improvement. In modern-day Philippines, this practice of sponsoring one's relatives from China to work in one's family continues.

Sharing business information is also a common practice among the Chinese kinsmen. Business information could be vital for their existence. It is important for them to understand what laws the government will implement and what businesses are open to expansion. The information about legal problems and methods of solving them is precious.

To consolidate one's business, some business families may marry each other and the affinal kinsmen developed from these marriages could be important for decision-making activities of the Chinese entrepreneurs. Some of the well-known marriages are those between the Dee family and Sycip family, and the Dee family and the Yutivo family. All these families own large businesses. George Dee Sekiat and Robert Dee Se Wee are the sons of the "lumber king" banker, C.Chuan Dee. George Dee married a daughter of Albino Sycip, the founder of China Banking Corp and a lawyer. Robert married Lilian Yu of the Yutivo family, which had a large hardware store and was the agent for General Motors.

The Role of Lineage and Clan

Contrary to Weightman (1960) and others, I found that business partnerships do not usually follow clan lines. Clan cooperation does not extend to business partnership. There is frequently cutthroat competition between clansmen in the field. The influential groups like the Sycip group, Yu Khe-tai group, the Peter Lim group and Gokongwei group are composed of family members but not of clansmen. Perhaps it is necessary to clarify the concept of clan. Technically, a clan is composed of members who are supposedly descendants of a common ancestor (Keesing 1974). But these descendants have no demonstrable genealogical links that connect them to the common ancestor. The various clan associations in the Philippines are realistically clan associations. They are common surname groups. A Lin surname association includes those named Lin who are not genealogically connected. Similarly a Wang surname association may have members who are not related consanguinially. However, in the case of the Philippine Chinese, in most of these surname associations, there are lineage cores (Amyot 1973:86). Thus, a clan in the Philippines is not a lineage. Not all the members are related. It is a fictive kin group. Members of the same surname "pretend" that they are related to a common ancestor. A similar phenomenon is found in other Overseas Chinese communities (B. Wong 1998; Chen 1998). Therefore, it is understandable why clanship cannot realistically be a basis for business partnerships. Certain blood ties, trust, and sentimentality need to exist first before the launching of any business enterprises.

In the homeland of the Philippine Chinese, the village was the basic unit of rural society. In Fujian province, village is normally composed of single or multiple lineages (Freedman 1958) The lineage group was composed of all the male patrilineal descendants of a founding ancestor, who is usually associated with a specific locality (H.Hu 1961). Lineage is a common descent group. Every male belongs automatically to his father's lineage. Every female is a member of her father's lineage until she gets married. Consequently, the members of the lineage are kinsmen and possess the same family name. However, an important distinction is that lineages are not families, but are composed of families. In Fujian and Guangdong, only the lineage and family could be considered an economic unit, because both own property. In the Philippines, the clan organization is larger than a lineage and has members who are not related to each other. In fact, very few of the members in the clan association are kinsmen originating from the same locality. The clan association in the Philippines has a different principle of recruitment because it groups people according to a given surname rather than to a given lineage. Only in this way can it recruit a sufficiently large membership. In the Philippines, the average size of surname association is 600. In traditional China, the lineage had political, economic and religious functions. The lineage may own common land, stores and pawnshops (Lang 1985). Members of the same lineage could also borrow money from the lineage. Furthermore, the lineage management had the obligation to defend the interests of the members and settle conflicts between different families (H. Hu 1961). The management of a lineage had the obligation to preserve the ancestor temples and graveyards. It was in the ancestor temples and graveyards that the ancestors of the lineage were worshipped (Lang 1985; H. Hu 1961; C. Hu 1960). In the Philippines, the nature of the lineage has changed. First, it is not possible to have enough members to organize a lineage organization, as it is not likely to have many immigrants from the same lineage migrating to one place. Migration is and was always an individual or family decision. It was never a lineage decision. Second, there is no common property owned by lineage member Philippines. Third, distant relatives or lineage members seldom enter into a partnership. However, in terms of employment, relatives or lineage members are given special consideration in many Philippine Chinese firms.

In the Philippines, as well as in many overseas Chinese communities (Wong 1988; 1998), the use of fictive kinship or "common mythical origins" as principle or social organization is quite common. There are single-surname or multi-surname associations that use a family name or several family names to organize surname or clan associations. The first clan associations in

Manila were established in the 1920s (Amyot 1973). The clan associations numbered 47 in 1966 and had a total membership of 15,000. Sometimes, a common certain surname is not the only pre-requisite for membership. Locality of origin, dialect and even possible genealogical linkage are factors for inclusions. Thirteen of the surname groups among the Chinese in the Philippines have more than one association for the same surname. Thus, for instance, Ch'en has four; Shih and Lin each has three; Tsai, Li, Yang, Kuo, Ting, Ma, Hsu, Liu, Chang, and Hsieh each have two associations. Among the Chinese in the United States, anyone who possess a family name 'Huang' can join the Huang Association (Wong 1998). However, among the Philippine Chinese, the surname or clan associations are segmented according to locality, dialect and blood ties.

The clan associations were conceived of by their founders as mutual aid associations for its members. Efforts were made to create a family spirit among the members. In the Chinese community, all members of the older generation are addressed as "uncle" or "aunt" and the young members of the same generation are addressed as "brothers" or "sisters." Some of the clans traced their genealogical connections to more than two or three thousand years ago. Thus, for instance, the Chan, Wu, Yuen and Wong families formed a multi-family name association, claiming that they were all offspring of Emperor Hsin. This, however cannot be proven historically. The contributions of the clan association to the entrepreneurial pursuit of the Chinese were more important in the past than it is now. From the 1920s to 1970s, the clan associations did provide credits and employment for the needy members. They mediated disputes over business matters and rendered legal assistance to those who encountered difficulties with the Philippine government. Other functions of the clan associations include social and charity functions. Members go to the association to exchange business or social information. Financial or material assistance is given to poorer members of the clan association. Thus, when a clan brother dies, flower wreaths and other expressions of sympathy are sent to the bereaved family while a delegation from the association attends the funeral. Some destitute clansmen are assisted financially in their funeral arrangements. A scholarship fund is also set up for children of the members. The destitute students may apply to the clan associations for a scholarship.

The most significant contribution of the clan association in the Philippines, however, is its effectiveness in mediating disputes over business matters. In this entrepreneurial community, disputes relate mainly to business problems—misappropriation of funds or property, unpaid debts, discord between employer and employee. Family quarrels are sometimes brought to the clan association for settlement, but less frequently (Ravenhold 1955; Amyot 1973). In the Chinese community of Manila, the disputes are first brought to the clan association by an injured party with a formal complaint. Justice is said to be very exacting. According to Amyot (1973), all disputes are investigated with care. Neighbors and fellow workers are questioned to learn all the circumstances. If resistance persists, relatives, fellow townsmen, members of the lineage, or friends of the litigants, will be brought in to intercede (Amyot 1973). If all these efforts fail, the case will go to the Philippine court of justice. The clan association's dispute mechanisms are always preferred, due to a number of reasons. The Chinese have customs and laws that are different from those of the Philippines. For example, only the sons can have claim to the inheritance. In dividing the inheritance, the eldest son is favored. But in the Philippines, daughters and sons share equal rights in claims towards the family inheritance. Another convenience offered by the clan court is the use of the Chinese language. This is particularly convenient for first generation immigrants who are not proficient in either Tagalog or English. Another factor is that the congestion of court cases in the Philippine court will always delay prosecution. In addition, the adverse publicity involved in a court case will bring injury to the reputation of the firm. However, those Chinese who are assimilated to the Philippine society prefer to use the Philippine courts. In a sense, the clan associations principally serve the cultural Chinese.

In traditional China, the lineage groups had to depend on their leaders for defense against bandits. The powerful lineage leaders and village gentry had influence in the government offices to help settle disputes quickly. In many such disputes within and between villages and lineages—such as those over water rights and local administration, lineage members could be certain of just treatment from other lineage members. In the Philippines, the clan management also provides legal consul for members who run into legal difficulties with the Philippine government. Each clan association has at least three legal advisors who are Philippine citizens. These Philippine Chinese lawyers give general advice to clan members. If further service is needed, the clansmen can get a discount from these advisors.

Some clan members could also get credit from each other. There are two reasons why credit is extended thus. First, there is a certain amount of trust among the members. Second, they can easily find out "who is who" through their clan association. Some need a character reference. They could obtain letters of recommendation from their leaders in the clan association. Strictly speaking, there is not business partnership established on the basis of clan. In fact, in modern day Manila, not every Chinese who is eligible to join their respective clan associations would actually join. According to my informants, there are three groups of people who will likely join their clan associations. First is the group of people who are more than 50 years old. The younger generations are not interested. Second, among the recent immigrants from China, some join the clan associations to meet their friends and village mates who share the same family name. The third group of people are those who are interested in obtaining prestige. They want to be "officials" or leaders of the clan associations for prestige. These rich businessmen give scholarships and donate money for social activities. In doing so, they may be elected as "leaders" and have their names published in the local Chinese newspapers, which carries prestige in the Chinese community.

All clan associations in the Philippines still practice ancestor worship. There are ancestral altars in the association halls. All members show their respect toward the ancestors by bowing to the ancestral tablets. However, not all the members of the clan associations in the Philippines go to the clan hall solely for worshipping the ancestor. Some go there for social and business purposes. Some go to meet their more prosperous clan brothers whom they rarely encounter in the regular course of social interaction. Some go to the association for nostalgia reasons. They feel better when they have a chance to chat and to see their distant relatives and clan members. The dyadic relationship contracted on these occasions could be valuable for their economic pursuits. The rich clansmen can enhance their prestige through holding offices and leading the various rituals. Similarly, the visits to the ancestor's grave in Manila are not merely for the purpose of ancestor worship. It has become a great occasion for a family picnic. It is a great occasion to show off the family wealth by inviting them to the family mausoleum. In the Chinese cemetery in Manila, a lot of conspicuous consumption is displayed in the cemetery. Some families have a two-story building to house their dead. There are rooms in these building for family members and friends to play mahjongg and to have dinners. The visit to the ancestor's mausoleum is also a great opportunity to talk about business deals and exchange business information.

In addition to clan associations, there are hometown or regional associations. Among the contemporary Chinese in the Philippines, localities of origin play an important role in economic cooperation. People from certain districts in Fujian, such as Fu-Chin and Jin-Jian would band together for economic activities. The Fu-chin group is composed of people who migrated from the area of Fu-Chin. They are an example of a successful organization. This group managed to have product exhibits produced by their members. The Chinese who migrated from Jin-Jian organized their own association. In fact, the Jin-Jian Chinese from the Philippines also use their hometown connection to invest in Jin-Jian in China. Locality ties thus are important in bringing hometown-mates together for economic activities.

While family, kinsmen and clansmen indeed play an important role in the activities of the Chinese entrepreneurs, this does not rule out the possibility of cooperation from friends and outsiders. The Roman Catholic Church rituals of Baptism and Confirmation are sometimes used to create social relationships between the Chinese and non-Chinese. Co-parenthood or the *Compadrazgo* system, as will be discussed later in this paper, is a social institution which could be utilized for entrepreneurial activities.

Cooperation with Outsiders

1. Chinese with Chinese

Business cooperation with outsiders does exit. There are several ways to launch business with outsiders. Amyot (1973) observed that it is important to first have trust between the individuals. Connections such as towns-fellows, schoolmates, or friends may get together and pool their resources to start a business and become shareholders. Same locality of origins, same hometowns, same teachers and the same alma maters could be very important among the Chinese. Another institution is called dry-parenthood. Individuals who like each other and get along well with each other may enter a relationship similar to father and son. This kind of relationship could be contracted between people of similar age and generation. It is a kind of fictive kinship or ritual kinship. These ritual brothers or sisters may start a business partnership. Sometimes business alliances are sealed by adoption or marriage. If a family does not have any children, they may adopt a son. The choice of the adopted son is not a random affair. It is highly selective in terms of his moral character, ability and family background. However, between the two families, the *confienza* or *Kan Chin* between the two families should exist first. The adopted son is groomed to succeed to the family business of the adopting family. However, marriage is used far more than adoption to seal business alliances. In fact, there is a tendency of intermarriage among the prominent Chinese families—the Dee family, the Sycip family, the Yu family and the Yao family

2. Chinese and Filipinos

Cooperation between Chinese and Filipinos is also found. However, most instances of interaction between Chinese and Filipinos are dictated by the principle of mutual benefits. The Chinese cannot operate a big business at times, because of legal restrictions. The Filipinos are hindered by their lack of capital. Thus, mutual needs explain many of the Chinese-Filipinos business cooperation. From the 1950s to the 1960s, there were laws against land-ownership, retail operations and even mining and lumber operations by the Chinese entrepreneurs who were not Philippines citizens. There was also a problem in getting their dollar quotas from the Central Bank. Partnership and cooperation with the Filipinos helped the Chinese to overcome these legal difficulties while giving assistance to Filipinos in gaining a share of their business.

To foster cooperation between the Filipinos and the Chinese, there is a need for some kind of social connection. Originally adopted from Catholicism, the system of ritual co-parenthood, or *Compadrazgo,* is a mechanism used in bridging the relationship between Filipinos and the Chinese businessmen. (The use of this institution was described by Mintz and Wolf 1950, B. Wong 1979, and Davila 1971.) During the Spanish Era, those Chinese who had become Christians were exempted from paying the customary tributes for ten years. They were also extended certain social and political privileges, including the right to hold public office (Liao 1964:25). Even today, the baptismal certificate is useful as a reference of good standing. For the purpose of naturalization, the baptismal certificate is also an important document for verification of parenthood, birthplace and birth date. The ritual of co-parenthood serves another important function, namely, to link the Chinese with the Filipinos socially. The non-related sponsor of the Baptism (Godfather) and the natural father become *compadres* (co–fathers). Two significant relationships developed from this institution. The Filipino godfather is a spiritual father and protector for the godson. The Filipino sponsor has become a friend and a ritual relative to the natural father of the son as well. The godfather is thus perceived to be a protector for both the son and the natural father. In the Spanish Era, some Chinese adopted the family name of their godfathers, which explains why some Chinese have names like Campos, Reyes and Rodriguez. It is possible to obtain the services of an influential Filipino godfather. Several of my informants' godfathers are influential Filipino politicians who are known to be "helpful" to their Chinese *compadres.*

Another mechanism in building connection between the Chinese and the Filipinos is through marriage. Intermarriage between the Chinese and Filipinos does occur. Some of these marriages are marriages of convenience. In the past, when the Chinese were not allowed to participate in the retail trades, marrying Philippine citizens would allow them to stay in business. Some of these marriages of convenience initially could end up as a marriage of love. There were also marriages between the rich Chinese and the rich Filipino families to consolidate their family wealth. Their children are called *meztizo.* In fact, at the end of the 19th century, there was a Chinese meztizo class that figured quite prominently in the Philippine history (Lynn Pan 1996). This also explains why some Chinese have surnames that are Spanish-sounding. They were the result of intermarriages.

Thus, I found that the Chinese entrepreneurs did use the *compadrazgo* system and marriage to further their economic goals. The interpersonal social network that developed from the *compadrazgo* and intermarriage is an important tool for entrepreneurial pursuit. Generally speaking, the Chinese tend to associate with family members, kinsmen, clansmen and people who are connected to them socially. Family, kinship, clanship, friendship and *compadrazgo* ties play an important role in the economic activities of the Chinese, especially during financial and legal crises. Thus, friendship between the Chinese and the Filipinos may also lead to economic cooperation.

Minority Group Factor and the Success of the Chinese

The success of the Chinese is also influenced greatly by their minority status. There is limited opportunity in economic sectors other than the commerce of the Philippines, particularly because of the legislative discrimination that excludes them from many professions such as medicine, law and engineering. Thus many young Chinese have no alternatives but to seek their fortune and their livelihood through their family business. Historically, it was difficult for them to become citizens. Without citizenship, they were not allowed to enter many professions and economic activities. They had to depend entirely on their family fortunes and family businesses. Thus, the discrimination resulting from the minority situation gives the second generation Chinese an incentive to work in family firms. Although the situation has changed since the 1970s, some of the trends are entrenched.

The minority factor also strengthens the community spirit of the Chinese in the Philippines. Many Chinese protective organizations and mutual aid societies were set up to fight discrimination and gain equality. As a protective device, many organizations that were oriented toward greater cooperation and mutual aid were established. The most effective of these organizations are the clan associations, the trade associations, and the Chinese Chambers of Commerce. The contributions of the clan associations have been pointed out. The Chinese trade associations are not substantially different from their Western counterpart but they are extraordinarily effective in protecting the business of the Chinese. They organized protests or boycotts against companies which are acting against the interest of their trade. The trade associations also regulate prices to avoid unnecessary competition between the Chinese tradesmen (Amyot 1973). Today, the trade associations remain important. They joined together for protection, for solidarity in dealing with the Government, to exchange information, and to help each other. These associations provide important information to their tradesmen about government regulations, product quality, shipping, and sales information.

The Federation of the Chinese Chamber of Commerce is the supreme authority for the Chinese community in the Philippines. It coordinates major commercial activities. It was also successful in persuading the Chinese not to compete with the wealthy Filipino groups and big American and Spanish interests in the 1950s, because these groups could command political hearings. The Federation is similar to the Chinese Consolidated Benevolent Association in the United States (Wong 1981, 1987a, 1988, 1998). The Federation of the Chinese Chamber of Commerce takes care of transactions between the Chinese community and the Philippine Government. Philippine politicians, including Ferdinand Marcos and others, frequently asked the

Federation for support. The important role played by the Federation is recognized by both the Chinese and Filipinos. The president of the Chamber of Commerce is the most prestigious post in the Chinese community and he is considered more powerful than the Chinese ambassador. The Chinese entrepreneurs did not find the Embassy helpful in solving their problems with the host country. On the other hand, the Federation could do much to alleviate the difficulties of the Chinese with the Philippine government. In the past, The Federation of the Philippine Chinese Chamber of Commerce was vocal about the various anti-Chinese policies, which included the Retail Trade Restriction, and the Naturalization Law. Many of my informants today claimed that as many of these laws have been abandoned or become non-applicable to the Chinese, the Federation has ceased to be critical about the government.

As a group, they are not accepted fully as cultural citizens of the Philippines and discrimination still exists in the Philippine society. The resentment against the Chinese is clearly demonstrated by the waves of kidnapping incidents in recent years. According to many writers (Cristina Szanton Blanc 1997; Pan 1996; Wickberg 1996; Teresita Ang See 1997: Interview), the kidnapping activities were conducted by the indigenous Filipinos and were often politically motivated. As a result of such discriminatory treatment against the Chinese, an organization called Kaisa Para Sa Launlarn was born in 1987. This organization pushed for adoption of the term *Tsino* (Chinese Filipinos) as opposed to *Pinoy* (Filipinos). The purpose of the organization is to overcome discrimination and to develop pride of Chinese heritage in Philippine society. The Credo of Kaisa is: "Our blood may be Chinese, but our roots grow deep in the Philippine soil and our hearts are with the Philippine People."

Kaisa Para Sa Kaunlaran also offers skills and entrepreneurship training to both the Chinese and the Filipinos, participates in charity projects and works towards the preservation of the Chinese heritage in the Philippines. The organization makes special effort to diffuse the antagonism between the Chinese and Filipinos. In 1993, Kaisa launched anti-kidnapping efforts by having the Movement of Restoration of Peace and Order in 1993. These efforts in fighting for equality and minority rights also unify the Chinese. In a paradoxical way, it also propels the Chinese to work harder to obtain more wealth. My informants in 2003 told me that wealth is power. They said, "If you have more wealth, you have more protection in the Philippines."

The establishment of and the reliance on the various mutual aid and ethnic organizations in this community is a defensive reaction to the minority situation (Amyot 1973; T.S. Chen 1998; Wong 1992). They feel that they need to band together to give each other support. Thus, the minority situation, contrary to the findings of Benedict (1968) in Africa, helps economic cooperation among the ethnic entrepreneurs.

Summary and Conclusion

In this paper I have tried to indicate the reciprocal relationship between kinship and entrepreneurship. Kinship does not necessarily inhibit the activities of the entrepreneurs. Kinship, friendship, *compadrazgo,* and other informal social relationships have contributed greatly to the success of the Chinese entrepreneurs. In particular, the family provides efficient training for the second generation Chinese by enculturating the risk-taking habit, and the spirit of industry and frugality. Economic gain is maximized in the family firm through the use of family labor and common expenditure. Through the employment of kinsmen, the Chinese entrepreneurs can obtain the maximum amount of service and loyalty. The greatest contribution of the clan association is its effectiveness in mediating business disputes. Kinship, friendship and *compadrazgo* relationships can provide financing, joint economic ventures, and expansion of business interests.

The Chinese kinship organization is also changed as a consequence of entrepreneurial activities. In addition to nuclear, stem and the extended family (under one roof), among the Philippine Chinese, there is the non-residential-extended family. Traditionally, the Chinese extended family was always patrilineal and patrilocal. Only married sons and their families stay while married daughters move away. In the Philippines, some of the extended Chinese families have their sons' families as well as their daughters' families living under one roof. There is more equality between the sexes in the Philippine Chinese. As for the non-residential–extended–family, some of the Chinese do not live together in a compound or under one roof. In the urban areas of the Philippines, some individual family units are distributed throughout the city. However, these families still function as one large unit and own common property. When circumstances permit, they still live together in a single neighborhood. The success of their enterprises demands cooperation in both manpower and capital.

Significant change is found on the level of the lineage. Strictly speaking, there are no lineage associations. The so-called clan associations are not lineages or descent groups. The clan organization is no longer a homogeneous common descent group. It has a new identity. It is a fictive kinship grouping composed of people who are supposedly related to each other. Members are not necessarily related by traceable descent. Participation is voluntary. They are not the traditional face-to-face kinship groups. They have become voluntary groups with myths and fictions underlying their organizations. However, family and kinship remain to be important in the urban environment. Contrary to the "Chicago School" of urban studies (Robert Redfield 1947; Wirth 1938; Park, Burgess and Mackenzie 1925), kinship is not "dead" in Manila.

The third related question raised was, "What are the factors contributing to the success of the Chinese entrepreneurs?" From analysis of their economic behavior, several major interrelated factors can be found. First, there is flexibility on the part of the Chinese in their response to the need of the Philippine economic environment. This ability is provided by family firms and the informal decision-making process in the family firms. Entrepreneurs of these family firms can seize economic opportunity quickly. A second factor is due to their occupational role as merchants. From the very beginning, the Philippine Chinese have been predominantly merchants. The macro-economic structure and Spanish Colonialism, as demonstrated in this paper, favored the presence of the Chinese merchants. As merchants, they are forced to be alert to the market as well as to the economic resources. As middlemen merchants, they are sensitive to the information network in the political and the business world. They are sensitive to the demands of the macro-economic environment. They also learned how to use social relations and social network—kinship, friendship, locality of origins, *compadrago* and the like, to exploit the macro-economic environment.

Third, the family structure and its transactional patterns have brought numerous advantages. This was also demonstrated in the works of Barnett (1960), Benedict (1968), Dewey (1962a), Wolf (1966), Wong (1979, 1981, 1987a, 1998), and Wong McReynolds and Wong (1991). Gain is maximized through the use of family, kinsmen, and clansmen. Credit and business information is provided by their extensive family and kinship network. Fourth, their willingness to work long hours increases their volume of sales. Fifth, the habit of frugality helps generate savings and the accumulation of wealth. Sixth, the minority status strengthens their sense of community, thus enabling greater economic cooperation. The minority situation induces incentive to maximize wealth to gain social prestige as well as power. Wealth helps their fight for equality and enables cultural acceptance. Thus their "cultural citizenship" (Rosaldo 1992) is to be obtained through wealth. Finally, the establishment of the various mutual aid organizations in this community is a defensive reaction to the minority situation. Thus, the minority situation of the Philippine Chinese has played an important role in the success of the Chinese entrepreneurs.

This paper has shown the reciprocal relationship between kinship and entrepreneurship. Kinship influences the activities of the Chinese entrepreneurs. On the other hand, kinship is also influenced by the entrepreneurial activities. In the process of demonstrating the economic behavior of the Chinese, we find that their success is due to a complex interweaving of factors in which kinship is one of the most significant.

Bibliography

Adams, Bert. 1968. *Kinship in an Urban Setting*. Chicago. Markham Publishing Co.

Agpalo, Remigio E. 1962. *The Political Process and the Nationalization of the Retail Trade in the Philippines*. Quezon City: University of the Philippines.

Alip, Enfromio. 1959. *Ten Centuries of Philippine-Chinese Relations*. Manila: Alip and Sons. Inc.

Appadurai, Arjun. 1990. "Disjuncture and Difference in the Global Cultural Economy." *Theory, Culture, and Society* 7:295-310.

———. 1996. Modernity at Large: Cultural Dimensions of Globalization. Minneapolis: University of Minnesota Press.

Applaton, Sheldon. 1960. Overseas Chinese and Economic Nationalization in the Philippines. *Journal of Asian Studies* 19(2): 151-161.

Amyot, Jacques. 1973. *The Manila Chinese: Adaptation of Familism to the Philippine Environment*. Quezon City: Institute of Philippine Culture, Ateneo de Manila University.

Aubey, Robert T. 1969. Entrepreneurial Formation in El Salvador. *Explorations in Entrepreneurial History*. 6(3):268-285.

Baker, Hugh D.R. 1980. *Chinese Family and Kinship*. New York: Columbia University Press.

Barnett, Milton L. 1960. Kinship as a Factor Affecting Cantonese Economic Adaptation in the United States. *Human Organization* 19(1):40-46.

Barranco, Vicente. 1961. "The Chinese Questions" In Schubert Liao, ed., *Chinese Participation in Philippine Culture and Economy*. Manila: Bookman Inc., pp. 184-190.

Barth, Fredrik. 1960. Models of Social Organization. Royal Anthropological Institute. Occasional Paper No. 23.

Basch, Linda, Nina Glick Schiller and Cristina Szanton Blanc. 1994. *Nations Unbound: Transnational Projects, Postcolonial Predicaments and Deterriotorialized States*. Amsterdam: Gordon and Breach.

Benedict, Burton. 1968. Family Firms and Economic Development. *Southwestern Journal of Anthropology*, 24(1):1-19.

Blanc, Cristina Szanton. 1997. "The Thoroughly Modern 'Asian': Thailand and the Philippines." In *Ungrounded Empires*, Aihwa Ong and Donald Nonini, eds., pp. 261-286. London: Routledge.

Blair, Emma H. and Robertson, James A. 1903-09. *Philippine Islands 1493-1898*. Cleveland: Arthur Clark.

Brown Ampalavanar Rajeswary, Ed. 1996. *Chinese Business Enterprise in Asia*. London: Routledge.

Carroll, John J. 1965. *The Philippine Manufacturing Entrepreneur: Agent and Product of Change*. Ithaca: Cornell University Press.

Castillo, Andres V. 1964. "The Chinese Role in Philippine Economic Progress" In *Chinese Participation Philippine Culture and Economy*, Schubert Liao, ed., pp 172-177. Manila: Bookman, Inc.

Chen, Ching-Ho. 1962. The Overseas Chinese in the Philippines During Sixteen Centuries. Hong Kong: Southeast Asia Studies Section, New Asia Research Institute. *Monograph Series* No. 2.

Chen, Ta. 1940. Emigrant Communities in South China: A Study of Overseas Migration and Its Influence on Standard of Living and Social Change. New York: Institute of Pacific Relations.

Chen, Tien-Shi. 1998. "Overseas Chinese in Japan: Transitions of Community and Identities in Yokohama Chinatown." Unpublished manuscript.

Coller, R.W. 1960. A Social-Psychological Perspective on the Chinese as a Minority Group in the Philippines. *Philippine Sociological Review*, 1960 8(1-2): 9-58.

Davila, Mario. 1971. *Compadrazgo*: Fictive Kinship in Latin America. In *Readings in Kinship and Social Structure*, Nelson Graburn, ed. New York: Harper & Row Publishers.

Dewey, Alice G. 1962a. *Peasant Marketing in Java*. New York: The Free Press.

———. 1962b. Trade and Social Control in Java. *Journal of Royal Anthropological Institute* 92: 177-190.

Espina, Vicente. 1957. *Immigration Rulings and Regulations: Including Laws, Rulings, and Regulations on Philippine Citizenship*. Manila: Educational Bookstore.

Felix, Alfonso Jr. ed. 1965. *The Chinese in the Philippines 1570-1770*. Manila: Solidaridad Publishing House.

Fox, Robin. 1984. *Kinship and Marriage*. New York: Cambridge University Press.

Freedman, Maurice. 1958. *Lineage Organization in Southeastern China*. London: London School of Economics and Political Science Monographs on Social Anthropology, No. 18.

———. 1959. The handling of money: A note on the background to the economic sophistication of overseas Chinese. *Man*, 59: 65.

———. 1960. Immigrants and Associations: Chinese in Nineteenth Century Singapore. *Comparative Studies in Society and History* 3: 25-48.

———. 1967. *Chinese Lineage and Society: Fukien and Kwangtung*. London: London School of Economics and Political Science Monographs on Social Anthropology. No. 33.

Greenfield, Sidney, Arnold Strickon and Robert Aubey, eds. 1979. *Entrepreneurs in Cultural Context*. Albuquerque: University of Mexico Press.

Glade, William P. 1968. Approaches to a Theory of Entrepreneurial Formation. *Exploration in Entrepreneurial History* 4(3):245-259.

Guerrero, Milagros, C. 1966. The Chinese in the Philippines, 1570-1770. In *The Chinese in the Philippines 1570–1770*, Alfonso Felix, ed. pp. 15-39. Manila: Solidaridad Publishing

Hsu, Francis L.K. 1971. *Under the Ancestors' Shadow: Kinship, Personality and Social Mobility in China*. Stanford: Stanford University Press.

———. 1981. *Americans and Chinese*. Honolulu: The University Press of Hawaii.

Hu, Hsien-chin. 1961. The Common Descent Group in China and Its Functions. *Viking Fund Publication in Anthropology* No. 10.

Hu,. Chang-tu. 1960. *China: Its People, Its Society, Its Culture*. New Haven: HRAF Press.

Kaisa Para Sa Kaunlaran, Inc. 1999. Credo of Kaisa. `http://www. philonline. com.ph/~kaisa/ kaisa_credo.html`

Keesing, Roger. 1974. *Kin Groups and Social Structure*. Fort Worth: Harcourt Brace.

Lang, Olga. 1985. *Chinese Family and Society*. New York: Oriental Book Store.

Lee, Rose Hum. 1960. *The Chinese in the United States of America*. Hong Kong: Hong Kong University Press.

Liao, Shubert, ed. 1964. *Chinese Participation in Philippine Culture and Economy*. Manila: Bookman Inc.

McPhelin, Michael. 1964. The Chinese Question. In *Chinese Participation in Philippine Culture and Economy*, Schubert Liao, ed. pp. 184-190. Manila: Bookman Inc.

Mintz, Sydney and Eric Wolf. 1950. An Analysis of Ritual Co-parenthood (Compadrazgo). *Southwestern Journal of Anthropology* 6(4):341-368.

Ng Kwee Choo. 1967. *The Chinese in London*. London: Oxford University Press.

Omohundro, John T. 1980. *Chinese Merchant Families in Iloilo: Commerce and Kin in a Central Philippine City*. Quezon City: Ateneo de Manila University.

Ong, Aihwa and Donald Nonini. 1996. *Ungrounded Empires*. London: Routledge.

Palanca, Ellen. 1995. "Chinese Business Families in the Philippines since the 1890s." In *Chinese Business Enterprise in Asia*. Rajeswary Ampalvavanar Brown, ed., pp. 197-213. London: Routledge.

Palmier, Leslie H. 1961. Batik Manufacture in a Chinese Community in Java. In *Entrepreneurship and Skills in Indonesia Economic Development: A Symposium*. Monograph Series No. 1. Southeast Asian Studies, Yale University. Pp. 75-97.

Pan, Lynn. 1996. *The Encyclopedia of Chinese Overseas*. Cambridge, MA: Harvard University Press.

Park, Robert, Ernest Burgess and Roderick Mackenzie. 1925. *The City*. Chicago: University of Chicago Press.

Phelan, John L. 1959. *Hispanization of the Philippines*. Madison: University of Wisconsin Press.

Purcell, Victor. 1951. *The Chinese in Southeast Asia*. London: Oxford University Press.

Ravenholt, Albert. 1955. Chinese in the Philippines: An Alien Business and Middle Class. American Universities Field Staff Reports. December 9, 1955.

Redding, Gordon S. 1990. *The Spirit of Chinese Capitalism*. New York: Walter de Gruyter.

Redfield, Robert. 1947. The Folk Society. *The American Journal of Sociology*. Vol. LII, (1947):293-306.

Reynolds, Harriet R. 1963. *Continuity and Changes in the Chinese Family in the Ilocos Province, Philippines.* Ann Arbor: University Microfilms.

———. 1966. Continuity and Changes as Shown by Attitudes of Two Generations of Chinese in the Ilocos Province, Philippines. *Sillian Journal* 13:12-21.

Reynolds, Ira Hubert. 1964. Chinese Acculturation in Ilocos: Economic, Political, Religious. Unpublished Ph.D. Dissertation. Ann Arbor: University Microfilm.

Rosaldo, Renato. 1990. *Culture and Truth.* Boston: Beacon Press.

Santamaria, Albert O.P. 1966. The Chinese Parian. In *The Chinese in the Philippines 1570–1770*, Alfonso Felix, ed., pp. 67-118. Manila: Solidaridad Publishing.

Schumpeter, Joseph A. 1934. *The Theory of Economic Development. Cambridge*, MA: Harvard University Press.

Schurz, William L. 1939. *The Manila Galleon.* New York: E.P. Dutton and Co.

See, Teresita Ang. 1997. Personal Interview.

Skinner, G. William. 1939. *Leadership and Power in the Chinese Community of Thailand.* Ithaca: Cornell University Press.

Strickon, Arnold. 1962. Class and Kinship in Argentina. *Ethnology*, Vol. 1 (4). pp. 500-515.

Tan, Antonio. 1988. "The Changing Identity of the Philippine Chinese, 1941-1984." In *Changing Identities of Southeast Asian Chinese Since World War II*, Jennifer Cushman and Wang Guangwu, eds. Hong Kong: Hong Kong University Press.

Tien, Ju-kang. 1952. The Chinese of Sarawak: A Study of Social Structure. London: London School of Economic Monographs of Social Anthropology No. 12.

Topley, Marjorie. 1960. The Emergence and Social Functions of Chinese Religious Associations in Singapore. *Comparative Studies in Society and History* 3:289-314.

Waldinger, Rober, Howard Aldrich and Robin Ward. 1990. *Ethnic Entrepreneurs.* Newbury Park: Sage Publications.

Weightman, George H. 1964. A Study of Prejudice in Personalistic Society: Analysis of an Attitude Survey of College Students—University of the Philippines. *Asian Studies*, 1964 (2): 87-101.

———. 1966. The Chinese Family and Sib in the Philippines. *Asian Studies*, 1(1):9-16.

Wickberg, Edgar. 1964. The Chinese Mestizo in Philippine History. *Journal of Southeast Asian History* 5(1):62-100.

———. 1965. T*he Chinese in Philippine Life, 1850-1898.* New Haven: Yale University Press.

———. 1991. "Note on Some Contemporary Social Organization in Manila Chinese Society." In *The Chinese Across the Seas: The Chinese as Filipinos*, Aileen S-P Baviera and Teresita Ang See, eds., Philippine Association for Chinese Studies.

———. 1996. "The Philippines" In *The Encyclopedia of Chinese Overseas*, Lynn Pan, ed., pp. 187-199. Cambridge, MA: Harvard University Press.

Wirth, Louis. 1938. Urbanism as a Way of Life. *American Journal of Sociology*, 44:1-24.

Wolf, Eric R.. 1938. Kinship, Friendship and Patron-Client Relationship in Complex Societies. Michael Benton, ed. Pp 1-20.

Wong, Bernard. 1979. *A Chinese American Community: Ethnicity and Survival Strategies.* Singapore: Chopmen Enterprises.

―――. 1981. *Chinatown: Economic Adaptation and Ethnic Identity of the Chinese*. New York: Holt, Rinehart and Winston.

―――. 1987a. The Role of Ethnicity in Enclave Enterprises: A Study of the Chinese Garment Factories in New York City." *Human Organization* 46(2):120-130.

―――. 1987b. The Chinese: New Immigrants in New York's Chinatown. In Nancy Foner, ed., *New Immigrants in New York*. New York: Columbia University Press.

―――. 1988. *Patronage, Brokerage, Entrepreneurship and the Chinese Community of New York*. New York: AMS Press.

―――. 1992. Hong Kong Immigrants in San Francisco. In *Reluctant Exile*, Ronald Skeldon, ed., pp. 235-255. New York: M.E. Sharpe.

―――. 1998. *Ethnicity and Entrepreneurship: The New Chinese Immigrants in the San Francisco Bay Area*. Boston:Allyn and Bacon.

Wong, Bernard, Becky McReynolds and Wynnie Wong. 1991. Chinese Family Firms in the San Francisco Bay Area. *Family Business Review* 5(4):355-372.

Wong, S.L. 1985. The Chinese Family Firm: A Model. *British Journal of Sociology* 36(1):58-72.

Wu, Ching-Hong. 1959. A Study of References to the Philippines in Chinese Sources from the Earliest Time to the Ming Dynasty. *Philippine Social Science and Humanity Reviews*. Vol. 24 (1-2).

Yoshihara, Kunio. 1988. *The Rise of Ersatz Capitalism in South-East Asia*. Singapore: Oxford University Press

Zaide, Gregorio F. 1953. Contributions of Aliens to Philippine Economy. In *Chinese Participation in Philippine Culture and Economy*, Schubert Liao, ed., pp 150-171. Manila: Bookman, Inc.

Zarco, Ricardo M. 1966. The Chinese Family Structure. In *The Chinese in the Philippines 1570–1770*, Alfonso Felix, ed., pp. 211-222. Manila: Solidaridad Publishing.

Part Three

Alternative Lifestyles and New Kinship Patterns

Introduction

The substantive and sometimes controversial topic of new kinship systems generated in contemporary cultures is the focus of this section. As the world changes, so does the definition of kinship itself adapt to new concepts of family and kin. Robert Thompson shows how, as a result of frequent divorce, the "unclear family" system has developed in modern Western society. Jankowiak's article on the Mormon community demonstrates how ideology and religion not only influenced the formation of polygamous households, but the development of new rationale for an old system of multiple-partner marriages. How polygamous members of the Mormon community deal with internal and external conflict makes for fascinating discussion.

Transnationalism and globalization are two hot phenomenon changing the nature of the family in the 21st century. Bernard Wong's article discusses the relationship between Chinese transnational migration and changing patterns of kinship. Wong shows how the traditional Chinese kinship system has been dramatically altered as a result of massive overseas migration in the 20th century. Most recently, economic globalization has further reshuffled the kinship system, creating new household patterns: patrifocal, matrifocal, non-residential extended and parent-absent households. Furthermore, economic globalization does not diminish the formation of kinship and social networks.

Modern technology also plays a role in the formation of kinship ties. The new reproductive technology not only has had a deep impact on the meaning of incest, it creates many difficult family and kinship issues that society never had to face before. Linda Stone shows how modern technology is creating new lifestyles and new family patterns. The question is not whether kinship is still important, but how the kinship system is adapting to changes in modern culture and technology.

What does it mean "to be family"? Within the context of this section, students can write papers on the various new kinship systems, which are already familiar to them or immersed in controversy. For example, lesbian or gay families, children dealing with multiple-kin relations engendered from divorced parents, polygamous families and alternative lifestyles run the gamut of possibilities for deep discussion. The various kinds of new reproductive strategies, from surrogate mothers, in-vitro fertilization, sperm and egg clinics, to what it means to be a parent today (biological vs. psychological/social?), even the pushing back of "the physical age limits for bearing children," and their resounding impact on American society, are all stimulating, investigative, and even controversial topics for classroom use. Kinship is evolving and we are a part of defining its modern parameters.

CHAPTER 13

Harmonious Love and Passionate Love in an American Polygamous Community

—— *William Jankowiak, University of Nevada-Las Vegas* ——

Introduction[1]

L ove and sex, albeit separate emotions, are inextricably intertwined and intimately connected. The critical question then must be whether they will be institutionalized inside or outside of marriage, or ignored and left to the individual to reinvent anew in each generation. In each pairing it is not the singular appearance therefore of romantic love, monogamy, or individual choice, but the combination of all three occurrences *inside* the institution of marriage that is historically significant. What accounts for romantic love's emergence as the primary basis, as opposed to a possible consideration, for marriage?

Every culture highlights either sexuality or love, but has a very difficult time in blending the two together. Every culture, including its intellectuals, prefer to speak in idioms that stress the benefits of either love or sex, but rarely both. This is especially true of the intellectual history of the Western world, which has repeatedly demonstrated a continuous and pronounced ambivalence toward sexuality and love. It is romantic passion's ability to provoke socially unacceptable behavior that makes it such a turbulent and complex human emotion (Jankowiak 1995). It is romantic attraction's ability to engender new social relations, often in the face of negative sanctions, that makes it such a volatile catalyst of resistance to cultural convention and communal harmony.

This volatility is especially prevalent in an ongoing experiment in family living in Angel Park, a Mormon fundamentalist polygamous community. This community seeks to "create heaven on earth" by organizing family relations around the two often competing notions of romantic and harmonious love. In embracing both notions of love, the community and its membership often become confused, uncertain, and emotionally twisted while striving to integrate the two, often, competing emotional orientations. Harmonious love is often challenged by other

---

Reprinted by permission of the author.

desires that undermine efforts to create a family order organized around the notion of selfless love. This is especially true in the case of romantic passion, a complex emotion that can, and often does, disrupt a family's and even society's sense of the "order of things." Romantic passion is unique in the realm of human emotions in that it forces an active response; as a nearly irresistible call to action it creates a catalyst for cultural change. In effect, emotionality provokes action.

In this chapter I hope to make this statement clearer by focusing on the relationship between fundamental Mormon theological notions of spiritual salvation, harmonious love, and romantic love. I want to explore how these somewhat lofty ideals establish the more concrete cultural and political systems that not only foster the shape of the fundamentalist polygamous family, but also accounts, in large part, for the variation in behavior found within the family. Specifically, I will examine romantic passion as a remembered, anticipated, feared, regretted, and articulated reality. By exploring romantic passion as the community's most volatile value, I will illustrate some of the dynamics of American polygamous family life. In this way, the study of Angel Park, a small township located in the intermountain region of the Western United States, provides an excellent opportunity to explore the interplay between romantic passion, harmonious love, and religiously sanctioned social obligations. How they shape the collective and personal expectations, in what, Paul Bohannan (1985) calls, "America's most unusual experiment in family living," is discussed.

Fundamentalist Theology and American Society

It is necessary to discuss several elements of the Fundamentalist Mormon religious creed as it provides significant and salient components of the culture's cosmology. Fundamentalist Mormon theology is grounded in the teachings of three books: the Bible, the Book of Mormon, and the Doctrine and Covenants. The latter two books are prescribed as Holy Scripture, the word of God revealed directly to Joseph Smith (Musser 1944).

American psychologists have long noted that, for American children of both sexes, the mother is the most important figure. Because families tend to be organized around the mother, there is a general tendency, especially among white American middle-class families, toward developing greater emotional ties between mother and children than between father and children (Sered 1994:57). Sered points out that matrifocal units often arise within patrilineal social organizations. In Angel Park, this American tendency toward matrifocality is outlawed by the cultural emphasis on the spiritual and administrative authority of the father.

There are several non-negotiable tenets that form the core of Mormon theology. For instance, that God is a polygamous man who loves all his children but confers on men, in particular, an elevated spiritual essence which insures that men who live "righteously" will obtain a higher spiritual standing. Men occupy leadership positions in their families and on the Church Council as well as having the potential, in the next life, to become god-heads with dominion over all their descendants. Within this cosmological framework, the father is charged with the duty to constantly expand his kingdom by entering into the institution of plural marriages (Musser 1944).

Women's official standing, on the other hand, is determined by their performance in the highly-valued complimentary roles of mother and wife. Like the southern Baptists church leadership, Mormon fundamentalists literally interpret the scripture, "A woman should submit herself graciously" to her husband's leadership, and that a husband should, "provide for, protect and lead his family" (*New York Times*, June 11, 1998, p. A1).

Women achieve salvation through obedience, first to their fathers and then to their husbands, by becoming sister-wives (i.e., co-wives) in a celestial, or plural, family. The marriage contract "seals" a man and woman together, "for time and eternity" in the Heavenly Kingdom (Musser 1944). Because this family unit extends beyond the grave into an eternal world, it is in a woman's "best interest to advance her husband's interests, (i.e., she should bear a large number of children) (Bohannan 1985, p.81), while also striving to uphold her husband's authority, especially in front of his children.

A second tenet holds that the father-son relationship is the core axis for the transmission of cultural and spiritual essence. This notion, first articulated by Joseph Smith in 1832, is a "theme that predominates throughout the Book of Mormon" (Clark and Clark 1991:286). It is based on the belief of a Melchizedek priesthood whose lineage, extended back to Adam, is the only legitimate religious authority. This notion is the primary legitimization of the church's insistence that the only acceptable foundation of religious expression is a patriarchal social organization.

The polygamous family's behavioral expectations are derived from these theological axioms which uphold men as the religious specialist and authority in the family. From an organizational perspective, intense and persistent familial attention should be on the father as the ultimate adjudicator of family affairs, as well as the representative of spiritual authority. The father's authority is reinforced as he leads the family in Sunday school service, conducts daily family prayers, arranges the marriages of his children, and disburses the family's income.

In contrast, mothers are seen as an emotional constant: warm, nurturing and intimate. They embody strength and continuity and are not perceived to be a force to contend with. This perception is imposed by the church's teachings, which hold that reproduction and childcare are a woman's primary duties. This qualified value of mother's relative place in the official culture quickly becomes an unqualified one whenever a male or female interacts with his or her own birth mother. In this domain, mothers, unlike fathers, are seldom feared or rejected. They are the emotional, rather than the symbolic, glue that holds the polygamous family together. More importantly, they are spared the difficult, and often troubling, pressures of adoration or reverence that fathers are subjected to.

Women's unofficial or earthly status is much higher than their theological status. This arises from the realities of the polygamous marriage system where there is always a shortage of women. The scarcity of women contributes to the readiness of the community to forgive and welcome back wayward women, both the young and mature, who had left. The community is less open to accepting back wayward young men who are often regarded with suspicion. They will have a difficult time finding a wife from within the community.

Church doctrine dictates that women should be taken care of. Any woman who requests to remarry will immediately be assigned and accepted into another man's family. Since men's social standing is based on the number of wives and offspring they have, the additional wife with her children serves only to enhance a man's relative social status. It is also understood that women, through work or public assistance, will bring income into the family. Women are seldom therefore perceived of as being an economic drain on family resources.

The Fundamentalists' conviction is that they are God's chosen people, born to live "the fullness of the Gospel," and thus create God's ideal, the polygamous family (Baur 1988). It lies at the heart of the Fundamentalist communities' communitarian impulses to create a spiritually unified and socially harmonious system of order. The creation of this order depends upon the strength and vitality of not only the father-son relationship and mother-children relationship, but also the relationship between co-wives. The plural family is held together as much by a collective effort to maintain a strong image of a harmonious family as it is by anything else.

Angel Park and American Culture

Given the unusualness of the community's family system, it is easy to overlook the commonalties that fundamentalist Mormons share with mainstream American culture. Forged out of 19th century American frontier experience, fundamentalist Mormonism embraces many American culture values that range from frugality to personal autonomy.

Although the residents of Angel Park feel that certain aspects of the larger culture are immoral (e.g., X-rated movies), most members of the community participate as interested spectators and, at times, disgruntled critics of national and international events. Several polygynous families have even appeared on various talk shows to defend their religiously-based life style. Others have discussed their lifetyle with magazine and television reporters. Contemporary fundamentalists are not like the Hutterites, who disapprove of, and strive to withdraw from, mainstream America culture. For Angel Park's residents, life is to be enjoyed and they do not hesitate to partake of some of life's many delights (e.g., drink coffee and alcohol, visit national parks, shop at a nearby shopping mall, and feast at all you can eat $4.99 buffets). Common dinner topics range from religious issues, current events, the entertainment value of *The Mask of Zorro* and *Saving Private Ryan*, Clinton's impeachment trial and its reflection on changes in American culture, to the benefits of taking flax seed oil to prevent illness.

Fundamentalist Mormons never rejected mainstream culture as much as they feared provoking its wrath. Nonetheless, for most of its 80-year existence, the community has repeatedly encountered social harassment and political persecution. From 1882, Federal and State governments sought to disenfranchise the Mormons in Utah. As a result, many polygynists went into hiding, fleeing into remote areas of Utah, Idaho, Arizona, and into Mexico. By 1897, almost 200 Mormons were sent to prison for practicing polygyny (Bohannan 1985:81). However, despite the arrests and the opposition from Americans outside the community, several church leaders, including some of the founders of the Angel Park community, believed that the Church would be compromising fundamental religious principles and therefore refused to cease forming plural marriages. Their refusal has resulted in more than two-generations of strife between Angel Park and the mainstream Mormon Church, which after 1890, officially prohibited polygamy.

Thus began an ongoing antagonistic and sometimes bitter conflict between Mormon fundamentalists, the mainstream Mormon church, and state and federal governments. From the 1930s until the 1950s, Angel Park was the site of numerous governmental raids. The last and largest took place in 1953, which resulted in the arrest of 39 men and 86 women, while their 263 children were placed in foster homes for up to two years (Bradley 1993: 110; Von Wagner 1991). An unintended consequence of the raids was to "strengthen everyone's conviction and dedication to maintain their life-style. Outside pressure had in effect turned everyone into a community of believers" (Bradley 1993:110). In this way, Angel Park remains an "enclave culture."

Since the late 1960s, there has emerged a greater tolerance, albeit a reluctant one, between the State of Arizona and the polygamous community. Although the State remains adamant in its insistence that the polygamous life style is illegal, it has tacitly adopted a "live and let live" posture toward Angel Park. Given American mainstream culture's tolerance toward cohabitation, alternative child rearing practices, and other related social experiments in family living, the polygamist community has become a public secret and as such, is culturally tolerated.

Angel Park: The Religious Community

Angel Park is a sectarian religious community that forms one of five polygamous communities found in Western North America and Northern Mexico. Each community is separately governed and maintains only nominal, if any, contact with the others. The population of Angel Park is approximately 6,500, with over half of the population under the age of 12.

Angel Park is a planned community whose members live, or expect to live, in a plural family. Unlike 19th century Mormonism, where an estimated 10 to 20 percent of the families were polygamous (Foster 1992), more than forty-five percent (158 out of 350 families) form polygamous households.

On the whole, Angel Park is a town that, from first appearance, appears quaint and rather ordinary. Like other small American rural communities, all of its main roads (seven in all) are paved, whereas its side streets are not. Its houses, however, are anything but ordinary. Because people practice "Big House" polygamy, where everyone lives together, the houses range in size from three bedroom mobile trailers to huge 35,000 square feet mansions, many in various stages of completion or renovation.

Because of its location, Angel Park's economy cannot support all of its residents. Therefore, most work outside the community in a variety of professions. Most men work in the booming regional construction and inter-state trucking industries, while women and other men work in a variety of jobs that include accountants, architects, janitors, masseuses, caretakers, principals, teachers, nurses, and mechanics. The lack of a well-developed local infrastructure necessitates that most residents find employment outside the community. Despite the inconvenience of working outside the community, most people find employment, and the town boasts a remarkable zero unemployment rate. Overall, it is not a wealthy town. Angel Park's $14,500 average median income is higher than Appalachia's $8,595, but is still one of the lowest median incomes in the Western United States (Zoellner 1998, p. A1).

Politically, Angel Park, like other small rural Mormon communities (Bennion 1998), is a closed system organized around a male theocratically-oriented system. Few town officials are selected without proper religious credentials (Parker et al. 1975:693).[2] Disagreements within the community in 1986, resulted in the town fissioning into two rival religious branches, which formed separate groups organized around their own churches and schools. The split resulted in the formation of two distinct postures toward religious authority and the mainstream culture. The largest factions embraced a reformist-conservative orientation, which resulted in the alteration of the fundamentalist religious doctrine away from collective authority to authority based in one man's guidance. The other faction espoused an orthodox-liberal posture, whereby they maintained adherence to strict interpretation of fundamentalist doctrine of priesthood authority, while adopting a more open attitude toward interacting with mainstream society.

The orthodox-liberal faction encourages personal agency and responsibility, while the reformist-conservative faction insists on absolute obedience to religious authority. Significantly, the liberal faction which is smaller (around 1000 members), is more educated, with a sizable number of businessmen who daily interact with outsiders. Regardless of its posture adopted toward mainstream society, both factions agree that their community should operate with each individual's primary allegiance to their theologically governed religious body, rather than to civil authority.

Placement Marriage, Passionate Love and Religious Authority

The Mormon conception of true love closely resembles the 19th century Victorian England's conception of platonic love, which Seidman, tells us, was "essentially spiritual, not physical or carnal in origin and essence" (1991:45). In practice, however, sexual love in fundamentalist Mormon society, as it was in Victorian society, is often highly eroticized. Sexual pleasure is an appropriate desire provided it is the by-product of spousal affection and hence, marital love. Angel Park fundamentalists, while disapproving of pre-marital sex, believe firmly that sexual pleasure should be an enjoyable aspect of every marriage.

Mormon cosmology holds that, before birth, everyone lives with God as a spirit. In this pre-existence state, men and women were promised to one another, for time and eternity. Individuals must therefore strive to find their "true love" and, in a sense, remarry his or her eternal, pre-ordained soul mate. Failure to strive in such a way can potentially lead to an awkward situation whereby one's earthly spouse will differ from one's heavenly spouse. To ensure that death will not result in the separation of the spouses, it is imperative that the couple follows God's will. To this end, the priesthood's council members act as God's representatives, and their council is eagerly sought in matters of the heart. One of the council's most important functions is to help community members find their celestial mates. The priesthood council is continuously involved in ongoing dialogues within itself in its effort to sort out individual matters of the heart and ultimately, marital placement.

It should not be inferred that romantic passion is a prerequisite for marriage. More than half of the marriages in Angel Park are placement marriages, with 85 percent of all elite families following this practice. In these marriages, individuals, particularly teen-aged women, followed the matrimonial recommendations of their parents and the priesthood council. These marriages may or may not result in intergenerational conflict or personal turmoil. Not being deeply emotionally involved with a spouse, the individual enters marriage expecting, as in many cultures, that in time, "Love will come." A 27-year-old woman, said, on the eve of her tenth wedding anniversary, "During the first three years of my marriage, I did not even like my husband, but now I can say I truly love him." Her's is not an atypical opinion.

Nevertheless, dilemmas do arise. There are times when parents disapprove of a daughter's (though seldom a son's) choice or, more importantly, the priesthood council considers the relationship inappropriate. When this occurs, individuals must reconcile their romantic feelings with their deep-seated religious beliefs, which include the priesthood council's importance in guiding the community and its members to spiritual salvation and eternal happiness. This is never an easy task. The following is an account of a lower-class Angel Park woman who repeatedly told me her hopes, fears, and anguish over being lost in the world and then saved through following the advice of a religious leader. The process and complexities found in the marital discussion (below) is typical.

As a young woman she "turned herself over to the priesthood" and asked them to help her discover "where she belonged" (i.e., who she should marry). One of the church elders, a highly respected man, after listening to her recount life's sadness, advised her to pray for an answer.

She recounts that Brother J read her a Patriarchical Blessing and started to pray.

He told me to go home and pray and to see what I come up with. Well, I didn't come up with nothing because all I started doing was getting scared. I was afraid that the priesthood brethren would give me away to anybody, and how was I suppose to know whether it was right or wrong, you know. So I started getting fear again, which is normal, but evil spirits started trying to bother me again. So finally, I just quit worrying about it, I started praying and I asked the Heavenly Father to just take all the confusion away, because I didn't really want to really get married, I really wanted to go back and make things up with Jim and everybody that I hurt their feelings, all the guys, and I didn't really feel like I wanted to get married. But I felt like if I did that, I would just start getting emotionally all into everything, cause I really didn't know what to do. Anyway, so finally I just went down and I told Brother J, I said, 'I ain't coming up with nothing, except I'm getting really confused.' And he said, 'OK, then just quit praying about a certain man and start praying that God will give you the intelligence that you will know when the time is right.'

So I went home, and actually, I didn't pray for a week because I was just, I would get too many mixed feelings, too many mixed thoughts, and I just felt like my prayers really weren't doing that much good for me. And that sounds weird and that's just how I felt emotionally about things. And then after about a week, I went in my room and I knelt down and prayed. But still got nothing. I then went to see Brother J and asked him if he had come up with a name. He said he hadn't. He asked if I had come up with a name. And I told him, 'No,' and I had quit praying, because I was getting too confused. And so he told me to go back home and pray because I needed to have an open channel with

God, which is true. I needed to make it for myself. Later, he told me that he came up with a man's name three times, and every time he prayed he would get the same name. What made him confused was what I said to him the last time we met. I told him I don't give a shit who you pick, I will never marry a Roberts, so don't you tell me that I'm going to marry a Roberts, because I will not marry him. Then he looked at me and said it was a Roberts who he saw me with. I was amazed. He told me to discuss marrying a Roberts with my parents. My father was neutral, he liked the Roberts family, but my mother was upset. After awhile I thought maybe I should meet Roberts and when I did an amazing calmness came over me and I felt that this is where I belong—so I agreed to become Roberts' second wife.

Not every encounter runs this smoothly. If an individual's love is more deeply felt, the council's recommendation is often resisted. There are numerous precedents of individuals asserting that their romantic experience is authentic and thus sanctioned by God.

Because Mormon theology is derived, in part, from 19th century transcendentalism, it holds that God's will can be known through acts of private introspection and personal revelation. Accordingly, it honors individual conviction. This religious tenet gives romantically entangled couples solid ground on which to argue that the council might be mistaken in its judgment. Although an individual's testimony of being divinely-inspired is never directly challenged, the common response is to wonder whether God or the Devil is the real source of the inspiration. Still, the notion of "agency," or personal choice, serves as an effective counterpoint to the community's formal organization, its male-centered Priesthood Council.

Although it is understood that the Priesthood Council's duty is to assist, guide, and instruct the community in its collective and personal endeavor to achieve salvation, it is equally understood that personal visions are of profound religious significance and must be taken very seriously. To this end, individuals seek to understand God's will through the aid of visions and dreams. Given these religious and secular values, it is accepted that the individual has the right to agree or disagree with any recommended marriage proposal.

Marriage negotiations are just that—negotiations which take place between the Priesthood Council and the couple—with the woman serving as both the object, and the arbitrator, of the negotiations. If the bride-to-be cannot be persuaded to change her mind, the council will often, albeit reluctantly, support her marital choice. For, as one informant said, "Who can deny God and God's love?" (i.e., choice). However, in those instances where either the parents or the Council refuse to sanction the marriage, the individual will either recognize and submit to the council's authority or the couple will elope and marry outside the community. Then, once a suitable time has elapsed, they will return as a duly-legitimized couple.

A 27-year-old man, who eloped with his present wife, told us that, "My wife's parents liked me until they found out that I wanted to marry their daughter. Her father wanted her to marry someone else. But we loved each other and knew we were meant to be together. My wife was only 26 and I was 16 when we left the community and married. A few months later we returned and were accepted back into the family." In this instance, the disagreement was between the bride's parents and the boy, and not the Council which had taken no strong position in the matter.

Another example of inter-generational antagonism is found in the tale of a young woman, who at the age of 15, refused her parents and the Priesthood Council's insistence that she marry a sixty-two year-old man. She recalls that, "He was so sure that I would agree that he immediately began to build a new house for me, while keeping his first wife in an old trailer. After six years of waiting and pleading, he finally got the hint and accepted the fact that I never would marry him. I wanted to marry someone who I love, and I did." In this way, marriages in Angel Park are often quasi-arranged, but only with the tacit support of some members of the younger generation. These are people who were not able to find someone on their own, and so had no difficulty acceding to the wishes of their parents or the Priesthood Council's marital recommendations.

Romantic Experience: Male-Female Commonality

Fundamentalist polygamists customarily use the quality of affection, and not duty, to assess and measure the overall quality of their family life. For analytical purposes, I have distinguished the range of feelings that men and women characteristically express concerning their experience with love. Angel Park residents have feelings similar to those found in 19th century Mormon polygamist love letters, which are typically filled with romantic yearnings, emotional turmoil, and heart-rending disclosures. At a bio-psychological level, these contemporary romantic yearnings and emotional longings resemble those found not only in mainstream America, but also those reported in other cultures around the world. It is important to remember that most people, at some point in their lives, experience some of these emotional high and low swings, and often with the same spouse.

The accounts presented below illustrate the importance of romantic love as a desirable personal emotional state, while at the same time reflecting a deep-seated ambivalence. For women, romantic love's presence or absence—much more than role equity—constitutes the primary measure of the quality of their relationship. Its primacy is movingly revealed in the following personal accounts of what happens when a husband's love is lost.

In one case, a husband told one of his wives that he no longer loved her. Sinking into a deep despondency, she took rat poison, crying that she no longer wanted to live. Although she became very sick, she survived. Instead of growing more sensitive and supportive, her husband was horrified and refused to talk to her. Another example of the power of love can be seen, by negative inference, in the habitual cynicism of many mature women who often privately counsel engaged women not to fall in love with their husband. A bitter romantic experience makes for a repeated warning among Mormon wives. One woman told a prospective bride, "If you do fall in love, he will hurt you." In this instance, the young bride confessed that it was too late as she had, "already fallen in love."

The ambivalent attitude held towards romantic love is further illustrated by the following episode. One Sunday afternoon, after church, a young girl announced her engagement by showing her new wedding ring to her friends. When asked if her husband had any other wives, she said, "No, I am the first." An older sister-in-law, who was a second wife, overheard the comment, and replied, "She is the first wife. She is the one who gets to go through all the heartache."

Fundamentalist women are not the only gender, however, that fears emotional vulnerability, although men maintain a more stoic, if not cynical, posture toward romantic love. Many men dismissed the emotion altogether, stressing that it was, at bottom, an illusion and not the best basis for a marriage. More in-depth probing, however, found that two-thirds of the men interviewed had been romantically rejected as young men in high school. The experience was so distressing that they became determined never to become emotionally involved again. For example, when I asked one man if, on his wedding day, he was in love with any of his three wives, he indicated that he was not, but acknowledged that, when in high school, he had fallen in love with two women who rejected his overtures. He admitted that, "It hurt so much I decided never again to let myself experience that feeling." His attitude sounds a familiar male chord in Angel Park. Men's anxiety over the possibility of losing emotional intimacy and being abandoned is a propensity revealed in the following account.

A middle-aged woman recalls the anxiety of her beloved husband and his words on their wedding night, "Have you ever wanted something your whole life and, when you finally have it, you feel that it is going to be taken away from you?" "No," she replied, "I guess I have not lived long enough to desire something that much." Then he told her he was, "so afraid of losing me because he loved me so much." That night she promised never to leave him. Twenty years later her husband, bedridden from old age could no longer control his bowel movements. Whenever she grew weary of the tedious duties involved in bathing, feeding, and cleaning him, she remembered her wedding night promise never to leave him. She asserted that "I stayed with him because in the end I realized that I love him. I know right now he is preparing a place for me on the other side and, when I die, he will come and take me back with him, but only if I am worthy."

Mormon fundamentalist men's reaction to the loss of love, whether through death, divorce, or abandonment, resembles their American mainstream male counterparts who tend to slowly recover from emotional separation. Men's capability for extended sadness, due to the absence of romantic love, is revealed in the following account.

A middle-aged woman unexpectedly met the son of a former high school classmate who had asked to marry her years ago. Much to her surprise, she discovered that the man had, for more than twenty years, harbored a love crush, which he only recently revealed to his young son who upon meeting her, blurted out, "So you are the woman that my father always talks about. He was so crushed when you married that older man."

Another example of men's propensity to quietly endure emotional loss is found in the torment of a man whose second wife left him to join another polygamous community. The man did not want to discuss the incident for fear of emotionally retrieving it. However his son told us that, "My father was depressed for months. He lost the woman he loved." Another wife revealed that her husband was devastated when his third wife left the family, remarking that, "When Sam's third wife left him for another man who had been secretly courting her, it affected his health. He cried for three straight weeks and simply deteriorated into an invalid. We buried him six months later."

Polygamist men and women, when discussing the benefits of arranged marriages, often mention the avoidance of emotional entanglements as being foremost. What is significant is that no one takes these discussions seriously. Everyone knows that each man and woman will have to reconcile, in their own way, the desired, feared, and often deeply troubling emotional experience that is romantic love.

Sex Differences: The Search for True Love

Because marriage is a reality that faces women at an earlier age than men, women more than men are preoccupied with finding one's "true love." It is a goal that is thought about and discussed with a genuine intensity and singleness of purpose. For young men, however, marriage remains a kind of abstraction that will not involve them until later in life. At this point in their lives, (16–17-years-old), many young women realize that they do not want to live in a plural marriage and decide to leave the community. For women who decide to remain, however, they must confront the dueling demands of romance, marital happiness, and family harmony.

Unlike polygamist men who can and, often do, find romantic passion by taking an additional wife, women's opportunities are more restricted. They can marry only one man at a time. Although more than 30 percent of women in Angel Park will divorce over the course of their lives, it is not the preferred solution to a loveless marriage.[3] It is far better to choose wisely and form a good marriage and thus "add to the Lord's flock." To this end, prayer, visionary dreams, and one's own inner prompting are evaluated in an attempt to understand God's will—processes that are not unlike the American approach taken by American Puritans to spiritual problems. The validity of dreams as a vehicle of truth is so strong that they are often the critical guide one uses in making important decisions. A middle-aged woman, for example, who had recently terminated a short but difficult marriage and was temperamentally hesitant to become emotionally involved again, changed her mind when she, by chance, met a man who resembled a man that she dreamed about as a young girl. She recalls that, "I dreamt of a man with blue eyes and curly blond hair. Neither of my first two husbands had blue eyes or curly hair. When I saw him standing with blond hair and blue eyes, I knew he was the man in my dreams and I wanted to immediately marry him. It did not matter what others might think, he was my true love."

Another woman prayed for a sign of whom she would marry. After several weeks of intense prayer, she had a vision that revealed her "promised love, "a married man who she had never spoken to." Immediately she sought out a member in the priesthood council for confirmation as to the authenticity of her vision. He informed her that it was a good sign. A few days later he approached the man and suggested that her vision was God's sign that he take another wife. Although he did not know the woman very well, he agreed. The woman was filled with anticipation and excitement over being united with her true love. The man, however, took a reserved, almost emotionally-guarded, attitude toward his new bride. For him marriage was more of a duty—in this case, a duty derived from a true visionary dream.

Younger men, more than older, mature men, are consistently concerned with finding one's true love. This is not unusual. Without the financial backing of their families, young men are economically unable to compete with the more established mature males. The only resources they have, being unmarried, are those not immediately available to older married men: access and the opportunity to offer exclusive attention to a particular woman. Because most male-female relationships begin in high school, many young men are able to form substantial emotional bonds. Although lacking economic means of support, a young man can often convince a woman that she would be happier marrying him rather than a middle-aged man with several wives. The pattern is that if the young woman falls in love with the young man, she will probably marry him. On the other hand, if he is unsuccessful in attracting a high school sweetheart, he will ultimately leave the community to find a wife.

There is always a shortage of eligible women in every polygamous society, and Angel Park is no exception. Young women leave because they reject the polygamous life style and want to live outside the community. The community is, therefore, always seeking ways to attract outsiders to convert to their religion and embrace their life style. The primary boosters are men, who, on their own accord, seek to marry women outside the community who will convert to their religion. To this end, men invoke religious scripture and secular ideals of harmonious love to justify the life they have to offer. Many women find these courtship persuasions intriguing and, provided they also enjoy the man's personality, often decide to marry the man and adopt his lifestyle. In these instances, it is not religious doctrine per se that is attractive, though it is a useful support, as much as it is the man himself and his alternative lifestyle.

Women who become a plural wife are drawn from three backgrounds: widows, divorcees, and persons who are open to a polygamous lifestyle. Their motivations range from deeply felt emotional and/or religious commitment to the pragmatic need for support of themselves and their children. Regardless of motivation, polygamist men are willing to marry them as it increases the size of their earthly family and thus their celestial rank in the heavenly kingdom. Despite this, it is young nubile women who are preferred over middle-age mature women. The reasons rest on reproductive pragmatics and male erotic aesthetics. Men want to have sex and children and they prefer to have both with young women.

As in other cultures, physical attraction is the hook that pulls men into the relationship (Symons 1979). Angel Park women are acutely aware that men find younger women more attractive than older women. Some wives relate stories of their husbands going, in their words, "crazy and chasing young girls." As a mature woman explained, "My husband went through a mid-life crisis and began chasing a young fourteen-year-old around. During the courtship my husband would spend his money on her, instead of giving it to me and the children. I hated that young girl for the neglect she caused my family." Another middle-aged woman, when asked what the difference was between men and women replied, "Men and women." She added, "Men desire young girls and women, friendship." Although women emphasize lust as the primary motivation for men's involvement with a younger wife, men report that it is not sexual desire per se that "drives a man crazy." Rather, it is the anticipation and enjoyment of being with an attractive woman that seems to invoke romantic idealization. As one man noted, "I was obsessed with her in ways that I did not understand. She became my life." Youth is the catalyst that provokes male idealization, transforming lust into passionate love.[4]

Men justify their interest in building a plural family entirely on the premise of religious tenets. They are hesitant to admit that they find erotic pleasure in sexual variety. It is, however, a pleasure often acknowledged in moments of private humor and spontaneous (and sometimes drunken) asides. This is not a recent occurrence. Kimball Young, writing about polygamous life in the 1930s, observed that "older men got a thrill out of courting a younger woman" (1954:282). Most men in Angel Park would concur, though some more loudly than others. They are adamant in their insistence, however, that their primary motive for entering into a plural marriage is one of religious conscientiousness. This notion is not self-deception. It is the fundamental reason why men and women strive to live "the principle" and, hence, create God's model human family system.

Politics of Romance: Inside a Polygamous Family

Angel Park is a community organized around a set of religious standards and secular principles that emphasize the pursuit of salvation through the avoidance of sin, selfishness, and arrogance. Within the family, the religious principles are centered on the notion we call harmonious or familial love. Harmonious love is somewhat akin to communitas in being unbounded in its potential for forging, strengthening, and sustaining affectionate bonds. Because it encourages respect, empathy, helpfulness, and lasting affection, harmonious love often serves as the principal means to bind and unite the polygamous family. Its non-dyadic focus stands in sharp contrast to romantic love, a tolerated but seldom glorified emotional experience. Although harmonious love is fervently stressed as the preferred ideal, it is vulnerable, as we have seen, to personal desires.

Angel Park distinguishes between two types of families: "united polygamy" (i.e, live together in one house) and "divided polygamy" (i.e., living in separate homes). The cultural ideal is to live together in one large house but the reality is that more than 60 percent of the Angel Park's polygamous families live in separate households.

Social relations in the Mormon polygamous family, unlike other polygamous societies, revolve around personal sentiment as much as duty. There is a twin pull of almost equal force. Whenever a conflict arises, an individual response is unpredictable and thus threatening to the social order: Will he or she uphold family harmony or seek to satisfy personal gratification? This is especially so of romantic love which, more than any other emotional experience, not only overwhelms a person's judgment but also can reorder his or her priorities for an uncertain period of time.

There is a continuum in both men's and women's involvement in plural marriages that ranges from shared equality to outright favoritism. Men, as the symbolic center of the family, must balance each wife's emotional and economic interests. Conscious of the impact of favoritism on the family harmony, men strive to modify some of its harmful impact. To this end, most husbands are diligent in spending quality time (e.g., dinners and trips), if not equal time, with each co-wife. In this regard, women intently study and assess their husband's actions and are quick to note acts that suggest favoritism. If a husband can avoid pursuing his interests and struggle or, in their words, "sacrifice" in order to uphold the religious principles, the household ambience will be relatively harmonious and content.

The most delicate and potentially dangerous situations arise whenever a new wife enters the family. This is the most unstable time in a fundamentalist household and often tests a woman's religious convictions and, in turn, her willingness to participate in a plural marriage. During this liminal state, the new wife usually receives the husband's undivided attention, and co-wives do not complain about their husband spending a lot of time with the new wife. It is understood that the honeymoon intimacy will continue once the couple returns from their trip. However, if the intimacy continues beyond a few weeks, it will engender a round of questions and doubts and, ultimately, generate into intense jealousy among the co-wives.

Mormon polygamous wives who are not the central focus of their husband's attention and love, like their counterparts in other cultures (Bell 1995), deeply resent the "favorite" wife. If the favoritism persists, a wife will assume that her husband has grown emotionally distant and is no longer interested in her. Whenever this happens, a wife will respond in one of three ways: 1) seek to rekindle her husband's interest through romantic love; 2) resign herself to the loss of affection and seek emotional fulfillment exclusively in her children; 3) divorce and seek love in another marriage; or 4) focus exclusively on enhancing their social standing amongst other co-wives. Clearly, for all concerned, it is imperative that the husband and his wives avoid favoritism and work together to sustain a harmonious family ambience.

As we have seen, it is romantic passion's volatility that makes it a feared, resented, and admired emotional experience. For the fundamentalists of Angel Park, it tests the faith and commitment of long term co-wives as well as newly-weds' religious faith. For example, in the case of a new wife, her emotions and expectations are often challenged by the reality of sharing a spouse. The adjustment is never easy. A young woman, who had recently taken a new sister wife, told us that, "Sometimes I want to always be with my husband, but I know that it is selfish so I encourage him to see his other wife." Not every wife is as generous or as noble. Some are confused, experiencing doubt and distress. A young woman told us that, "I did not think my husband's second marriage would bother me—I was ready to live the principle. But I stayed awake at nights, unable to sleep. I felt so alone and abandoned." Other co-wives cease believing in the spiritual nobility of harmonious love and focus entirely on getting their fair share of emotional attention. This attitude is exemplified in the following account of a new wife's surprise and eventual resignation that the other co-wife did not believe in, nor want to work to create a "united polygamous" family. She reported that, "Right before I married my husband, he, his first wife, and myself went for a walk. My husband had his arms around both of us as we walked down the street. As we walked, I put my arm around my husband's waist, just below the first wife's arm who was already holding on to him. Later that evening the first wife told me, "When I felt your arm around our husband's waist it made my blood boil." I was shocked at her comment because I thought she wanted to live the principle and create a harmonious large family. (pause) This marriage has been a challenge from that day forward, because the first wife refuses to accept God's law" (i.e., polygyny).

An uneasy and perennial tension exists between a woman's desire to receive exaltation by participating in the plural marriage and her fear of losing her husband's interest and attention. This accounts for the continuous evaluation of every potential marital prospect. Wives are keen to discover shortcomings of a potential wife and become annoyed and, at times, paranoid whenever their husband is considering another wife. How unsettling this transition can be is illustrated by the following account. A woman had been staying with a polygynous family for a short period of time. Although she assured everyone that she was not interested in a plural marriage, the wives of the family were leery of her true intentions. After the visit, the woman explained to a co-wife that she had a boyfriend and only wanted to stay with them for a short vacation, whereupon the wife immediately reported the conversation to her husband and then watched, in delight, his surprise and disappointment. Another example of the tension between religious conviction and pragmatic interest is found in the various ways that co-wives often seek to discourage a prospective wife from joining the family. These can range from ignoring her presence whenever she visits to asking her assistance in performing a particularly odious domestic chore. After a young woman who was being courted, had spent the entire night talking with her potential husband, the next morning a co-wife requested that she wash the family's Sunday dinner dishes. It was a task that required washing by hand more than 100 dishes and taking more than an hour-and-a-half. The point that the co-wife wanted to communicate to the potential wife was that plural marriage did not involve stimulating discussions of love, religious philosophy, and family harmony.

If polygamist women are emotionally vulnerable, particularly to psychological abandonment, so are the men. If a polygamist husband becomes too attached, he knows that he will disrupt family bonds and do damage to his reputation within the community for being unable to manage his family. The burden of this management falls heavily on the man. Men know that, if the family has the reputation of being disharmonious, he will lose honor and social standing in the community, which can result in difficulty in attracting a future wife.

A man is dependent on his wife's (or wives') assistance in attracting another spouse. Even if the Priesthood Council recommends a marriage partner, the woman still must decide. Her decision is often based on three factors: 1) the quality of family harmony (actual and potential) represented in the cooperation between co-wives; 2) the intensity of affection held for the husband; 3) the number of wives, especially young wives, in the family. It is a cultural given that it is often in a young woman's short-term interest to marry a middle-aged man with mature wives. This is a powerful motivation and requires assessment.

Mature wives are not powerless. They are respected, valued, and loved not because of seniority, but rather for either the quality of marriage or their access to valuable resources (e.g., a deceased husband's retirement funds, social security benefits, or some other forms of inheritance or income). This wealth, while not considerable, is often sufficient to assist a man to attract another wife. With this supplementary source of income, a man can buy a used car or build a home for his new wife. If a wife withholds her income, it can undermine her husband's ability to attract another wife. A polygamist husband depends on his co-wife's (or co-wives) assistance to sustain a friendly household environment and to provide economic aid in helping him build his heavenly kingdom.

It is a dilemma for men and women. They embrace the polygamous principle and its call for plurality, while simultaneously seeking to hold onto, or rekindle, the romantic passion once felt toward a particular spouse. The tensions that erupt around this dilemma are the source of drama found in daily life at Angel Park. The reality is that the majority of Angel Park's polygamous families seldom achieve genuine long lasting harmony, but remain, at best, a cauldron of competing interests that periodically rupture the fragile balance that unites a man, his wives, and children together in their religiously-inspired and unified cultural system. In seeking to fulfill God's law and create the polygamous family, the residents of Angel Park endure "sacrifices" that they believe will ultimately enable them to achieve salvation. The domestic tensions serve to build character, which in the eyes of the Lord, will make them worthy to enter his Heavenly Kingdom.

In summary, nineteenth century Mormons strove to achieve a spiritual community based on the institution of plural or celestial marriage, which exalts harmonious love as the center of family life. This ideal stands in sharp contrast to romantic love, which Angel Park has neither rejected nor encouraged, but recognized. Furthermore, the competing 19th century notions of agency and collectivism contributes to ongoing tensions within Angel Park, often pulling the individual in opposite directions.

Since this community honors the individual's freedom to determine which emotional orientation—harmonious or romantic love—is the more important, there is tremendous variation in response. In this way, romantic love constitutes both an authentic, creative force, and a potentially disruptive emotion. As such, it is an experience that challenges collective religious conviction and the individual will to participate in America's most unique experiment in family living.

Notes

1. The data that forms much of this research is part of a larger ongoing research project that began in 1992. The work is partially supported by a mini-grant from the Nevada National Endowment for the Humanities and a UNLV Research Grants and Fellowships Award. I would like to thank Emilie Allen, Hans Baur, Jim Bell, Janet Bennion, Philip Kilbride, Lee Munroe, Thomas Paladino, Elizabeth Whitt, and Bernard Wong for their encouragement, suggestions, and comments.

2. In the early 1970s Parker et al. (1975) found that every family in "Weston," a polygamist community in northern Utah, was polygamous.

3. Janet Bennion (1998) found that the Harker fundamentalist polygamous community, about 700 miles north of Angel Park, was around 35 percent, with "40% of all marriages ended in release, divorce, or abandonment" (1998:89). I found that the abandonment rate in Angel Park to be higher—it was near 51% of all marriages.

4. Although many 19th century Mormons argued that sexual intercourse was for procreation and not personal enjoyment, this is not always the case. Sexuality is not an embarrassing topic in Angel Park. Although modesty is stressed, men and women are not sexual prudes. Given the frequency of childbirth, reproduction and sexuality are simply taken as a natural aspect of life.

References

Baur, H. 1988. *Utopia in the Desert.* New York: SUNY.

Bohannan, P. 1985. *All The Happy Families.* New York: McGraw Hill.

Bradley, M. 1993. *Kidnapped From that Land.* Provo: University of Utah Press.

Bennion, J. 1998. *Women of Principle.* Oxford: Oxford University Press.

Cancian, F. 1987. *Love in America.* New York: Cambridge University Press

Cannon, J. 1992. "My Sister, My Wife: An Examination of Sororal Polygyny in a Contemporary Mormon Fundamentalist Sect," *Syzygy*: 1:4:315-320.

Foster, L. 1992. *Women, Family and Utopia*. Syracuse: Syracuse University Press.

Musser, J. 1944. *Celestial or Plural Marriage*. Salt Lake City: Truth Publishing Co.

New York Times, June 11, 1998. "Women Should Submit."

Parker, S, Janet Smith, and Joseph Ginat. 1973. "Father Absence and Cross-Sex Identity: The Puberty Rites Controversy Revisited." *American Ethnology*: 687-706.

Seidman, S. 1992. *Romantic Longings*. London: Blackwell.

Van Wagoner, R. 1986. *Mormon Polygamy: A History*. Salt Lake City: Signature Books.

Symons, D. 1979. *Human Sexuality*. Oxford: Oxford University Press.

Young, K. 1954. *Isn't One Wife Enough?* New York: Crown.

Zoellner, T. 1998. "Polygamy on the Dole." *The Salt Lake Tribune* (June 28: A1).

CHAPTER 14

Plotting the Contours of the "Unclear" Family

Bob Simpson

R ising rates of divorce and separation in Britain over the last twenty years have gener- ated a considerable amount of debate and engaged the perspectives of lawyers, sociolo- gists, theologians, feminists, politicians and policy-makers. The ground over which this highly contested discourse ranges takes in changes in familial residential patterns, gender roles, socialisa- tion and patterns of inheritance, as well as the way in which changes in each of these relate to broader patterns of cultural and social interaction. In other words, precisely the area which an- thropologists tend to subsume under the heading of kinship.

To date however, discussion of divorce has been solidly cast in the idiom of family and, as I have suggested in the introduction, this ideologically loaded concept proves wholly inadequate to capture the social complexities it is made to encompass. To talk of family in a non-contested and uncritical way is to obscure the creative possibilities inherent in kinship for the structuring and organisation of inter-personal relations (cf. Weston 1991). The study of divorce as a cultural ex- pression of kinship rather than a social problem with the family demonstrates the distinctiveness of western patterns of relational organisation and transformation; it offers the prospect of locat- ing distinctively Euro-American (Edwards et al. 1993:7–8) ideas of parenthood, relatedness and the transmission of identity within the wider continuum of societies studied by anthropologists. In this chapter consideration is given to the kinship implications of divorce and re-marriage. Consideration of the way in which particular kinds of networks are asserted and maintained after divorce enables us to begin the process of plotting the contours of the unclear family. First, how- ever, it is important to locate the study of divorce within the anthropological study of family and kinship.

Anthropological Perspectives on Divorce

Divorce has long been a pre-occupation of social anthropologists studying non-western societies. Classical structural-functionalist concerns with the reproduction and maintenance of social and political order meant that marriage and its dissolution were of central importance. Just as marriages, in a general sense might be said to be formally marked by the transfer of goods, rights and people, so the ending of marriages involves the reallocation of these. The strategies for this reallocation proved illuminating for understanding broader questions of filiation, legitimacy, inheritance and authority in traditional societies. Apparent differences in the stability of marriage across cultures, and particularly those of African tribal societies, were noted and attempts made to explain these in terms of the variability of bridewealth practices. Large bridewealth meant that a substantial bundle of rights were acquired by a husband and his kin in the productive and reproductive capacities of a woman and this, in turn, tended to produce "low divorce" societies. This contention laid the grounds for the much vaunted and latterly much criticised "bridewealth and stability of marriage" debate which raged throughout the 1950s (see Comaroff 1980 and Hutchinson 1990 for a review of the issues). Although this debate is instructive in that it focuses on the question of how rights and obligations are reallocated following marital dissolution, in other ways it is singularly unhelpful. Its predominantly jural focus and concomitant concern with male rights obscures the processual aspects of marital dissolution and the extent to which women act as agents within these processes (Hutchinson 1990: 394). The anthropological interest in divorce was thus in terms of what it revealed about marriage in broadly functionalist terms rather than as a process in itself which involved actual relationships and arrangements concerning people and property, negotiated in particular contexts of power and gender relationships. An important exception to this view is to be found in Esther Goody's seminal piece on separation and divorce among the Gonja (1962). In this work, the place of divorce within the developmental cycle of the domestic group is made clear, as are the strategies for incorporating its consequences into everyday life (cf. also Stenning 1958 & Cohen 1971). Marriages are ended either *de facto* or *de jure* at various points in the life-cycle and this results in dispersal of kin; a woman may return to her natal village, perhaps with young children, but leaving older ones with their father and his kin.

What is of note here is that in Goody's account, divorce relocates people and relationships in space and time. It does not result in the ending of all relationships between the separating couple. The ties created by the birth of children, for example, continue to bind parents long after they cease to live together. The particular dynamics of Gonja kinship also mean that the splitting of the sibling group is common and this gives rise to a wide range of parenting and caring arrangements. The Gonja case provides a useful illustration of what Goode describes as a "stable high divorce rate system" (Goode 1993: 16). As he points out, even though the instability of individual marriages is very high in such systems the overall patterning of relationships is remarkably stable for the simple reason that customary arrangements are in place to deal with the economic and kinship consequences of marital dissolution.

The interest in divorce in traditional societies is in stark contrast to the lack of attention paid to divorce in contemporary western society; anthropologists have been slow to respond to the kinship implications of large-scale divorce in contemporary western society.[1] This is a serious omission. Kinship provides a context in which people make sense of the relational dimensions of their lives. Divorce entails a fundamental reordering of this context which invites public and private concern. However, given the way that anthropologists have tended to approach the study of English kinship it is hardly surprising that radical changes in this system have escaped attention. As Bouquet has highlighted (1993:13), the centrality of the study of kinship within the British anthropological tradition makes for a revealing contrast when placed alongside the relative paucity of anthropological studies of English kinship. In a similar, and somewhat wry observation, Barnes (1980:297) contrasts the study of kinship by anthropologists with the study of family by sociologists. For the former, the study of kinship in non-western societies is a rather serious and esoteric pursuit which forms one of the central planks of the discipline. For the latter, the study of the family has often been treated as rather more lightweight and marginal to central sociological concerns with class, mobility and industrialisation in modern society. Suffice it to say that for a long time anthropologists were not particularly aware that there was anything to study under the heading of kinship in English society. Notable exceptions are the classic monographs of Firth and his colleagues (Firth, Hubert and Forge 1969) who mapped middle-class kinship in London and Young and Willmott who tracked working-class communities in transition with a particular eye on kinship (Young and Willmott 1957). However, the dominant view appears to have been that the family was best left to the attentions of sociologists and psychologists. Beyond the nuclear family in western societies, relations seemed to fall into the rag-bag of bilateral or cognatic systems with an emphasis on fluidity in the ascription of roles and identities. The rich vocabulary of classical anthropological kinship studies, with its ideological focus on descent and group formation, could offer little by way of illumination when considering western kinship in general and English kinship in particular. As a result, English kinship and its consequences for ideas of personhood, community and economy was for a long time lost to anthropological enquiry to the extent that Bouquet has deemed it necessary to "reclaim" it (1993). Indeed, the lack of analytical rigour in the area of family studies has obscured more than it has revealed about the operations of kinship and household in contemporary society. In a recent review of A.F. Roberston's book *Beyond the Family*, Paul Bohannan was moved to point out the diffuse and unsatisfactory nature of literature on the western family: "almost never have the lurking assumptions been examined" (1993:175). In similar vein, Wilson and Pahl (1988) have drawn attention to the overly narrow focus on conjugal and parental roles within the family. Some family sociologists, such as Bernardes (1988) and Scanzioni (Scanzioni et al. 1989), have gone so far as to advocate the total abandonment of family as a meaningful concept in sociological discourse.

The anthropological study of divorce and separation put forward here is in some senses part and parcel of the reclamation process advocated by Bouquet (ibid). As such, consideration of divorce as a revealing manifestation of kinship has strong affinities with the study of other domestic and inter-personal contexts in contemporary British society. As Strathern has suggested there is a "vanishing effect" in operation. The point at which kinship "disappears" into class or consumption (Strathern 1992a) or into the classrooms of Portuguese undergraduates (Bouquet 1993) is the point at which the implicit is made explicit. Divorce provides a similar occasion for analytical reflection and revelation. Divorce is the point at which marriage is officially dissolved but is also the point at which the principles, assumptions, values, attitudes and expectations surrounding marriage, family and parenting are made explicit. The reason they are made explicit is that these fundamental and implicit cultural tenets are all, in one way or another, confounded and conflicted and have to become the subject of a rather public and painful process of negotiation and calculation. The apparent certainties of the life-cycle are rapidly and irreversibly replaced by the vicissitudes of an individualised life-course. We, along with our informants, can no longer assume that kinship and biology provide immutable, common-sense baselines for the understanding of contemporary English kinship but must endeavour to construct our knowledge of human relations "after nature" (Strathern 1992a), that is, as a kaleidoscope of connected cultural contexts rather than as a layering of discourses upon a solid foundation of immutable connections. For example, the rhetoric of the enterprise culture, so fundamental to British conservatism through-out the l980s, provides just such a context. Freedom, fulfilment and authenticity of the individual are shaped through choice. The enterprising self (Rose 1992) is but one step away from enterprising kinship (Strathern l992b) and the expansion of choice in the conduct of personal relations carries profound implications for the way that we think of relationships of intimacy and friendship, nurture and parenthood as well as obligations to kin in general. Recent efforts to illuminate these processes include Strathern's comprehensive account of new reproductive technologies and their impact on conceptualisations of kinship relations (Strathern 1991, 1992a, 1992b; Edwards et al. 1993). La Fontaine has provided a detailed analysis of child abuse in the light of anthropological theories of incest avoidance as well as a broader commentary on changing family (La Fontaine 1985, 1988, 1990). Such studies provide an important point of departure for the study of divorce in that they begin to probe the culturally distinct patterns of procreation, nurture and parenthood found in Britain which have hitherto been treated as opaque and self-evident science social science discourse.

Important as studies of new reproductive technologies, sexual abuse and incest undoubtedly are, they do tend to reproduce an anthropological preoccupation with the marginal if not the exotic. Divorce and its longer-term consequences on the other hand are pervasive and are bringing about fundamental transformations in patterns of kinship, parenting and what is thought of as family life in contemporary Britain. Yet, these transformations are ones about which we know relatively little. In many ways the debates which currently surround the family suggest a point similar to the one identified in the 1970s by Pahl (1984) regarding unemployment. In the preface to *Divisions of Labour* he points to the absence at that time of any clear understanding regarding the relationship between work and household provisioning on the one hand and unemployment on the other. Then, as now, the absence of good ethnographic research on a politically loaded topic makes it difficult to separate what is actually happening from the fog of ideological pronouncements about what might be happening or, as is more often the case, what pundits feel should be happening on the ground.

What is readily apparent from even a cursory examination of recent divorce statistics is that divorce has become an increasingly common part of the life-course for men and women in contemporary society. In the not too distant past divorce was a relatively isolated and anomalous incident in a world of "normal" families. It was perceived as evidence of deviance and pathology and invited attention of a therapeutic kind (Dominian 1965). Nowadays, this sense of anomaly and stigma has been greatly diluted. Today, divorce and family reconstitution are an increasingly distinctive weft running through the fabric of society, linking households through the movement of children and property from former marital relationships and generating new and complex variations in the ordering of kinship relations. The result for many divorced men and women is that they find themselves at the centre of extensive kindreds based as much on the negative affinities of divorce, as on the positive relationships one normally attributes to relations between kin. Connections, albeit negative and unwelcome, must be directly or indirectly incorporated into networks based on more conventional notions of family and kinship. Unlike the compact and predictable sociality of the nuclear family, the post-divorce kindred is fashioned out of a dispersed and rather less predictable sociality in which kinship, residence and the economics of household are substantially refigured. From the perspective of any one individual several layers of kin may have to be ordered as new constellations of relatives appear and disappear as a result of divorce and re-marriage. But, just as families are zipped together through acts of recombination they may be just as easily unzipped at some later date compounding even further the confusions over the significance of others. Similarly, the discrete family residence may for the child become radically de-centred as children pass through multiple family spaces in which they might well also have their own private spaces. Indeed, the identification of the post-divorce family with two or even more households is presented in many divorce "self-help" books as the "ideal" solution to the problem of ensuring parental continuity in the face of conjugal discontinuity (Ricci 1980; Burrett 1993). Resourcing the family may be similarly fragmented with household income a patchwork of wage, state benefits and the formal and informal inter-household transfer of money, labour and commodities. Such arrangements I have dubbed the unclear family.

The Unclear Family: A Case in Point

Steve is a man in his mid-thirties. He is a local government caretaker living in tied accommodation and, by his own estimation, "happily" married to Karen. They have three children. This is the family as it would appear to be on a tax return or census form or on a typical evening in front of the television. However, when Steve met Karen she was a single-parent caring for her daughter (see Figure 1). She was not in contact with the child's father. When they married in 1990, Steve took on the role of "father" to Karen's daughter, that is, by virtue of co-residence, his marriage to Karen and his economic support for the two of them, he became what is commonly referred to as the child's step-father or, rather more formally, her *pater*. Steve and Karen went on to have two children together. Steve also came to the marriage with previous commitments. He was earlier married to Kath, from whom he divorced in 1985. Together they had produced two daughters with whom Steve was still in regular contact and who came to stay with Steve and Karen on a regular basis. Steve also spoke of a relationship he had had in his teens which resulted in the birth

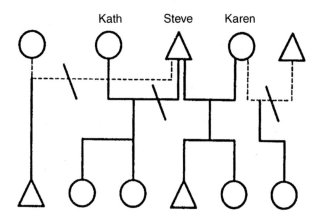

Figure 1. Kinship diagram showing the marriages and children of Steve. (Divorces are shown by oblique lines. Dotted lines represent non-marital relationships.)

of a son who lived close by and whom he saw from time to time. However, he neither lived with the boy's mother nor had had any permanent relationship with her.

Steve's narration of his "family life" places him at the centre of a network of relationships which carry varying loads in terms of affect and commitment. For example, he sees himself as a "father" to six children. However, the way in which fatherhood is expressed and experienced by Steve in relation to each of his children is variable. The simple label "father" condenses and conceals varying levels of financial and emotional commitment, different residential arrangements and variable quantities of contact with these six children.

In being a "father" to his children, Steve also comes into contact with the three women who are the mothers of the five children to whom he is *genitor*. He co-habits with his present wife Karen but also regularly meets with his ex-wife, Kath and has helped her with domestic and relationship problems. He also sees the mother of his eldest son from time to time, with whom he claims to "get on well." To complete the picture, he also claims to have good relationships with the current partners of both his ex-partners, that is, the step-fathers of the children who do not live with him.

Steve also likes to present his children as being part of "one big happy family." He encourages them to treat the various full-, half- and step-sibling relationships as if they were all "brothers and sisters." He sees this as having considerable potential when it comes to future patterns of friendship, support and obligation between them. However, not everyone understands and interprets the pattern and meaning of sibling relations as Steve does. From the perspective of grandparents, for example, there is considerable impetus to deny such patterns as they seek to establish their own sense of boundary and structure to their "family" after divorce. Steve's parents speak of having six grandchildren while Karen's parents speak of having three. This discrepancy in reckoning has become a source of conflict between Steve and his in-laws, because it translates into actions on their part which Steve sees as divisive of the sibling group. The principle of treating all the children equally, which is espoused by Steve and Karen, is contradicted when Karen's mother ignores Steve's children from his earlier marriage and only gives treats and gifts to the children actually born to Karen. The children for their part can find themselves with four, six or possibly eight relatives at the grandparental level.

Steve provides us with a summary account of what constitutes family life for a growing number of men, women and children in Britain today. Measured against the cereal-packet norm of the nuclear family it is complex, with children and resources linking households across space and time, in ways which render the identification of family with a single, discrete household wholly misleading. Indeed, the whole vocabulary of western kinship is woefully inadequate when it comes to making intelligible the complex arrangements which lie beneath the simple notions of mother, father, family, home, son and daughter in contemporary contexts.

What was once part of the habitus of domestic organisation—"a system of durable transposable dispositions" (Bourdieu 1977)—must, because of divorce, necessarily be transposed in such a way that structures and values are made conscious and explicit. The practical mastery of the domestic habitus is undermined; actions, strategies and intentions have to be thought about in ways that would not normally occur in the family prior to divorce. Pragmatic decisions have to be taken about where children should live, how often they should see the other parent, who should support whom and at what level. Emotional and economic contributions previously invisible in the implicit and private ordering of home and hearth become subject to exacting and explicit public classification and calculation; they are described and transformed by a whole new vocabulary. For example, a father's contribution to the domestic budget thus becomes "maintenance" or "support" while his role as a parent is likely to be expressed as "access" or "contact." There is nothing new in the distinction between *pater* and *genitor* which emerges from these transformations and neither is there anything new in the idea that the tenuousness of physiological paternity is apt to render its social constructions somewhat diverse across cultures (Barnes 1973). What is new in this account is the way essentialist notions of fatherhood, as a coherent repertoire of assumptions, attitudes, emotions and relationships, are rendered partial and fragmented. The emerging patterns of serial monogamy mean that fatherhood is enacted and embodied differently according to situation and circumstance. Fatherhood is thus simultaneously a grand iconic image as well as a multiplicity of situated and specifiable possibilities. Steve's account of fatherhood can thus be seen as an attempt to orchestrate multiple narratives relating to other marriages, other relationships and other parenting, within a single narrative. As I demonstrate in considerably more detail in later chapters, the cultural scripts which shape how such narratives ought to be are highly contested. Steve provides one version of how ideas of hegemonic masculinity (Carrigan et al. 1985; Cornwall and Lindisfarne 1994) and the emergent habitus of family life after divorce are brought together in practice.

Where familial arrangements fall outside the temporally stable, co-resident, nuclear model, external and normative factors such as the form and extent of state economic and welfare support following marital breakdown or the legal machinery to process divorce and civil dispute come into play to shape relational continuities. Adjusting to relationship breakdown and divorce, despite the illusion of private ordering, thus amounts to a series of personal choices and negotiations conducted within state-controlled parameters about the way that kinship ought to be. Just what these parameters are, and the models to which people turn in order to make sense of their circumstances in the wake of divorce, are only beginning to emerge.

Continuity and Discontinuity after Divorce

Marital breakdown necessitates dismantling the joint edifice of family life and divorce is the legal mechanism sanctioning this process. Putting asunder, however, does not have the dire consequences that it had in the nineteenth century when divorce brought shame and ostracism, particularly to women. Far from being the social death that it once was, divorce is nowadays more likely to be framed in terms of liberation and social rebirth; "an acute version of the process of 'finding oneself' which the social conditions of modernity force upon us all" (Giddens 1991:12). However, divorce is not entirely the unfettered quest for personal freedom and individual autonomy which such comments imply. On the contrary, personal destiny and family history are deeply entwined and in practice divorce is just as likely to reproduce continuities in social relationships as it is to establish discontinuities. From an anthropological perspective the interesting problem is what continues and what does not, what kin relations are preserved and developed and which ones attenuate and atrophy? The terminologies applied in popular discourse tend to mask such continuities whilst emphasising the discrete households and family forms that emerge. Categories such as "lone" or "single" parent, "second family" and "absent father" all emphasise the separateness of persons rather than the ways in which they retain connections economically, socially and emotionally after divorce.

In terms of the wider network of relatives the patterns are difficult to predict and often run counter to expectations of a conjugal chasm held by onlookers or, indeed, by participants themselves. In a study of middle-class families in London, a case is presented in which the person a woman was closest to after divorce was her ex-husband's sister and her daughter (Firth et al. 1969:288). This rather arbitrary process has been referred to by Finch as "working out" (Finch 1989:194–211); it is a process of evaluating relationships on the basis of shared histories and future expectations rather than rigid role prescriptions. The networks which are established once a couple cut loose from the moorings of affinity thus appear to owe more to voluntarism than to expectation: more to process than to structure. However, "working out" relationships and identifying an ego-centred post-divorce kindred is not without its problems for there are no clear expectations as to how one should treat an ex-husband's new wife or what one's attitudes should be to affines who were, prior to divorce, close and supportive relatives (Finch and Mason 1990). Indeed, for a divorcing couple "working out" is far too neat a description of this process and the idea of disentangling or disaggregating social relations might be a better conceptualisation. Speaking of notions of personhood among the Are'are of Melanesia, Strathern sees this process as being achieved "via funerary, bridewealth and similar prestations, transactions that lay out the person in terms of the claims diverse others have" (Strathern 1996:527). Divorce necessitates similar processes of disaggregating persons in terms of their interests, rights and claims in one another. Such processes are invariably characterised by high levels of confusion and ambivalence over how and whether these processes should take place. The difficulties raised by this process are further compounded by the form which Euro-American kinship takes. The capacity for extension of the kinship network is an important feature of bilateral kinship systems; they appear to have "no in built boundaries" (Strathern 1996:529). Chains of potential relationships span out from the individual person in all directions and can be activated according to a wide range of apparently arbitrary contingencies. The capacity for relatives to become "distant," "lost" or "forgotten" is an important indicator of this process in operation. The prevalence of divorce has now added the kin prefix "ex-" to this list. Just as marriage generates a universe of kin who are like one's consanguineous kin but are related "in-law," divorce converts these relatives into "ex" relations. People will thus talk of their "ex-mother-in-law" or "ex-sister-in-law." Conversely, relatives also retain their potential for resurrection at some point in the future despite the absence of active contact or communication. As the following examples illustrate, disaggregating persons is not simply a linear process but one in which parties may have radically different ideas about how networks and boundaries should be constituted.

In the first example, the couple in question had evolved a reasonably communicative relationship despite a painful and highly conflicted divorce some six years earlier. In the passage below the man is reflecting on his ex-wife's relationship with his relatives:

> The only thing that is odd is that Kate [ex-wife} tends to pop up at my family gatherings. I find that most odd. To me it's a source of extreme resentment. It makes T [new partner] feel terribly awkward. I find it embarrassing. I used to say "I can't go to any formal occasion without that bloody woman being there!" During the time that we were married she tried to draw me away from my family and into her family and she put all sorts of obstacles in the way of us going to any kind of functions with my family. Yet as soon as we separate she's trying to home in on my family—it's most odd. And I find it insensitive of the people sending the invitations to invite her. And secondly I find it insensitive of her to accept the invitations.

His ex-wife, for her part, claimed not to see her husband's family very often—*"we haven't fallen out or anything, we just don't keep in touch."* However, she did point out that one of her ex-husband's sisters does still consider her "as family" and invites her to family functions such as weddings and christenings. Her occasional inclusion in collective family rituals amounts to an uncomfortable blurring of boundaries for her ex-husband who is anxious to incorporate his new partner and children publicly into his wider network of relatives without the anomalous presence of his ex-wife. He is quick to attribute to his former wife a proactive rather than a reactive role in this and sees her as wishing "to home in" on his family.

In a second example, a similar unease is in evidence as the woman interviewed questions her ex-husband's motives for visiting her parents:

> . . . he's cultivated my mother and father since the break up and he often goes to see them on a Sunday afternoon with the boys, so that's very cosy. Now he hadn't that much

time for them when we were married, so again it's a sort of ingratiating way of niggling me I suppose because I think "well why is he doing that?" The boys see my parents as often as they want. They ought really to go of their own account and actually see their grandparents.

The implication is clear. The woman's ex-husband's visits to her parents with her sons create the blurring of a boundary which she would rather keep as discrete: the affection, interaction and exchange which animate his networks run on in ways which spill into the networks of his former wife. Furthermore, this unwelcome overlap of networks causes tensions with her own parents who still, much to the woman's chagrin, continue to keep up relationships that grew out of the first marriage:

> Well it does annoy me because even after John (her new husband) and I were married, for a good 18 months my mother wouldn't let me bring him to the house—even when we were married. And although she idolises Keith (the child of her second marriage) . . . [ ] . . . I found that very hurtful, and she said "well, you know I've got nothing against him (first husband) and he didn't do anything wrong to us, you were the one that wanted the marriage ended, you know "why should I turn my back on him?" and I said "well, don't you really . . . can't you see my side of it, that you're actually keeping away Keith's father and my husband" you know, "excluding him in favour of someone who, you know, didn't particularly have a great deal of er, social graces, when you used to come and visit us."

Examples such as these illustrate the divergence of perspectives over the meaning and significance of adult kin relations and contacts between relatives after divorce. Whereas at one time marriage brought a set of seemingly indissoluble relationships, with divorce there is the possibility for individuals to make particular selections from this set. This is no doubt part of a broader pattern of uncouplings in which sex has been largely uncoupled from marriage and marriage uncoupled from reproduction. With the advent of New Reproductive Technologies, the uncoupling of sex from reproduction is now also an option. With divorce the options available appear to be getting wider, such that, as in the example above, one might have in-laws even though one no longer has a spouse. Indeed, it would appear that an important expression of personal progress and development after divorce is the right to construct one's network of significant others. Good, wholesome, gratifying relationships can be preserved whereas the people to whom one was previously yoked by the mere accident of affinal relationship can be distanced and forgotten.

As we have seen, the making and un-making of networks is achieved through statements of inclusion and exclusion which are likely to prove highly contentious. Nevertheless, where a former partner's kin are concerned a sense of personal history rather than a sense of duty or ascribed role would appear to prevail. However, where kin relationships involving children are at issue, questions of continuity and discontinuity become significantly more contentious and emotive. The desire to construct networks which maximise inclusion of one's children yet limit the inclusion of a former partner is particularly acute. As we shall see in the next chapter, these circumstances makes all the more difficult the business of disaggregating persons from the rights, interests and responsibilities in which they were previously enmeshed. First, however, it is necessary to consider some of the cultural under-pinnings of parent-child relationships after divorce.

Disentangling "Love" from "Blood"

For couples without children who divorce, the separation might well be total and the process of adjustment an entirely personal affair achieved without reference to a former partner. It is often characterised by those concerned as "sad," rather than as a problem which invites wider public concern. Where there are children from a marriage, however, the problem is acute. Notions of continuity, connectedness and extension are fundamental to kinship and hence to the relational context through which people identify themselves. These must be disentangled from the notions of curtailment, discontinuity and severance which it is the object of divorce to achieve. Feelings and sentiments which previously flowed more or less freely are subject to multiple and conflicting interpretations. Furthermore, attempts to clarify, or at least make workable, relationships between mothers and fathers and their children after divorce are the objective of a wide range of informal and statutory agencies to say nothing of parents and children themselves.

Schneider's account (1968, 1984) of American kinship is a useful starting point in an attempt to understand this problem, not least because it invites reflection upon the cultural construction of western kinship systems. The account is premised on two major constructs. One corresponds to the order of nature, metaphorically expressed as ties of blood, and otherwise referred to as consanguinity or descent. The other corresponds to the order of law, in which culture is contrasted with nature. In the order of law the formation of relationships is based upon affinity and the extension of kin networks is through marriage. This particular construct is paradigmatic in the organisation and development of western family law. Schneider goes on to describe two kinds of "love," conjugal and cognatic, both of which he considers are central to American kinship. The latter is associated with parental ties and the former with adult conjugal relationships. These strands are woven together and subsumed under the elastic and common-sense label of "family"; within which they come all of a piece. The integration of marriage, procreation and parenthood lies at the heart of the western tradition of "family" and has been evident in philosophical discourse at least since the time of Aquinas (Blustein 1982:234). Human offspring need attention and nurturance for greater lengths of time than non-human counterparts and the indissolubility of marriage, as a divinely ordained construct, strengthens conjugal love in a way that promotes the collaborative and long-term endeavour of procreation and parenting. However, what happens at divorce, amongst other things, is that these two closely integrated polarities of kinship, the legal and the natural, the conjugal and the cognatic, the affinal and the consanguineal, have to be unpicked with the result that the roles of mother, father, and parent are constructed anew. There is continuity, yet also transformation. Conjugal relationships are sanctioned by law and are therefore capable of reversal, that is, the married can return to being unmarried. However, these must be disentangled from those relationships which are seen as essentially irreversible, that is, the set of *natural* relationships which are brought into being by the birth of a child.

Viewed in these terms, the history of divorce is one of a growing reversibility of affinal relationships. In the past, relationships, whether consanguineal or affinal, were never reversible—Christian marriage was indeed "till death us do part" with the couple, in terms of identity and estate, becoming "one flesh." The possibilities of the legal reversal of what were hitherto irreversible ties of procreative marriage has gradually widened from obscure grounds based on the failure to consummate, argued in the ecclesiastical courts of the Middle Ages, through eighteenth-century acts of parliament which enabled adulterous aristocrats to divorce and on into the humiliating and inquisitorial divorce courts of the 1940s and 1950s intent on divining "fault" amongst errant middle-class couples. However, replacement of "fault" with the notion of "irretrievable breakdown" in the 1969 Divorce Reform Act meant the way was virtually open for the pursuit of individual fulfilment beyond marriage, unfettered by legal and moral constraints. As Wolfram (1987:148) has argued, what was previously available only to the rich has, since the Matrimonial Causes Act of 1857, gradually been made more available, through legal reform and liberalisation, to all sections of society.

However, along with these changes have also come changes in ideas about parental rights and responsibilities. In the nineteenth century, the legal position of fathers vis-à-vis their legitimate children was unassailable with that of mothers correspondingly weak. Lowe (1982) cites the case of R. v De Manneville 1804 in which a man who had separated from his wife "forcibly removed an eight month old child while it was actually at the breast and carried it away almost naked in an open carriage in inclement weather. Despite this the court said it could draw no inferences to the disadvantage of the father and upheld his right to custody" (Lowe 1982:27). Over the last fifty years the pendulum has swung in the opposite direction with mothers experiencing a seemingly natural ascendancy when it comes to decisions over custody. It is estimated that as many as 90 percent of fathers who divorce do not retain custody of their children (Richards and Dyson 1982).

With this increasing reversibility of affinal ties the perceived irreversibility of consanguineal relations has become problematic, especially for a society with high investment in the ideology of patriarchy and patrifiliation (La Fontaine 1980:340). What should be the relationship between a non-resident father and his children from a former marriage? As we shall see the answers of mothers, fathers and children to this question are often seriously at odds. However, the "official" solution to the question of parental continuities and discontinuities after divorce is neatly summed up by a judge with whom I was able to sit during his day long processing of Children's Appointments (also known at that time as Section 41 Appointments). Such meetings normally took place in his chambers; there were no wigs and no oaths, just a few minutes" avuncular chat in which the judge elicited more information from a sad and often fearful parade of mothers and fathers about their proposed arrangements for their children after the divorce. In the absence of a more rigorous divination, the arrangements so described are quickly rubber-stamped and one case ushered out as the next is ushered in. However, this judge ended each of his meetings with his own particular incantation: "you may not be husband and wife anymore but you are mum and dad for the rest of your lives."

The judge's statement carries with it an important cultural expectation about patterns of kinship post-divorce. Being "mum and dad for the rest of your lives" invites reflection on the perceived irreversibility of certain relationships and consideration of their long-term implications. The distinction is one that parents who divorce readily articulate: "I mean he's a good father to him (the son) but he were a bad husband." Indeed, it is likely to be the basis for parents to rationalise their separation in the first place as one young woman recalled:

> Dad carted off Anna (sister) and I for a walk along the sea front with the dog and he explained that, although he loved us very dearly, he couldn't stand living with mother anymore and he was moving out . . .

However, being "mum and dad for the rest of your lives" handed down as free advice from on high is easy to say but notoriously difficult to achieve in practice. Maintaining relationships with children across the conjugal divide is often stressful and unsatisfactory for all participants (Simpson et al. 1995). Under these circumstances, parenting all too easily becomes an exhausting round of conflict and attrition rather than the rewarding and constructive experience described in the "how to do it" books. Navigating the life-course after divorce can be a perilous undertaking with many important reference points rendered dysfunctional or entirely absent. In the next section some of the predominant ways in which post-divorce relations are patterned are considered. This exploration of the distinctive ways that new relationships are grafted onto the old is developed with reference to two extended case studies of the post-divorce kindred.

Two Variants of the Unclear family

The post-divorce kindred may take many forms. It is shaped and re-shaped over time by an interplay of emotions and public and private interests. To plot this complex social form in space and over time will be a major theoretical and methodological challenge for the study of kinship in contemporary European society in the years to come. As a preliminary move in this direction, the remainder of this chapter is taken up with a discussion of two forms of post-divorce family relations which appear to be at opposite ends of a spectrum. At one end of the spectrum there is a propensity for discontinuities in post-divorce relations, at the other, choice and the possibilities for continuity in social relations would appear to be maximised. The first account is given by Sally Thomas, a working-class housewife living in council accommodation. The second account is provided by Stuart Smith, a middle-class, self-employed builder living in the home of his new partner. Each case demonstrates how cultural expectations and economic constraints shape relational possibilities in practice. Each typifies a pattern of kinship which is clearly derivative of family life before the separation but which is, in crucial ways, also distinct and emergent.

The Nuclear Mould: The Case of Sally Thomas

When Sally married Stephen Thomas he had been married before and already had a young daughter, Sharon. Sally took on the role of primary carer for Sharon (see Figure 2.) and the couple went on to have two children together, Andrew and Dawn. Towards the latter stages, their marriage became increasingly problematic because in Sally's view Stephen was mostly unemployed, occasionally violent and always financially irresponsible.

Sally left the matrimonial home in April 1987, taking with her the two younger children—Andrew and Dawn—into bed and breakfast accommodation and leaving Sharon behind in the matrimonial home with Stephen. There followed a complex and protracted wrangle over the terms and conditions of custody and access. This was exacerbated by the fact that not only were the couple trying to make arrangements for Andrew and Dawn to see their father, Stephen, they were also trying to enable Sharon to see her step-mother, Sally, as well as seeking to preserve some continuity of the sibling group, that is, allowing all three children to spend some time together. Courts and conciliation services were involved in trying to make this exploded and highly conflicted nuclear family hang together in some form, but without success. Despite the best intentions of all concerned, the attempted arrangements repeatedly collapsed in acrimony. This was further fuelled by Stephen being ousted from the matrimonial home in order to allow Sally to move back in. Stephen was eventually re-housed on the same estate within a couple of hundred yards of his former home.

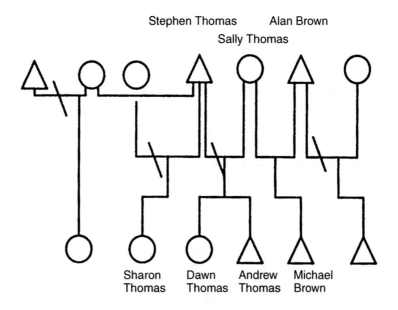

Figure 2. The "family" of Sally Thomas

By the time of the second interview in 1991, Sally and Stephen, now divorced, had each taken up residence with partners who had also been previously married. Sally had recently given birth to a son, Michael, by this new relationship. The contact between Andrew and Dawn and their father was continuing to be a source of major conflict and anxiety. Sally's assessment of the situation was that things had deteriorated since her new partner had moved in, at which point Stephen had become jealous, vindictive and obstructive.

> . . . we were talking quite well and then he found another partner and that was OK, I even went over there for a Tupperware party, but when I found myself a new partner that was when the trouble started. He started making trouble over the children and that's when the communication stopped.

As a result, and at Stephen's insistence, they only communicated through solicitors, despite living very close to one another. Also, Dawn refused to visit her father ever again. Her allegiances had been substantially transferred to her mother's new partner:

> . . . my daughter, as far as she is concerned that [i.e., the new partner] is her dad, she thinks the world of him. She calls him dad and her dad over there Stephen, she calls him by his first name. As far as she is concerned my new partner brings her up, he buys all her clothes and food, he gives her the love and attention she wanted from her other father but never got. So far as she is concerned, that's it, that's her dad.

The intensely negative feelings of Dawn towards her father were further exacerbated by the fact that she disliked both her father's new wife and her daughter and also was upset at the shabby treatment that Sharon, her half-sister, received in their father's house. Stephen had accused Sally of putting pressure on Dawn to effect this break in relations. However, Sally was adamant that anger and resistance was coming entirely from Dawn.

Andrew's position was less clear. Whereas Dawn had opted for the newly emergent nuclear family group, Andrew felt ambivalence. He had a history of emotional and behavioural problems which were attributed by Sally to her first husband's inconsistent and inept handling of his relationship with the boy. The availability of two father figures, a seemingly inept *genitor* on the one hand and a perfect *pater* on the other, was proving a major dilemma. As Sally said "Andrew is at the stage where he's split between the two dads." Later she added he sometimes gets "torn" between the two.

Sally's image of the splitting and tearing of her child suggests an understanding of the situation in terms of something that should be in one place or the other but not in both. The polarities between which Andrew is drawn are those of his mother's husband and his "real dad" as Sally described her first husband. Pater and genitor are no longer one and the same and Andrew can seemingly have one but not both. Sally's use of the term "stage" implies structured process and possibly preferred outcome in the resolution of this conflict. However, Andrew is not of an age where he can assert his opinions with quite the impact that his sister seems to have done. He remains caught in a prolonged liminality.

> [when with his father] he gets spoilt rotten . . . [ ] . . . one minute I'm confident, he's happy here and at other times perhaps I think he would like to be with his dad . . . [ ] . . . but there again if that made him happy I'd have to let him go—not that I think his father's capable of looking after him because I don't think he knows how to, and his partner don't seem to know how to either.

Any possible future decision to allow Andrew to live with Stephen is based upon the cultural elaboration of the irreversible fact of bio-genetic parenthood. Stephen, in Sally's words, is Andrew's "real dad," a potent relationship especially in view of the fact that the relationship in question is one between a male parent and a male child. This dictates that there will always be the element of legitimacy and legality in the desire of Stephen and Andrew to have a relationship. This consideration is powerful enough for Sally to consider taking steps which are not necessarily in Andrew's own best emotional and material interests as she sees them. The outcome hoped for is the child's happiness realised through his own conscious choice. However, in her deliberations as to which parent Andrew should be living with, there can be discerned a subtle shift from Sally's use of "dad" to describe Andrew's relationship with Stephen to her use of "father" to describe Stephen's relationship with Andrew. It is this latter aspect that Sally sees as problematic.

This point is further emphasised by examining the position of Sharon, Sally's step-daughter. Sharon continued to be a frequent visitor to Sally's house where, it was claimed, she was given the kind of care and attention that she did not receive at home with her father, Stephen and his new partner. Sally described how she had often thought of having Sharon to live with her but how this was rejected on the grounds that, whatever her circumstances in Stephen's house, he was her "real father." Furthermore, it would not be "right," that is natural, for her to be a part of Sally's newly constituted family as she would not be biologically related to either of the adults with whom she would be living. However, the memory and indeed the continuity of caring provided by Sally for Sharon was clearly an unresolved issue for them both.

In the case outlined above there are numerous points at which the threat of discontinuities seem to outweigh the fact of continuities as relationships slide back into the nuclear family mould. For Sally, the breakdown of one "family" was followed by the creation of another "family" in which efforts were made to make it appear a neat and seamless co-resident grouping. Yet, the continuity of external form in the way Sally presents her "family" conceals internal discontinuities. The roles may appear to stay the same but the personnel have in fact changed. As a consequence the role expectations which are implied by specific kinship terms are highly significant. For example, Sally is keen to point out that Dawn has in effect relegated Stephen from his status as "dad" by referring to him by his first name and giving the title of "dad" to Alan, Sally's new partner. The shift from category to person is seen by Sally as an illustration both of the distance that has developed between Dawn and Stephen and her closeness to her new step-father. Thus, the breaking of ties between husband and wife also brings the role of *genitor* as *pater* into question. The roles of husband and father are too closely bound together in terms of sentiment and practice for either Sally or her ex-husband to discontinue one without undermining the continuity of the other. Thus it was difficult for Sally to establish continuity with Alan as a husband without also inviting him to take up the role of "father" and "dad" vis-à-vis her children, particularly when their new baby arrived. Although Stephen was persistent about maintaining his role and relationship with his children, most of the economic and emotional gaps left by his departure were effectively filled by another.

There are numerous alternative explanations which could be developed as to why the relationships between children and parents who no longer live together are so problematic. Sally's narrative centres on an ex-husband who, although recalled with compassion, was seen as irresponsible, inconsistent and immature. Although Stephen was not interviewed, he might well have identified an ex-partner keen to play "happy families," as an interviewee in similar circumstances described his ex-wife's attempts to exclude him from contact once she had formed a new relationship. Attention could be drawn by either party to a system of welfare support which, in housing and social security terms, makes life very difficult for those who end their marriages but seek to develop patterns of parenting across multiple residences rather than according to bureaucratically straightforward intra-household patterns. Running through these potential explanations is the problem already mentioned, that of disentangling blood and patrifiliation from conjugal love and affinity. The ease with which the rupture of marital relationships can bring about discontinuities of conjugality do not sit so easily with the expected continuities of parenthood. There is a recurrent conflict between matrifocal residence on the one hand and notions of patrifiliation on the other. The matrifocal orientation is clearly apparent in the unity of the sibling group, that is, the belief that children born of the same mother should remain co-resident with her. The ethnographic record reveals that this belief operates at both the parental level and at the judicial level with contested hearings tending to support what is usually the matrifocal status quo. This status quo however is in conflict with notions of patrifiliation. This is most clearly seen in the scattering of surnames across the different residence groups. For example, when Sally re-married it was likely she would adopt the surname of her new partner, Brown. This name would also be given to their son but her own two daughters would retain the name of Thomas, the surname of their father. The whole sibling group would be domestically united by maternal care and residence but publicly divided by the patronyms they received from their respective fathers.

The Extending Family: The Case of Stuart Smith

Stuart was married for ten years before he left his wife, Rachel and took up residence with another woman. The decision to leave was extremely traumatic and protracted because, although clear about his desire to be with the woman with whom he had been having an affair, he was far from happy about moving away from his three young sons. This was made worse by the fact that the matrimonial home was located in a very isolated part of the country and his new partner's home was some sixty miles away. The situation was further exacerbated by the fact that Stuart's new partner was also friendly with his wife (see Figure 3).

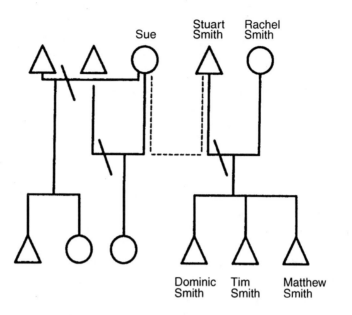

Figure 3. The "family" of Stuart Smith

Stuart recalls that the early years of the separation were extremely grim for all concerned. For him it involved long weekend trips between his new home and the former matrimonial home. Meetings with his sons took place at the homes of friends where he would stay overnight, or in whose gardens he would camp. The role of friends in providing support was seen as crucial in enabling him to maintain contact at a time when it might easily have ceased. The contact with the boys did indeed continue, and although extremely bitter over the treatment she had received, Stuart's ex-wife was generally supportive of him as "the boys' father" and recognised the important part that he played in the children's lives.

Where this case differs profoundly from that of Sally Thomas is that the separation took place in the midst of a strong and long established network of mutually supportive friends and relatives. Rachel brought into her marriage the support of a large extended family, although Stuart was apt to see this as interference. Following the divorce, the involvement of these relatives in the lives of both Rachel and her three sons became even greater, raising anxieties for Stuart about his sons being raised in a "claustrophobic" and "hermetic" group, although acknowledging that they were "good" people who had a lot to offer his children. Stuart did not have particularly strong "family ties" but spoke of a series of important "family-like" relationships which he had been able to draw upon following the separation. As Stuart commented "my children are exposed to a wide, varied circle of people."

As far as the three children were concerned there remained a degree of unity in the circle of kin following the divorce. The two kinship worlds of *mum* and *dad* did not simply bifurcate but continued to function with some degree of coherence. Thus, for example, Rachel took the boys for a Christmas meal with their paternal grandparents. Her father visited the house where Stuart and his new partner lived. More recently, both Stuart and Rachel attended social gatherings hosted by mutual friends, something unthinkable in the early days of their separation. Stuart did odd jobs at Rachel's house and occasionally ate there:

> . . . I've sat down and had meals with them basically for symbolic purposes not formally, just snacks, but it all helps.

"But it all helps" refers to Stuart's desire to establish a network of relations that is not fragmented by divorce but merely re-arranged. Consequently, his efforts are primarily aimed at providing evidence of overlap and continuity of parental relationships for his children.

However, the social networks of Stuart and Rachel have not only become more-scrambled and intensified, they have also been extended. Stuart's relationship with Sue, his new partner, brings his children into contact with her as a step-parent-figure, with her three children who range from nine to twenty-one and to a certain extent with her family, in this case her siblings, parents and cousins. Whereas in the Thomas case the family of orientation appeared to close down and start up again, here there is a process of accretion whereby functioning relationships are added on to it. These relationships are not perceived as in any way problematic for, or contradictory of, existing relationships. As far as Stuart is concerned, they constitute an expanding network of social opportunity for his children.

In further contrast to the Thomas case, the emphasis throughout the discussion with Stuart focused on persons rather than roles. There was an active attempt by him to eschew kinship roles and thereby flatten kinship hierarchies and power relations which might characterise relationships been him and his children or indeed between him and his new partner's children. Friendship and a history of shared experience provided the basis for relationships and this is typified in the extensive use of first name terms which here mark intimacy and familiarity rather than a dislocation of the relationship between parent and child as in the Thomas case. Consequently, in this case there is a recognition of the value of individual persons in their roles and no question of displacement. Thus, despite a bitter separation, Stuart remains the children's "father" and has been recognised and supported as such by their mother (although whether this would continue to be the case were she to establish a permanent relationship may be another matter). These feelings are reciprocated by Stuart regarding Rachel's capacities as a "good" mother. In short, there is considerable mutual trust between them both regarding their ongoing abilities as parents.

Finally, the most distinctive feature of the extending family as illustrated by the Smith case is the desire on the part of all the key actors to ensure the continuity of virtually all those relationships that existed in the past, as well as the new relationships established after divorce. For example, with reference to step-siblings Stuart observed:

> It's quite involved because there's six children between us and all six children have a relationship between them . . .

> . . . they like the complication of it, working out who's who. The children are familiar with the extended family and they can look at relationships in the same light.

One immediate implication of this view of "extended family" is the immense amount of energy which is put into the maintenance of relation-ships on the children's behalf. When with their mother, they are drawn into a large extended family, when with their father they do the rounds of an established network of close friends who Stuart, in the absence of any relatives with whom he would like to be in contact, regards as "family." From the children's perspective this can make for an exhausting schedule of movement and socialising.

For Sally Thomas, our first case, there is considerable unease with the messiness of relation-ships. The unfolding of relationships after divorce took place in circumstances where there was high dependency on the state and few individuals in the "family" network were in employment. Her ability to shape the configurations of relationships beyond the narrow parameters of the household was greatly limited. Indeed, low-income families may have considerable problems in maintaining kin relations in anything other than the discrete nuclear family variant.[2] Absence of resources for the material expression of relations, whether this be in terms of formal payments of maintenance or informal donations of gifts and money to spend on socialising, may well render relationships precarious and liable to atrophy.[3] Difficult economic circumstances appear to foster a rigidity in the way that family relations are conducted. In ways that are reminiscent of Bernstein's notion of a restricted or closed communication system (Bernstein 1973:177–80), tender feelings may well be expressed in "tough terms" precisely because there is no other vocabulary available. Identities and relationships within the changing kinship systems of the poor are positional and context dependent. In network terms, there are numerous points where networks are severed or closed off. Money, goods, favours and sentiments do not flow across the conjugal divide. On the contrary, the way this flow is re-routed at divorce becomes a potent statement of the narrow and tightly bound networks which characterise the nuclear family.

This is in contrast to the Smith case, our second example, in which the re-ordering of kinship relations takes place against a backdrop of relative affluence with most of the adults in employment. For Stuart Smith there was a certain exuberance in his description of post-divorce relationships. For him there was the sense of a controlled expansion of relationship possibilities and permutations consonant with Bernstein's elaborated or open communication systems. Sally Thomas, five years after divorce, appears to be serially recasting her new family in the image of a traditional nuclear family. Stuart Smith on the other hand pays only fleeting reference to conventional family forms. For him the emphasis is on an extending kindred founded on personal identities and relationships; continuities bridge the conjugal divide at numerous points. Throughout Stuart Smith's account there is an apparent denial of material interest when it comes to kinship relations. The narratives he presents portray a network of relationships which are voluntary, individualised and personalised; they are presented as running on and on with very few external constraints.

The Unclear Family

In this chapter it has been my intention to identify and bring into anthropological focus the complex and varied patterns of inter-personal and kinship arrangements which emerge over time as a result of divorce and family reconstitution in Britain. I have referred to these patterns collectively as the unclear family and attempted to locate them within a broader anthropology of marital dissolution. Implicit in this approach has been a critique of the conceptual heritage which emanates from essentialist, ideal-type models of the bourgeois nuclear family. Such models are built on a powerful alignment of co-residence, temporally stable conjugal/parental relationships and the social recognition of fatherhood. Such an alignment leaves little room for agency and the under-pinnings of family life appear to be all but natural.

When viewed against the broader canvas of human social and domestic organisation, however, such arrangements may well be the exception rather than the norm. As Seccombe has recently argued (1993), in the West we may be emerging from a "golden age" of the family, a period of exceptional stability which reached its zenith in the 1950s and which is now giving way to a period of familial instability. The concentricity of parenting, residence and authority is being progressively de-centred and we are witnessing, if not directly experiencing in our own lives, novel re-arrangements and reconstructions of what were hitherto the certainties of Euro-American kinship. Indeed, Robertson has suggested that in recent times, notions of filiation and responsibility for bringing up children in the West have progressively shifted from the "compact household to the wider social domain" (1991:122). The evidence he cites is the fact that increasingly aspects of reproduction are being mediated by civil and market institutions. Here we might draw attention to the considerable machinery which has appeared to assist couples in dealing with marital breakdown, much of which is geared towards sanitising divorce and bringing about an "embourgeoisement" of its consequences. Divorce law reform, the growth of conciliation services geared to resolving conflict and dispute, the growing expectation of amicable relationships and the emphasis on continued parenting after divorce all point to external pressures to bring particular shape to the form that social and kinship networks take after divorce. In short, divorce generates a host of questions regarding the form and viability of parenthood in circumstances in which family is dispersed and in which there is state participation in key aspects of social reproduction (Donzelot 1979; Goody 1982).

Viewed against such a backdrop, the study of the variations in domestic arrangements after divorce poses some major analytical challenges. The identification of a private domain which is the preserve of the family and a public domain which is characterised by impersonal, market transactions has obscured the two-way traffic between them. Consideration of the arrangements which couples themselves devise or otherwise have imposed upon them requires that we re-think the way that kinship articulates with economy. In other words, the re-shaping of the kinship framework over time is not an arbitrary process. The disaggregation of persons takes place within parameters set by public interests. Fundamental in this regard is the question of resourcing the unclear family. Divorce renders the material underpinning to family life quite explicit; the "maintenance" of relationships costs money. A network of households in which there are adequate or substantial resources and incomes may be extremely effective in enabling finance and children to flow between households, thus maximising choice and potential in the relational framework which divorce allows. However, in the absence of resources to disperse and disburse, sentiment and the pragmatics of household subsistence often pull in opposite directions. This is nowhere more clear than in the underlying philosophies of the Children Act 1989 and the Child Support Act 1991. Whilst in the Children Act there is an expectation and encouragement of continuing parental involvement after divorce, even though a mother and father do not live together, the Child Support Act sees the non-resident parent as "absent" and his or her relationship rather more in terms of the pragmatics of financial support. In terms of the case studies presented here one might characterise the Children Act as a piece of legislation ideally suited to a world of Stuart Smiths and the Child Support Act similarly suited to a world of Sally Thomas's. Equally we might begin to understand the fierce and critical reaction that is aroused when these pieces of legislation are applied across all contexts seemingly extending and cutting networks in ways that are favoured in economic, social and moral terms by the state. Thus, as a result of the Child Support Act the likes of Stuart Smith are affronted by being characterised as "absent" and pursued for maintenance in ways which overlook the quality of their existing relationships with children and former spouse. Conversely, the Children Act means that the likes of Sally Thomas are confronted with a legal framework which puts pressure on them to allow ex-husbands to have contact with their children even though the general climate of economic and cultural expectation moves them to the opposite conclusion, that is, divorce is not just conjugal but parental. In each instance, the law provokes a sense of indignity, because it is attempting to influence and inform areas of family life which are believed to be autonomous, discrete and the object of private ordering.

The unclear family also poses some major methodological challenges. How do we study change in sets of relationships which are themselves characterised by qualitative change and transience? Whereas the nuclear family was usually assumed to speak with one voice, a master narrative, if you will, the unclear family is characterised by a polyphony of voices. The roles, spaces, boundaries and classifications which previously mapped relationships through space and time are subtly transformed to produce competing, contested and often contradictory versions of the kinship network.

In the next three chapters, these challenges, analytical and methodological, are taken up in more detail. Chapters 4 and 5 take up the question of disputes between parents after divorce and in particular the disputes they have over their children. These disputes reveal the fundamental unclearness of family relations after divorce and show the way multiple narratives surrounding parental relationships result in new and complex forms of kinship. Chapter 6 deals with the closely related question of financial support and the role of the non-resident parent.

Notes

1. A notable exception here is Bohannan (1971a) who provides a useful if disjointed collection of articles on divorce in the USA and "around the world." Bohannan (1971b) also engages in a series of speculations regarding the longer-term consequences of divorce which pre-figure the idea developed in this paper of the post-divorce kindred as the unclear family. One of the few sociological studies of divorce in Britain is Hart's (1976) participant-observation study of a singles club frequented by divorcees. Hart focused specifically on divorce as a status passage which for most people constitutes a brief but highly anomalous phase between broadly similar married statuses.

2. In the study of non-custodial fathers carried out by myself and colleagues, clear gradients were identified in the levels of contact across social class and income with non-manual workers earning over £300 per week having the highest levels of contact and most likely to have their children on overnight stays. This is in contrast to unemployed men whose relationships with their children from previous marriages appeared to be particularly at risk (Simpson et al. 1995: 5).

3. Such an inference is hardly a new one, it has resonances of the culture of poverty debate (Lewis 1966) and more recent discussions regarding the rise of households headed by women (e.g., Ross and Sawhill 1975) in which paternal relations are largely characterised by their transience.

References

Alanen, L. (1993. "After 'the family': Childhood, Gender and Family Change." Paper presented at the XXXth Committee of Family Research, *Gender and Families: Choices, Challenges and Changing policy,* Annapolis, Maryland. USA.

Anderson, D., Lait, J. and Marsland, D. 1981. *Breaking the Spell of the Welfare State.* London: Social Affairs Unit.

Arendt, H. 1958. *The Human Condition.* Chicago: University of Chicago Press.

Aries, P. 1979 [1962]. *Centuries of Childhood.* Harmondsworth: Penguin.

Backett, K. 1982. *Mothers and Fathers: A Study of the Development and Negotiation of Parental Behaviour.* London and Basingstoke: Macmillan.

———. 1987. "The Negotiation of Fatherhood" in C. Lewis and M. O'Brien (eds), *Reassessing Fatherhood.* London: Sage Publications.

Bakhtin, M.M. 1986. *Speech Genres and other Late Essays* (translated by Vern McGee and edited by Caryl Emerson and Michael Holquist). Austin: University of Texas Press.

Barnard, A. and Good, A. 1984. *Research Practices in the Study of Kinship.* London: Academic Press.

Barnes, J.A. 1973. "Genitor: Genetrix: Nature: Culture" in J. Goody (ed.), *The Character of Kinship.* Cambridge: Cambridge University Press.

———. 1980. "Kinship Studies: Some Impressions on the Current State of Play." *Man* (n.s.), 15.2: 293–303.

Barrett, M. and MacIntosh, M. 1982. *The Anti-Social Family.* London: Verso.

Becker, G. 1981. *Treatise on the Family.* Cambridge, Mass: Harvard University Press.

Beck, U. and Beck-Gernsheim, E. 1995. *The Normal Chaos of Love.* Cambridge: Polity Press.

Belk, R.W. and Coon G.S. 1993. "Gift-giving as Agapic Love: An Alternative to the Exchange Paradigm based on Dating Experiences." *Journal of Consumer Research*, 20: 393–417.

Bell, D. 1997. "Defining Marriage and Legitimacy." *Current Anthropology*, 38, 2: 237–54.

Bellah, R. N., Madsen, R., Sullivan, W.M., Swidler, A. and Tipton, S.M. 1985. *Habits of the Heart: Individualism and Commitment in American Life*. New York: Harper and Row.

Berger, B. and Keilner, H. 1964. "Marriage and the Construction of Reality: An Exercise in the Microsociology of Knowledge." *Diogenes*, 46: 1–23.

Bernard, J. 1972. *The Future of Marriage*. Harmondsworth: Penguin Books.

Bernardes, J. 1985. "'Family Ideology': Identification and Exploration." *The Sociological Review*, 33: 275–97.

———. 1988. "Founding the *new* 'Family Studies.'" *The Sociological Review*, 36: 57–86.

Bernstein, B. 1973. *Class, Codes and Social Control: Volume One. Theoretical Studies Towards a Sociology of Language*. St. Albans: Paladin.

Bloch, M. 1973. "The Long-Term and the Short-Term: The Economic and Political Significance of the Morality of Kinship" in J.R. Goody. (ed.), *The Character of Kinship*. Cambridge: Cambridge University Press.

Blustein, J. 1982) *Parents and Children: The Ethics of the Family*. New York: Oxford University Press.

Bohannan, P.J. (ed.), 1971a. *Divorce and After*. New York: Doubleday.

———. 1971b. "Divorce Chains, Households of Re-marriage and Multiple Divorcers" in P.J. Bohannan (ed.), *Divorce and After*, New York: Doubleday.

———. 1993. "Review of A.F. Roberston: Beyond the Family: The Social Organisation of Human Reproduction." *American Anthropologist*, 95:175.

Bott, E. 1971. *Family and Social Network*. London: Tavistock.

Bouquet, M. 1993. *Reclaiming English Kinship: Portuguese Refractions of British Kinship Theory*. Manchester: Manchester University Press.

Bourdieu, P. 1977. *Outline of a Theory of Practice*. Cambridge: Cambridge University Press.

Bradshaw, J. and Millar, J. 1991. *Lone-Parent Families in the UK*. London: HMSO.

Brophy, J. 1989. "Custody Law, Child Care and Inequality in Britain" in C. Smart and S. Sevenhuijsen (eds), *Child Custody and the Politics of Gender*. London and New York: Routledge.

Bruner, J. 1986. *Actual Minds: Possible Worlds*. Cambridge MA: Harvard University Press.

———. 1990. *Acts of Meaning*. Cambridge MA: Harvard University Press.

Buisson. M. and Mermet, J-C. 1986. Des circulations des enfants: De la famille a la familialité. *Le groupe familial*, 112; 38–43.

Burgess, A. 1997. *Fatherhood Reclaimed: The Making of the Modern Father*. London: Vermillion Press.

Burgess, E. 1926. "The Family as a Unity of Interacting Personalities." *The Family*, 7 March: 3–9.

Burgoyne, J. and Clark, D. 1984. *Making-a-go-of-it*. London: Routledge, Kegan and Paul.

Burrett, J. 1993. *To and fro Children: Co-operative Parenting after Divorce*. London: Thorson (Harper Collins).

Butler-Sloss, Lord Justice 1988. *Report of the Inquiry into Child Abuse in Cleveland*. Cmnd 412. London: HMSO.

Campbell, B. 1993. *Goliath: Britain's Dangerous Places*. London: Methuen.

Carrier, J. 1992a. "The Gift in Theory and in Practice: A Note on the Centrality of Gift Exchange." *Ethnology*, 31: 186–93.

———. 1992b. "Occidentalism: The World Turned Upside Down." *American Ethnologist*, 19: 195-2 12.

———. 1995. *Gifts and Commodities: Exchange and Western Capitalism since 1700*. London: Routledge.

Carrigan, T., Connell, B. and Lee. J. 1985. "Towards a new Sociology of Masculinity." *Theory and Society*, 14: 551–603.

Carrithers, M.B. 1992. *Why Humans have Cultures*. Oxford: Oxford University Press.

Carsten, J. 1991. "Children in between: Fostering and the Process of Kinship on Pulau Langkawi, Malaysia." *Man* (n.s.) 26: 425–43.

———. 1995. "The Substance of Kinship and the Heat of the Hearth: Feeding, Personhood and Relatedness among Malays in Pulau Langkawi." *American Ethnologist*, 22(2): 223–41.

Caughey, J.L. 1984. *Imaginary Social Worlds: A Cultural Approach*. Lincoln: University of Nebraska Press.

Child Support Agency 1994. *Press Pack*. London: Child Support Agency.

Children Come First 1990. Government White Paper, 2 vols. Cmn 1236. London: HMSO.

Cochrane, M., Lamer, M., Riley, D., Gunnarson, L. and Henderson C.R. Jnr. 1990. *Extending Families*. Cambridge: Cambridge University Press.

Cohen, R. 1971. "Brittle Marriage as a Stable System: The Kanun Case" in P.J. Bohannan (ed.), *Divorce and After*. New York: Doubleday.

Collier, R. 1995. *Masculinity, Law and the Family*. London: Routledge.

Collins, J. 1994. "Disempowerment and Marginalisation of Clients in Divorce Court Cases" in S. Wright (ed.), *Anthropology of Organisations*. London: Routledge.

Coltrane, S. and Hickman, N. 1992. "The Rhetoric of Rights and Needs: Moral Discourse in the Reform of Child Custody and Child Support Laws." *Social Problems*, 39: 400–20.

Comaroff, J.L. (ed.) 1980. *The Meaning of Marriage Payments*. New York: Academic Press.

Cornwall, A. and Lindisfarne, N. 1994. "Dislocating Masculinity: Gender, Power and Anthropology" in A. Cornwell and N. Lindisfarne (eds), *Dislocating Masculinity: Comparative Ethnographies*. London and New York: Routledge.

Corlyon, J., Simpson, R., McCarthy, P. and Walker, J. 1991. *The Links Between Behaviour in Marriage, the Settlement of Ancillary Disputes, Arrangements for Children and Post-Divorce Relationships*. Report to the Nuffield Foundation.

Davies, J. (ed.)1993. *The Family: Is it Just Another Life Style Choice?* London: Institute of Economic Affairs.

Davis, G. and Murch, M. 1988. *Grounds for Divorce*. Oxford: Clarendon Press.

Day-Sclater, S. 1997. "Creating the Self: Stories as Transitional Phenomena." Unpublished MS (presented at the Auto/Biography Study Group Annual Conference).

De'Ath, E. 1992. "Step-families in the Context of Contemporary Family Life." in E. De'Ath (ed.), *What do We Know? What do We Need to Know?* Croydon: Significant Publications.

Dennis, N. 1996. "Men's Sexual Liberation" in R. Humphrey (ed.), *Families Behind the Headlines*. Newcastle: British Association for the Advancement of Science/Department of Social Policy, University of Newcastle upon Tyne.

Dennis, N. and Erdos, G. 1992. *Families without Fatherhood*. London: Institute of Economic Affairs, Health and Welfare Unit.

Denzin, N.K. 1989. *Interpretive Biography*, Qualitative Research Methods vol. 17. Newbury Park: Sage.

di Leonardo, M. 1987. "The Female World of Cards and Holidays: Women, Family and the Work of Kinship." *Signs*, 12(3): 440–53.

Dizard, J.E. and Gadlin, H. 1990. *The Minimal Family*. Amherst: University of Massachusetts Press.

Dominian, J. 1965. *Marital Breakdown*. Harmondsworth: Penguin.

Dominian, J., Mansfield, P., Dormor, D. and McAllister, F. 1991. *Marital Breakdown and the Health of the Nation: A Response to the Governments Consultative Document for Health in England*. London: One plus One Marriage and Partnership Research.

Donzelot, J. 1979. *The Policing of Families*. London: Hutchinson.

Dormor, D. 1992. *The Relationship Revolution: Cohabitation, Marriage and Divorce in Contemporary Europe*. London: One plus One.

Edwards, J., Franklin, S., Hirsch, E., Price, F. and Stratbern., M. 1993. *Technologies of Procreation: Kinship in the Age of Assisted Conception*. Manchester: Manchester University Press.

Eekelaar, J. 1984. *Family Law and Social Policy*. London: Weidenfeld and Nicolson.

Eekelaar, J. and Maclean, M. 1986. *Maintenance after Divorce*. London: Oxford University Press.

Elliot, F. Robertson, 1986. *The Family: Change or Continuity?* Hound-Mills: Macmillan.

Ellis, R. 1983. "The Way to a Man's Heart: Food in the Violent Home" in A. Murcott (ed.), *The Sociology of Food and Eating*. Aldershot: Gower.

Emery, R.E. 1988. *Marriage, Divorce and Children's Adjustment*. Beverly Hills. CA: Sage Publications.

Finch, J. 1989. *Family Obligations and Social Change*. Oxford: Polity Press.

Finch, J. and Mason J. 1990. "Divorce, Re-marriage and Family Obligations." *The Sociological Review*, 38: 219–46.

Firth, R., Hubert, J. and Forge, A. 1969. *Families and their Relatives*. London: Routledge, Kegan and Paul.

Flandrin, J.L. 1979. *Families in Former Times*. Cambridge: Cambridge University Press.

Fletcher, R. 1973. *The Family and Marriage in Britain*. Harmondsworth: Penguin.

Fortes, M. 1969. *Kinship and the Social Order*. Chicago: Aldine.

Franklin, S., Levy, C. and Stacey, J. (eds) 1991. *Off-Centre: Feminism and Cultural Studies*. Hammersmith: Harper and Collins.

Freeman, M. D. A. 1983. *The Rights and Wrongs of Children*. London: Frances Pinter.

Furstenberg, F.F., Petersen, J.L., Nord, C.W. and Zilli, N. 1993. "The Life Course of the Children of Divorce: Marital Disruption and Parental Contact." *American Sociological Review*, 48: 656–8.

Geertz, C. 1983. *Local Knowledge: Further Essays in Interpretative Anthropology*. New York: Basic Books.

Gergen, K. 1991. *The Saturated Self: Dilemmas of Identity in Contemporary Life*. New York: Basic Books.

Gerstel, N., Reissman, C.K. and Rosenfeld, S. 1985. "Explaining the Symptomology of Separated and Divorced Women: The Role of Material Conditions and Social Networks." *Social Forces*, 64: 84–101.

Gibson, C.S. 1994. *Dissolving Wedlock*. London & New York: Routledge.

Giddens, A. 1991. *Modernity and Self-Identity: Self and Society in the Late Modern Age*. Cambridge: Polity Press.

———. 1994. "Living in a Post-traditional Society." in U. Beck (ed.), *Reflexive Modernity: Politics, Tradition and Aesthetics in the Modern Social Order*. Cambridge: Polity Press.

Gilligan, C. 1982. *In a Different Voice*. Massachussetts: Harvard University Press.

Gillis, J.R. 1985. *For Better, for Worse: British Marriages 1600 to the Present.* Oxford: Oxford University Press.

Goffman, E. 1969. *The Presentation of Self in Everyday Life.* Harmondsworth: Penguin.

———. 1981. *Forms of Talk.* Philadelphia: University of Pennsylvania Press.

Goode, W.J. 1984. "Individual Investments in Family Relationships over the Coming Decades." *The Tocqueville Review,* VI(1): 51–83.

———. 1993. *World Changes in Divorce Patterns.* New Haven and London: Yale University Press.

Goody, J. and Mitchell, J. 1995. "The Child Support Agency: Changing Family Structures in Contemporary Britain." Paper given at the Department of Anthropology, Durham. Nov. 1995.

Goody, E.N. 1962. "Conjugal Separation and Divorce among the Gonja of Northern Ghana" in Meyer Fortes (ed.), *Marriage in Tribal Societies.* Cambridge: Cambridge University Press.

———. 1982. *Parenthood and Social Reproduction.* Cambridge: Cambridge University Press.

Gregory, C.A. 1982. *Gifts and Commodities.* London: Academic Press.

Greif, J. 1979. "Fathers, Children and Joint Custody." *American Journal of Orthopsychiatry,* 49: 311–19.

Grief, G.L. 1985. *Single Fathers.* New York: Free Press.

Gubrium, J.F. and Holstein J.A. 1990. *What is Family?* California: Mayfield Publishing Company.

Gullestadt, M. 1996. "From Obedience to Negotiation: Dilemmas in the Transmission of Values between the Generations in Norway." *The Journal of the Royal Anthropological Institute,* 2(1): 25–42.

Gutman. H.G. 1984. "Afro-American Kinship before and after Emancipation in North America" in H. Medick and D.W. Sabean (eds), *Interest and Emotion: Essays on the Study of Family and Kinship.* Cambridge: Cambridge University Press.

Harré, R. 1986. *The Social Construction of Emotion.* Oxford: Blackwell.

———. 1993. *Social Being.* Oxford: Blackwell.

Harris, C.C. 1983. *The Family and Industrial Society.* London: Allen and Unwin.

———. 1990. *Kinship.* Buckingham: Open University Press.

Harris, J.R. 1995. "Where is the Child's Environment? A Group Socialisation Theory of Development." *Psychological Review,* 102(3): 45 8–89.

Harris, O. 1981. "Households as Natural Units" in K. Young, C. Walkowitz and R. McCullagh, (eds), *Of Marriage and the Market.* London: CSE Books.

Hart, N. 1976. *When Marriage Ends: A Study in Status Passage.* London: Tavistock.

Harvey, D. 1989. *The Condition of Post-modernity; An Enquiry into the Origins of Cultural Change.* Oxford: Basil Blackwell.

Haskey, J. 1988. "Trends in Marriage and Divorce and Cohort Analyses of the Proportions of Marriages ending in Divorce." *Population Trends,* 54: 21.

———. 1989. "Current Prospects for the Proportion of Marriages ending in Divorce." *Population Trends,* 55: 34.

Hermans, H.J.M~ and Kempen, H.J.G. 1993. *The Dialogical Self: Meaning as Movement.* New York: Academic Press, Inc.

Hetherington, E.M. 1979. "Divorce: A Child's Perspective." *American Psychologist,* 34(10): 85 1–8.

Hockey, J. 1990. *Experiences of Death: An Anthropological Account.* Edinburgh: Edinburgh University Press.

Hockey, J. and James, A. 1993. *Growing Up and Growing Old: Ageing and Dependency in the Life-Course.* London and New York: Sage Publications.

Hoggett, B. 1989. "The Children Bill: The Aims." *Family Law,* 19: 217–21.

Holmes. T.H. and Rahe, R.H. 1967. "Holmes-Rahe Social Re-Adjustment Rating Scale." *Journal of Psychosomatic Research,* 11: 213–18.

Holquist, M. 1990. *Dialogism: Bakhtin and his World.* London: Routledge.

Holt, J. 1975. *Escape from Childhood.* Harmondsworth: Penguin.

Holy, L. 1996. *Anthropological Perspectives on Kinship.* London: Pluto Press.

Houseman, M. 1988. "Towards a Complex Model of Parenthood: Two African Tales." *American Ethnologist,* 15: 658–77.

Humm, M. 1987. "Autobiography and Bellpins" in V. Griffiths (ed.), *Feminist Biography II: Using Life Histories.* Manchester: Studies in Sexual Politics, University of Manchester.

Hutchinson, S. 1990. "Rising Divorce among the Nuer, 1936–1983." *Man* (n.s.), 25: 393–411.

James, A., Hockey, J. and Dawson, A. 1997. *After Writing Culture: Epistemology and Praxis in Contemporary Culture* (ASA Monograph 34). London: Routledge.

Kaplan, E.A. 1992. *Motherhood and Representation: The Mother in Popular Culture and Melodrama.* London and New York: Routledge.

Kelly, J. 1988. "Adjustment in Children of Divorce." *Journal of Family Psychology,* 2(2): 119–40.

King, M. 1987. "Playing the Symbols—Custody and the Law Commission." *Family Law,* 17: 186–91.

King, M., and Piper, C. 1990. *How the Law Thinks about Children.* Aldershot: Gower.

Kruk, E. 1993. *Divorce and Disengagement: Patterns of Fatherhood within and beyond Marriage.* Halifax, Nova Scotia: Fernwood Publishing.

La Fontaine, J.S. 1980. "The Domestication of the Savage Male." *Man,* (n.s.), 16: 338–49.

———. 1985. "Anthropological Perspectives on the Family and Social Change." *Quarterly Journal of Social Affairs,* 1: 29–56.

———. 1988. "Child Sexual Abuse and the Incest Taboo: Practical Problems and Theoretical Issues." *Man,* (n.s.), 23: 1–18.

———. 1990. *Child Sexual Abuse.* Cambridge: Polity Press.

Lamb, M.E. 1987. "Father and Child Development: An Integrative Overview." in M.E. Lamb (ed.), *The Father's Role: Applied Perspectives.* New York: Wiley.

Lasch, C. 1977. *Haven in a Heartless World: The Family Besieged.* New York: Basic Books.

Laslett, P. 1972. "The History of the Family" in P. Laslett and R. Wall (eds), *Household and Family in Past Time.* Cambridge: Cambridge University Press.

Lauer, R.H. and Lauer, J.C. 1994. *Marriage and Family: The Quest for Intimacy,* Dubuque, IA: Brown Communications Inc.

Law Commission 1988. *Family Law Review of Child Law: Guardianship and Custody.* Law Commisssion No 172. London: HMSO.

Law, J. 1994. *Organising Modernity.* Oxford: Blackwell.

Leach, E.R. 1961. *Rethinking Anthropology*. London: Athlone Press.

———. 1967. "An Anthropologist's Reflections on a Social Survey" in D.C. Jongmans and P.C.Gutkind (eds), *Anthropologists in the Field*. Assen, Netherlands: Van Gorcum and Co.

———. 1968. "The Cereal-packet Norm." *The Guardian*, 29 January.

Legal Aid Board 1994. *Annual Report 1993–94: Report to the Lord Chancellor on the Operation of the Finance and Legal Aid Act 1988*. London: HMSO.

Lévi-Strauss, C. 1974. "The Principle of Reciprocity." in R. Laub-Coser (ed.), *The Family: Its Structure and Functions*. New York: St. Martin's Press.

Lewis, C. 1986. *Becoming a Father*. Milton Keynes: Open University Press.

Lewis, C., and O'Brien, M. 1987. "Constraints on Fathers: Research, Theory and Clinical Practice" in C. Lewis and M. O'Brien (eds), *Reassessing Fatherhood*. London, Sage Publications.

Lewis, J., Clark, D. and Morgan, D. 1992. *Whom God hath Joined together: The Work of Marriage Guidance*. London: Routledge.

Lewis, O. 1966. *La Vida: A Puerto Rican Family in the Culture of Poverty—San Juan and New York*. New York: Random House.

Linde, C. 1993. *Life Stories: The Search for Coherence*. Oxford: Oxford University Press.

Linell, P. 1990. "The Power of Dialogue Dynamics" in I. Markova and K. Foppa (eds), *The Dynamics of Dialogue*. New York: Harvester: Wheatsheaf.

Loizos, P. and Papataxiarchis. E. (eds) 1991. *Contested Identities: Gender and Kinship in Modern Greece*. Princeton: Princeton University Press,

Lord Chancellor's Department 1985–91. *Judicial Statistics*. London: HMSO.

Lowe, N. 1982. "The Legal Status of Fathers Past and Present" in L. Mckee and M. O'Brien (eds), *The Father Figure*. London: Tavistock.

McAllister, F. 1995. *Marital Breakdown and the Health of the Nation* (2nd edition). London: One Plus One.

McCarthy, P. 1996. "Marital Breakdown: Professional Shakedown" in R. Humphrey (ed.), *Families behind the Headlines*. Newcastle: British Association for the Advancement of Science/Department of Social Policy, University of Newcastle upon Tyne.

McCarthy, P., and Simpson, B. 1991. *Issues in Post-divorce Housing: Family Policy or Housing Policy?* Aldershot: Avebury.

McCarthy, P., and Simpson, R., Walker, J. and Corlyon, J. 1991. *A Longitudinal Study of the Impact of Different Dispute Resolution Processes on Post-divorce Relationships Between Parents and Children*. Report to the Ford Foundation (Fund for Research in Dispute Resolution).

Macfarlane, A. 1978. *The Origins of English Individualism*. Oxford: Basil Blackwell.

MacIntyre, A. 1981. *After Virtue*. London: Duckworth.

Maclean, M. 1991. *Surviving Divorce: Women's Resources after Divorce*. Basingstoke: Macmillan.

Maidment, S. 1982. "Law and Justice: The Case for Family Law Reform." *Family Law*, 12: 229–32.

———. 1984. *Child Custody after Divorce: The Law in Social Context*. London: Croom Helm.

Mair, L. 1971. *Marriage*. Harmondsworth: Penguin.

Mansfield, P. and Collard, J. 1988. *The Beginning of the Rest of your Life: A Portrait of Newly-Wed Marriage*. Basingstoke: Macmillan.

Markus H.R. and Kitayama, S. 1991. "Culture and the Self: Implications for Cognition, Emotion and Motivation." *Psychological Review*, 98: 224–53.

Marriage and Divorce Statistics 1977. Office of Population, Censuses and Surveys. London: HMSO.

———. 1986. Office of Population, Censuses and Surveys. London: HMSO.

———. 1990. Office of Population, Censuses and Surveys. London: HMSO.

———. 1994. Office of Population, Censuses and Surveys. London: HMSO.

Mauss, M. 1925[1954]. *The Gift: Forms and Functions of Exchange in Archaic Societies*. Trans. by I. Cunnison. London: Cohen and West.

Mead, G.H. 1936. *Mind, Self and Society*. Chicago: University of Chicago Press.

Medick, H. and Sabean, D.W. 1988. *Interest and Emotion: Essays on the Study of Family and Kinship*. Cambridge: Cambridge University Press.

Meyrowitz, J. 1984. "The Adult Child and the Child-like Adult." *Daedalus*, 113(3): 19–48.

Mitchell, J.C. 1969. "The Concept and Use of Social Networks" in J.C Mitchell (ed.), *Social Networks in Urban Situations*. Manchester: Manchester University Press.

Mnookin, R. and Kornhauser, L. 1979. "Bargaining in the Shadow of the Law: The Case of Divorce." *Yale Law Journal*, 88: 950–70.

Modell, J. 1986. "In search: The Purported Biological Basis of Parenthood." *American Ethnologist*, 13: 646–61.

Moore, H. 1988. *Anthropology and Feminism*. Cambridge: Polity Press.

Morgan, D.H.J. 1985. *The Family, Politics and Social Theory*. London: Routledge, Kegan and Paul.

———. 1988. "Two Faces of the Family: The Possible Contribution of Sociology to Family Therapy." *Journal of Family Therapy*, 10: 23 3–53.

Morgan, P. 1986. "Feminist Attempts to Sack the Father: A Case of Unfair Dismissal?" in D. Anderson and G. Dawson (eds), *Family Portraits*. London: Social Affairs Unit.

Mount, F. 1982. *The Subversive Family*. London: Jonathan Cape.

Needham, R. 1971. "Remarks on the Analysis of Kinship and Marriage" in R. Needham (ed.), *Rethinking Kinship and Marriage*. London: Tavistock Publications.

New, C. and David, M. 1985. *For the Children's Sake: Making Childcare more than Women's Business*, Harmondsworth: Penguin.

Newman, J. 1991. "Enterprising Women: Images of Success" in S. Franklin, C. Levy and J. Stacey (eds), *Off-Centre: Feminism and Cultural Studies*. Hammersmith: Harper and Collins.

Newson, J. and Newson, E. 1978. "Cultural Aspects of Child-rearing in the English-Speaking World" in M. Richards (ed.), *The Integration of a Child into a Social World*. Cambridge: Cambridge University Press.

Oakley, A. 1974. *The Sociology of Housework*. London: Martin Robertson.

Offer, A. 1996. "Between the Gift and the Market: The Economy of Regard." Unpublished MS, prepared for the Congress of the European Association of Historical Economics, Venice.

Ogus, A., Walker, J., Jones-Lee, M., Cole, W., Corlyon, J., McCarthy, P., Simpson, R. and Wray, S. 1989. *Report to the Lord Chancellor's Department on the Costs and Effectiveness of Conciliation in England and Wales*. London: Lord Chancellor's Department.

Osmond, M.W. 1986. "Radical-critical Theories." in M.B. Sussman and S.K. Steinmetz (eds), *Handbook of Marriage and the Family*. New York and London: Plenum Press.

Pahl, J. 1983. "The Allocation of Money and the Structuring of Inequality within Marriage." *The Sociological Review*, 31: 237–62.

Pahl, R. 1984. *Divisions of Labour*. Oxford: Blackwell.

Parkinson, L. 1981. "Joint Custody," *One-Parent Times*, No. 7. London: National Council for One Parent Families.

———. 1986. *Conciliation in Separation and Divorce*. London: Croom Helm.

———. 1988. "Child Custody Orders: A Legal Lottery." *Family Law*, 18: 26–30.

Phillips, R. 1988. *Putting Asunder: A History of Divorce in Western Society*. Cambridge: Cambridge University Press.

Pitt-Rivers, J. 1973. "The Kith and the Kin." in J.R. Goody (ed.), *The Character of Kinship*. Cambridge: Cambridge University Press.

Polkinghorne, D.E. 1988. *Narrative Knowing and the Human Sciences*. Albany, NY: State University of New York Press.

Priest, J. and Whybrow, J. 1986. *Child Law in Practice in the Divorce and Domestic Courts*. Supplement to Law Commission Working Paper No. 96. London: HMSO.

Rapport, N. 1997. *Transcendent Individual*. London: Routledge.

Reiss, D. 1981. *The Family's Construction of Reality*. Cambridge MA: Harvard University Press.

Ribbens, J. 1994. *Mothers and Their Children*. London: Sage.

Ricci, I. 1980. *Mom's House—Dad's House: Making Shared Custody Work*. London: Collier-Macmillan.

Richards M. 1982. "Post-Divorce Arrangements for Children: A Psychological Perspective." *Journal of Social Welfare Law*, 3: 133–51.

Richards, M., and Dyson, M. 1982. *Separation, Divorce and the Development of Children: A Review*. London: Department of Health and Social Security.

Riessman, C.K. 1990. *Divorce Talk: Women and Men Make Sense of Personal Relationships*. New Brunswick and London: Rutgers University Press.

———. 1993. *Narrative Analysis*. London: Sage Publications.

Robertson, A.F. 1991. *Beyond the Family: The Social Organisation of Human Reproduction*. Berkeley: University of California Press.

Rose, N. 1992. "Governing the Enterprising Self" in P. Heelas and P. Morris (eds), *The Values of the Enterprise Culture*. London and New York: Routledge.

Ross, H. and Sawhill, I. 1975. *The Growth of Households Headed by Women*. Washington DC: The Urban Institute.

Scanzioni, J. 1983. *Shaping Tomorrow's Family: Theory and Policy for the 21st Century*. Beverly Hills and London: Sage Publications.

Scanzioni, J. and Polonko,K., Teachman, J. and Thompson, L. 1989. *The Sexual Bond: Rethinking Families and Close Relationships*. Newbury Park: Sage.

Schneider, D.M. 1968. *American Kinship: A Cultural Account*. Englewood Cliffs: Prentice-Hall.

———. 1984. *A Critique of the Study of Kinship*. Ann Arbor: University of Michigan Press.

Schwartz, R. 1987. "Our Multiple Selves: Applying Systems Thinking to the Inner Family." *The Family Therapy Networker*, March/April: 25–83.

Seccombe, W. 1993. *Weathering the Storm: Working Class Families from the Industrial Revolution to the Fertility Decline*. London: Verso.

Segal, L. 1983. "Smash the Family? Recalling the 1960s" in L. Segal (ed.), *What is to be Done about the Family?* Harmondsworth: Penguin.

Seltzer, J.A., Schaeffer, N.C. and Charng, H. 1989. "Family Ties after Divorce: The Relationship between Visiting and Paying Child Support." *Journal of Marriage and the Family*, 1: 1,013–1,031.

Shorter, E. 1975. *The Making of the Modern Family*. London: Fontana/Collins.

Simpson, B. 1994a. "Access and Child Contact Centres in Britain: An Ethnographic Perspective." *Children and Society*, 8(1): 42–54.

———. 1994b. "Bringing the Unclear Family into Focus: Divorce and Re-marriage in Contemporary Britain." *Man* (n.s.), 29: 831–51.

———. 1997. "On Gifts Payments and Disputes after Divorce." *Journal of the Royal Anthropological Institute*, 3(4): 731-45.

Simpson, B., and McCarthy, P. and Walker, J. 1995. *Being There: Fathers after Divorce*. Newcastle: Relate Centre for Family Studies.

Smart, C. 1984. *The Ties that Bind: Law, Marriage and the Reproduction of Patriarchal Relations*. London: Routledge, Kegan and Paul.

———. 1989. "Power and the Politics of Child Custody" in C. Smart and S. Sevenhuijsen (eds), *Child Custody and the Politics of Gender*. London and New York: Routledge.

Smith, R.T. 1996. *The Matrifocal Family: Power; Pluralism and Politics*. New York and London: Routledge.

Social Trends 1991. Office of Population, Censuses and Surveys. London: HMSO.

———. 1994. Office of Population, Censuses and Surveys. London: HMSO.

Stacey, J. 1990. *Brave New Families: Stories of Domestic Upheaval in Late Twentieth Century America*. New York: Basic Books.

———. and Price, M. 1981. *Women, Power and Politics*. London: Tavistock.

Stack, C.B., and Burton, L.B. 1994. "Kinscripts: Reflections on Family, Generation and Culture" in E.N. Glen, G. Chang and L.R. Forcey (eds), *Mothering: Ideology, Experience and Agency*. New York & London: Routledge.

Steinberg, L. 1987. "Recent Research on the Family at Adolescence: The Extent and Nature of Sex Differences." *Journal of Youth and Adolescence*, 16: 191–7.

Stenning, D.J. 1958. "Household Viability among the Pastoral Fulani" in J.R. Goody (ed.), *The Developmental Cycle in Domestic Groups*. Cambridge: Cambridge University Press.

Stone, L. 1977. *The Family, Sex and Marriage in England 1500–1800*. London: Weidenfeld and Nicolson.

Strathern, M. 1982. "The Place of Kinship: Kin, Class and Village Status in Elmdon, Essex" in A.P. Cohen (ed.), *Belonging: Identity and Social Organisation in British Rural Cultures*. Manchester: Manchester University Press.

———. 1984. "Domesticity and the Denigration of Women" in D. O'Brien and S. Tiffany (eds), *Rethinking Women's Roles: Perspectives from the Pacific*. Berkeley: California University Press.

———. 1988. *The Gender of the Gift*. London and Berkeley: University of California Press.

———. 1991. *Reproducing the Future.* Manchester: Manchester University Press.

———. 1992a. *After Nature: English Kinship in the Late Twentieth Century.* Cambridge: Cambridge University Press.

———. 1992b. "Enterprising Kinship: Consumer Choice and the new Reproductive Technologies" in P. Heelas and P. Morris (eds), *The Values of the Enterprise Culture.* London and New York: Routledge.

———. 1996. "Cutting the Network." *Journal of the Royal Anthropological Institute,* 2: 5 17–32.

Stromberg, P.G. 1993. *Language and Self-Transformation: A Study of Christian Conversion Narrative.* Cambridge: Cambridge University Press.

Tannen, D. 1991. *You Just Don't Understand.* New York: William Morrow.

Utting, D. 1995. *Family and Parenthood: Supporting Families, Preventing Breakdown.* York: Joseph Rowntree Foundation.

Vitebsky, P. 1993. *Dialogues of the Dead: The Discussion of Mortality among the Sora of Eastern India.* Cambridge: Cambridge University Press.

Vygotsky, L.S. 1962. *Thought and Language.* Cambridge MA: MIT Press.

Wallerstein, J. 1985. "The Over-burdened Child: Some Long-term Consequences of Divorce." *Social Work* 30: 116–23.

Wallerstein, J., and Blakeslee, S. 1989. *Second Chances: Men, Women and Children a Decade Afterwards.* London: Bantam Press.

Wallerstein, J., and Kelly, J. 1980. *Surviving the Break-Up.* London: Grant McIntyre.

Watkins, M. 1986. *Invisible Guests: The Development of Imaginal Dialogues.* Hillsdale, NJ: The Analytic Press.

Weiss, C. 1986. "Research and Policy-making: A Limited Partnership" in F. Heler (ed), *The Use and Abuse of Social Science.* London: Sage.

Weitzman, L. 1985. *The Divorce Revolution.* New York: Free Press.

Wexler, P. 1990. "Citizenship in the Semiotic Society" in B. Wilson, (ed.), *Theories of Modernity and Postmodernity.* London and New Delhi: Sage.

Weston, K. 1991. *Families We Choose: Lesbians, Gays, Kinship.* New York: Colombia University Press.

Wicks, M. 1991. "Research Results of Lone Parent Families." Letter to *The Independent,* March.

Widdershoven, G.A.M. 1993. "The Story of a Life: Hermeneutic Perspectives on the Relationship between Narrative and Life History" in R. Josselson and A. Lieblich (eds), *The Narrative Study of Lives.* Newbury Park: Sage.

Wilson, P. and Pahl, R. 1988. "The Changing Sociological Construct of the Family." *The Sociological Review,* 36: 23–372.

Wolfram, S. 1987. *In-Laws and Out-Laws: Kinship and Marriage in England*. London: Croom Helm.

Yanagisako, S.J. and Collier, J.F. 1987. "Toward a Unified Analysis of Gender and Kinship" in J.F. Collier and S.J. Yanagisako (eds), *Gender and Kinship: Essays towards a Unified Analysis*. Stanford CA: Stanford University Press.

Young, M. and Wilmott, P. 1967 [1957]. *Family and Kinship in East London*. Harmondsworth: Penguin.

———. 1973. *The Symmetrical Family*. London: Routledge, Kegan and Paul.

CHAPTER 15

The Female World of Cards and Holidays: Women, Families, and the Work of Kinship

Micaela di Leonardo

> Why is it that the married women of America are supposed to write all the letters and send all the cards to their husbands' families? My old man is a much better writer than I am, yet he expects me to correspond with his whole family. If I asked him to correspond with mine, he would blow a gasket.
>
> —Letter to Ann Landers

> Women's place in man's life cycle has been that of nurturer, caretaker, and helpmate, the weaver of those net-works of relationships on which she in turn relies.
>
> —Carol Gilligan, In a Different Voice

Feminist scholars in the past fifteen years have made great strides in formulating new understandings of the relations among gender, kinship, and the larger economy. As a result of this pioneering research, women are newly visible and audible, no longer submerged within their families. We see households as loci of political struggle, inseparable parts of the larger society and economy, rather than as havens from the heartless world of industrial capitalism.[1] And historical and cultural variations in kinship and family forms have become clearer with the maturation of feminist historical and social-scientific scholarship.

Two theoretical trends have been key to this reinterpretation of women's work and family domain. The first is the elevation to visibility of women's nonmarket activities—housework, child care, the servicing of men, and the care of the elderly—and the definition of all these activities as labor, to be enumerated alongside and counted as part of overall social reproduction. The

---

From *Signs* 12, No. 3 (1987) by Micaela di Leonardo. The University of Chicago Press, publisher. Reprinted with permission.

second theoretical trend is the non-pejorative focus on women's domestic or kin-centered networks. We now see them as the products of conscious strategy, as crucial to the functioning of kinship systems, as sources of women's autonomous power and possible primary sites of emotional fulfillment, and, at times, as the vehicles for actual survival and/or political resistance.[2]

Recently, however, a division has developed between feminist interpreters of the "labor" and the "network" perspectives on women's lives. Those who focus on women's work tend to envision women as sentient, goal-oriented actors, while those who concern themselves with women's ties to others tend to perceive women primarily in terms of nurturance, other-orientation—altruism. The most celebrated recent example of this division is the opposing testimony of historians Alice Kessler-Harris and Rosalind Rosenberg in the Equal Employment Opportunity Commission's sex discrimination case against Sears Roebuck and Company. Kessler-Harris argued that American women historically have actively sought higher-paying jobs and have been prevented from gaining them because of sex discrimination by employers. Rosenberg argued that American women in the nineteenth century created among themselves, through their domestic networks, a "women's culture" that emphasized the nurturance of children and others and the maintenance of family life and that discouraged women from competition over or heavy emotional investment in demanding, high-paid employment.[3]

I shall not here address this specific debate but, instead, shall consider its theoretical background and implications. I shall argue that we need to fuse, rather than to oppose, the domestic network and labor perspectives. In what follows I introduce a new concept, the work of kinship, both to aid empirical feminist research on women, work and family and to help advance feminist theory in this area. I believe that the boundary-crossing nature of the concept helps to confound the self-interest/altruism dichotomy, forcing us from an either-or stance to a position that includes both perspectives. I hope in this way to contribute to a more critical feminist vision of women's lives and the meaning of family in the industrial West.

In my field research among Italian-Americans in northern California, I found myself considering the relations between women's kinship and economic lives. As an anthropologist, I was concerned with people's kin lives beyond conventional American nuclear family or household boundaries. To this end, I collected individual and family life histories, asking about all kin and close friends and their activities. I was also very interested in women's labor. As I sat with women and listened to their accounts of their past and present lives, I began to realize that they were involved in three types of work: housework and child care, work in the labor market, and the work of kinship.[4]

By kin work I refer to the conception, maintenance, and ritual celebration of cross-household kin ties, including visits, letters, telephone calls, presents, and cards to kin; the organization of holiday gatherings; the creation and maintenance of quasi-kin relations; decision to neglect or to intensify particular ties; the mental work of reflation about all these activities; and the creation and communication of altering images of family and kin vis-à-vis the images of others, both folk and mass media. Kin work is a key element that has been missing in the synthesis of the "household labor" and "domestic network" perspectives. In our emphasis on individual women's responsibilities within households and on the job, we reflect the common picture of households as nuclear units, tied perhaps to the larger social and economic system, but not to *each other*. We miss the point of telephone and soft drink advertising, of women's magazines' holiday issues, of commentators' confused nostalgia for the mythical American extended family: it is kinship *across households*, as much as women's work within them, that fulfills our cultural expectation of satisfying family life.

Maintaining these contacts, this sense of family, takes time, intention, and skill. We tend to think of human social and kin networks as the epiphenomena of production and reproduction: the social traces created by our material lives. Or, in the neoclassical tradition, we see them as part of leisure activities, outside an economic purview except insofar as they involve consumption behavior. But the creation and maintenance of kin and quasi-kin networks in advanced industrial societies is *work*, and, moreover, it is largely women's work.

The kin-work lens brought into focus new perspectives on my informants' family lives. First, life histories revealed that often the very existence of kin contact and holiday celebration depended on the presence of an adult woman in the household. When couples divorced or mothers died, the work of kinship was left undone; when women entered into sanctioned sexual or marital relationships with men in these situations they reconstituted the men's kinship networks and organized gatherings and holiday celebrations. Middle-aged businessman Al Bertini, for example, recalled the death of his mother in his early adolescence: "I think that's probably one of the biggest losses in losing a family—yeah, I remember as a child when my Mom was alive . . . the holidays were treated with enthusiasm and love . . . after she died the attempt was there but it just didn't materialize." Later in life, when Al Bertini and his wife separated, his own and his son Jim's participation in extended family contact decreased rapidly. But when Jim began a relationship with Jane Bateman, she and he moved in with Al, and Jim and Jane began to invite his kin over for holidays Jane single-handedly planned and cooked the holiday feasts.

Kin work, then, is like housework and child care: men in the aggregate do not do it. It differs from these forms of labor in that it is harder for men to substitute hired labor to accomplish these tasks in the absence of kinwomen. Second, I found that women, as workers in this arena, generally had much greater kin knowledge than did their husbands, often including more accurate and extensive knowledge of their husbands' families. This was true both of middle-aged and younger couples and surfaced as a phenomenon in my interviews in the form of humorous arguments and in wives' detailed additions to husbands' narratives. Nick Meraviglia, a middle-aged professional, discussed his Italian antecedents in the presence of his wife, Pina:

Nick: My grandfather was a very outspoken man, and it was reported he took off for the hills when he found out that Mussolini was in power.
Pina: And he was a very tall man; he used to have to bow his head to get inside doors.
Nick: No, that was my uncle.
Pina: Your grandfather too, I've heard your mother say.
Nick: My mother has a sister and a brother.
Pina: Two sisters!
Nick: You're right!
Pina: Maria and Angelina.

Women were also much more willing to discuss family feuds and crises and their own roles in them; men tended to repeat formulaic statements asserting family unity and respectability. (This was much less true for younger men.) Joe and Cetta Longhinotti's statements illustrate these tendencies. Joe responded to my question about kin relations: "We all get along. As a rule, relatives, you got nothing but trouble." Cetta, instead, discussed her relations with each of her grown children, their wives, her in-laws, and her own blood kin in detail. She did not hide the fact that relations were strained in several cases; she was eager to discuss the evolution of problems and to seek my opinions of her actions. Similarly, Pina Meraviglia told the following story of her fight with one of her brothers with hysterical laughter: "There was some biting and hair pulling and choking . . . it was terrible! I shouldn't even tell you. . . . Nick, meanwhile, was concerned about maintaining an image of family unity and respectability.

Also, men waxed fluent while women were quite inarticulate in discussing their past and present occupations. When asked about their work lives, Joe Longhinotti and Nick Meraviglia, union baker and professional, respectively, gave detailed narratives of their work careers. Cetta Longhinotti and Pina Meraviglia, clerical and former clerical, respectively, offered only short descriptions focusing on factors of ambience, such as the "lovely things" sold by Cetta's firm.

These patterns are not repeated in the younger generation, especially among young women, such as Jane Bateman, who have managed to acquire training and jobs with some prospect of mobility. These younger women, though, have added a professional and detailed interest in their jobs to a felt responsibility for the work of kinship.[5]

Although men rarely took on any kin-work tasks, family histories and accounts of contemporary life revealed that kinswomen often negotiated among themselves, alternating hosting, food-preparation, and gift-buying responsibilities—or sometimes ceding entire task clusters to one woman. Taking on or ceding tasks was clearly related to acquiring or divesting oneself of power within kin networks, but women varied in their interpretation of the meaning of this power. Cetta Longhinotti, for example, relied on the "family Christmas dinner" as a symbol of her central kinship role and was involved in painful negotiations with her daughter-in-law over the issue: "Last year she insisted—this is touchy. She doesn't want to spend the holiday dinner together. So last year we went there. But I still had my dinner the next day. . . . I made a big dinner on Christmas Day, regardless of who's coming—candles on the table, the whole routine. I decorate the house myself too . . . well, I just feel that the time will come when maybe I won't feel like cooking a big dinner—she should take advantage of the fact that I feel like doing it now." Pina Meraviglia, in contrast, was saddened by the centripetal force of the developmental cycle but was unworried about the power dynamics involved in her negotiations with daughters- and mother-in-law over holiday celebrations.

Kin work is not just a matter of power among women but also of the mediation of power represented by household units.[6] Women often choose to minimize status claims in their kin work and to include numbers of households under the rubric of family. Cetta Longhinotti's sister Anna, for example, is married to a professional man whose parents have considerable economic resources, while Joe and Cetta have low incomes and no other well-off kin. Cetta and Anna remain close, talk on the phone several times a week, and assist their adult children, divided by distance and economic status, in remaining united as cousins.

Finally, women perceived housework, child care, market labor, the care of the elderly, and the work of kinship as competing responsibilities. Kin work was a unique category, however, because it was unlabeled and because women felt they could either cede some tasks to kinswomen and/or could cut them back severely. Women variously cited the pressures of market labor, the needs of the elderly, and their own desires for freedom and job enrichment as reasons for cutting back Christmas card lists, organized holiday gatherings, multifamily dinners, letters, visits, and phone calls. They expressed guilt and defensiveness about this cutback process and, particularly, about their failures to keep families close through constant contact and about their failures to create perfect holiday celebrations. Cetta Longhinotti, during the period when she was visiting her elderly mother every weekend in addition to working a full-time job, said of her grown children, "I'd have the whole gang here once a month, but I've been so busy that I haven't done that for about six months." And Pina Meraviglia lamented her insufficient work on family Christmases, "I wish I had really made it traditional . . . like my sister-in-law has special stories."

Kin work, then, takes place in an arena characterized simultaneously by cooperation and competition, by guilt and gratification. Like housework and child care, it is women's work, with the same lack of clear-cut agreement concerning its proper components: How often should sheets be changed? When should children be toilet trained? Should an aunt send a niece a birthday present? Unlike housework and child care, however, kin work, taking place across the boundaries of normative households, is as yet unlabeled and has no retinue of experts prescribing its correct forms. Neither home economists nor child psychologists have much to say about nieces' birthday presents. Kin work is thus more easily cut back without social interference. On the other hand, the results of kin work—frequent kin contact and feelings of intimacy—the subject of considerable cultural manipulation as indicators of family happiness. Thus, women in general are subject to the guilt my informants expressed over cutting back kin-work activities.

Although many of my informants referred to the results of women's kin work—cross-household kin contacts and attendant ritual gatherings—as particularly Italian-American, I suggest that in fact this phenomenon is broadly characteristic of American kinship. We think of kin-work tasks such as the preparation of ritual feasts, responsibility for holiday card lists, and gift buying as extensions of women's domestic responsibilities for cooking, consumption, and nurturance. American men in general do not take on these tasks any more than they do housework and child care—and probably less, as these tasks have not yet been the subject of intense public debate. And my informants' gender breakdown in relative articulateness on kin-ship and workplace themes reflects the still prevalent occupational segregation—most women cannot find jobs that provide enough pay, status, or promotion possibilities to make them worth focusing on—as well as women's perceived power within kinship networks. The common recognition of that power is reflected in Selma Greenberg's book on non-sexist child rearing. Greenberg calls mothers "press agents" who sponsor relations between their own children and other relatives; she advises a mother whose relatives treat her disrespectfully to deny those kin access to her children.[7]

Kin work is a salient concept in other parts of the developed world as well. Larissa Adler Lomnitz and Marisol Perez Lizaur have found that "centralizing women" are responsible for these tasks and for communicating "family ideology" among upper-class families in Mexico City.

Matthews Hamabata, in his study of upper-class families in Japan, has found that women's kin work involves key financial transactions. Sylvia Junko Yanagisako discovered that among rural Japanese migrants to the United States the maintenance of kin networks was assigned to women as the migrants adopted the American ideology of the independent nuclear family household. Maila Stivens notes that urban Australian housewives' kin ties and kin ideology "transcend women's isolation in domestic units."[8]

This is not to say that cultural conceptions of appropriate kin work do not vary, even within the United States. Carol B. Stack documents institutionalized fictive kinship and concomitant reciprocity networks among impoverished black American women. Women in populations characterized by intense feelings of ethnic identity may feel bound to emphasize particular occasions—Saint Patrick's or Columbus Day—with organized family feasts. These constructs may be mediated by religious affiliation, as in the differing emphases on Friday or Sunday family dinners among Jews and Christians. Thus the personnel involved and the amount and kind of labor considered necessary for the satisfactory performance of particular kin-work tasks likely to be culturally constructed.[9] But while the kin and quasi-kin universes and the ritual calendar may vary among women according to race or ethnicity, their general responsibility for maintaining kin links and ritual observances does not.

As kin work is not an ethnic or racial phenomenon, neither is it linked only to one social class. Some commentators on American family life still reflect the influence of work done in England in the 1950s and 1960s (by Elizabeth Bott and by Peter Willmott and Michael Young) in their assumption that working-class families are close and extended, while the middle class substitutes friends (or anomie) for family. Others reflect the prevalent family pessimism in their presumption that neither working- nor middle-class families have extended kin contact.[10] Insofar as kin contact depends on residential proximity, the larger economy's shifts will influence particular groups' experiences. Factory workers, close to kin or not, are likely to disperse when plants shut down or relocate. Small business people or independent professionals may, however, remain resident in particular areas—and thus maintain proximity to kin—for generations, while professional employees of large firms relocate at their firms' behest. This pattern obtained among my informants.

In any event, cross-household kin contact can be and is affected at long distance through letters, cards, phone calls, and holiday and vacation visits. The form and functions of contact, however, vary according to economic resources. Stack and Brett Williams offer rich accounts of kin networks among poor blacks and migrant Chicano farmworkers functioning to provide emotional support, labor, commodity, and cash exchange—a funeral visit, help with laundry, the gift of a dress or piece of furniture.[11] Far different in degree are exchanges such as the loan of a vacation home, a multifamily boating trip, or the provision of free professional services—examples from the kin networks of my wealthier informants. The point is that households, as labor and income-pooling units, whatever their relative wealth, are somewhat porous in relation to others with whose members they share kin or quasi-kin ties. We do not really know how class differences operate in this realm; it is possible that they do so largely in terms of ideology. It may be, as David Schneider and Raymond T. Smith suggest, that the affluent and the very poor are more open in recognizing necessary economic ties to kin than are those who identify themselves as middle class.[12]

Recognizing that kin work is gender rather than class based allows us to see women's kin networks among all groups, not just among working-class and impoverished women in industrialized societies. This recognition in turn clarifies our understanding of the privileges and limits of women's varying access to economic resources. Affluent women can "buy out" of housework, child care—and even some kin-work responsibilities. But they, like all women, are ultimately responsible, and subject to both guilt and blame, as the administrators of home, children, and kin network. Even the wealthiest women must negotiate the timing and venue of holidays and other family rituals with their kinswomen. It may be that kin work is the core women's work category in which all women cooperate, while women's perceptions of the appropriateness of cooperation for housework, child care, and the care of the elderly varies by race, class, region, and generation.

But kin work is not necessarily an appropriate category of labor, much less gendered labor, in all societies. In many small-scale societies, kinship is the major organizing principle of all social life, and all contacts are by definition kin contacts.[13] One cannot, therefore, speak of labor that does not involve kin. In the United States, kin work as a separable category of gendered labor perhaps arose historically in concert with the ideological and material constructs of the moral mother/cult of domesticity and the privatized family during the course of industrialization in the eighteenth and nineteenth centuries. These phenomena are connected to the increase in the ubiquity of productive occupations *for men* that are not organized through kinship. This includes the demise of the family farm with the capitalization of agriculture and rural-urban migration; the decline of family recruitment in factories as firms grew ended child labor and began to assert bureaucratized forms of control; the decline of artisanal labor and of small entrepreneurial enterprises as large firms took greater and greater shares of the commodity market; the decline of the family firm as corporations—and their managerial workforces—grew beyond the capacities of individual families to provision them; and, finally, the rise of civil service bureaucracies and public pressure against nepotism.[14]

As men increasingly worked alongside of non-kin, and as the ideology of separate spheres was increasingly accepted, perhaps the responsibility for kin maintenance, like for child rearing, became gender-focused. Ryan points out that "built into the updated family economy . . . was a new measure of voluntarism." This voluntarism, though, "perceived as the shift from patriarchal authority to domestic affection also signaled the rise of women's moral responsibility for family life. Just as the "idea of fatherhood itself seemed almost to wither away" so did male involvement in the responsibility for kindred lapse.[15]

With postbellum economic growth and geographic movement, women's new kin burden involved increasing amounts of time and labor. The ubiquity of lengthy visits and of frequent letter-writing among nineteenth-century women attests to this. And for visitors and for those who were residentially proximate, the continuing commonalities of women's domestic labor allowed for kinds of work sharing—nursing, childkeeping, cooking, cleaning—that men, with their increasingly differentiated and controlled activities, probably could not maintain. This is not to say that some kin-related male productive work did not continue; my own data, for instance, show kin involvement among small businessmen in the present. It is instead to suggest a general trend in material life and a cultural shift that influenced even those whose productive and kin lives remained commingled. Yanagisako has distinguished between the realms of domestic and public kinship in order to draw attention to anthropology's relatively "thin descriptions" of the domestic (female) domain Using her typology, we might say that kin work as gendered labor comes into existence within the domestic domain with the relative erasure of the domain of public, male kinship.[16]

Whether or not this proposed historical model bears up under further research, the question remains. Why do women do kinwork? However material factors may shape activities, they do not determine how individuals may perceive them. And in considering issues of motivation, of intention, of the cultural construction of kin work, we return to the altruism versus self interest dichotomy in recent feminist theory. Consider the epigraphs to this article. Are women kin workers the nurturant weavers of the Gilligan quotation, or victims, like the fed-up woman who writes to complain to Ann Landers? That is, are we to see kin work as yet another example of "women's culture" that takes the care of others as its primary desideratum? Or are we to see kin work as another way in which men, the economy, and the state extract labor from women without a fair return? And how do women themselves see their kin work and its place in their lives?

As I have indicated above, I believe that it is the creation of the self interest/altruism dichotomy that is itself the problem here. My women informants, like most American women, accepted their primary responsibility for housework and the care of dependent children. Despite two major waves of feminist activism in this century, the gendering of certain categories of unpaid labor is still largely unaltered. These work responsibilities clearly interfere with some women's labor force commitments at certain life-cycle stages; but, more important, women are simply discriminated against in the labor market and rarely are able to achieve wage and status parity with men of the same age, race, class, and educational background.[17]

Thus for women informants, as for most American women, the domestic domain is not only an arena in which much unpaid labor must be undertaken but also a realm in which one may attempt to gain human satisfactions—and power—not available in the labor market. Anthropologists Jane Collier and Louise Lamphere have written compellingly on the ways in which varying kinship and economic structures may shape women's competition or cooperation with one another in domestic domains.[18] Feminists considering Western women and families have looked at the issue of power primarily in terms of husband wife relations or psychological relations between parents and children. If we adopt Collier and Lamphere's broader canvas, though, we see that kin work is not only women's labor from which men and children benefit but also labor that women undertake in order to create obligations in men and children and to gain power over one another. Thus Cetta Longhinotti's struggle with her daughter-in-law over the venue of Christmas dinner is not just about a competition over altruism, it is also about the creation of future obligations. And thus Cetta's and Anna's sponsorship and their children's friendship with each other is both an act of nurturance and a cooperative means of gaining power over those children.

Although this was not a clear-cut distinction, those of my informants who were more explicitly antifeminist tended to be most in vested in kin work. Given the overwhelming historical shift toward greater autonomy for younger generations and the withering of children's financial and labor obligations to their parents, this investment was in most cases tragically doomed. Cetta Longhinotti, for example, had repaid her own mother's devotion with extensive home nursing during the mother's last years. Given Cetta's general failure to direct her adult children in work, marital choice, religious worship, or even frequency of visits, she is unlikely to receive such care from them when she is older.

The kin-work lens thus reveals the close relations between altruism and self-interest in women's actions. As economists Nancy Folbre and Heidi Hartmann point out, we have inherited a Western intellectual tradition that both dichotomizes the domestic and public domains and associates them on exclusive axes such that we find it difficult to see self-interest in the home and altruism in the work place.[19] But why, in fact have women fought for better jobs if not, in part, to support their children? These dichotomies are Procrustean beds that warp our understanding of women's lives both at home and at work. "Altruism" and "self-interest" are cultural constructions that are not necessarily mutually exclusive, and we forget this to our peril.

The concept of kin work helps to bring into focus a heretofore unacknowledged array of tasks that is culturally assigned to women in industrialized societies. At the same time, this concept, embodying notions of both love and work crossing the boundaries of households, helps us to reflect on current feminist debates on women's work, family, and community. We newly see both the interrelations of these phenomena and women's roles in creating and maintaining those interrelations. Revealing the actual labor embodied in what we culturally conceive as love and considering the political uses of this labor helps to deconstruct the self-interest/altruism dichotomy and to connect more closely women's domestic and labor-force lives.

The true value of the concept, however, remains to be tested through further historical and contemporary research on gender, kinship, and labor. We need to assess the suggestion that gendered kin work emerges in concert with the capitalist development process; to probe the historical record for women's and men's varying and changing conceptions of it; and to research the current range of its cultural constructions and material realities. We know that household boundaries are more porous than we had thought—but they are undoubtedly differentially porous, and this is what we need to specify. We need, in particular to assess the relations of changing labor processes, residential patterns, and the use of technology to changing kin work.

Altering the values attached to this particular set of women's tasks will be as difficult as are the housework, child-care, and the occupational segregation struggles. But just as feminist research in these latter areas is complementary and cumulative, so researching kin work should help us to piece together the home, work, and public-life landscape—to see the female world of cards and holidays as it is constructed and lived within the changing political economy. How female that world is to remain, and what it would look like if it were not sex-segregated, are questions we cannot yet answer.

Notes

Acknowledgments: Many thanks to Cynthia Costello, Rayna Rapp, Roberta Spalter-Roth, John Willoughby, and Barbara Gelpi, Susan Johnson, and Sylvia Yanagisako of *Signs* for their help with this chapter. I wish in particular to acknowledge the influence of Rayna Rapp's work on my ideas. Acknowledgment and gratitude also to Carroll Smith-Rosenberg for my paraphrase of her title, "The Female World of Love and Ritual: Relations Between Women in Nineteenth-Century America," *Signs: Journal of Women in Culture and Society* 1, no. 1 (Autumn 1975): 1–29. The epigraphs are from Ann Landers letter printed in *Washington Post* (April 15, 1983); Carol Gilligan, *In a Different Voice* (Cambridge, Mass.: Harvard University Press, 1982), 17.

1. Heidi I. Hartmann, "The Family as the Locus of Gender, Class, and Political Struggle: The Example of Housework," *Signs* 6, no. 3 (Spring 1981): 366–94; and Christopher Lasch, *Haven in a Heartless World: The Family Besieged* (New York: Basic Books, 1977).

2. Representative examples of the first trend include Joann Vanek, "Time Spent on Housework," *Scientific American* 231 (November 1974): 116–20; Ruth Schwartz Cowan, A Case Study of Technological and Social Change: The Washing Machine and the Working Wife," in *Clio's Consciousness Raised*, ed. Mary Hartmann and Lois Banner (New York: Harper & Row, 1974), 245–53; Ann Oakley, *Women's Work: The Housewife, Past and Present* (New York Vintage 1974) Hartmann and Susan Strasser, *Never Done: A History of American Housework* (New York: Pantheon Books, 1982). Key contributions to the second trend include Louise Lamphere, "Strategies, Cooperation and Conflict Among Women in Domestic Groups," in *Women, Culture and Society*, ed. Michelle Zimbalist Rosaldo and Louise Lamphere (Stanford, Calif.: Stanford University Press, 1974), 97–112; Mina Davis Caulfield, "Imperialism, the Family and the Cultures of Resistance," *Socialist Revolution* 20 (October 1974): 67–85; Smith-Rosenberg; Sylvia Junko Yanagisako, "Women-Centered Kin Networks and Urban Bilateral Kinship," *American Ethnologist* 4, no. 2 (1977): 207–26; Jane Humphries, "The Working Class Family, Women's Liberation and Class Struggle: The Case of Nineteenth Century British History," *Review of Radical Political Economics* 9 (Fall 1977): 25–41; Blanche Weisen Cook, "Female Support Networks and Political Activism: Lillian Wald, Crystal Eastman, Emma Goldman," in *A Heritage of Her Own*, ed. Nancy F. Cott and Elizabeth H. Pleck (New York: Simon & Schuster, 1979); Temma Kaplan, "Female Consciousness and Collective Action: The Case of Barcelona, 1910–1918," *Signs* 7, no. 3 (Spring 1982): 545–66.

3. On this debate, see Jon Weiner, "Women's History on Trial," *Nation* 241, no. 6 (September 7, 1985): 161, 176, 178–80; Karen J. Winkler, "Two Scholars' Conflict in Sears Sex-Bias Case Sets Off War in Women's History," *Chronicle of Higher Education* (February 5, 1986), 1, 8; Rosalind Rosenberg, "What Harms Women in the Workplace," *New York Times* (February 27, 1986); Alice Kessler-Harris, "Equal Employment Opportunity Commission vs. Sears Roebuck and Company: A Personal Account," *Radical History Review* 35 (April 1986): 57–79.

4. Portions of the following analysis are reported in Micaela di Leonardo, *The Varieties of Ethnic Experience: Kinship, Class and Gender Among California Italian-Americans* (Ithaca, N.Y.: Cornell University Press, 1984), chap. 6.

5. Clearly, many women do, in fact, discuss their paid labor with willingness and clarity. The point here is that there are opposing gender tendencies in an identical interview situation, tendencies that are explicable in terms of both the material realities and current cultural constructions of gender.

6. Papanek has rightly focused on women's unacknowledged family status production, but what is conceived of as "family" shifts and varies (Hanna Papanek, "Family Status Production: The 'Work' and 'Non-Work' of Women," *Signs* 4, no. 4 [Summer 1979]: 775–81).

7. Selma Greenberg, *Right from the Start: A Guide to Nonsexist Child Rearing* (Boston: Houghton Mifflin Co., 1978), 147. Another example of indirect support for kin work's gendered existence is a recent study of university math students, which found that a major reason for women's failure to pursue careers in mathematics was the pressure of family involvement. Compare David Maines et al., *Social Processes of Sex Differentiation in Mathematics* (Washington D.C.: National Institute of Education, 1981).

8. Larissa Adler Lomnitz and Marisol Perez Lizaur The History of a Mexican Urban Family *Journal of Family History* 3, no. 4 (1978): 392–409, esp. 398; Sylvia Junko Yanagisako, "Two Processes of Change in Japanese-American Kinship," *Journal of Anthropological Research* 31 (1975): 196–224; Maila Stivens, "Women and Their Kin: Kin, Class and Solidarity in a Middle-Class Suburb of Sydney, Australia," in *Women United, Women Divided*, ed. Patricia Caplan and Janet M. Bujra (Bloomington: Indiana University Press, 1979), 157–84.

9. Carol B. Stack, *All Our Kin: Strategies for Survival in a Black Community* (New York: Harper & Row, 1974). These cultural constructions may, however, vary within ethnic-racial populations as well.

10. Elizabeth Bott, *Family and Social Network*, 2d ed. (New York: Free Press, 1971); Michael Young and Peter Willmott, *Family and Kinship in East London* (London: Routledge & Kegan Paul, 1957), and *Family and Class in a London Suburb* (London: Routledge & Kegan Paul, 1960). Classic studies that presume this class difference are Herbert Gans, *The Urban Villagers: Group and Class in the Life of Italian-Americans* (New York: Free Press, 1962) and Mirra Komarovsky, *Blue-Collar Marriage* (New York: Random House, 1962). A recent example is Ilene Philipson, "Heterosexual Antagonisms and the Politics of Mothering," *Socialist Review* 12, no. 6 (November–December 1982): 55–77. Edward Shorter, *The Making of the Modern Family* (New York: Basic Books, 1975), epitomizes the pessimism of the "family sentiments" school. See also Mary Lyndon Shanley, "The History of the Family in Modern England: Review Essay," *Signs* 4, no. 4 (Summer 1979): 740–50.

11. Stack; and Brett Williams, "The Trip Takes Us: Chicano Migrants to the Prairie" (Ph.D. diss., University of Illinois at Urbana-Champaign, 1975).

12. David Schneider and Raymond T. Smith, *Class Differences and Sex Roles in American Kinship and Family Structure* (Englewood Cliffs, N.J.: Prentice-Hall, 1973), esp. 27.

13. See Nelson Graburn, ed., *Readings in Kinship and Social Structure* (New York: Harper & Row, 1971), esp. 3–4.

14. The moral mother/cult of domesticity is analyzed in Barbara Welter, "The Cult of True Womanhood, 1820–1860," *American Quarterly* 18, no. 2 (Summer 1966): 151–74; Nancy Cott, *The Bonds of Womanhood: "Women's Sphere" in New England, 1780–1835* (New Haven, Conn.: Yale University Press, 1977); and Ruth Bloch, "American Feminine Ideals in Transition: The Rise of the Moral Mother, 1785–1815," *Feminist Studies* 4, no. 2 (June 1978): 101–26. The description of the general political-economic shift in the United States is based on Harry Braverman, *Labor and Monopoly Capital: The Degradation of Work in the Twentieth Century* (New York: Monthly Review Press, 1974); Peter Dobkin Hall, "Family Structure and Economic Organization: Massachusetts Merchants, 1700–1850," in *Family and Kin in Urban Communities, 1700–1950*, ed. Tamara K. Hareven (New York: New View points, 1977), 38–61; Michael Anderson, "Family, Household and the Industrial Revolution," in *The American Family in Social-Historical Perspective*, ed. Michael Gordon (New York: St. Martin's Press, 1978), 38–50; Tamara K. Hareven, *Amoskeag: Life and Work in an*

American Factory City (New York: Pantheon Books, 1978); Richard Edwards, *Contested Terrain: The Transformation of the Workplace in the Twentieth Century* (New York: Basic Books, 1979); Mary Ryan, *The Cradle of the Middle Class: The Family in Oneida County, New York, 1790–1865* (Cambridge: Cambridge University Press, 1981); Alice Kessler-Harris, *Out to Work: A History of Wage-Earning Women in the United States* (New York: Oxford University Press, 1982).

15. Ryan, 231–32.

16. Sylvia Junko Yanagisako, "Family and Household: The Analysis of Domestic Groups," *Annual Review of Anthropology* 8 (1979): 161–205.

17. See Donald J. Treiman and Heidi I. Hartmann, eds., *Women, Work and Wages: Equal Pay for Jobs of Equal Value* (Washington, D.C.: National Academy Press, 1981).

18. Lamphere (n. 2 above); Jane Fishburne Collier, "Women in Politics," in Rosaldo and Lamphere, eds. (n. 2 above), 89–96.

19. Nancy Folbre and Heidi I. Hartmann, "The Rhetoric of Self-Interest: Selfishness, Altruism, and Gender in Economic Theory," in *The Consequences of Economic Rhetoric*, ed. Arjo Kiamer, Donald McCloskey, and Robert M. Solow (New York: Cambridge University Press, 1988).

CHAPTER 16

Transnationalism and New Chinese: Immigrant Families in the United States

Bernard P. Wong

Migration for Chinese in the United States has changed significantly in the recent past, and these changes have in turn had considerable impact on migrants' families.[1] New Chinese immigrants differ significantly from old settlers in that many are highly educated professionals and affluent businessmen operating on a global stage. In response to changing economic opportunity structures throughout the world, Chinese immigrants have diversified from traditional ethnic niches and professional occupations into international trade. Various of these have become global, conducting business from different regions of the world and producing, distributing, and investing in different locales. For these new Chinese immigrants, long distance commuting has become common. Some migrants are required by their jobs to live temporarily in one country and conduct business in another; they have become transnationals.

Transnationalism implies that immigrants develop and sustain multiple social relationships that span geographic, political, and cultural borders (Basch et al. 1994; Rosaldo 1989). New Chinese immigrants use the term "astronaut" to refer to those transnational migrants among them who travel frequently between continents, families, and work places in various countries.

Traditional immigration, which proceeds unilineally from a mother country to a host country, requires rethinking. During the period from 1940 to 1970, scholars (e.g., Handlin 1951; Gans 1962; Gordon 1964) suggested that immigrants experienced initial uprooting, made gradual adjustments to the host country, and eventually settled down and became members of the host society. Transnational migrants, however, experience obstacles in adjustment and readjustment to both host and home societies due to the fact that they constantly are crossing borders.

From *Diasporic Identity,* Selected Papers on Refugees and Immigrants, Vol. VI., American Anthropological Association.

The social costs incurred in transnationalism are high. Migrants must negotiate, create, and maintain various social and other network relationships in two or more communities/countries. Intra-familiar relationships of husband-wife, sibling-sibling, father-child, and mother-child are altered and sometimes destroyed.

This chapter will examine types of family patterns created by transnationalism in relationship to four major types of transnational activities. All four types of families are known by the conspicuous absence of one or both parents. Structurally, the first type is headed by the mother, the second by the father. A third type is characterized by the absence of both parents, and a fourth by extended family members spanning two or more nations. The conclusions in this chapter are based on data obtained from fieldwork in New York City and the San Francisco Bay area from 1987 to 1997. Fieldwork included interviews with Chinese immigrants, visits to their families, and discussions with community leaders (Wong 1998).

Transnationalism as a Way of Life

In the past twenty years, Pacific Rim countries have become an important economic arena, linking numerous countries in manufacturing and distribution.[2] The rapid economic development of China, the political situation in Asia, uneven economic development of the third world, and the transformation of the first world economy from manufacturing to high tech and service have given rise to the activities of international itinerants among Chinese transnationals. These new Chinese immigrants who arrived after the 1990s have found that "America is not a paradise" for everyone. For many Chinese immigrants, the "American dream" must be redefined. After family soul-searching sessions, some Chinese have opted for a transnational lifestyle, returning to Asia or traveling to different parts of the world to seek their financial fortune.

The majority of these transnational migrants prefer to "grow roots" in the United States because, they say, of the better educational opportunities available to their children in America. Aspiring to settle comfortably in the United States and send their children to desirable schools or universities here, these immigrants travel for economic success, seeking high-income jobs in Asia. Social mobility requires that "bread winners" or "wage winners" commute cross-nationally.

Transnationalism has necessitated a series of changes in residence patterns, social relations, gender relations, and parent-child relations as well as relationships between immigrants and the receiving countries. Thus, the uprooting of social, economic, and cultural connections has created new family patterns.

Family Patterns of the Transnationals

New immigrants, whether rich, middle class, or poor, must travel long distances, undergo family separation, emotional upheaval, and the disruption of children's, parents', and friends' social lives. Nobel Prize winners, university presidents, white collar workers, blue collar workers, or paupers—all are subject to these upheavals.

Some distinguished immigrant scientists and professionals, who have enriched the West with their talents and contributions, are returning to work in Asia. Although many young Chinese students and professionals continue to come to the United States for university education and business opportunities, an increasing number are seeking employment in Asia where opportunities are expanding.

Some migrants are attracted by newfound opportunities in engineering, science, avionics, and computer design. Others are motivated by an entrepreneurial urge to start their own businesses. Some have felt the presence of a "glass ceiling" in American firms that has blocked their career advancement. Still, many of those who return to Asia retain their American citizenship or resident alien status as a way to keep their global options open.

Some Chinese businessmen also fear that the economic potential in the United States is limited, suggesting that growth is inhibited by high costs, high wages, and low productivity. By contrast, China and Taiwan's economies are growing rapidly, and their proximity to burgeoning Asian consumer markets may hold better promise for businessmen with expertise in both Asian and American markets and languages. Further, the American recession of the early 1990s affected California, where many immigrants live, more than many other states. Home to the defense and aeronautics industries, California was hit particularly hard during this recession. The loss of these industries multiplied the economic effects on other sectors such as real estate, tourism, and retail. In turn, the accompanying loss of consumer purchasing power has affected many Chinese businesses. Small businesses, larger firms, and professionals were all affected. At the same time, the Asia economy experienced unprecedented growth, triggering a new immigrant exodus, especially between 1990 and 1995 (*New York Times* 1995; *San Jose Mercury News* 1993).

Returning to Asia or traveling to other parts of the world to seek employment during the recession of the early 1990s was an adaptive strategy also of less educated newcomers. Many traveled to South Africa, Central America, Thailand, Nepal, Saudi Arabia, and China where they had social or economic connections. Long distance travel has become a necessity. Among newly-arrived immigrant families in the 1990s, it is common to see one or both parents constantly departing or arriving. This is the life of an "astronaut."

The "Astronaut" Trend

"Astronaut" (*tai kung ren*) has many meanings in Chinese. One connotes a cosmonaut; another alludes to a frequent flier. There is also a colloquial use of the word tai kung ren in Chinese, meaning a wife without her husband or vice versa. In the context of this chapter, "astronaut" refers to a transnational migrant who travels cross-nationally for his or her livelihood.

New Chinese immigrants tell numerous stories of itinerant businessmen to Hong Kong, Taiwan, or China who become entangled in new social relationships. Some of these men have two families: one in the United States and Taiwan or China. These bilocal polygamous households created through transnational migration, however, are not the normal pattern.

Matrifocal Families

Stack (1974), Guldin (1977), and a host of other authors have discussed the formation of matrifocal families. A matrifocal family refers to a family made up of a mother and her children This single parent household type is often the result of migratory labor. In her work on African

Americans, Stack (1974) demonstrates that the matrifocal household is an adaptive mechanism. In their father's absence, children must depend on their mother and her social network for survival. Guldin (1977) has described how Fujianese-Chinese in Hong Kong live, garnering support from their mothers rather than their fathers who were forced to travel to the Philippines to make their living overseas. Matrifocal families have existed also among Chinese immigrants in the past when families were separated by American exclusion laws (Wong 1985). The Immigration Act of 1924 specifically prohibited the entry of Chinese wives, and thus prevented the union of many Chinese families. In times past, many immigrants returned to China to marry and sire children.[3] They then returned to the United States. Their families in China continued to be tended by their wives there. Among today's Chinese transnational migrants, the situation has reversed itself. Now, wage earners leave their families behind in the United States. In these matrifocal families, men travel back and forth between America and other countries. In such cases, fathers may return once or twice a year to visit their families. Rather than developing a father-son bond, the dominant dyadic relationship is that between mother and son. This is a change from the traditional Chinese kinship pattern which emphasizes father-child relationships in a patrilineal kinship system (Hsu 1988). Among transnational Chinese families today, communication between a father and his family is often carried out by telephone and fax machine rather than face-to-face interaction.

Some transnational migrants who have left their children and spouses behind have acquired a new sense of freedom. They suddenly become "new bachelors," free and undisciplined in their daily regimen. After work, they frequent restaurants and entertainment establishments, changing their eating and sleeping habits. When they return to America, they find their family reunions boring. Children may have become strangers, and vice versa. The constant separation strikes a major blow to intra-family relationships. A traditional, complete, nuclear family household has now become an incomplete, truncated one. Children are emotionally tied to their mothers, and the dominant mother-child bond persists even after the child's reunion with his or her father.

The decision to return to Asia is often initiated by the husband, usually with the consent of his wife. After considering the financial advantages of a move, a husband may depart with the reluctant blessing of his wife. The following story is shared by men who have become "astronauts."

Mr. Zee was an accountant in Hong Kong. He and his family immigrated to San Francisco in 1992 by way of his wife's family connection. Fearing the uncertain future of Hong Kong after its eventual return to the People's Republic of China in 1997, Mr. Zee and his wife, who had been a teacher in Hong Kong, decided to move to the United States. After their arrival, Mr. Zee spent more than six months looking for suitable employment in his field. His accounting degree from Hong Kong University could not land him a job with any white accounting firms. The only job he could find was as bookkeeper in a Chinese restaurant. After receiving a "green card," he returned to Hong Kong for a visit and to try to win his old job back. To his surprise, Mr. Zee was welcomed back with open arms by his former employers. When I met Mr. Zee, he had been working in Hong Kong for three years.

Mrs. Zee continued to live in the United States caring for their two children. When Mrs. Zee first came to the United States, she stayed home with the children, but once they began high school she decided to look for work outside the home. She found a job working part-time as a cashier in a Chinese firm. The Zee family is reunited only twice a year. Mr. Zee comes back from Hong Kong each summer to stay with his family in San Francisco for two or three weeks. During the Chinese New Year, Mr. Zee returns to California once again to pay them a brief visit.

This family separation has created many problems in their lives. Mr. Zee's children have a hard time relating to their father because he is not around most of the time. Mrs. Zee told me they will continue this arrangement for only two more years. Both Mr. Zee and his wife believe that he should continue to work m Hong Kong until 1999 when, the two feel, he will no longer have the opportunity to make as much money. Mr. Zee hopes that by 1999 he will have accumulated sufficient savings to start a business in the United States.

The *San Jose Mercury News* (1993) reported on the experiences of the Tsenshau Yang and Samuel Liu families. Mr. Yang, an engineer in his late 30s, moved from Taiwan to the United States for university studies. After obtaining his doctoral degree in engineering from Stanford University, Mr. Yang stayed on to work in California's Silicon Valley. In 1993 he returned to Taiwan to work as vice president of a start up company designing integrated circuits His wife, Shyun, and their two children remain in Cupertino. Mr. Yang comes back to his family several times a year. For him, Taiwan offers better opportunities in his field. However, for his wife, an accountant, finding equivalent work in Taiwan is difficult. Although Mr. Yang returned to Taiwan with the blessing of his wife, she later had second thoughts. She said: "I didn't want him to come to me in 10 years and tell me he regretted not starting his own business. . . . But now, I am beginning to regret it because he is not home most of the time."

Another Taiwanese engineer, Mr. Samuel Liu, has had similar experiences *(San Jose Mercury News* 1993). After receiving an American education and working as president of a Silicon integrated systems firm for a number of years, Mr. Liu returned to Taiwan to take over a troubled semiconductor company which had made him an attractive job offer. Mr. Liu is able to return home about seven times a year to see his wife and children, but he misses his family. Global immigrants do, indeed, make sacrifices in pursuit of career advancement, as can be seen in the many single-parent Chinese "astronaut" families residing in the San Francisco Bay area. Many families are not as lucky as the above three families. In some "astronaut" families, children go unsupervised, experiencing problems in school and at home. Some children join gangs; many families experience emotional and marital problems. New immigrants pay a high price if they choose to lead the lives of "astronauts."

Patrifocal Families

Patrifocal families, which are headed by a single male parent, are relatively new and still rare among new Chinese immigrants. Children in patrifocal families derive their emotional support mainly from their fathers rather than from absentee mothers. Some women among new Chinese immigrants are known as *nu chiang ren* (in Mandarin) or *nuey kiong yan* (in Cantonese), meaning "strong woman." These women are extremely talented or have better family connections (*guanxi*), social capital, or professional training than their husbands. Some had good salaried jobs in Hong Kong or Taiwan prior to their migration to the United States. After arrival, they become impatient with the downward social mobility they are experiencing because they cannot find suitable employment. Some return to China or Hong Kong to look for better economic opportunities. Mrs. A was one such woman.

After much "brain storming" and discussion, Mrs. A decided to leave San Francisco for Hainan Island to help with the development of a power plant there. She leased a hotel room in Hong Kong as a long-term resident and from there traveled to Hainan Island to conduct her business. Hong Kong was her business center; the United States was her home. Her husband was an engineer and was in charge of raising their school age children since Mrs. A was able to return only twice a year to see her family. Here existed a reversal of the traditional gender role, with the man rather than the wife running the household. The husband had to go to work daily while supervising his children's schoolwork and doing household chores. He was family head, wage earner, and homemaker. His children were thus more connected to their father than to their mother. However, both husband and wife were unhappy with this separation. After three years, Mrs. A successfully completed her business project and returned to the United States with substantial savings. The family purchased a large house in the San Francisco Bay area. Concluding that the family had suffered enough, the wife vowed not to travel anymore.

The difficulty in maintaining patrifocal and matrifocal households can cause disintegration of the family. This is particularly so when the relationship between the husband and wife is strained prior to the departure of one for Hong Kong or other parts of the world. These marriages often end in divorce.

Matrifocal households are more numerous than patrifocal ones because men are the traditional wage earners in Chinese families. Chinese immigrants consider it more appropriate for a husband than a wife to travel overseas seeking economic advancement (Hsu 1983). The increase in women traveling for economic reasons, leaving husbands to care for families, represents a change in Chinese kinship relationships, with a husband now assuming the wife's role. The American women's liberation movement, increased education, and "social capital" have encouraged Chinese immigrant women to shift, at least temporarily, their traditional sex roles. Thus, transnational migration can change sex roles as well as kin relations among Chinese immigrants.

Pasternak et al. (1997) note that the development of residence rules or patterns is intimately connected to the division of labor by gender. Murdock (1965) noted the same phenomenon long ago. Matrifocal households develop when husbands' careers necessitate long distance travel. When wives commute internationally for a living, patrifocal households develop. In either case, separations between spouses and between parents and children occur and cause human and emotional suffering.

No-Parent Households

The so-called "no-parent" household is a new phenomenon among Chinese transnational migrations. Some well-to-do Chinese immigrants from Hong Kong or Taiwan, after obtaining immigrant status, set up households for their children, then return to work in their homeland. In effect, they "drop-off" their children in America to pursue their education. These parents typically purchase a house and find a school for their teenage children. Extra-curricular activities may also be arranged for them. Relatives or friends are asked to visit or keep an eye on these children whenever possible. Younger children may live near their aunts and uncles. The authority figure in these cases is the uncle; he "checks" on his nephews and nieces and reports back to their parents. In reality, supervision is often nominal. After the arrangement is made, the parents return to their home of origin either in Taiwan or Hong Kong. This phenomenon is called "Family of Parachuted Children." With schoolwork, housework, social activities, cooking, and playing, the children are on their own. Some of these teenage children are doing well; others are not. Loneliness and a lack of parental supervision create problems. These youngsters' parents remain uninformed about their children's problems, such as being bullied by gang members or experiencing conflicts with their friends. Frequently, these children and their parents cease having common interests. Often, on the occasion of family reunions, they have trouble engaging in ordinary conversations with one another. Children's ties to the family grow increasingly weak, except in financial matters.

There are many reasons for "dropping off" one's children. The first is the educational opportunities available in America. Many parents believe their children will be able to attend a better university in the United States than in their country of origin. The second reason is investment. Parents are worried about the political stability of Asia. Many reason that they should use their savings to invest in real property in the United States in which their children can live and oversee. In case of an emergency, parents can always fly back to the United States and have a comfortable home already available to them. "Plan before it rains" and "Don't wait to dig a well until you are thirsty" are common Chinese sayings given in response to my questions about parents leaving their children alone in America.

Transnational Extended Families and Global Business Strategies

The world has changed in that what was once considered a collection of independent and often isolated states is today an interdependent world. Processes of production span national boundaries and items of consumption may be assembled in more than one country. Modern communication and transportation technologies have shortened the distances of international travel. In this new world, some citizens have become transnational migrants, living their lives across national borders. A number of extended families now have members traveling and residing in different parts of the world.

A transnational extended family refers to a large family, headed by a patriarch, in which family members are scattered throughout the United States and other parts of the world. Transnational extended families are not units of consumption. They are principally units of economic activity coordinated by a patriarch. Extended families may coincide with family firms. For instance, a transnational corporation may have branches in different parts of the world, each administered by a different child and the child's family, while the headquarters continue to be run by the founder/patriarch in Hong Kong, Taiwan, or Singapore.

Contrary to the claims of many economists about the negative role of the family in business (Okun 1961; Donckels and Frohlich 1991), kinship is important in conducting international business. Some economists argue that particularistic social relations like kinship inhibit economic development and retard productivity. In contrast, Gallo and Sveen (1991), Whyte (1996), and Wong (1998) find that kinfolk can be engines for economic growth and can facilitate the internationalizing of business in the global economy.

Chinese family firms have been important in the economic activities of Chinese in the Philippines (Amyot 1973), China (Redding 1990; Yang 1994), Southeast Asia (Weidebaum and Hughes 1996), and the United States (Wong et al. 1992). The development of transnational extended families among the Chinese, however, is a relatively new phenomenon. Some business tycoons in this global economy think that a joint family venture, with various world branches run by family members and their spouses, is a necessity. In these ventures, strategic information is kept within the family. Decisions can be made quickly because of the family's centralization of authority and control. In certain circumstances, the chiefs of these family businesses can delegate decision-making powers to their family members in different local offices.

The transnational extended family occurs only among the very rich. Chinese interested in enlarging their family businesses can do so by enlarging their sphere of economic activity and developing transnational networks. These business strategies can be employed to capture a larger share of the market.

In the 1980s, new Chinese immigrants began to form multinational corporations. The principal organizers of these corporations were wealthy Hong Kong Chinese who lived in different parts of the world. Many of these corporations are now globalized. An example of a multinational corporation is the Chinese restaurant chain known as Harbor Village which has branches in Los Angeles, Hong Kong, Kowloon, and San Francisco.

Some multinational corporations have been created by Chinese businessmen to develop shopping centers, office buildings, and other commercial real estate businesses. Other corporations are building residential housing. This type of business venture is a recent phenomenon among the Chinese from Hong Kong, Thailand, Taiwan, and the United States.

Multinational corporations are also a way of enlarging financial networks. Diversifying their investments in different parts of the world is common among extremely wealthy Chinese immigrants. Thus, for example, Alexander Lui owns Anvil International Properties, Inc. in San Francisco and acts as board director of Furama Hotel Enterprises, Ltd. in Hong Kong. Mr. Lui is also on the Board of Directors of the Trans Pacific Bancorp in San Francisco. *The San Francisco Examiner* (1989a, 1989b) reported that the Lui family has investments and development interests throughout Asia. Anthony Chan is another example of this role of the phenomenon. His family has extensive investments in China, and he himself has been a general partner of WorldCo. Ltd. since 1972. He and his partners developed a 12-story office building in San Francisco. They also built shopping centers around the Bay area, especially in the South Bay region. These Hong Kong businessmen have connections and businesses in different parts of the world. Moreover, they have personal contacts in various Chinese communities throughout the world. An example is Robert Chan Hing Cheong, former chairman of HK-TVB, a Hong Kong cable company. Mr. Chan has been making connections in San Francisco, and has taken many business trips to the city to visit his former schoolmate, Deputy Mayor James K. Ho. With his international contacts and financial resources, Mr. Chan Hing Cheong has become a successful commercial and residential real estate developer in northern California.

Diversifying and globalizing family businesses into different fields and locations has become a common response of wealthy Hong Kong business people to cope with globalization trends in the business world. Employing this strategy can also help move a business's capital from one place to another in a crisis. The Ho Tim family is an example of wealthy Hong Kong immigrants utilizing global strategies. This family runs Honorway Investment Company, which developed a 26-story office and condominium building in San Francisco. The family firm also owns the Brooks Brothers Building, located in popular Union Square. The family patriarch is the chairman of the Miramar Hotel in Hong Kong. His son, Hamilton Ho, commutes frequently between Hong Kong and San Francisco on family business. Another well-known Bay area family is the Ma family, which owns a 26-story building in the San Francisco financial district, built in 1985. The Ma family also owns and controls Tai Sang Land Development Company in San Francisco and Tai Sang Bank in Hong Kong. The brother is chairman of Tai Sang in Hong Kong and his sister, Joy Ma, is in charge of Tai Sang in San Francisco. The Kwok Ta-seng family owns a large Chinese restaurant in Millbrae in the South Bay area, as well as valuable downtown real estate in San Francisco. This family also owns a successful real estate company in Hong Kong, known as Sun Hung Kai Properties, Ltd. The Chan Chak-fu family owns the Parc 55 Hotel in San Francisco, the Hyatt Regency in Oakland, and the Park Lane Hotels in Hong Kong and San Francisco. The Lui Che Woo family owns numerous businesses in San Francisco and Hong Kong.

Many business tycoons are concerned with preserving their wealth in the family and thus hire only family members to run their businesses. Sons and daughters are trusted helpers in dealing with transnational family enterprises. Thus, the very rich, out of economic necessity, have globalized their families along with their businesses. These are "transnational" families with family members living globally in order to run global enterprises.

To cope with rapid world changes, some rich Hong Kong businessmen send their children to be educated in different parts of the world. The Chang family, for example, sent their oldest son, William, to a boarding school in Somerset, England called the Millfield Institute before being sent to Harvard to study economics. In another example, Mr. Chan grew up in Hong Kong and now lives in San Francisco. He is a former San Francisco port commissioner. His family has investments in Shanghai, San Francisco, and Oakland. The Chan family's Westlake Development Company of San Mateo is influential in commercial real estate in the South Bay area and Nevada. Lawrence Chan was sent by his family to Switzerland, and then to Denver, to study and prepare for a career in hotel management as he was expected to continue the family's hotel business. The Chan family owns hotels in Hong Kong, Sydney, New York, Phoenix, Hawaii, San Antonio, and San Francisco. International experience is thought to be important in certain businesses. Thus, globalizing a child's education is recognized by these wealthy Hong Kong business families as an advantage in conducting business.

The movers and shapers of these big Chinese businesses and multinational corporations, however, are small in numbers. They do not represent the majority of Chinese immigrants. Class differences do exist among the immigrants. Some Chinese immigrant capitalists possess both the power and money to pursue global business strategies otherwise available only to very wealthy white Americans. Only about two or three dozen Chinese families in the entire Bay area participate in such large-scale international business ventures. The majority of transnational Chinese immigrants return to Asia for employment opportunities.

Other new immigrants use their connections in China and other parts of Asia to establish international trading companies selling heavy equipment, medical instruments, and American products in China, then purchasing consumer goods in China to sell in the American market. Many grocery stores and restaurants in Chinatown sell foodstuffs and products from China supplied by immigrant importers. Other Chinese products are produced in Canada and are shipped by land transport to bypass American regulations or to gain tax advantages. For instance, some Chinese-style sausages are made in Vancouver or Toronto in Chinese communities there. Similarly, it is easier to import sharks' fins and other marine products from Mexico than from Asia.

In summary, transnational economic activities have induced the development of transnational families with family members living in different parts of the world. The data obtained from this study demonstrate that family members can facilitate internationalization of their family businesses. Among the transnational extended families are adaptive responses to economic globalization. With trusted family members overseeing economic transactions in different parts of the world, international family firms can achieve more control and economic gain. However, some transnational family members are unhappy with their newly fashioned lifestyles. Some must travel constantly, thus forcing a separation between themselves and their spouses and children. Some complain about their lack of "grounding," commenting that they are not tied closely to any nation or community Some feel isolated from their parents and siblings in Hong Kong, Taiwan, and elsewhere. Discontentment and isolation are social costs of transnational migration.

Conclusion

Realizing that the world has gradually developed into a global production system, many Chinese businessmen and educated professionals have become players in the global economy. In so doing, they are not hesitant in using family, kinship, and friendship connections to organize business firms, locate employment, and invest and expand their business activities. Some have built international social networks that have successfully responded to the changing economy of the world. Among these new Chinese immigrants, one sees dynamism and ingenuity: they are truly global migrants and shapers of their own destinies.

Even immigrants who are not particularly wealthy or educated have benefited from their ability to travel to and from Asia establishing lucrative businesses, seeking employment, participating in economic joint ventures, or launching special business projects. As transnational migrants, they have had to leave their families in the United States and make personal sacrifices in order to earn a living for their families and themselves. They have done so at considerable social cost. These migrants have rearranged family relations, changing the composition of the Chinese domestic group called family.

Not all Chinese immigrants are transnational migrants.[4] Nuclear families, stem families, extended families, and non-residential extended families continue to exist among Chinese immigrants.[5] But, as this chapter demonstrates, transnationalism has created new structural arrangements among some immigrants: separated nuclear families which have transformed into patrifocal or matrifocal families, no-parent households, and transnational extended families.

Transnational migration demonstrates that the relatively durable Chinese institution of family is diverse and fluid. This fluidity has outdated the concept of a fixed, unitary, and bounded culture and its one-sided influence on the family. Family types and relationships are influenced by the cultural constraints and reinforcements of the global economy. For example, extended families do not necessarily atrophy or disappear in contemporary societies. On the contrary, they may be used as tools by Chinese businessmen to adapt to economic globalization.

Return Chinese migration also indicates that attempting to attain the "American dream" takes many forms. For some migrants, attaining social mobility in America may require many trips back home to Asia. The social and gender relations of these transnational immigrant families then must be viewed in a larger context which includes global, national, and local components. In the case of Chinese transnationals, household patterns and intra-familial relations result principally from the dynamic interplay between personal, cultural, and global economic factors.

Notes

1. *Acknowledgments.* A short version of this paper was presented at the 96th Annual Meeting of the American Anthropological Association in Washington D.C, November 1997. The research fieldwork was supported by a grant from the Ministry of Education in Japan.
2. This trend started in the 1980s, but gained momentum in the 1990s. Several factors explain the increase in the number of transnationals. First is the restructuring of the global economy, in general, and the American economy in particular In the past 20 years increasing numbers of companies have moved from industrial countries to Pacific Rim countries. As a consequence, Asia has become an important global center of manufacturing, a phenomenon discussed at length by Fong (1994). The second factor was the recession of the American economy in the early 1990s, which propelled many Chinese immigrants to look for economic opportunities overseas.
3. Reasons for men returning to China to get married in the pre-1945 era were (1) miscegenation laws that prohibited Chinese from marrying white American women; (2) an imbalanced sex ratio, with males outnumbering females among Chinese in the United States; and (3) exclusion laws, such as the Chinese Exclusion Act of 1882 and the Immigration Act of 1924 that prohibited immigration of Chinese women to America.
4. Some Chinese immigrants followed the traditional migration pattern, namely, they left China and settled in the United States for good. This is the "old model" of immigration pursued also by many European immigrants who migrated from, but never returned to, their old countries.
5. See Wong (1985) for a detailed discussion on nuclear, stem, extended, and non-residential extended families among Chinese immigrants who arrived in the United States between 1880 and 1980.

References Cited

Amyot, Jacques. 1973. *The Manila Chinese.* Quezon City: Institute of Philippine Culture.

Basch, Linda, Nina Glick Schiller, and Christina Szanton Blanc. 1994. *Nations Unbound: Transnational Projects, Postcolonial Predicaments and Deterritorialized National-States.* Langhorne, PA: Gordon and Breach.

Donckels, Rik, and Erwin Frohlich. 1991. Are Family Businesses Really Different? European Experience from STRATOS. *Family Business Review* 4(2):149-160.

Fong, Timothy P. 1994. *The First Suburban Chinatown*. Philadelphia: Temple University Press.

Gallo, Miguel A., and Jannicke Sveen. 1991. Internationalizing the Family Business: Facilitating and Restraining Factors. *Family Business Review* 4(2):181–190.

Gans, Herbert. 1962. *Urban Villagers: Group and Class in the Life of Italian-Americans*. New York: Free Press.

Gordon, Milton. 1964. *Assimilation of American Life: The Role of Race. Religion, and National Origins*. New York: Oxford University Press.

Guldin, Gregory. 1977. Overseas At Home: The Fujianese of Hong Kong. Ph.D. dissertation. University of Wisconsin-Madison.

Handlin, Oscar. 1951. *The Uprooted: The Epic Story of the Great Migrations that Made the American People*. Boston: Little, Brown.

Hsu, Francis L. K. 1981. *Americans and Chinese*. Honolulu: University Press of Hawaii.

———. 1988. *Rugged Individualism Reconsidered*. Knoxville: University of Tennessee Press.

Murdock, George Peter. 1965. *Social Structure*. New York: The Free Press.

New York Times. 1995. Skilled Asians Leaving U.S. for High-Tech Jobs at Home. February 21:A1.

Okun, Bernard. 1961. *Studies in Economic Development*. New York: Rinehart and Winston.

Pasternak, Burton, Carol R. Ember, and Melvin Ember. 1997. *Sex, Gender, and Kinship*. Englewood Cliffs, NJ: Prentice Hall.

Redding, S. O. 1990. *The Spirit of Chinese Capitalism*. Berlin: Walter de Gruyter.

Rosaldo, Renato. 1993. Borderlands of Race and Inequality. Paper presented at the Spring Meeting of the Society for Cultural Anthropology. Washington DC, May.

San Francisco Examiner. 1989a. A New Money Elite. August 20:A1, 12-14.

———. 1989b. Asia Influence Comes of Age. August 21:Al, 6-7.

San Jose Mercury News. 1993. Time of Opportunities Turns for Taiwanese Engineers. August 2:A1, 8.

Stack, Carol. 1974. *All Our Kin: Strategies for Survival in a Black Community*. New York: Harper Colophon.

Weidebaum, Murray and Samuel Hughes. 1996. *The Bamboo Network*. New York: The Free Press.

Whyte, Martin K. 1996. The Chinese Families and Economic Development: Obstacle or Engine? *Economic Development and Culture Change* 45(1): 1–30.

Wong, Bernard. 1985. Family, Kinship and Ethnic Identity of the Chinese in New York City, with Comparative Remarks on the Chinese in Lima, Peru and Manila, Philippines. *Journal of Comparative Family Studies* 16(2):231–254.

———. 1998. *Ethnicity and Entrepreneurship: The New Chinese Immigrants in the San Francisco Bay Area*. Boston: Allyn and Bacon.

Wong, Bernard, Becky McReynolds, and Wynnie Wong. 1992. The Chinese Family Firms in the San Francisco Bay Area. *Family Business Review* 5(4):355-372.

Yang, Mayfair. 1983. *Gifts, Favors and Banquets: The Art of Social Relationships in China*. Ithaca, NY: Cornell University Press.

CHAPTER 17

Kinship, Gender, and the New Reproductive Technologies: The Beginning of the End?

Linda Stone

ome, home—a few small rooms, stiflingly overinhabited by a man, by a periodically teeming woman, by a rabble of boys and girls of all ages. No air, no space; an understerilized prison. . . . Psychically, it was a rabbit hole, a midden, hot with the frictions of tightly packed life. . . . What suffocating intimacies, what dangerous, insane, obscene relationships between the members of the family group! Maniacally, the mother brooded over her children . . . brooded over them like a cat over its kittens; but a cat that could talk, a cat that could say, 'My baby, my baby' over and over again" (Huxley 1946 [orig. 1932]:24). This passage from Huxley's science fiction novel, *Brave New World*, gives a society's comment on its past, a despicable past when humans reproduced their own offspring and lived in families. In this brave new world reproduction is entirely state-controlled and carried out in test tubes and incubators. There is no kinship whatsoever in this new society. There is also no marriage. Women and men are equally expected to be sexually promiscuous, and sex is solely for pleasure. But apart from this, rather amazingly, there are few changes in gender. Women of the brave new world appear passive and fluffy-headed. Men apparently run the new society and hold all the prestigious or powerful jobs. In real life, meanwhile, new modes of reproduction are very definitely challenging conventions of both gender and kinship, as this chapter will show.

In 1978 the first "test-tube" baby, Louise Brown, was produced in England. Human conception had taken place inside a petri dish, outside the womb, and without sexual intercourse. By now, thousands of babies have been created in this way. About a decade after Louise Brown was born, we began to see cases of "surrogate" mothers and complex legal battles over the fate of their children. In 1987 Mary Beth Whitehead sought custody of a child, the famous Baby M, whom she had borne through a surrogacy contract. She had agreed to bear a child for William Stern, using his "donor" sperm. Stern's wife, Elizabeth, felt that because she had a mild case of multiple sclerosis, a pregnancy would be too great a risk to her health. The case went through two New Jersey courts. Both awarded custody of Baby M to Stern, although the higher court ruled that the surrogacy contract was invalid.

Surrounded by controversy, these and other New Reproductive Technologies (NRTs) have raised thorny legal and moral issues. They also present a challenge to our deepest ideas and values concerning kinship, and carry profound implications for gender. What are these NRTs, how do they work, and what implications do they have? In this chapter I discuss the new technologies and trace their overall impact.

The New Reproductive Technologies

Reproductive technologies, as such, are not new. Various forms of contraception, abortion, fertility-enhancing concoctions, cesarean surgery, and so on have existed for a long time. As far as I know, every human culture in the world offers local techniques for assisting conception as well as some methods of contraception, effective or not. But the NRTs go beyond promoting or preventing conception, or inducing or ending pregnancy. Some, for instance, provide knowledge about particular reproductive acts, knowledge that humans have never had before. Other NRTs open up new reproductive roles that humans have never played before. What follows is a listing of the new technologies along with explanations of how they work. The first two are technologies that give us new—and, in some contexts, problematic—knowledge.

Determining Biological Fatherhood

Throughout most of human history biological motherhood was taken for granted, but an equivalent "paternal certainty" did not exist. Then, around 1900, some techniques were developed that were capable of specifying, with certainty, who could *not* have fathered a particular child. Thus these tests could *exclude* individuals from a group of potential fathers but could not determine which particular individual was the actual father. The most common test performed back then was based on the well-known ABO blood group system. All humans are phenotypically either A, B, AB, or O. The A phenotype corresponds to an $I^A I^A$, or $I^A I^O$ genotype; B corresponds to an $I^B I^B$ or $I^B I^O$ genotype; AB is always $I^A I^B$; and O is always $I^O I^O$. Let us assume that a child belongs to the A blood group and that its mother is in the O group. This means that the mother is $I^O I^O$ and the child is either $I^A I^A$ or $I^A I^B$. We know that this child could not possibly have inherited the I^A gene from the mother and, therefore, that the I^A gene had to have come from the father. Let us then assume that a particular man is thought to be the father and that the mother is suing him for child support The ABO blood test is performed and the man is found to belong to the B group. In other words, the man's genotype is $I^B I^B$ or $I^O I^B$, meaning that he could not have contributed the I^A gene. This man could not possibly be the father, and he is excluded.

But even if the suspected man turns out to belong to the A blood group (making it possible for him to have contributed an I^A gene), he is not proven to be the biological father. Indeed, since the whole human population is subdivided into only four blood groups, hundreds of millions of men can be found in each category. But obviously not all A-type men should be suspected, as it would be impossible for the mother to have had sexual intercourse with hundreds of millions of men from all over the planet.

The new so-called DNA fingerprinting technique has considerably altered this situation. The technique relies on amplifying portions of human DNA in a test tube using the polymerase chain reaction (PCR) and identifying DNA fragments based on restriction fragment length polymorphism (RFLP). DNA can be isolated easily from a small quantity of blood taken from the individual in question. The general principle here is that human individuals differ in their DNA in many subtle ways and that no two individuals (except identical twins) have exactly the same DNA patterns. The PCR and RFLP techniques are capable of discerning these subtle variations and thus can provide a genetic (DNA-based) "fingerprint" of an individual that *corresponds to that individual only,* to the exclusion of all others. Genetic fingerprinting is now widely used to determine paternity with a very high degree of certainty, up to 99.99 percent or better. It has also been used to trace the parentage of orphans whose parents were killed and buried in known locales during wars. Under proper conditions, DNA can survive, even in bones, for thousands of years. Had DNA fingerprinting existed during the life of Anastasia, who claimed to be the sole surviving daughter of Tzar Nicholas II, her bluff would have been uncovered at the time. Recently, DNA analysis applied to bone material showed that Anastasia was indeed an impostor.

Determining biological fatherhood may be of great interest or advantage to many individuals in a variety of situations. But what are the broader implications of the fact that this determination can now be made so easily; and so "scientifically?" Many people have argued that paternity uncertainty in many ways shaped human culture, around the globe. They suggest that a whole host of practices in different regions of the world—having to do with female seclusion, restrictions on female behavior, medieval chastity belts, and so on—were all predicated on the principle of paternity uncertainty. But such uncertainty is now a thing of the past. We do not yet know what the long-term consequences of this may be for women or men.

As noted in Chapter 6, the polyandrous Nyinba are very concerned with biological fatherhood. But culturally they have constructed a rather efficient and normally satisfying way of designating paternity to husbands. Wives simply announce which husband is the father of a given child, even though in some cases this could not have been "scientifically" known; or husbands and wives together determine which brother the child most closely resembles. The process of designating paternity gives women a lot of power and, in cases of successful marriages, serves to equitably distribute children to husbands. But what will happen to this system when "real" paternity can be easily and quickly determined through a simple blood test? Will it bring discord between brothers? Will it result in the loss of power and influence for women? And what will happen to women in societies where the accepted punishment for proven infidelity is severe beating or death?

Determining the Sex of the Unborn Child

Sex determination techniques are by-products of a technology first developed to screen for genetic defects. These defects are detectable at the chromosomal level. The basic procedure involves harvesting fetal cells *in utero* (from inside the uterus), preparing their chromosomes, and looking at them under a microscope. The resulting chromosome spread is called a **karyotype**, and the process of characterizing chromosomes from an individual is called karyotyping. It turned out to be the case that, while karyotyping chromosomes to detect for genetic defects, technicians found it also very easy to see what sex the fetus was going to be. Karyotyping readily identifies the sex of the fetus since the Y chromosome (unique to males) is very small whereas X is large.

Two techniques are used to sample fetal cells. One is **amniocentesis**, the process of inserting a needle into the uterus (through the abdomen) and harvesting fluid from the amniotic sac that surrounds the fetus. Fetal skin cells are normally shed into this fluid. Usually only a few cells are present in the fluid, so it has to be cultured *in vitro* (i.e., in an artificial environment outside the living organism) to allow for cell manipulation. These cells are then karyotyped. Amniocentesis cannot be applied before the twelfth week of pregnancy since sufficient amniotic fluid is not present until that time.

The other technique, **chorionic villus sampling**, is less invasive because the abdomen is not punctured. In this case, a sample of **chorion** is taken by introducing a tube through the vagina into the uterus. The chorion is fetal tissue that lines the uterine cavity and surrounds the amniotic sac. Since this tissue is abundant, no cell culture is necessary and karyotyping can be done right away. There is enough chorion to allow the procedure as early as the eighth week of pregnancy.

In societies that do not express a cultural preference for male or female children, a couple's knowledge of the sex of a fetus is without much consequence. But, as we have seen, there are some societies that strongly prefer male children. In India, for example, amniocentesis is a major social issue. When the test became available, female fetuses were aborted at a very high rate. Many women underwent amniocentesis, either voluntarily or at the insistence of husbands and in-laws, with the idea that their pregnancy would be terminated unless the fetus was male. Many Indian women's organizations have fought to protect women and unborn females from this abuse. In some Indian states amniocentesis is now illegal (except in cases where genetic defects are an issue), but the test is still widely used illegally.

In the United States amniocentesis is a common procedure used to detect genetic defects. Rayna Rapp's (1990) study of amniocentesis in New York City showed that this test carries cultural meanings that vary among the people involved in it. Biomedical personnel discuss amniocentesis using an abstract, authoritative, impersonal language that contrasts sharply with the personal, emotional discourse of many women undergoing, or refusing to undergo, the test. Rapp also found that women talked about amniocentesis in ways that varied according to their class and ethnic backgrounds. For example, compared with others, white middle-class women spoke about amniocentesis in much the same way that biomedical personnel did, supporting a positive image of science assisting reproduction. Yet the same women spoke about their experiences with great ambivalence and self-criticism, especially when tests indicated a genetic defect and thus brought up the issue of abortion. Rapp's study relates these and other findings to the changing constructions of womanhood and motherhood among the diverse groups of women who consider technological reproductive interventions.

Artificial Insemination and In Vitro Fertilization

Certain NRTs are used in cases of infertility of an individual or a couple. In males, infertility is usually caused by either sperm defect (low count or immotile sperm cells) or impotence (physiological or psychological). In females, the situation is more complicated. A woman may be sterile, meaning that she is unable to conceive a child, due to absence of ovulation (either no eggs are produced or the egg cannot travel through fallopian tubes that are blocked). However, a sterile woman may still be able to carry and bear a child. Another problem is that a woman may be fertile (i.e., able to conceive a child), but the fertilized egg fails to become implanted in her uterus. Some reproductive problems can be corrected by surgery, drugs, or, in some cases of male impotence, psychotherapy. But if these treatments do not work, there are two other procedures that can allow an individual or couple to have a child. These procedures are **artificial insemination (AI)** and **in vitro fertilization (IVF)**.

Artificial insemination can be used when a couple seeks to have a child but the male is infertile. In this case the biological father may be an anonymous sperm donor whose sperm is stored in a sperm bank. The sperm bank categorizes sperm according to the physical characteristics of the donors (skin, eye and hair color, height and general body features) so that the future parents can roughly determine the looks of their offspring. For example, the parents may seek a child who will look something like its legal father.

Artificial insemination is a simple technique. Donor sperm is simply placed into the uterus of the female at the proper stage of her menstrual cycle. Nature does the rest. Artificial insemination has long been routinely used in animal husbandry to ensure production of animals with desired characteristics. Its average cost ranges from $200 to $400, and its success rate is about 30 percent if fresh sperm is used and about 15 percent if frozen sperm is used.

Artificial insemination can also be used by women who seek pregnancy without sexual intercourse. For example, a single woman may wish to have a child without involvement of the biological father beyond anonymous sperm donation. Or a woman may wish to serve as a "surrogate" mother for a married couple who cannot have a child of its own due to the wife's infertility. In this case the surrogate is artificially inseminated with the husband's sperm. The sperm donor is obviously not anonymous, but sexual intercourse between the husband and the surrogate is unnecessary.

The technique of in vitro fertilization (IVF) is much more complicated and expensive (about $25,000); it also has a lower success rate than AI with fresh sperm (about 14 percent). It was developed for humans in the late 1970s. In this case, oocytes (immature eggs) are surgically removed from the ovaries of a woman and incubated with sperm in a sterile petri dish in the presence of a nutrient medium. After fertilization occurs, the embryo is allowed to undergo cell division for a few days. The embryo is then removed from the dish and implanted into the uterus of a woman, where, if all goes well, it will grow to term.

Usually, several oocytes are removed, fertilized in vitro at the same time, and implanted together. Often only one embryo, or none, will continue to develop. However, cases of multiple birth have occurred. Excess embryos resulting from IVF and not implanted can be frozen and used at a subsequent time, even many years later. One current problem concerns the fate of all the frozen embryos now in existence and the question of who has rights over them. In the United States alone there are tens of thousands of frozen embryos; and throughout the world, hundreds of thousands.

With both IVF and AI, the biological father can also be the would-be legal father of the child, or the biological father may be a sperm donor. With AI, too, one woman may be the legal mother while another woman is the biological mother. But with IVF, something altogether new happens to "motherhood." The woman who contributes the oocytes may or may not be the woman who carries the child and gives birth. Once the eggs of one woman are fertilized outside the womb, they may be implanted back either into her or into another woman. This is an important point to which we will return later.

Table 1 summarizes the different forms of AI and IVF, and shows what options are available depending on the reproductive problem involved. Note that the "father" (F) is designated as either fertile or sterile, whereas the "mother" (M) may exhibit different combinations of sterility (unable to conceive) or fertility, and be either able or unable to bear a child. The table indicates the circumstances under which a couple would need a "donor" egg, sperm, or womb. It also shows what genetic connection the child will have with either or both parents, given the various options. In preparing this table I have assumed that it is a couple, rather than an individual, who is seeking a child; that to the extent possible the couple seeks to have a child genetically related to at least one of its members; and that, if possible, the mother seeks to give birth. In real life, some alternative possibilities may also exist. For example, in case 1 of the table, the mother cannot conceive but can bear a child. Although the table specifies the use of IVF, an actual couple in this situation might elect to avoid the expense and trouble of IVF and use AI instead (as in case 5).

The table also shows three different circumstances under which a so-called surrogate mother might be used, along with the different outcomes involved. In case 2 the surrogate not only carries the child but is the genetic mother, whereas the father is also genetically contributing to the child. In case 3 the surrogate has no genetic relation to the child, and the child is the genetic product of both of the parents. Finally, in case 6, the surrogate has no genetic connection to the child, and the child is genetically related to only one parent, the mother.

Table 1: NRTs: Contributions of Egg, Sperm, and Womb, with Genetic Outcomes

	Problem	Donation Needed			Technique	Genetic Result
		Egg	Sperm	Womb		
1.	F fertile, M sterile but can bear child	X			IVF	child = ½ F
2.	F fertile, M sterile and cannot bear child	X		X	AI	child = ½ F
3.	F fertile, M fertile but cannot bear child			X	IVF	child =½ F + ½ M
4.	F sterile, M sterile but can bear child	X	X		IVF	child = 0% parents
5.	F sterile, M fertile and can bear child		X		AI	child = ½ M
6.	F sterile, M fertile but cannot bear child		X	X	IVF	child ½ M

Note: F stands for Father; and M for Mother.

As this table clearly shows, IVF can be used to assist reproduction in a greater variety of situations than AI. At the same time, however, it is more problematic than AI. For one thing it is not always safe for women. Depending on her particular role in the process, a participating woman may have to take fertility drugs, some with possible side effects. If she is using or donating her eggs, these must be removed from her through invasive laparoscopy; and if the IVF procedure fails to result in fertilized eggs, it must be performed again. Some women argue that the real beneficiaries of IVF are the highly paid medical professionals who exploit the desperation of childless couples and offer them false hope (Raymond 1993). Based on her own experience, one woman asserted that IVF programs encourage couples to seek their identity in genetic reproduction rather than considering other options for their lives. As she put it: "I look back in amazement at the person I was, traversing the country from one IVF program to another, in search of an infertility 'fix.' . . . I found IVF an extremely arduous, life-dominating experience, involving some eight unsuccessful attempts" (Bartholet 1992:254).

Some Additional NRTs

Among the NRTs available, a few are not widely used as yet but may become more prevalent in the future. One, called **embryo adoption**, would apply to the situation of case 1 in Table 1. Here, the mother cannot conceive but can bear a child. Instead of using IVF with donor eggs, the husband could artificially inseminate another woman who serves as a very temporary surrogate.

After a week, the embryo is flushed out of the surrogate's uterus and inserted into the uterus of the mother. Another type of reproductive technology is called oocyte freezing, a procedure in which oocytes, or eggs, are taken from a woman and frozen for later use. So far this procedure has not proven very successful; but if perfected, it could open a whole range of reproductive options. For example, a woman could freeze her oocytes when she is young and healthy and use them later in life when her fertility would otherwise be lower. Technically, she could use them even past menopause. Alternatively, a much older woman could take oocytes donated by a young women. These could be thawed, fertilized in IVF, and then' implanted in the older woman. Already one woman aged fifty-nine has given birth through oocyte donation. Some people are repulsed by the image of very old women giving birth or becoming mothers. Others point out that men have all along been able to reproduce at any age.

Social, Legal, and Moral Implications

NRTs are becoming available just when other options for reproduction seem to be diminishing. Fewer children are now available for adoption both because effective contraception has decreased unwanted births and because a more accepting social climate has allowed more single women to keep their children. At the same time, natural fertility has been decreasing—at least in the United States, where about one in six couples suffers some fertility problem. The sperm count of the American male has fallen by 30 percent over the last fifty years and continues to decline (Blank 1990:13–14), possibly due to environmental pollution. Female fertility is also decreasing.

Although NRTs clearly assist the infertile, they are also bringing about some new kinds of social relationships. Some ramifications of these technologies are easy to imagine—and many of these have already occurred. For example, through the use of frozen embryos, two genetic twins could be—and, indeed, have been—born years apart. By means of the same technology, a woman could give birth to her own genetic twin, or to her own genetic aunt or uncle. In 1991, a forty-two-year-old woman in South Dakota, Arlette, gave birth to twins who are her genetic grandchildren. Her own daughter could not bear a child, but she and her husband desperately wanted children. Through IVF, the daughter's eggs were fertilized with the husband's sperm, and later the pre-embryos were implanted into Arlette's uterus. Another woman, Bonny, donated an egg for her infertile sister, Vicki. Bonny's egg was fertilized with the sperm of Vicki's husband and implanted into Vicki's uterus. A male child, Anthony, was born. In this case the genetic mother, Bonny, is a, social aunt; her sister, Vicki, gave birth to Anthony who is her social son but her genetic nephew. Even more disconcerting, through the use of frozen embryos it is also possible for dead people to reproduce.

As confusing as these and other cases may be, they have had some happy results, at least for those couples blessed with children they desperately desired. Usually all of the participants in the making of a baby fully agree about its social and legal status. But as we know from the many cases covered in the media, this does not always happen. Baby M was just one such case. Other problems have emerged with the use of frozen embryos. In a famous case of 1989, *Davis v. Davis*, a Tennessee couple attempted IVF because Mrs. Davis was able to conceive but could not bear a child. Nine eggs were fertilized. Two were implanted, unsuccessfully, in Mrs. Davis' uterus, and the remaining seven were frozen for a later try. But then the couple divorced. They went to court over the fate of these embryos. Mrs. Davis wanted to have them implanted, but Mr. Davis wanted them destroyed. He argued that he had a right *not* to be a father. In the end, Mrs. Davis remarried and requested that the embryos be donated to some other infertile couple. Thus the case was resolved; but it opened the difficult question: Who should have rights over frozen embryos? Or, for that matter, should frozen embryos have any rights, protected by the law? In another interesting case from Australia, a woman's eggs were fertilized in IVF by an anonymous donor. One of these was unsuccessfully implanted in the woman and the other two were frozen. This woman and her husband then died in a plane crash. It turned out that the couple left a sizable fortune. Should the embryos have rights of inheritance? This was a question that troubled the couple's adult children. Even more pressing, morally speaking, are the larger questions of whether frozen embryos should have rights to be born, or who should decide if, when, and under what circumstances human embryos are to be donated to medical research. Should frozen embryos even be produced in the first place? Certainly, embryo freezing is a useful NRT for infertile couples; and in the case of IVF, a woman is spared repeated laparoscopies through the option of freezing the extra embryos produced the first time. But is embryo freezing a form of irresponsible reproduction? What kind of society, with what views of human life, are we constructing? How should we even think about frozen embryos? Sarah Franklyn (1995:337) argues that the frozen embryo straddles the boundary between science and nature, giving it an ambivalent status such that its identity and meaning will be contested:

> The embryo is a cyborg entity; its coming into being is both organic and technological. Though it is fully human (for what else can it be?) it is born of science, inhabits the timeless ice land of liquid-nitrogen storage tanks. . . . At once potential research material (scientific object), quasi-citizen (it has legal rights) and potential person (human subject), the embryo has a cyborg liminality in its contested location between science and nature.

Moral and legal difficulties also surround the practice of surrogacy, particularly "contract" or "commercial" surrogacy. This form of surrogacy, though permitted in the United States, is illegal in most countries that have laws regulating the NRTs (Blank 1990:157). Some people have severely censured surrogates, calling them "baby sellers." Others have merely wondered what sort of woman would contract to carry a baby for another woman or couple. Surrogates typically receive a fee of about $10,000 for their service. Yet most surrogates insist that they do it not for the money but because they're genuinely motivated to provide a child to an infertile couple. Apparently some women also enjoy the experience of pregnancy and seek to experience it again after they have had all the children they want for themselves. Helena Ragoné's (1994) study of surrogate motherhood in America shows how the surrogate role gives women confidence and a sense of self-importance and worth. These women, she says, are adding meaning to their lives by going beyond the confines of their own domestic situations or their unrewarding jobs to do something vital for others.

Other studies have shown that surrogates are usually not poor women in desperate need of cash but, rather, working-class women. According to Ragoné's (1994:54) study, the personal income of unmarried surrogates ranged from $16,000 to $24,000, and the average household income of married surrogates was $38,000. Still, in the context of surrogacy the issue of social class and economic inequality is easily raised. The couple seeking a surrogate is generally wealthy, at least wealthy enough to be able to afford a surrogate plus the other expenses ($20,000 or more) that they will pay to doctors and a fertility clinic. But surrogates, though not poor, are not of this privileged social class. They may feel rewarded by the attention, care, gifts, and positive social treatment they receive from the couples they are assisting (Ragoné 1994:64–66). Is this all well and good, or is contract surrogacy enmeshed in a new type of class exploitation?

In a discussion of surrogacy, Sarah Boone (1994) invokes both racial and class inequality by drawing some disturbing cultural parallels between contemporary surrogate motherhood and the former practice of slavery in America. Boone describes black slave women as "bottom women" in the gender and racial hierarchy of earlier American society, a hierarchy that placed white males on top, followed by white females and black males. One measure of the "bottom" status of black slave women was wide sexual access to them, for in their position in slave society white male slaveholders could easily exploit them sexually. In addition, black women were themselves considered property and had no legal rights to their children. Meanwhile, "the white woman as top woman became the physically delicate asexual mother/wife, subordinate helpmate" (Boone 1994:355). Boone asks whether the surrogate mother is another kind of "bottom woman," one whose status is measured not by sexual access to her but by reproductive access to her body: After all, "CCM [commercialized contract motherhood] allows men and privileged women to purchase or rent the gestational capacities of other women in order to produce a genetic heir" (Boone 1994:358).

A new "top woman" thus emerges here too, but she is still a wife and the member of a privileged class. Yet this is a "top woman" with a new twist: "Now a career woman in her own right but naturally drawn to motherhood, she is fully appropriate for the more refined roles of genetic contributor and rearer of children," whereas the "bottom woman" surrogate is given "the 'unrefined' work of gestation and childbearing for men and more privileged women who are incapable or unwilling to do this work" (Boone 1994:358). We may argue that, unlike slave women, surrogates choose their "work" and, as we have seen, are not poor or disadvantaged persons. Still, Boone's observations suggest that surrogacy occurs not in a vacuum but in a sociocultural context where it is inseparable from issues of gender and social inequality.

Moral concerns, debates, and controversies rage on over the NRTs. But it is on kinship and gender that these new technologies may yet have their greatest impact.

Kinship and Gender

We have already seen how the use of frozen embryos confounds some conventional notions of kinship relation. Is the woman who gives birth to her genetic uncle his niece or his mother?

What happens to our kinship system when the boundaries of our core concepts of "kin," set long ago by our ancestors and taken for granted for so many centuries, are blurred? Even more jolting, perhaps, is the fragmentation of motherhood that results from the technological ability to separate conception from birth and eggs from wombs. Robert Snowden and his colleagues (1983:34) claim that, with the advent of NRTs, we now need a total of ten different terms to cover the concepts of "mother" and "father." The terms they propose are as follows:

1.   Genetic mother
2.   Carrying mother
3.   Nurturing mother
4.   Complete mother
5.   Genetic/carrying mother
6.   Genetic/nurturing mother
7.   Carrying/nurturing mother
8.   Genetic father
9.   Nurturing father
10.   Complete father

The first three terms cover the distinct stages of conception, gestation, care for a child. These three aspects of motherhood can be carried out by one, two, or three different women. If one woman does all three, she is the "complete" mother. Note that a child could conceivably have five different persons as "parents" in this system (1–3 as mothers and 8 and 9 as fathers), even without including stepparents (Blank 1990:10). But it is really only motherhood that has fragmented as a result of the NRTs, since we have long been accustomed to the idea that a child can have one man as its "genetic" or "biological" father and another as its "nurturing" (or perhaps a better word here might be "legal") father. Similarly, we are familiar with the idea that "legal" or "nurturing" mothers can be different from "natural" or "biological" mothers. What is new is the division of biological motherhood into two parts: conception and gestation.

In comparison to our society, a people like the Nuer (Case 1) would perhaps have had different conceptual problems with kinship in relation to the NRTs. For them, legal rights to children were held by fathers (and their patrilineal kin groups), not by mothers. Also, these rights were clearly established by cattle payments, not by concerns with biological fatherhood. Recall that Nuer culture constructed kinship such that children belonged to fathers, defined as the men who paid bridewealth for the mothers.

In American society, however, ideas about kinship have been based on cultural notions of biology (Schneider 1968). Americans have strongly defined "real" parenthood as biologically based. And they have taken for granted that this way of thinking about kinship is in line with "science." But now science itself has thrown a wrench into the American system of kinship by showing that unitary "natural" motherhood is actually divisible. In the courts and in our own minds we thus face the challenge of reconstructing motherhood and, hence, reconstructing kinship. Will we need to devise a nonbiologically based definition of the *mater* as the Nuer have done for the *pater*? Marilyn Strathern (1995) discusses how the NRTs challenge Euro-American notions of "nature" itself as well as fundamental ideas about what constitutes personal "identity."

We do not know what the future may bring. But what seems to be happening at present is that those involved with the NRTs are not discarding the old American ideas about kinship but, on the contrary, are making every effort to preserve the cultural notions of "real" biological parenthood. Toward this end, they are reinterpreting the NRTs and their tricky implications so as to reconcile them with these core cultural notions of biological parenthood and the resulting American family ideal. This process has played out in two very interesting contexts.

One context concerns, lesbian couples. Those seeking to have children and to become a family in the conventional sense have of course benefited by the NRTs. At a minimum, one member of the couple may become impregnated with donor sperm. Corinne Hayden's (1995) study of American lesbian couples shows that some lesbian couples with children are constructing something truly new in kinship: double motherhood. They are raising their children to perceive that they have two mothers. One way to support this perception is to have the children call both of them "mother." Another way is to hyphenate the co-mothers' names to form the children's surname. In short, these couples seek to raise their children in an environment of parental equality—a process that, in their view, constitutes a true challenge and alternative to the conventional husband-dominant household of broader American society. Of course, the creation of equal, dual motherhood is confounded by the fact that only one woman can be the biological mother. Even if the lesbian couple themselves perceive their motherhood to be equal, the surrounding society, and courts of law, may not.

In trying to create new forms of kinship and family, lesbian couples are not so much rejecting biology as a basis for kinship as making use of the NRTs to bring their situation into line with biologically based kinship. For example, they may strive for a more equitable double motherhood by getting pregnant by the same donor. In this way, each partner becomes a mother, their children are born genetically related to one another, and they all more closely resemble a family in the conventional American sense. Another possibility is for one woman to be artificially inseminated using the sperm of the other woman's brother. Each woman would then have some genetic relation, as well as a conventional kinship relation, to the child. Even more creative is what Hayden (1995:55) refers to as the "obvious and 'perfect' option for lesbian families: one woman could contribute the genetic material, and her partner could become the gestational/birth mother." Thus even the idea that homosexual unions are "inherently non-procreative" (Hayden 1995:56) is challenged, now that a woman can give birth to the genetic child of her female partner. Going a step further, a lesbian couple could combine the last two options: One woman could contribute an egg to be fertilized by the brother (or, for that matter, son) of her lesbian partner, after which the egg would be implanted in her partner.

The other context in which efforts are being made to reconcile the NRTs with core cultural notions, especially American ideas about kinship, concerns surrogate motherhood. As Ragoné (1994:109) concluded from her study of surrogate mothers in America, "Programs, surrogates and couples highlight those aspects of surrogacy that are most consistent with American kinship ideology, deemphasizing those aspects that are not congruent with this ideology. Thus, although the means of achieving relatedness may have changed, the rigorous emphasis on the family and on the biogenetic basis of American kinship remains essentially unchanged." One way in which surrogates and their couples maintain this emphasis is to downplay the relationship between the husband and the surrogate in cases where the surrogate has been impregnated with the husband's sperm. Indeed, since the surrogate is carrying the husband's (and her) child, there are disturbing parallels with adultery. In some surrogate programs the relationship that is given priority and becomes strong is that between the surrogate and the wife. This arrangement is obviously more comfortable for the surrogate; it also allows the wife to feel that she is participating in the process of creating the child. In addition, the wife, or the adoptive mother, in such cases may emphasize her role in the creation of the child as one of intention, choice, and love: "One adoptive mother . . . described it as conception in the heart, that is, the belief that in the final analysis it was her desire to have a child that brought the surrogate arrangement into being and therefore produced a child" (Ragoné 1994:126).

The NRTs have spurred debates among women in general and feminists in particular over how these technologies are affecting women and relations between the sexes. Some feminists approve of the NRTs precisely because they fragment motherhood and in many ways distance women from "nature" and "natural" reproduction. Their argument is that women have been trapped by their reproductive roles, that their lower status has been due all along to their entrenchment in reproduction and motherhood. According to this view, the NRTs not only expand reproductive choices for individual women and men but can help to liberate women from the inferior status that their biological roles have given them. Other feminists have argued that the legal use of NRTs supports women's right to control their own bodies. They also approve of contract surrogacy because it allows a surrogate to use her body as she wishes for her own economic benefit.

Yet another argument is that the NRTs are potentially good for women but need to be subjected to proper controls and approached with caution (Purdy 1994). Thus, for example, regulations should be implemented to ensure that surrogate mothers retain control of their pregnancies and, by extension, that contracting fathers not be given rights to say how a surrogate should behave while pregnant, to decide whether she should have a cesarean, to sue her for miscarriage, and so on. With such controls in place, according to this argument, contract pregnancy can considerably benefit infertile women or women with high-risk pregnancies. As for accusations of "baby selling" by surrogate mothers, those taking this position raise an important question: Why are there no parallel objections against the payments made to men who donate their sperm? Laura Purdy (1994:316) also questions the view that "women can be respected for altruistic and socially useful actions only when they receive no monetary compensation, whereas men—physicians, scientists, politicians—can be both honored and well paid."

Perhaps the strongest feminist criticism of the NRTs has come from Janice Raymond (1993). In her book, *Women As Wombs*, Raymond describes the NRTs as a form of "violence against women": Since a male-dominant "medical fundamentalism" defines both the problem (infertility) and the cure (the NRTs), application of the new techniques entails "appropriation of the female body by male scientific experts" (1993:xx). Raymond argues directly against the position that NRTs liberate women by freeing them from their previous reproductive roles. On the contrary, she says, the fragmentation of motherhood, the conceptual wedge that the NRTs place between a woman and a fetus, results in the loss of women's control over reproduction. When the fetus is seen as so separable from a woman, the fetus itself becomes the focus of attention, and, in the process, male rights over reproduction are increased: "Reproductive technologies and contracts augment the rights of fetuses and would-be fathers while challenging the one right that women have historically retained some vestige of—mother-right" (Raymond 1993:xi).

Raymond notes that in the case of Baby M, even though William Stern and Mary Beth Whitehead were equally the genetic parents and Whitehead was also the birth mother, Stern was continually referred to in the media as "the father" whereas Whitehead was always "the surrogate." The courts also awarded custody to Stern. About this situation Raymond (1993:34) wrote: "A woman who gestates the fetus, experiences a nine-month pregnancy, and gives birth to the child is rendered a 'substitute' mother. On the other hand, popping sperm into a jar, is 'real' fatherhood, legally equivalent, if not superior, to the contribution of egg, gestation, labor, and birth that is part of any woman's pregnancy."

Of course, one could retort that the genetic/birth mother in the Baby M case did sign a surrogacy contract, thus bringing about the whole trouble in the first place. But Raymond's point is that the NRTs are changing our society's perceptions of motherhood and fatherhood, conceptually and legally, and that women may be losing out in the process. Legally speaking, what Raymond (1993:30) calls "ejaculatory fatherhood" does appear to be gaining ground—in part, perhaps, because ideas about biological fatherhood have not been fundamentally changed by the NRTs whereas ideas about motherhood most definitely have been. In the American biogenetic ideology of kinship, fatherhood is still simple, but motherhood is no longer so.

And what of future reproductive technologies? Cloning and the growing of a fetus outside a uterus may be a long way off. Much closer, and possibly far more radical in terms of the implications for gender, is male pregnancy. As Blank (1990:29) notes, "There is increasing evidence that the embryo might be transferred to the abdominal cavity of a male, thus enabling male pregnancy. The birth of a baby from a New Zealand woman who had no uterus, and successful male procreation in other species, contribute to the expectation that IVF will soon permit human male pregnancies."

Continuities

In this book we have examined a variety of ways in which kinship and gender are culturally constructed and interrelated. This analysis has involved us in discussions of sexuality and reproduction, and of the interests of many people and groups in exercising control over women's reproductive capacities. We have seen cases, specifically among the Nuer and the Nyinba, in which female sexuality is largely unrestricted but cultural rules allocate a woman's children to her legal husband or husbands and their kinship groups. And among the matrilineal Nayar, female sexuality is unrestrained (except for sexual intercourse before the tali-tying ceremony and at any time with a lower-class man) but children are allocated to a woman's own kinship corporation under the leadership of her senior matrilineal kinsmen. In all three societies, female sexuality and female fertility are separate social concerns.

We have also seen cases in which a woman's sexuality is, or was, ideally restricted to one man, her husband: Examples include the Nepalese Brahmans, the ancient Romans, and early Europeans and Americans. In these societies, a woman's "inappropriate" sexual behavior (premarital sex or adultery) could result in devaluation of her person, dishonor to her family, and, among the Nepalese Brahmans, devaluation of the woman's future fertility. The Nayar, sharing some of the Hindu caste ideas related to female purity and pollution, also showed this connection between female sexuality and fertility, inasmuch as sex with a lower-caste man would expel a woman and her future children from her caste and kin group. In all of these Eurasian cases we have seen that the concern with female sexual "purity" is interwoven with concerns over property and its transmission, as well as with the maintenance of class and caste divisions; in other words, they are bound up with larger issues of socioeconomic inequality.

Many of the cases discussed in this book have dealt with male-led kin groups seeking control over women's reproduction. We have also seen a few' cases where a woman's reproduction was not of much concern to larger groups of kin. Among the Navajo, for instance, although a woman reproduces for her own and her husband's matriclans, clan continuity is not a strong concern. Navajo culture venerates women for their reproductive powers, but it does not punish women for childlessness. Another group, the early Christians in Europe, valued celibacy over reproduction and held that sexuality was equally unspiritual for women and men. As noted, one historian argued that early Christian women found in Christianity a welcome liberation from both marriage and reproduction.

By and large, white, middle-class Euro-American women have not had to contend with the interests of kin groups in their reproduction, nor have they been under pressure to reproduce for anyone but themselves and their partners. Furthermore, over the centuries, restrictions on their sexuality have relaxed. Yet, paradoxically, these Euro-American women have expressed problems and tensions of their own in the process of trying to reconcile their sexuality, fertility, and personhood in a meaningful and satisfying way.

With the emergence of the NRTs, we cannot fail to ask ourselves who we will become, as women, as men, as persons, and as kin. But this is not a new question. All human groups throughout history have continually constructed kinship and gender, seeking meaning and identity within these cultural constructions. And along the way, the constructions themselves have been contested between men and women, young and old, powerful and powerless. Now, as we face the development of new (and newer) reproductive technologies, the struggle continues. In this way, perhaps the NRTs are not taking us into a brave new world so much as dealing out new cards in an older dynamic human game of self, kin, and gender definition.

References

Bartholet, Elizabeth. 1994. In Vitro Fertilization:, The Construction of Infertility and of Parenting. In Helen Bequaert Holmes, ed., *Issues in Reproductive Technology*, pp. 253–260. New York: New York University Press.

Blank, Robert H. 1990. *Regulating Reproduction*. New York: Columbia University Press.

Boone, Sarah S. 1994. Slavery and Contract Motherhood: A "Racialized" Objection to the Autonomy Argument. In Helen Bequaert Holmes, ed., *Issues in Reproductive Technology*, pp. 349–366. New York: New York University Press.

Franklyn, Sarah. 1995. Postmodern Procreation: A Cultural Account of Assisted Reproduction. In Faye D. Ginsburg and Rayna Rapp, eds., *Conceiving the New World Order: The Global Politics of Reproduction*, pp. 323–345. Berkeley: University of California Press.

Hayden, Corinne P. 1995. Gender, Genetics, and Generation: Reformulating Biology in Lesbian Kinship. *Cultural Anthropology* 10(1): 41–63.

Huxley, Aldous. 1946 [orig. 1932]. *Brave New World*. New York: Bantam Books

Purdy, Laura M. 1994. Another Look at Contract Pregnancy. In Helen Bequaert Holmes, ed., *Issues in Reproductive Technology*, pp. 303–320. New York: New York University Press.

Ragoné, Helena. 1994. *Surrogate Motherhood: Conception in the Heart*. Boulder: Westview Press.

Raymond, Janice G. 1993. *Women As Wombs: Reproductive Technologies and the Battle over Women's Freedom*. San Francisco: Harper San Francisco.

Schneider,. David M. 1968. *American Kinship: A Cultural Account*. Englewood Cliffs: Prentice-Hall.

Snowden, Robert, G. D. Mitchell, and E. M. Snowden. 1983. *Artificial Reproduction*. London: Allen and Unwin.

Strathern, Marilyn. 1995. Displacing Knowledge: Technology and the Consequences for Kinship. In Faye D. Ginsburg and Rayna Rapp, eds., *Conceiving the New World Order: The Global Politics of Reproduction*, pp. 346–363. Berkeley: University of California Press.

Glossary

affinal related through marriage.

age-set a lifelong affiliation of similar-aged persons who pass through various life stages together as a unit; age-sets are characteristic of East African pastoral societies.

altruistic acts individual behaviors that enhance others' reproductive success while simultaneously reducing one's own.

ambilocal referring to a postmarital residence pattern in which a married couple can choose to live with or near the kin of either the groom or the bride.

amniocentesis a procedure for drawing a sample of amniotic fluid from a pregnant woman by inserting a needle into the uterus; the results provide genetic information about the fetus.

artificial insemination (AI) a process of placing donor sperm into the vaginal cavity of a female at the proper stage of her menstrual cycle in an attempt to achieve pregnancy.

avunculocal referring to a postmarital residence pattern in which a married couple moves to or near the household of the groom's mother's brother(s).

bilateral kinship the recognition of kin connections through both parents; virtually all societies exhibit bilateral kinship.

bilateral society a society that traces kin connections over the generations through both males and females, but without the formation of descent groups.

bridewealth the transfer of wealth from the kin of the groom to the kin of the bride at marriage.

chorion fetal tissue that lines the uterine cavity and surrounds the amniotic sac.

chorionic villus sampling a technique for retrieving chorionic cells from the uterine cavity by introducing a tube into the uterus through the vagina.

clan a group or category of people who claim to share descent through a common ancestor, but whose genealogical links with one another are obscured and no longer traceable; the common ancestor of the group is often a mythical figure.

class endogamy marriage within a given social class.

cognatic descent descent based on any combination of male or female links.

consanguineal related through descent (or "blood" ties).

corporate group a group of people who collectively share rights, privileges, and liabilities.

cross cousins the children of two opposite-sex siblings.

descent group a kin group based on descent (patrilineal, matrilineal, or cognatic).

domestic group people who live together and share resources for their subsistence.

double descent the existence in one society of both matrilineal and patrilineal descent groups; each person simultaneously belongs to two descent groups.

dowry wealth that accompanies a bride to her marriage.

embryo adoption the result of artificial insemination achieved by using the uterus of a surrogate, from which the embryo is then flushed and inserted into the uterus of the mother-to-be.

endogamy marriage inside a certain social group or category.

exogamy marriage outside a certain social group or category.

fitness reproductive success; the more fertile offspring a person has, the greater his or her fitness is considered to be.

fraternal polyandry a marriage union in which two or more brothers share one wife.

genitor the biological father of a child.

ghost marriage the practice whereby a patrilineal kinsman takes a wife in the name of a deceased man in order to have children by the woman in that man's name.

hominid a family-level classification that includes modern humans and their extinct ancestors.

hominoid a superfamily-level classification of primates that includes apes and humans.

hypergamy marriage of a woman upward into a higher-status group.

inclusive fitness the process whereby an individual enhances his or her reproductive success through altruistic acts that favor the fitness of others who share some genes in common with that individual, as in the case of close relatives.

in vitro fertilization (NP) the process of incubating oocytes with sperm in a petri dish to produce a fertilized embryo.

karyotype a chromosome spread prepared for microscopic examination.

kindred a set of relatives traced to a particular ego.

kin selection the process whereby natural selection acts on inclusive fitness.

levirate the practice whereby a man marries the widow of his deceased brother.

lineage a group of people who trace their descent to a common ancestor through known links.

matrilineage a group of people who can trace descent from a common ancestor through female links and who can trace the links among themselves.

matrilineal descent descent based on links through females only.

matrilocal referring to a postmarital residence pattern in which a married couple lives in the household or place of the bride's kin; also called *uxorilocal*.

monogamy marriage between two persons, generally a man and a woman.

mother-in-law avoidance an interaction between a man and his wife's mother characterized by respectful restraint.

multimale, multifemale units groupings of primates that consist of numerous males living and mating with numerous females.

natolocal referring to a postmarital residence pattern in which husbands and wives reside with their own respective natal groups and so do not live together.

neolocal referring to a postmarital residence pattern in which a married couple moves to a new location, living with the kin of neither the groom nor the bride.

nonfraternal polyandry a marriage union in which one woman has two or more husbands who are not brothers.

one-male units primate units in which one adult male lives and mates with several females.

oocytes immature eggs.

oocyte freezing the process of taking oocytes from a woman's uterus and then freezing them for later use.

parallel cousins the children of two same-sex siblings.

parental investment the contributions of parents to the fitness of their offspring.

pater the legal father of a child.

patrilineage a group of people who can trace descent from a common ancestor through male links and, who can trace the links among themselves.

patrilineal descent descent traced through males only.

patrilocal referring to a postmarital residence pattern in which a married couple lives in the household or place of the groom's kin; also called *virilocal*.

phratries groupings of two or more clans.

polyandry marriage of one woman to two or more men at the same time.

polygyny marriage of a man to two or more women at the same time.

postmarital residence the location in which a newly married couple will reside.

primogeniture a pattern of inheritance in which only the eldest son receives a patrimony.

sexual dimorphism the external physical differences between males and females.

sexual selection the process by which one sex (usually male) competes for sexual access to the other sex.

sororal polygyny a marriage of two or more sisters to one man.

sororate the practice whereby a man marries the sister of his deceased wife.

totemism the symbolic identification of a group of people with a particular plant, animal, or object.

unilineal descent descent traced through only one sex, as in the case of matrilineal or patrilineal descent.

woman-woman marriage the marriage of a barren woman (who counts as a "husband") to another woman; a genitor is arranged for the "wife," and the barren woman becomes the legal father of the children.

Appendix 1

Sample Exam Questions

Part I: Continuity and Change

1. DEFINE the following kinship concepts:

   a. Patrilineal:

   b. Matrilineal:

   c. Nuclear family:

   d. Bilateral:

   e. Extended family:

   f. Primogeniture:

   g. Unigeniture:

2. Kinship studies:
   Choose one of the following:

   a. Were developed in the 19th century by anthropologists into a new discipline.
   b. Was one of the earliest fields to be developed in social science.
   c. Deals only with exotic 3rd world countries.
   d. Has become a dead issue (unimportant) in Anthropology.

3. (True / False). In terms of family size and mobility, the American kinship system is similar to that of the Eskimo tribal groups.

4. (   ) believed that the study of kinship structure is not useful. He argued that structure is an artifact and is the result of social transaction. Therefore, it is important for us to look at the activity system, which created the structure. Name the author.

5. (True / False). "The Chicago School" of kinship believed that kinship is dead in urban society.

6. (   ). Name the type of kinship terminological system that is highly descriptive. Each kinsman is labeled by a separate term.

7. (   ). In this type of kinship terminological system all the males (excepting the father) in the parental generation is known by one term and all the females (excepting the mother) of the parental generation is known by another term. Name it.

8. (   ) is the author of the Alliance Theory for the study of kinship.

9. (   ) is the author of the Dominant Dyad Hypothesis.

10. According to Francis Hsu, American kinship is characterized by the (   ) dyad.

11. According to Francis Hsu, India is characterized by the (   ) dyad.

12. (True / False). The decision-making approach to kinship emphasizes human interaction.

13. (   ). Revolution in China has created one of the following:

    a. The 1954 marriage law which names monogamy as the only legal form of marriage and forbids divorce
    b. Patrilocal household
    c. Matrilocal household
    d. Social relationships between the daughter-in-law and mother-in-law

14. Name two factors that made the Chinese immigrants to the USA different from Japanese immigrants to Hawaii.

    a. _____

    b. _____

15. What aspect of kinship relations was most important to the Japanese in Hawaii:

    a. *IE* system and Banto succession
    b. Mother-in-law to daughter-in-law relation
    c. KEN (prefecture) association
    d. Mother and son relation
    e. Religious affiliation

16. Which of the following statements is FALSE for Japanese Americans in Hawaii?

    a. The Japanese came to Hawaii to replace the Chinese laborers.
    b. The Japanese have been able to successfully assimilate.
    c. Immigration still plays a major part in the formation of kinship for Japanese.

17. What is the OBON Festival? Describe its function in maintaining kinship relations for the Japanese in Hawaii.

18. (True / False). Diane Hoffman, in her research on American middle class families, found that the family is no longer important in the formation of self in the U.S.

19. (True / False). In Japanese society, the adult and child are not conceptualized as separate or distant entities, but share an overlapping space.

20. AMAE means:

    a. a kind of sweet candy
    b. to be independent
    c. to be dependent and indulgent
    d. to be selfish and stubborn

21. Name two factors or situational actions that differ in American and Japanese societies:

    a. _____

    b. _____

22.   (   ). A marriage pattern among villages that looks like this: a-b-c-d-a is
       called:

       a.   circular
       b.   rectangular
       c.   asymmetrical

23.   Malinowski's approach to kinship is called (   ).

24.   Radcliffe-Brown's approach to kinship is called (   ).

25.   Name a cognitive component in American kinship. (   ).

26.   (   ) argued that marriage can be seen as an exchange system and a way of cre-
       ating alliances. Name the creator of **the Alliance theory.**

27.   (True / False). The Alliance theory changed the focus of kinship studies from descent to
       marriage.

28.   (True / False). David Schneider argued that kinship is a cultural construct.

29.   (True / False). According to Jankowiak, political change could not alter the kinship sys-
       tem in China.

30.   (True / False). In a comparative study on Mexican-American families and Anglo-Amer-
       ican families, Susan Keefe found that Mexican-American and Anglo-Americans visited
       other families at the same rate.

Essay Questions

1.   What is the dominant dyad approach to kinship? Why did Francis L.K. Hsu advocate this approach over the functional, structural-functional and structural approaches to kinship?

2.   Do you agree with David Schneider's analysis of American kinship? Take a position and defend it.

3.   What is the "kinscripts" approach of Carol Stack and Linda Burton? Discuss the strength and weaknesses of this approach.

4.   How does political change affect the family and kinship system in China? How has revolution changed the family size, husband and wife relations, patterns of affection preference for son and daughter-in-law and mother-in-law relations in China?

5.   How is the American middle-class family generating the image of self among the young?

6. How has immigration changed the Japanese kinship system in Hawaii?

7. How has modern technology and the economy system affected the resident patterns, social mobility, and interaction patterns of the Mexican-Americans and Anglo-Americans in the United States?

8. How did the Chicago School of urban studies affect the study of kinship?

9. What is the OBON Festival? Describe its function in maintaining kinship relations for the Japanese in Hawaii.

10. What were the options available for NISEI (2nd generation) Japanese women in Hawaii if they were in an unhappy marriage? WHY?

Part II: The Use of Kinship in Contemporary Life

1. (True / False). Researchers have noted that immigrants often reconstitute their family ties in their new countries for practical reasons.

2. (   ) is the author who studied kinship in Turkey.

3. Carol Delany argued that the study of kinship should include the study of (   ) relations.

4. According to Ramu, many of the ethnic businesses in the Third World countries are founded by (   ).

5. The Norwegian Deed is:

    a. A marriage certificate
    b. Not a legal document recognized in Wisconsin.
    c. An agreement protecting a PARENT'S rights to land ownership.
    d. An agreement protecting only a CHILD'S rights to land ownership.

6. Why are there many spinster and bachelor siblings running farms in Wisconsin?

    a. It's too far from urban areas for them to find mates.
    b. There are too many females per males in Wisconsin.
    c. The inheritance laws of property in Wisconsin make them not want to marry.
    d. No one wants to marry farmers in today' society.

7. Define lineage:

8. Define clan:

9.   Define fictive kinship:

10.   Affinal kin refers to:

11.   Ritual brotherhood is:

12.   Consanguinity means:

13.   (True / False). Kinship provides a model for organization in social, education and religious activities in many contemporary societies.

14.   (True / False). The study of modern kinship includes the study of consanquineal, affinal, fictive and other social networks.

15.   (True / False). Kinship is detrimental to economic activities.

16.   (True / False). Informal ties and social networks disappeared in contemporary societies .

17.   (True / False). The "farm family" played an important role in the rural economy of Wisconsin.

18.   (True / False). In India, G.N. Ramu found that children who obtained their training in business school are likely to continue to their family businesses.

19. (True / False). Family firms are incompatible with economic development in the Third World

20. Identify the two anthropologists who studied family and kinship in London in the 1950s. _____ and _____.

21. (True / False). Isolation in modern life, according to Graham Allan maybe an important reason for people to treasure their old friendship and social network.

22. (True / False). Robert Park argued that kinship is dead in the cities.

23. (True / False). Both Raymond Firth and Elizabeth Bott studied kinship in England.

24. (   ) Urbanization tends to perpetuate one of the following residence patterns.

    a.   patrilocal residence
    b.   matrilocal residence
    c.   bilocal residence
    d.   avunculocal residence
    e.   neolocal residence

25. Name three important factors that determine "Norwegianess" in Wisconsin:

    a.   _____

    b.   _____

    c.   _____

26. (True / False). Modern kinship studies distinguish the concept of lineage from the concept of clan.

27. In developing societies such as India, do extended family and kinship ties facilitate or hinder the process of economic development? _____

28. Define these Turkish concepts:

    a. Devlet Baba:

    b. Anavatan:

29.   What are the 5 types of support networks of Wenger (In Allan)?

   a.   _____

   b.   _____

   c.   _____

   d.   _____

   e.   _____

30.   (True / False). The study of friendship is included in the study of kinship today.

31.   The kin of the Chinese are those relatives for whom one has to wear mourning a symbol like a black ribbon. These are three groups of relatives from:

   a.   _____

   b.   _____

   c.   _____

32.   A Chinese clan in the Philippines is composed of members who are

   _____ .

33.   A Chinese lineage in the Philippines is composed of members who are

   _____ .

34.   Co-parenthood or the *Compadrazgo* system are created between the Chinese and non-Chinese through the use of two Roman Catholic rituals of

   a.   _____ and

   b.   _____

35. Between marriage and adoption, which is frequently used to seal business alliances among the Chinese in the Philippines?

       _____ .

Essay Questions

1. According to Delaney, how does one become a member of a family, kinship unit, religion or nation?

2. How does kinship help the understanding of nationalism in modern Turkey?

3. Are social networks and informal ties important in contemporary societies? Take a position and defend it. Use concrete data to substantiate your arguments.

4. Is kinship an impediment for economic development in the Third World countries? Use materials from your reading to discuss this issue.

5. How do family and kinship constitute the Norwegian community in Wisconsin?

6. What is the image of women in Turkish society? Discuss the concepts of "seed," "soil" and sex rôle in their society.

7. Compare the role of women in Turkish society with Chinese, American or Japanese society. What kinship factors contribute to their status?

8. The British believe that "marriage, children and the construction of a satisfactory home life are high on the list of people's priorities." (In Graham Allan). How does this compare with American society today? Have these values towards kinship and family changed for Americans or are they still important? Why?

9. Who are the Marwaris? How did kinship play a role in their society?

10. What is the "monogenetic" theory of procreation? How does it define men's and women's roles in Turkish society?

11. In what way can the study of gender help us understand the biases in traditional kinship studies.

12.   What are the major functions of the Chinese family and kinship in the entrepreneurial activities of the Chinese in the Philippines?

13.   What is the changed nature of the Chinese kinship organization in the Philippines?

14.   What are the kinship and non-kinship factors contributing to the economic success of the Chinese in the Philippines?

15.   Does urbanism as a way of life cause the "dead of kinship" in Manila? Use the article of Bernard Wong on the Chinese in the Philippines to argue your case.

16.   Does kinship play any role in the global economy of the Philippine Chinese? Take a position and use relevant material data to illustrate your points.

Part III: Alternative Lifestyles and New Kinship Patterns

1.   (True / False). Globalization may have an impact on the residence patterns of the Chinese immigrants.

2.   (True / False). A culture's kinship system may affect its gender relation system.

3.   (True / False). Kinship is an important social unit in both traditional and modern societies.

4.   (   ). Surname Association in Chinatown is an example of one of the following:

     a.   friendship
     b.   clanship
     c.   compadrazgo system
     d.   adoption system

5.   (   ) is a result of the economic globalization of some Chinese business people.
    Choose one of the following:

     a.   Non-residential transnational extended family
     b.   Patrilineal kinship
     c.   Matrilineal kinship
     d.   Bilateral kinship

6. (True / False). Wong found that Transnational migration IS RESPONSIBLE FOR THE MULTIPLICATION OF SINGLE PARENT HOUSEHOLDS.

7. (True / False). Focusing on how kinship system is used is one of the trademarks of modern kinship studies.

8. (True / False). The new Chinese immigrants maintain a tightly closed network of kinship, favoring affinal kin over others.

9. Which of the following are important values to the Chinese entrepreneur?

    a. trust
    b. connections
    c. family
    d. all of the above
    e. none of the above

10. Urbanization tends to perpetuate one of the following residence patterns:

    a. patrilocal residence
    b. matrilocal residence
    c. bilocal residence
    d. avunculocal residence
    e. neolocal residence

11. (   ) is a result of the economic globalization of some Chinese business people.
     Choose one of the following:

    a. Non-residential transnational extended family
    b. Bilateral kinship
    c. Matrilineal kinship
    d. Hawaii kinship system

12. What are the three types of work or labor that American women are primarily involved in? (di Leonardo)

    a. _____

    b. _____

    c. _____

13. Kin work, according to di Leonardo, is characterized by
cooperation and _____, by guilt and _____.

14. (True / False). Yanagisako distinguishes between realms of domestic and public kinship in order to draw attention to anthropology's relatively "thin descriptions" of the female domestic domain. (di Leonardo)

15. Name three types of new reproductive technology:

    a. _____

    b. _____

    c. _____

16. What is surrogate motherhood? Define it.

17. What relationship between kinship and gender is changed by reproductive technology?

    a. motherhood
    b. sibling relations
    c. genetic father
    d. all of the above
    e. none of the above

18. In-vitro means:

    a. a new TV program on infertility
    b. impregnation using natural means
    c. impregnation using test-tube technology
    d. when a couple is sterile

19. (True / False). Robert Park argued that kinship is dead in the cities.

20. Bob Simpson argues that the study of divorce may be useful in locating ideas of three of the following :

    a. _____

    b. _____

    c. _____

21. (True / False). Divorce has not been the focus of anthropological research on non-Western societies.

22. (True / False). Bridewealth may be one of the factors for low divorce rate in tribal societies.

23. (True / False). British social anthropologists, with the exception of a few, for a long time were not aware that there may be anything to study under the head of kinship in English society.

24. (True / False). It is the opinion of Paul Bohannan that there was a lack of serious study on kinship in Western family.

Essay Questions

1. How does political ideology affect the size of family, type of marriage, intral-familial relations and kinship system. Cite material from Jankowiak's paper to discuss the above issues.

2. Discuss how immigration have changed the kinship of the Chinese in the United States? How the various kinds of households and intra-familiar relationships are developed as a result of transnational migration.

3. How globalization has created a group of "astronauts" and their transnational extended families? Cite concrete examples from Wong's article to demonstrate your points.

4. Discuss the impact of NRT on modern kinship studies.

5. Name three problems that women in polygynous marriages in Angel Park face.

6. What do you think of the Angel Park marriage system? Do you agree or disagree with their religious beliefs and social practices? WHY?

7. How does gender play a role in kinship? Use the article by Micaela di Leonardo to discuss this issue.

8. What are the contributions of Bob Simpson's study on divorce? How does the study of divorce enrich kinship studies in anthropology?

9. How can class be an factor in the formation of a certain household? Cite materials from your readings and your experience to demonstrate the relationship between class and kinship.

10. Is kinship structure immutable? Under what circumstances may the traditional kinship systems have to change?

 # Appendix 2

Suggested Additional Readings

Part I

Allan, Graham
 1996 Kinship and Friendship in Modern Britain. London: Oxford University Press.

Baker, Huge
 1980 Chinese Family and Kinship. New York: Columbia University Press.

Davis, Debrah and Stevan Harrell, ed.
 1993 Chinese Families in the Post-Mao Era. Berkeley: University of California Press.

di Leonardo, Macaela
 1984 The Varieties of Ethnic Experience: Kinship, Class, and Gender Among California Italian-Americans. Ithaca: Cornell University Press.

Goody, Jack, ed.,
 1973 The Character of Kinship. New York: Cambridge University Press.

Hsu, Francis L.K.
 1975 *Iemoto*: the Heart of Japan. Cambridge, Mass: Schenkman Publishing Co.
 1983 Rugged Individualism Reconsidered. Knoxville: The University of Tennesse Press.

Hsu, Francis L.K. and Hendrick Serrie, ed.
 1998 The Overseas Chinese: Ethnicity in National Context. Lanham: University Press of America.

Keesing, Roger
 1975 Kin Groups and Social Structure. Fort Worth: Harcourt Brace.

Lévi-Strauss, Claude et al.
 1971 The Elementary Structutes of Kinship. Boston: Beacon Press.

Levine, Nancy
 1988 The Dynamics of Polyandry. Chicago: University of Chicago Press.

Pasternak, Burton et al.
 1997 Sex, Gender, and Kinship: A Cross-Cultural Perspective. New Jersey: Prentice Hall.

Schneider, David
    1980   American Kinship: A Cultural Account. Chicago: University of Chicago Press.

Strathern, Marilyn
    1992   After Nature: English Kinship in the late Twentieth Century. New York: Cambridge University Press.

Stone, Linda
    1997   Kinship and Gender: An Introduction. Boulder: Westview Press.

Yanagisako, Sylvia and Carol Delaney, ed.
    1992   Naturalizing Power: Essays in Feminist Cultural Analysis. London: Routledge.

Part II

Borneman, John
    1992   Belonging in the Two Berlins: Kin, State, Nation. New York: Cambridge University Press.

Brusco, Elizabeth
    1995   The Reformation of Machismo: Evangelical Conversion and Gender in Columbia. Austin: University Texas Press.

Lamphere, Louise et al.
    1993   Sunbelt Working Mothers: reconciling Family and Factory. Ithaca, New York: Cornell University Press.

Noguchi, Paul
    1994   Delayed Departures, Overdue Arrivals: Industrial Familialism and the Japanese Railways. Honolulu: University of Hawaii Press.

Singerman, Diane
    1996   Avenues of Participation: Family Politics, and Networks in Urban Quarters of Cairo. Princeton: Princeton University Press.

Stack, Carol
    1975   All Our Kin. New York: Harper & Row.
    1996   Call to Home: African Americans Reclaim the Rural South. New York: Basic Books.

Wong, Bernard
    1997   Ethnicity and Entrepreneurship: The New Chinese Immigrants in the San Francisco Bay Area. Boston: Allyn & Bacon.
    1998   The Chinese in New York City: Kinship and Immigration. *In* The Overseas Chinese: Ethnicity in National Context. Francis L.K. Hsu and Hendrick Serrie, eds. Pp. 143-172. Lanham: University Press of America.

Wong, Bernard and Becky McReynolds and Wynnie Wong
    1992   Chinese Family Firms in the San Francisco Bay Area. Family Business Review 5(4):355-372.

Yanagisako, Sylvia
    1992   Transforming the Past: Tradition and Kinship Among Japanese Americas. Stanford: Stanford University Press.

Young, Michael and Peter Willmott
    1992   Family and Kinship in East London. Berkeley: University of California Press.

Part III

Franklin, Sarah
    1999   Embodied Progress: A Cultural Account of Assisted Conception. New York: Routledge Press.

Henderson, J. Neil and Maria Vesperi, eds.
    1995   The Culture of Long Term Care: Nursing Home Ethnography. Westport: Bergin & Garvey

Jankowiak, William
    1997   Romantic Passion. New York: Columbia University Press.

Kertzer, David I.
    1996   Sacrificed for Honor: Italian Infant Abandonment and the Politics of Reproductive Control. Boston: Beacon Press.

Modell, Judith
    1994   Kinship with Strangers: Adoption and Interpretations of Kinship in American Culture.

Robertson, A.F.
    1991   Beyond the Family: The Social Organization of Human Reproduction. Berkeley: University of California Press.

Scheper-Hughes, Nancy
    1992   Death Without Weeping: The Violence of Everyday Life in Brazil. Berkeley: University of California Press.

Shokeid, Moshe
    1997   A Gay Synagogue in New York. New York: Columbia University Press.

Strathern, Marilyn
    1993   After Nature: English Kinship in the Late Twentieth Century. New York: Cambridge University Press.

Stone, Linda
    1998   Kinship and Gender. Boulder: Westview Press.

Van Den Berghe, Pierre L.
    1990   Human Family Systems: An Evolutionary View.

Weston, Kath
    1991   Families We Choose: Lesbians, Gays, Kinship. Boston: Beacon Press.